Gender in the Middle Ages

Volume 13

POPULAR MEMORY AND GENDER
IN MEDIEVAL ENGLAND

Gender in the Middle Ages

ISSN 1742-870X

Series Editors
Jacqueline Murray
Diane Watt

Editorial Board
Clare Lees
Katherine J. Lewis
Liz Herbert McAvoy

This series investigates the representation and construction of masculinity and femininity in the Middle Ages from a variety of disciplinary and interdisciplinary perspectives. It aims in particular to explore the diversity of medieval genders, and such interrelated contexts and issues as sexuality, social class, race and ethnicity, and orthodoxy and heterodoxy.

Proposals or queries should be sent in the first instance to the editors or to the publisher, at the addresses given below; all submissions will receive prompt and informed consideration.

Professor Jacqueline Murray, Department of History, University of Guelph, Guelph, Ontario, N1G 2W1, Canada

Professor Diane Watt, School of Literature and Languages, University of Surrey, Guildford, Surrey GU2 7XH, UK

Boydell & Brewer Limited, PO Box 9, Woodbridge, Suffolk IP12 3DF, UK

Previously published volumes in the series are listed at the end of this book.

POPULAR MEMORY AND GENDER
IN MEDIEVAL ENGLAND

MEN, WOMEN, AND TESTIMONY IN THE CHURCH COURTS, c.1200–1500

Bronach C. Kane

THE BOYDELL PRESS

© Bronach C. Kane 2019

All Rights Reserved. Except as permitted under current legislation
no part of this work may be photocopied, stored in a retrieval system,
published, performed in public, adapted, broadcast,
transmitted, recorded or reproduced in any form or by any means,
without the prior permission of the copyright owner

The right of Bronach C. Kane to be identified as
the author of this work has been asserted in accordance with
sections 77 and 78 of the Copyright, Designs and Patents Act 1988

First published 2019
The Boydell Press, Woodbridge
Paperback edition 2021

ISBN 978-1-78327-352-2 hardback
ISBN 978-1-78327-596-0 paperback

The Boydell Press is an imprint of Boydell & Brewer Ltd
PO Box 9, Woodbridge, Suffolk IP12 3DF, UK
and of Boydell & Brewer Inc.
668 Mt Hope Avenue, Rochester, NY 14620-2731, USA
website: www.boydellandbrewer.co.uk

A CIP catalogue record for this book is available
from the British Library

The publisher has no responsibility for the continued existence or accuracy of
URLs for external or third-party internet websites referred to in this book, and
does not guarantee that any content on such websites is, or will remain, accurate
or appropriate

This publication is printed on acid-free paper

For Simon, Miri, and Jeremy

CONTENTS

List of Abbreviations	viii
Introduction	1
Chapter 1. Pastoral Care, Canon Law, and Social Relations	31
Chapter 2. Gender, Narrative, and Testimony	57
Chapter 3. Bodily Practices	81
Chapter 4. Sexuality and Generation	109
Chapter 5. Marriage, Kinship, and Widowhood	137
Chapter 6. Orality, Written Memory, and Custom	171
Chapter 7. Place, Landscape, and Gender	211
Conclusion	245
Bibliography	259
Acknowledgements	285
Index	287

ABBREVIATIONS

BI	Borthwick Institute, York
C	Gratian, *Decretum*, cited from *Corpus iuris canonici*, ed. E. Friedberg, 2 vols. (Leipzig, 1879–81; repr. Union, NJ, 2000)
CCA	Canterbury Cathedral Archives
Ch. Ant.	Chartae Antiquae
Councils and Synods	*Councils and Synods with Other Documents Relating to the English Church II: A.D. 1205–1313*, eds. F. M. Powicke and C. R. Cheney (Oxford, 1964), Parts I and II
CP	Cause Paper
EETS	Early English Texts Society
E.S.	Ecclesiastical Suit
KALHS	Kent Archives and Local History Service
MED	*Middle English Dictionary*, ed. H. Kurath et al. (Ann Arbor, 1952–2001)
Select Cases	*Select Cases from the Ecclesiastical Courts of the Province of Canterbury c.1200–1301*, ed. N. Adams and C. Donahue, Jr., Selden Society, 95 (London, 1981)
SVSB	Sede Vacante Scrapbook
VCH	Victoria County History
X	*Liber Extra*, cited from *Corpus iuris canonici*, ed. E. Friedberg, 2 vols. (Leipzig, 1879–81; repr. Union, NJ, 2000)
YMA	York Minster Archive

INTRODUCTION

In 1270, Sibilla de Hinteworth testified in a matrimonial suit that reached the Court of Canterbury on appeal from the archdeaconry of Huntingdon. Despite the preference for male witnesses in most cases in the English ecclesiastical courts at the time, a large number of women remembered the birth of the female party in the case, Cecilia, daughter of Bartholomew, to prove that she was under the approved age of twelve at the time of the marriage. Sibilla told the clerical examiner that she remembered the child's birth as she 'was deflowered during the Lent that next followed'.[1] She gave no further details about the circumstances surrounding her experience, an absence compounded by the shifting meaning assigned to the act of deflowering in this period. In manorial communities, 'deflorata' was most commonly used to describe women's loss of virginity outside marriage, appearing in fines made upon bondwomen and the female poor for fornication or illegitimate children. It also surfaced in some accounts of rape and sexual assault, accompanied by language that implied physical force, and lay behind payments of compensation for damage to women's marital value.[2]

The fragmentary nature of Sibilla's memory alludes to the marginalisation of women's voices in a range of suits in the medieval church courts. The focus of her account simultaneously underscores the potential for female memories to subvert clerical assumptions about women's speech and sexual shame. Other women witnesses in the case recalled childbirth, marriages, work, and the deaths of kin in patterns that diverged to an extent from the recollections of men in comparable situations. Yet Sibilla's memory implies the ability for non-elite women not only to testify in suits that mattered in their local communities, but also to articulate rather than suppress gendered sexual experiences that involved contact with manorial or Church authorities.

This book traces everyday perceptions and uses of the past among non-elite men and women in England from the early thirteenth century to the end of the fifteenth century. It draws on the wealth of detailed legal testimony on a variety of issues that survives for the church courts of Canterbury and York,

---

[1] CCA E.S. Roll 10. 'deflorata fuit in carniprimo proximo sequente'.

[2] J. M. Bennett, 'Writing Fornication: Medieval Leyrwite and its Historians', *Transactions of the Royal Historical Society*, 6th series, 13 (2003), 131–62, at pp. 142, 150.

Popular Memory and Gender in Medieval England

and opens up these archives for further study by medievalists in various areas. This is not a procedural history of canon law in the English church courts, although it speaks to many of the themes that concern scholars in that field.[3] Rather, it provides a cultural and social history of the use of the church courts, and explores how men and women recalled the past in this setting. The chronological extent of the study begins with early ecclesiastical proceedings from the provincial and diocesan court of Canterbury, which illuminate nascent practices in the courts and their interaction with canon law and pastoral literature. It closes on the eve of the Reformation, as the relationship between memory, history, and identity in these decades of profound religious change is another book entirely, and are themes that have received some attention in several existing studies.[4]

A number of pioneering works have dealt with women's participation in the creation and maintenance of memory in medieval contexts, particularly the way in which aristocratic laywomen and female religious contributed to the preservation of family and local histories.[5] The study of memory in medieval culture remains vibrant and now includes aspects of individual and collective identity, such as religion, kinship, and commemoration. The rich intersections of gender and memory among people below the level of elites, however, are mapped in much sparser detail.[6]

Manorial records and cases from the Chancery and borough courts illuminate many elements of women's social experiences in England during the period which this book covers. Pioneering studies in these areas reveal women involved in a vast array of activities relating to work, crime, sexuality, and marriage.[7] Legal depositions from the church courts, however, provide unpar-

---

[3] For foundational treatments of canon law in English contexts, see: R. H. Helmholz, *Marriage Litigation in Medieval England* (Cambridge, 1974); *Canon Law and the Law of England* (London, 1987); *Roman Canon Law in Reformation England* (Cambridge, 1990); *The Ius Commune in England: Four Studies* (Oxford, 2001); *The Oxford History of the Laws of England: The History of the Canon Law and Ecclesiastical Jurisdiction from 597 to the 1640s* (Oxford, 2004).

[4] See, for example, A. Walsham, *The Reformation of the Landscape: Religion, Identity, and Memory in Early Modern Britain and Ireland* (Oxford, 2011); A. Wood, *The Memory of the People: Custom and Popular Senses of the Past in Early Modern England* (Cambridge, 2013); J. Pollman, *Memory in Early Modern Europe, 1500–1800* (Oxford, 2017).

[5] E. van Houts, ed., *Medieval Memories: Men, Women and the Past, 700–1300* (London, 2001); E. van Houts, *Memory and Gender in Medieval Europe, 900–1200* (Basingstoke, 1999); E. Cox, L. H. McAvoy, and R. Magnani, eds., *Reconsidering Gender, Time and Memory in Medieval Culture* (Cambridge, 2015).

[6] S. L. Einbinder, *No Place of Rest: Jewish Literature, Expulsion, and the Memory of Medieval France* (Philadelphia, 2009).

[7] J. M. Bennett, *Women in the Medieval English Countryside: Gender and Household in Brigstock before the Plague* (Oxford, 1987); B. A. Hanawalt, 'Peasant Women's Contribution to the Home Economy in Late Medieval England', in B. A. Hanawalt, ed., *Women and Work in Preindustrial Europe* (Bloomington, IN, 1986), pp. 3–19; H.

Introduction

alleled evidence of the ways in which men and women presented themselves as individuals during these cases. Although many secular courts restricted the involvement of women, in some actions female jurors and witnesses were employed as legal experts, albeit in ways informed by prevailing attitudes to gender. Yet the more extensive nature of testimony from the church courts demonstrates in greater detail the extent of women's agency in pursuing courses of action, how they managed social expectations and understood the intricacies of canon law. These records form the principal sources for this study, supplemented by literature on religious instruction (*pastoralia*), ballads and other lyrics, and canon-law treatises. The book foregrounds the witness statements of men and women, situating them in the wider framework of the ecclesiastical courts, and tracing the emergence of memory as an integral form of proof in this jurisdiction.

Thanks to the richness of these records, we can study here depictions of the past by servants, agricultural labourers, married and single women, and the unfree, while analysing the nature of gender relations in non-elite cultures. Normative social hierarchies produced visions of the past which depended on literate practices of ordering memories that were less available to women and lower-status men. These habits developed through the overlapping categories of gender and social background, yet they were also ingrained in layers of personal experience. Men and women's memories in testimony underscored the incremental nature of their identities, simultaneously adapted to acknowledge points of law and their current legal experiences.

The beliefs and habits that sustained these distinctive ways of remembering often related to the patriarchal ideologies and practices that saturated aspects of everyday life. Female nature was associated with passivity and subservience in opposition to the active and governing role usually ascribed to men. Patriarchal beliefs and practices were ubiquitous in numerous areas of life, deriving 'strength from ideology, custom and affective relations as well as from politics, law and society'.[8] These attitudes not only influenced the language that men and women used and appropriated in the courts, but also shaped patterns of selecting witnesses and reporting the presence of women in male and

---

Jewell, 'Women at the Courts of the Manor of Wakefield, 1348–1350', *Northern History*, 26 (1990), 59–81; J. M. Bennett, *Ale, Beer, and Brewsters in England: Women's Work in a Changing World, 1300–1600* (Oxford, 1996); K. Jones, *Gender and Petty Crime in Late Medieval England: The Local Courts in Kent, 1460–1560* (Woodbridge, 2006); N. J. Menuge, ed., *Medieval Women and the Law* (Woodbridge, 2000); C. Beattie, 'Your Oratrice: Women's Petitions to the Late Medieval Court of Chancery', in B. Kane and F. Williamson, eds., *Women, Agency and the Law, 1300–1700* (London, 2013), pp. 17–30.

8 J. M. Bennett, 'Medieval Women, Modern Women: Across the Great Divide', in D. Aers, ed., *Culture and History, 1350–1600: Essays on English Communities, Identities, and Writing* (London, 1992), pp. 147–75, at p. 165; for a useful outline of patriarchy as a concept, see K. Barclay, *Love, Intimacy and Power: Marriage and Patriarchy in Scotland, 1650–1850* (Manchester, 2011), pp. 6–9.

female testimony. While women were absent from many types of cases, they were often active agents outside the courts in the initiation and progression of disputes, and as witnesses in suits they depicted their experiences with great awareness of the law and its implications.

GENDER AND MEMORY STUDIES

The past three decades have seen the proliferation of works on gender in contemporary and historical societies, with several intellectual offshoots that include the analysis of masculinity and the emergence of queer theory. Formative in the development of gender history was the work of Joan Scott, which, although critiqued and developed in various ways, became the standard point of reference for many historians of gender relations. Scott situated manifestations of gendered behaviour within the dynamics of power relations, arguing that gender should be understood as the 'perceived differences between the sexes'.[9] This interpretation outlined methods for tracing the components of gender through the symbols, concepts, and institutions that structure personal identity and collective behaviour.

Despite its widespread acceptance as a primary approach to gender and its invigorating force in historical studies, the central tenets of Scott's analysis have been profoundly questioned. Acknowledging the importance of Scott's intervention, Jeanne Boydston notes that the model only shifted emphasis from 'the naturalised body to the perceived body, but this was a deflection, not a displacement, for perception now became the real subject'.[10] This approach qualified the nature and operation of gender, but simultaneously reified the oppositional binary in earlier works focused on the body. The reception of gender as a fixed category retained little flexibility for non-Western and premodern variants of gender in which power relations were enacted in less oppositional and detrimental ways. Boydston also proposed the interrogation of gendered behaviour through an appreciation of 'genderqueer-ness' that unshackles the term from binary terminology and imagines gender as a more expansive process with countless variations that change over time.[11] This book is influenced by this reconceptualization and interprets gendered patterns associated with memory within their cultural and social settings, rather than as stable categories. The study does not anticipate the centrality of gender in every depiction of the past, but instead traces its presence and absence to understand more fully the nexus of memory, gender, and testimony in daily settings during this period.

---

[9]   J. Scott, 'Gender: A Useful Category of Historical Analysis', *The American Historical Review*, 91 (1986), 1053–75, at p. 1067.

[10] J. Boydston, 'Gender as a Question of Historical Analysis', *Gender & History*, 20 (2008), 558–83, at p. 563.

[11] Boydston, 'Gender as a Question', pp. 577–8.

Introduction

The fields of gender history and memory studies possess analogous histories. Intersections between these areas of scholarship illuminate the points of contact that shaped gendered differences in memory in late medieval England. Feminist and gender theorists, like many scholars of memory, question pasts which are depicted as static, identifying areas of fluidity, uncertainty, and fragmentation.[12] In particular, both fields probe prevailing historical narratives and aim to attribute agency and an autonomous remembered past to groups which are most excluded from traditional history.

Concepts of collective or shared memory have long been central to the advent of memory studies as a way of tracing the social elements of recollection. The work of Maurice Halbwachs emerged as the most prominent theorisation of group memory, particularly his pioneering but blunt assertion that memory is entirely social and cannot exist outside the social group.[13] Addressing themes which had already interested Émile Durkheim, Halbwachs's theories were tied intimately to studies on the formation of identity and the concept of collective memory that placed the individual within the wider group. The family was the most recognisable example, but religious and class settings were also considered as primary channels for acquiring and locating memories.[14] Halbwachs's theories have been critiqued as determinist due to their tendency to subsume the individual into an amorphous group.[15] James Fentress and Chris Wickham are two of the most prominent heirs to the approaches that Durkheim and Halbwachs pioneered. In their path-breaking study, they proposed 'social memory' as a more appropriate analytic term to 'collective memory', arguing that it better describes how the individual remembers past events and allows room for the acquisition and transmission of memory.[16] Fentress and Wickham also emphasised the intimate connections between memory and identity, noting that '[w]hen we remember, we represent ourselves to ourselves and to those around us'.[17] In the work of Hermann Ebbinghaus, Frederic C. Bartlett, and others, forgetting also retains creative elements, influencing what is remembered and its representation in

---

[12] M. Hirsch and V. Smith, 'Feminism and Cultural Memory: An Introduction', *Signs: Journal of Women in Culture and Society*, 28.1, special issue: *Gender and Cultural Memory* (2002), 1–19, at p. 12.

[13] M. Halbwachs, *On Collective Memory*, ed. and trans. L. A. Coser (Chicago, 1992), pp. 56–166; see also K. M. Baker, 'Memory and Practice', *Representations*, 11 (1985), 134–59, at pp. 156–8.

[14] É. Durkheim, *The Elementary Forms of Religious Life*, trans. C. Cosman (New York, 1995).

[15] S. A. Crane, 'Writing the Individual Back into Collective Memory', *The American Historical Review*, 102.5 (1997), 1372–85.

[16] J. Fentress and C. Wickham, *Social Memory* (Oxford, 1992); M. S. Weldon, 'Remembering as a Social Process', *The Psychology of Learning and Motivation*, 40 (2001), 67–120.

[17] Fentress and Wickham, *Social Memory*, p. 7.

the present.[18] Despite their inherent value for exploring the social dynamics of remembrance, these theories tend to marginalise female experiences as their contributions to the production of official monuments and histories can be hard to perceive.

The absence of women's memories from collective remembrance guided early attempts among sociologists, historians, and theorists to locate women's pasts through oral history and autobiography.[19] Gender was recognised in these works as an influence on the structure and content of recollection, but, as Sherna Berger Gluck remarks, initial feminist works on oral history depended on 'the principle of women's unitary experience'.[20] As post-structuralism became embedded in many fields, new methods for interpreting women's words developed, 'casting a postmodernist eye on languages, silences, and interpretation'.[21] In attempting to reincorporate the memories of women and other marginalised groups, feminist theorists established techniques that were finely attuned to the gender dynamics of power relations and subjective experience. The patriarchal impulse inherent in traditional ways of viewing the past has also been criticised, underlining the potential for feminist memory 'to disturb, subvert and transform the existing paternal order'.[22]

In tracing the power relations involved in the suppression and amplification of different pasts, oral history has gained import in the study of popular memory. Focusing on the Turin working classes during the twentieth century, Luisa Passerini explored the subjectivities that were produced within memories of collaboration with fascism and its collective traditions.[23] Feminist scholars have also embraced the related concepts of popular memory and counter-memory, drawn initially from Michel Foucault's work on remembrance and later influential in a variety of fields.[24] Both theories aimed to refocus attention upon marginalised versions of the past. The recollections of

---

[18] M. de Montaigne, *Les Essais* (Paris, 2007), II.ix; Fentress and Wickham, *Social Memory*, pp. 14–15.

[19] S. Geiger, 'What's So Feminist About Women's Oral History', *Journal of Women's History*, 2.1 (1990), 161–82.

[20] S. Berger Gluck, 'Women's Oral History: Is it So Special?', in T. L. Charlton, L. E. Myers, and R. Sharpless, eds., *Handbook of Oral History* (Lanham, MD, 2006), pp. 357–83, at p. 366.

[21] S. Armitage, 'The Stages of Women's Oral History', in D. A. Ritchie, ed., *The Oxford Handbook of Oral History* (Oxford, 2011), pp. 169–85, at p. 175; S. Berger Gluck and D. Patai, eds., *Women's Words: The Feminist Practice of Oral History* (New York, 1991).

[22] M. A. Lourie, D. C. Staunton, and M. Vicinus, 'Introduction: Women and Memory', *Michigan Quarterly Review*, 26.1 (1987), 1–8, at p. 3.

[23] L. Passerini, *Fascism in Popular Memory: The Cultural Experience of the Turin Working Class* (Cambridge, 1987).

[24] M. Foucault, 'Film and Popular Memory: An Interview with Michel Foucault', trans. Martin Jordan, *Radical Philosophy*, 11 (1975), 24–9; G. Lipsitz, *Time Passages: Collective Memory and American Popular Culture* (Minneapolis, 1990), p. 213.

Introduction

lower-status people, especially groups who lacked influence in society, could cohere into popular memory due to their shared position. The associated concept of countermemory refers to acts of remembering that more explicitly undermine dominant or official narratives, although both categories possess common features.[25] Feminist approaches to memory and their sensitivity to issues of hegemony informed the efforts of the Popular Memory Group, allowing closer scrutiny of the elements that contributed to the 'social production of memory'. The 'real processes of domination' that shaped accounts of the past were rooted in experiences of authority – its routines, language, and material and emotional effects.[26]

Conceiving of women's memories, and those of more marginal men, as forms of popular memory situates competing ideas of the past within prevailing sets of power relations. In this sense, memory can work against ideological and structural forms of forgetting where erasure of the past carries gendered meaning in the present.[27] In the period explored in this book, male witnesses were preferred in church-court suits, and officials in some cases suppressed the presence of women from testimony entirely. Yet non-elite people did not always undermine dominant narratives, and complex social and economic hierarchies meant that men and women sometimes reinforced normative ideologies where these coincided with their own interests. The experiences of the peasantry and urban workers emerge as heterogeneous, driven by a sense of self and a purposeful awareness of their own gendered worlds.

Men and women communicated aspects of their identities in legal testimony through conversation and other forms of oral exchange.[28] As the Popular Memory Group has noted, senses of the past are transmitted and adapted in situations that involve 'everyday talk and … personal comparisons and narratives'.[29] Some of these memories were recounted orally in group settings. Paul Connerton emphasises the importance of 'acts of transfer' in the development of family memory, arguing for greater understanding of how kin-based accounts of the past circulated.[30] Narratives transmitted to younger generations were marked by gender differences related to social experience.

---

[25] For a summary, see B. A. Misztal, *Theories of Social Remembering* (Maidenhead, 2003), pp. 62–3.

[26] Popular Memory Group, 'Popular Memory: Theory, Politics, Method', in R. Perks and A. Thomson, eds., *The Oral History Reader* (London, 1998), pp. 75–86, both quotes at p. 77.

[27] For an important taxonomy of forgetting, see P. Connerton, 'Seven Types of Forgetting', *Memory Studies*, 1 (2008), 59–71.

[28] D. Middleton and D. Edwards, 'Conversational Remembering: A Social Psychological Approach', in D. Middleton and D. Edwards, eds., *Collective Remembering* (London, 1990), pp. 23–45.

[29] Popular Memory Group, 'Popular Memory', p. 77.

[30] P. Connerton, *How Societies Remember* (Cambridge, 1989), pp. 38–40.

Popular Memory and Gender in Medieval England

Isabel Hofmeyer examines oral histories of a Boer siege of the Ndebele people in mid-nineteenth-century Lebowa, a South African chiefdom in the North Transvaal. The Ndebele people's memory of the incident passed through three or four generations, but whereas the men's stories of the siege concentrated on political and military activities, women's memories focused on the misery and distress which the villagers endured.[31] In later medieval England men and women's legal testimony was more comparable, reflecting their social experiences that usually occurred in everyday settings. Social memory that mattered to local families centred on histories and traditions communicated between family members and neighbours, such as past events, collective rituals, and uses of the land, that were passed down by parents, kin, and the elderly.

The concept of time has also been discussed from a gendered perspective, as earlier approaches to temporality depicted its passage as linear and characterised by historical time, particularly in modern cultures.[32] Feminist theorists have critiqued the patriarchal and heteronormative tone of these initial studies, drawing attention to their coexistence with temporalities that are otherwise excluded from mainstream ways of recalling the past. Julia Kristeva maintains that an appreciation of feminine experiences of the past, or 'women's time', facilitates the resurgence of memories suppressed within patriarchal and linear memory.[33] This kind of time appears composed of 'cycles, gestation, the eternal recurrence of a biological rhythm that conforms to that of nature', and conveys ideas of time connected with the eternal. Yet, as Kristeva notes, it underpins temporality in many cultures, and does not necessarily oppose more masculine perceptions of time.[34] Queer theory also exposes traces of other time lines that diverged from normative ways of viewing the past. In late medieval culture, this included memories from childless women of reproductive age, unmarried, and widowed women testifying outside patriarchal control, as well as memories from men and women of impoverished and unfree backgrounds. These groups used markers of temporality arising from events beyond childbearing, marriage, and labour patterns in order to measure the passage of time.

This book concentrates on personal and social memory in particular, analysing the former in two ways. First, it considers the mnemonic markers that men and women used when questioned explicitly on their memories of past events. As shown in Chapter 1, this was a common form of examination in early Canterbury cases and in depositions from the fourteenth- and

---

[31] I. Hofmeyer, '*We spend our years as a tale that is told': Oral Historical Narrative in a South African Chiefdom* (Johannesburg and London, 1994), pp. 167–70.

[32] For a recent and important study of time in late medieval Europe, see M. S. Champion, *The Fullness of Time: Temporalities of the Fifteenth-Century Low Countries* (Chicago, 2017).

[33] J. Kristeva, 'Women's Time', *Signs*, 7 (1981), 13–35.

[34] Kristeva, 'Women's Time', pp. 16–17.

Introduction

fifteenth-century courts of York. It produced a rich body of responses from men and women who purported to represent their memories of specific points in time. Second, the study explores the social and cultural contexts of these mnemonic strategies, thus considering individual memory in relation to shared reconstructions of the past. The approaches noted above offer an implicit scaffold for this study, but, as Matt Matsuda remarks, 'memory has too often become another analytical category to impose on the past; the point should be to re-historicize memory and see how it is so inextricably part of the past'.[35] These forms of remembrance were an integral part of everyday life in medieval England and need to be situated in a social as much as a theoretical context.

MEMORY IN MEDIEVAL CULTURE

Medieval society maintained numerous forms of mnemonic signifiers, and the history of memory in this period is associated with several interpretive traditions. During the early and high Middle Ages in particular, *memoria* represented the liturgical use of memory in the remembrance and commemoration of the dead, including its expression through texts, objects, and rituals.[36] The art of memory, comprising numerous practices aimed at training recollection, has received attention from pioneering historians whose work has examined its intellectual foundations. Frances Yates provided an important study of these architectural memory techniques, describing their genesis from classical traditions of rhetoric and oratory to the Renaissance memory palaces of Giordano Bruno.[37] Memory work was intimately connected to the understanding and *praxis* of reading and writing, as Mary Carruthers notes, with pictures and diagrams that were mnemonic in function and intended to complement text often congesting books and manuscripts. Images and the written word coexisted through the concepts of *painture* and *parole*, the ocular and aural pathways to memory.[38] Aside from these compositional forms of memory, meditation on the past was fundamental in theological terms. Contemplative prayer and a focus on the Passion were the cornerstones of Christian worship, and the Eucharist itself recreated Christ's suffering and resurrection. The significance of introspection was also demonstrated in

---

[35] M. K. Matsuda, *The Memory of the Modern* (New York, 1996), p. 16.

[36] P. J. Geary, *Phantoms of Remembrance: Memory and Oblivion at the End of the First Millennium* (Princeton, 1994), p. 18; see also C. M. Barron and C. Burgess, eds., *Memory and Commemoration in Medieval England* (Donington, 2010); E. Brenner, M. Cohen, and M. Franklin-Brown, eds., *Memory and Commemoration in Medieval Culture* (Farnham, 2013).

[37] F. A. Yates, *The Art of Memory* (Chicago, 1966); see also P. H. Hutton, *History as an Art of Memory* (Hanover, 1993), especially pp. 30–2.

[38] M. Carruthers, *The Book of Memory: A Study of Memory in Medieval Culture* (Cambridge, 1990), pp. 221–9.

Popular Memory and Gender in Medieval England

pastoral and judicial realms of the Church as men and women were instructed to mine their own memories for the remnants of sin and wrongdoing.

The twelfth and thirteenth centuries saw a substantial growth of another type of memory in the form of written records from royal and episcopal administration. Michael Clanchy detailed the shift in mentalities which had previously privileged oral memory over written memory, as patterns of record keeping filtered out from royal government, influencing civic and episcopal administration.[39] Under the direction of clerks and lawyers who appreciated the utility of writing to preserve essential records, civic government began to make use of registers, annals, and chronicles.[40] Despite the growth in written records as a means to preserve the past, oral culture remained crucial to the transmission of memory and tradition. Patrick Geary and Matthew Innes both argue that writing and literate abilities were more central to early medieval culture than Clanchy and others have acknowledged, noting that societies are seldom strictly oral or literate.[41] Memory based on written records could also be restricted to the memorising of text, rather than the compositional and inventive functions of the learned *ars memoria*. The learning of material by rote was common among students and masters of the law, as legal maxims and other elements of the law were committed to memory.[42]

Memory and commemoration were integral to civic identity and record keeping as towns and cities recorded and memorialized past events to produce distinctive histories.[43] In early fifteenth-century York, for instance, a copy of the chronicle of the archbishops of York found its way into the city register, perhaps compensating for the absence of a history akin to the chronicles of London.[44] Clerks engaged in recording civic pasts often worked as lawyers and notaries for ecclesiastical administrations, offering a channel for the mutual exchange of scribal practices.[45] These forms of memory were produced in

---

[39] M. T. Clanchy, *From Memory to Written Record: England 1066–1307*, 2nd edition (Oxford, 1993), p. 74.

[40] D. Cannon, 'London Pride: Citizenship and the Fourteenth-Century Custumals of the City of London', in S. Rees Jones, ed., *Learning and Literacy in Medieval England and Abroad* (Turnhout, 2003), pp. 179–98; S. Rees Jones, 'York's Civic Administration, 1354–1464', in S. Rees Jones, ed., *The Government of Medieval York: Essays in Commemoration of the 1396 Royal Charter* (York, 1997), pp. 108–40.

[41] M. Innes, 'Memory, Orality and Literacy in an Early Medieval Society', *Past & Present*, 158 (1998), 3–36, at p. 9.

[42] P. Hyams, 'The Legal Revolution and the Discourse of Dispute in the Twelfth Century', in A. Galloway, ed., *The Cambridge Companion to Medieval English Culture* (Cambridge, 2011), pp. 43–65, at pp. 55–6.

[43] H. M. Carrel, 'Civic Government and Identity in the Provincial Towns of Late Medieval England, c. 1370–c. 1500' (PhD thesis, University of Cambridge, 2007).

[44] Rees Jones, 'York's Civic Administration', p. 108.

[45] B. Dobson, 'Contrasting Chronicles: Historical Writing at York and Durham at the Close of the Middle Ages', in I. Wood and G. A. Loud, eds., *Church and Chronicle in the Middle Ages: Essays Presented to John Taylor* (London, 1991), pp. 201–18, at p. 215 n. 47.

Introduction

masculine spheres, concentrating mainly on the activities and appointments of men. Women entered these records primarily through appearances in court rolls and in statutes that were seen to pertain to female experience and via their occasional involvement in civic processions.

Different temporal systems shaped the way that men and women imagined and located events in this period.[46] The most common method was the use of religious feasts, including saints' days; this served as a basic way for people to anchor specific dates in testimony from the church courts. In 1464 Michael Coke recalled events in relation to the Saturday before the feast day of St Denis, which he claimed to know well as he was born in France and consulted a calendar in his chamber for other saints' days.[47] The measurement of time through the feast days of saints or by regnal years was augmented by other modes of quantification. For example, Jacques Le Goff noted the growing significance of mercantile culture in supplementing religious perceptions of time from the fourteenth century in particular.[48] Multiple temporalities shaped men and women's experiences, including cycles which were 'corporeal, seasonal, devotional, familial or vocational' in nature.[49] The practical and symbolic use of memory extended beyond the church courts to other jurisdictions which non-elite men and women encountered on a routine basis. By the late thirteenth century, legal memory under common law was seen to begin in 1189, with customs and events prior to this date regarded as occurring 'time out of mind' or beyond the 'memory of man'.[50] The apprehension of the past through the law produced methods that measured the past in relation to the length of legal procedures and specific dates.[51] A variety of registers for remembering thus coexisted and intersected in this period. As the masculine tone of many forms of legal and civic memory implies, their nature and production should be situated in gendered contexts and explored in relation to a broader range of mnemonic strategies.

---

[46] B. Kane, 'Women, Memory and Testimony in the Medieval Ecclesiastical Courts of Canterbury and York', in Kane and Williamson, eds., *Women, Agency and the Law*, pp. 43–62; B. Kane, 'Custom, Memory and Knowledge in the Medieval English Church Courts', in R. Hayes and W. J. Sheils, eds., *Clergy, Church and Society in England and Wales, c. 1200–1800* (York, 2013), pp. 61–81.

[47] BI CP.F.203.

[48] J. Le Goff, *Time, Work and Culture in the Middle Ages*, trans. A. Goldhammer (Chicago and London, 1980); see also Champion, *The Fullness of Time*.

[49] L. H. McAvoy, 'Introduction. *In Principio*: The Queer Matrix of Gender, Time and Memory in the Middle Ages', in Cox, McAvoy, and Magnani, eds., *Reconsidering Gender, Time and Memory*, pp. 1–12, at p. 5.

[50] P. Brand, '"Time out of mind": The Knowledge and Use of the Eleventh- and Twelfth-Century Past in Thirteenth-Century Litigation', *Anglo-Norman Studies* XVI (1994), 37–54.

[51] P. Brand, 'Lawyers' Time in England in the Later Middle Ages', in C. Humphrey and W. M. Ormrod, eds., *Time in the Medieval World* (York, 2001), pp. 73–104.

Popular Memory and Gender in Medieval England

MEMORY, GENDER, AND STATUS

The dynamics of memory in medieval society have been explored increasingly through the interrelated themes of family and gender.[52] Kinship networks provided a forum for the creation and maintenance of recollections, serving to connect individual memory with family identity.[53] In some contexts, the desire to cultivate ancestry found expression in the form of genealogies, while in Renaissance Florence, private *ricordanze* were employed which extended outwards to the wider family.[54] Geary suggests that women, particularly widows, were assigned the role of memory specialist in family commemoration of the dead, a responsibility he notes from the ninth century, but which apparently fell into decline some three centuries later.[55] Elisabeth van Houts challenges this argument, observing that women's participation did not recede in the face of monastic involvement in family memory.[56] The maternal line was often able to trace its genealogy back farther than the male line whether or not lands passed along these channels.[57] Elite marriage patterns ensured a smaller age-gap between mothers and their children, causing living memory to extend farther back in the female as opposed to the male line. Family memory and ancestries could be recorded in monastic muniments and chronicles, as Chris Given-Wilson remarks, with women regarded as responsible for their maintenance receiving assistance from monastic houses.[58] The majority of works on memory in late medieval England centre on gentry and aristocratic circles or monastic and clerical contexts, shedding light on practices prevalent in the Church and among the highly literate laity, but overlooking the ways that men and women outside these groups thought about the past.[59]

---

[52] S. Leydesdorff, L. Passerini, and P. Thompson, eds., *Gender and Memory*, 2nd edition (New Brunswick, NJ, and London, 2007); G. Ciappelli and P. Rubin, eds., *Art, Memory and Family in Renaissance Florence* (Cambridge, 2000); Fentress and Wickham, *Social Memory*, pp. 112–13.

[53] Fentress and Wickham, *Social Memory*, p. 113.

[54] G. Ciappelli, 'Family Memory: Functions, Evolution, Recurrences', in Ciappelli and Rubin, eds., *Art, Memory and Family*, pp. 26–38, at p. 31.

[55] Geary, *Phantoms of Remembrance*, pp. 52–73; B. Jussen, 'Challenging the Culture of *Memoria*: Dead Men, Oblivion, and the "Faithless Widow" in the Middle Ages', in G. Althoff, J. Fried, and P. J. Geary, eds., *Medieval Concepts of the Past: Ritual, Memory, Historiography* (Cambridge, 2002), pp. 215–32, at pp. 229–30.

[56] van Houts, *Memory and Gender*, pp. 13–14.

[57] van Houts, *Memory and Gender*, pp. 148–9.

[58] C. Given-Wilson, *Chronicles: The Writing of History in Medieval England* (London and New York, 2004), p. 79; J. Bedell, 'Memory and Proof of Age in England, 1272–1327', *Past & Present*, 162 (1999), 3–27, at pp. 24–5.

[59] J. T. Rosenthal, *Telling Tales: Sources and Narration in Late Medieval England* (Philadelphia, 2003), pp. 1–62; M. Cassidy-Welch, *Monastic Spaces and their Meanings: Thirteenth-Century English Cistercian Monasteries* (Turnhout, 2001).

Introduction

Habits of memory among non-elites have begun to be addressed, but the tone and breadth of popular memory in this period remain underexplored.[60] A number of studies map the dynamics of personal and social memory below the level of elites, mining proof-of-age inquests and other legal archives, including ecclesiastical court records, for traces of attitudes towards the past.[61] Joel Rosenthal and John Bedell have examined proofs of age for the thirteenth and fourteenth centuries in order to analyse the memories of jurors who gave evidence on the birth of the prospective heir.[62] Statements from these inquests depict men recalling children's births, social occasions, their own marriages, and other incidental details, though recycled and stock memories appear increasingly in later statements. Jurors involved in these proceedings were exclusively male, occasionally family servants, and often low in status. Evidence from male jurors implies much about men's behaviour in late medieval England, revealing gendered practices around life-cycle events. Men remembered the birth of children, baptisms, and churching ceremonies, but, as Fiona Harris-Stoertz demonstrates, women's accounts formed the bedrock of male evidence and 'played a vital role in creating the community memories' in these records.[63]

Normative ideas about gender meant that men were regarded as more authoritative witnesses in most legal contexts, while women were seldom named as sources of evidence in chronicles. There were exceptions where miraculous knowledge was attributed to women, but a reliance on male memory was much more typical.[64] Old age, which often endowed men's testimony with authority, could afford women's personal memories greater credibility in the absence of living kinsmen.[65] For instance, Judith Everard

---

[60] See, for example, D. M. Owen, 'White Annays and Others', in D. Baker, ed., *Medieval Women: Dedicated and Presented to Professor Rosalind M. T. Hill on the Occasion of her Seventieth Birthday*, Studies in Church History Subsidia, 1 (Oxford, 1978), pp. 331–46, at pp. 336–9; B. R. Lee, 'Men's Recollections of a Women's Rite: Medieval English Men's Recollections Regarding the Rite of the Purification of Women after Childbirth', *Gender & History*, 14 (2002), 224–41; P. J. P. Goldberg, 'Gender and Matrimonial Litigation in the Church Courts in the Later Middle Ages: The Evidence of the Court of York', *Gender & History*, 19 (2007), 43–59; F. Harris-Stoertz, 'Remembering Birth in Thirteenth- and Fourteenth-Century England', in Cox, McAvoy, and Magnani, eds., *Reconsidering Gender, Time and Memory*, pp. 25–59.

[61] Rosenthal, *Telling Tales*; Bedell, 'Memory and Proof of Age', pp. 3–27; Goldberg, 'Gender and Matrimonial Litigation'.

[62] Rosenthal, *Telling Tales*; Bedell, 'Memory and Proof of Age'; J. T. Rosenthal, *Social Memory in Late Medieval England: Village Life and Proofs of Age* (New York, 2018).

[63] Lee, 'Men's Recollections of a Women's Rite'; B. R. Lee, 'A Company of Women and Men: Men's Recollections of Childbirth in Medieval England', *Journal of Family History*, 27 (2002), 92–100; Harris-Stoertz, 'Remembering Birth'.

[64] Given-Wilson, *Chronicles*, pp. 12–13.

[65] E. van Houts, 'Gender and Authority of Oral Witnesses in Europe, 800–1300', *Transactions of the Royal Historical Society*, 6th series, 9 (1999), 201–20, at p. 209; J.

shows that in twelfth- and thirteenth-century Brittany women may have testified when widowed or as the oldest family member regardless of their gender.[66] Women testified in the English church courts, but usually in suits concerning marriage and defamation, rarely featuring as witnesses in cases over parish rights, tithes, and ecclesiastical appointments. As Chapters 1 and 2 emphasise, their treatment and function as deponents depended on notions of female reputation which arose from their perceived sexual behaviour, social status, and the occupation they practised.

Women's testimony was assigned particular value in cases involving activities that were regarded as feminine, where it was treated as a gendered form of expertise. During the high and late Middle Ages, women gave evidence in disputes related to virginity, rape, and motherhood, where their knowledge of childbirth and women's sexual organs served legal purposes.[67] P. J. P. Goldberg suggests that female witnesses in suits from the church courts of York were able to locate past events in reference to pregnancy and childbirth in a manner which may have been unavailable to men.[68] Yet while personal memories of marriage contracts, sexual encounters, and childbirth reflect intimate events associated with the household, memories of marital disputes and violence imply coexisting masculine control over domestic life.

This book explores memory in areas beyond those traditionally associated with each gender, demonstrating that men and women's uses of the past were highly variegated in content. Women retained specialist roles in suits that required knowledge of marriage, sexual activity, childbirth, and ancestry, but also recalled details of customs, economic matters, and events that resonated locally, contributing substantially to the social memory of their communities. Men's recollections covered a broader range of areas, yet they predominated in disputes over ecclesiastical customs and rights, including tithes and appointments to benefices. Aside from differences in the selection of witnesses, the tone of men and women's memories also diverged in specific senses. Embodied memories of childbirth – the accompanying physical trauma, and its frequent association with infant death and parental grief – were woven through women's memories of attending and experiencing labour. Men's recollections were characterised more by movement and demonstrate a greater degree of physical autonomy, with memories of its restriction seen as a marker of unfreedom in manors where serfdom persisted.

Everard, 'Sworn Testimony and Memory of the Past in Brittany, c. 1100–1250', in van Houts, ed., *Medieval Memories*, pp. 72–91, at p. 81; van Houts, *Memory and Gender*, p. 25; see also K. Thomas, 'Age and Authority in Early Modern England', *Proceedings of the British Academy*, 62 (1976), 205–48.

[66] Everard, 'Sworn Testimony', pp. 80–1.

[67] van Houts, 'Gender and Authority', p. 204.

[68] Goldberg, 'Gender and Matrimonial Litigation', pp. 49–50; Owen, 'White Annays'.

Introduction

Perceptions of the past in non-elite settings have received more attention among social and cultural historians of early modern England. Andy Wood explores how memories of rights and customs allowed labourers and peasant communities to challenge the erosion of their livelihoods and means of survival in sixteenth- and seventeenth-century England.[69] At the same time, the relationship between local and central legal systems was increasingly a site of contest, as Simon Sandall argues in the industrial context of the Forest of Dean.[70] Despite the masculine tone that imbued many forms of social memory, Nicola Whyte notes the myriad ways that rural women participated in the development of custom in early modern England and Wales.[71] These avenues hold potential for mapping popular perceptions of the past at a point when the seigneurial system was placed under growing pressure, prior to the social, economic, and religious shifts of the sixteenth century.

Non-elite ways of remembering drew on the routines and ideologies that marked everyday life, although these were not isolated from wider traditions more readily associated with other status groups. The social organisation of medieval and early modern culture has often been interpreted in binary terms, with the labels popular and elite initially constructed in opposition to one another, despite ample evidence of the 'messy, uneven, dynamic, creative interplay between official and non-official discourses'.[72] Early modernists in particular have observed a growing divergence in the habits and attitudes of lower-status and more elite people from the sixteenth to the late eighteenth centuries.[73] For the medieval period, the precise remit and meaning of an identifiable popular culture can be difficult to establish. Indeed, as Aaron Gurevich remarks, popular culture did not operate as a 'single identity distinct from official or "learned" culture' but was instead 'composed of widely divergent components and tendencies'.[74] Everyday encounters between the

---

[69] Wood, *The Memory of the People.*

[70] S. Sandall, *Custom and Popular Memory in the Forest of Dean, c. 1550–1832* (Saarbrücken, 2013); see also S. Sandall, 'Custom, Common Right and Commercialisation in the Forest of Dean, c. 1605–1640', in J. P. Bowen and A. T. Brown, eds., *Custom and Commercialisation in English Rural Society, c. 1350–c. 1750: Revisiting Tawney and Postan* (Hatfield, 2016), pp. 161–79.

[71] N. Whyte, 'Custodians of Memory: Women and Custom in Rural England c. 1550–1700', *Cultural and Social History*, 2 (2011), 153–73; N. Whyte, '"With a sword drawne in her hande": Defending the Boundaries of Household Space in Early Modern Wales', in Kane and Williamson, eds., *Women, Agency and the Law*, pp. 141–55.

[72] Wood, *The Memory of the People*, p. 21; B. Reay, *Popular Cultures in England, 1550–1750* (London and New York, 1998), p. 1.

[73] K. Wrightson and D. Levine, *Poverty and Piety in an English Village: Terling, 1525–1700* (London, 1979); A. Fletcher and J. Stevenson, 'Introduction', in A. Fletcher and J. Stevenson, eds., *Order and Disorder in Early Modern England* (Cambridge, 1985), pp. 1–40.

[74] A. Gurevich, *Medieval Popular Culture: Problems of Belief and Perception*, trans. J. M. Bak and P. A. Hollingsworth (Cambridge, 1988), p. xviii.

clergy and laity, and the peasantry and gentry, were defined by processes of exchange – of knowledge, habits, perceptions, and beliefs. This 'internal acculturation', noted Le Goff, shaped and appropriated strands of cultures which not only coexisted but also coincided through particular points of contact.[75] In local situations, these networks and belief systems overlapped to such an extent that their experiences were often inseparable. From the perspective of Annales historians like Le Goff, this influence flowed from the Church to lay society, but Gramscian interpretations emphasise the capacity for power structures to appropriate the language and customs of non-elites.[76] Popular cultures could perhaps withstand the ideological incursions of the Church and Crown, prompting official and unofficial responses that aimed to standardise their beliefs.[77]

Other categories based on status, such as clerical and lay, intersect with accounts of popular cultures, implying a similar oppositional dynamic expressed through people's relationship with the Church.[78] These identifiers also carry connotations of literacy, theological knowledge, and occasionally, social background. Perceived differences in status or literacy were often encoded in these terms, which sometimes but not always corresponded with other related categories. The language in which texts and documents were written and through which ideas were spoken and diffused mattered in this context, and the absence of Latinity in certain contexts opened up only some genres to the laity. Literary texts aimed at the levels below the aristocracy were more likely to be composed in the vernacular, but many of these, such as devotional works and the Middle English popular romances, were read and heard primarily in mercantile and gentry households.[79] In practice, though, laypeople were acquainted with documentary cultures to different degrees of familiarity, whether these were expressed orally or in written form, and in Latin or the vernacular. This book shows that non-elite men and women were involved in a range of activities more traditionally associated with clerical, gentry, and aristocratic cultures, including literate practices and formal uses of the law. Cultural beliefs and traditions sometimes derived from written texts, especially where these related to piety and the law, yet this knowledge was also

---

[75] J. Le Goff, 'The Historian and the Ordinary Man', in Le Goff, *Time, Work and Culture*, pp. 225–36, at p. 235.

[76] T. F. Ruiz, 'Elite and Popular Culture in Late Fifteenth-Century Castilian Carnivals: The Case of Jaén', in B. Hanawalt and K. Reyerson, eds., *City and Spectacle in Medieval Europe* (Minneapolis, 1994), pp. 296–318, at p. 307.

[77] R. F. Green, *Elf Queens and Holy Friars: Fairy Beliefs and the Medieval Church* (Philadelphia, 2016), pp. 49–50.

[78] For a critique of these terms, see also C. Watkins, *History and the Supernatural in Medieval England* (Cambridge, 2007), p. 21.

[79] For a study of the growth of vernacular reading, see K. Breen, *Imagining an English Reading Public, c. 1150–1400* (Cambridge, 2010).

Introduction

articulated in the liturgy, material culture and habits, and everyday patterns of communication.

To overstate similarities in memory practices across social groups underestimates the dynamics of status and the role of conflict in shaping views of the past. Uses of the past in non-elite and middling contexts derived from the organisation of social hierarchies as well as gender, with the rights and customs of the poor, unfree, and labouring groups often tied to their social position. Power relations upheld through social and economic disparity impinged on the everyday lives of non-elites, notwithstanding the unified nature of many cultural experiences across the social strata. Local disputes concerning boundaries and resources often emerged from the socio-economic relationships that shaped everyday life on the parish and manor. The Church asserted its rights over the collection of tithes, oblations, and other offerings, providing memories of the past that reinforced its hegemonic status. The remembrance of the landscape and its use also magnified elements of social conflict in manorial society, especially during the thirteenth and fourteenth centuries. Rodney Hilton emphasised the extractive nature of seigneurial power, whereby lordly authorities appropriated workers' surplus labour from the agrarian system in ways that produced unequal economic standards.[80] Men and women's legal status could thus be indicated in testimony through accounts of their historical interactions with manorial lords and their officials.

Memory practices were marked by plurality in this period, aside from instances where agreed versions of the past were proffered during legal disputes. Non-elite memory was far from homogeneous, and this book will demonstrate that popular perceptions of the past were multi-faceted in composition. The material conditions of these groups could vary vastly in towns and cities in medieval England, and memories of past events reflected both the divisions and cohesion that arose from social and economic difference. Miriam Müller has detected competition over land and resources within peasant communities in the fourteenth and fifteenth centuries, but the 'experience of lordship' perhaps unified interests enough to ease everyday tensions.[81] Internal stratification could generate moments of conflict rather than solidarity and harmony, ensuring that few memories of events and relationships went uncontested in their local environment.

Although the present study takes memory among non-elites as its primary area of focus, ideas of the past at this social level were not forged in a vacuum. People remembered in relational ways as contact with other social groups

---

[80] R. H. Hilton, *Bondmen Made Free: Medieval Peasant Movements and the English Rising of 1381* (New York, 1973; repr., London and New York, 2003).

[81] M. Müller, 'A Divided Class? Peasants and Peasant Communities in Later Medieval England', in C. Dyer, P. Coss, and C. Wickham, eds., *Rodney Hilton's Middle Ages: An Exploration of Historical Themes*, Past & Present Supplement, 2 (Oxford, 2007), pp. 115–31, at p. 131.

Popular Memory and Gender in Medieval England

gave rise to cooperation and discord, ensuring that '[p]rivate memories … cannot be readily unscrambled from the effects of dominant historical discourses'.[82] In this context, popular memory refers to the widely available ways in which lower-status people, urban labourers, servants, and peasantry – and occasionally the groups with which they interacted – thought about and positioned themselves in relation to past events. Gendered experiences of authority were expressed in social, economic, and religious disparities that shaped everyday routines. It is more appropriate, then, to refer to popular *memories* in this period, acknowledging that these developed in the midst of complex and intertwined socio-economic relationships.

LAW, EXPERIENCE, AND SUBJECTIVITY

Gendered uses of the law were multifaceted and mutable in a number of jurisdictions during the centuries which this study explores.[83] A series of socio-economic shifts both preceded and accompanied the demographic disaster of the plague in the mid-fourteenth century, facilitating a more dynamic land market, a growth in workers' wages, and a general improvement in living standards among labourers and other non-elites.[84] The question of whether women also benefited from these advancements or remained subject to entrenched patriarchal structures continues to enliven scholarship on the experience of gender in late medieval England. These concerns are especially marked in studies that trace long-term trends in wages, gendered patterns of work and marriage, speech crime, and compulsory service. In the context of late medieval London, Caroline Barron observed a growth in economic power and autonomy among some urban women from the early fourteenth century onwards. Goldberg posited a comparable expansion in opportunities in post-plague Yorkshire, where high mortality rates brought higher numbers of young single women into the labour market, and urban service in particular, perhaps fostering a culture of financial independence in which marriage and childbearing could be deferred.[85] The benefits of these shifts were transitory

---

[82] Popular Memory Group, 'Popular Memory', p. 78.

[83] See, for instance, Jones, *Gender and Petty Crime*; Menuge, ed., *Medieval Women and the Law*; P. J. P. Goldberg, *Women, Work, and Life Cycle in a Medieval Economy: Women in York and Yorkshire c. 1300–1520* (Oxford, 1992), pp. 217–79.

[84] B. M. S. Campbell, ed., *Before the Black Death: Studies in the 'Crisis' of the Early Fourteenth Century* (Manchester, 1991); L. R. Poos, *A Rural Society after the Black Death: Essex, 1350–1525* (Cambridge, 1991); J. Hatcher, 'England in the Aftermath of the Black Death', *Past & Present*, 144 (1994), 3–35; B. M. S. Campbell, *The Great Transition: Climate, Disease and Society in the Late-Medieval World* (Cambridge, 2016).

[85] C. M. Barron, 'The "Golden Age" of Women in Medieval London', *Reading Medieval Studies*, 15 (1989), 35–58; for a discussion of migration to towns in this context, see Goldberg, *Women, Work, and Life Cycle*, pp. 280–304; F. Riddy, 'Mother Knows Best: Reading Social Change in a Courtesy Text', *Speculum*, 71 (1996), 66–86; for an

Introduction

and geographically uneven, as Barron and Goldberg have noted. The broader notion of improvement has been rejected in a series of studies by Judith Bennett and Sandy Bardsley, both of whom emphasise the endurance of a 'patriarchal equilibrium' in relation to women's experiences after the Black Death.[86]

The label 'golden age', often applied to these differing perspectives, tends to elide the wide-ranging social, economic, and cultural developments which these studies address, including women's interactions with the law. The patchwork of economic gains for London women in the fourteenth and fifteenth centuries did not translate into participation in civic governance, as Barron noted, although wives on occasion circumvented legal theories like conjugal unity to make testaments and exercise widows' customs.[87]

The interpretation of legal testimony must also be situated within the growing body of work that has emerged in the 'new legal history' over the past two decades. These studies mark a profound shift from public and criminal law as primary areas of study to a broader approach that acknowledges the wide range of areas in which the law was experienced and developed.[88] A number of works address popular uses of the law in medieval and early modern English society. Garthine Walker, for example, explores the role of women within the 'broad participatory base of the legal system' in early modern England, and non-elite engagement with the law in general has produced works on themes including crime, marital violence, economic worth, and attitudes towards women's bodies and reputations.[89] As Walker observes, the content and register of testimony depended on the legal situation, while the language used in the courts drew on 'concepts, images, metaphors and vocabulary that themselves were part of or variously conditioned by ideas about gender, class,

---

important study of single women, see C. Beattie, *Medieval Single Women: The Politics of Social Classification in Late Medieval England* (Oxford, 2007).

[86] Barron, 'The "Golden Age" of Women', pp. 35–58; P. J. P. Goldberg, 'Female Labour, Service and Marriage in the Late Medieval Urban North', *Northern History*, 22 (1986), 18–38; S. Bardsley, *Venomous Tongues: Speech and Gender in Late Medieval England* (Philadelphia, 2006), p. 7; J. M. Bennett, 'Compulsory Service in Late Medieval England', *Past & Present*, 209 (2010), 7–51.

[87] Barron, 'The "Golden Age" of Women', pp. 48–9.

[88] For a survey, see A. Hunt, 'The New Legal History: Prospects and Perspectives', *Crime, Law, and Social Change*, 10 (1986), 201–8.

[89] G. Walker, *Crime, Gender and Social Order in Early Modern England* (Cambridge, 2003), p. 3; for key studies, see Goldberg, *Women, Work, and Life Cycle*; L. Gowing, *Domestic Dangers: Women, Words, and Sex in Early Modern London* (Oxford, 1996); L. Gowing, *Common Bodies: Women, Touch and Power in Seventeenth-Century England* (New Haven, 2003); S. Butler, *The Language of Abuse: Marital Violence in Later Medieval England* (Leiden and Boston, 2007); Wood, *The Memory of the People*; A. Shepard, *Accounting for Oneself: Worth, Status, and the Social Order in Early Modern England* (Oxford, 2017).

Popular Memory and Gender in Medieval England

law, religion and more'.[90] In the medieval church courts, the memories of witnesses developed in a similar nexus of experiences, and included perceptions of the law and its operation.

The specificities of language and rules of the law affected the substance and tone of testimony in these suits. Chapter 1 traces the ways in which pastoral theology and court practice fostered a growing interest in memory as a method of establishing proof. The complexity of canon law increased at the same time, with treatises advancing new and more detailed rules on testimony and legal actions. Yet lower-status men and women engaged with various legal processes in their lifetimes, sometimes on a regular basis, and in different jurisdictions simultaneously.[91] This knowledge was accumulated from personal experience as well as through discussion in local communities, and much of this practical expertise reflected the gendered positions that people adopted under the law.

In this book, I focus on the relationship between witnesses and their testimonies, tracing the extent to which their evidence reflected aspects of their identity.[92] Early theorists of memory emphasised its subjective and imaginative tone as a process. For example, Bartlett applied the method of 'repeated reproduction' to analyse how students recalled the same prose story at intervals. Past experiences were crucial to the formation and reshaping of memories as men and women created their own experiences of the tale. Bartlett concluded that 'both the manner and the matter of recall are often predominantly determined by social influences'.[93] Although stories are often remembered through imagery and motifs already circulating in societies, individual identity also contributes to their narrative focus and structure.[94]

The analysis of memory must also be located in the context of the linguistic turn, where figures such as Hayden White suggested that historical texts should be viewed as an 'extended metaphor' rather than a literal telling of events.[95] The emergence of linguistic analysis forced a conflict between experience and discourse, where interest in the former waned as the latter was seen to better reflect the ideological construction of language. Feminist historians were early proponents of post-structuralist theory as a way of parsing the

---

[90] Walker, *Crime, Gender and Social Order*, p. 7.

[91] P. R. Hyams, 'Deans and their Doings: The Norwich Inquiry of 1286', *Proceedings of the Sixth International Conference on Canon Law, Berkeley* (Vatican City, 1985), pp. 619–46.

[92] A. Musson, *Medieval Law in Context: The Growth of Legal Consciousness from Magna Carta to the Peasants' Revolt* (Manchester, 2001).

[93] F. C. Bartlett, *Remembering: A Study in Experimental and Social Psychology*, 2nd edition (Cambridge, 1964), p. 244; Weldon, 'Remembering as a Social Process', p. 73.

[94] Fentress and Wickham, *Social Memory*, p. 88.

[95] H. White, 'The Historical Text as Literary Artefact', in H. White, ed., *Tropics of Discourse: Essays in Cultural Criticism* (Baltimore, 1978), pp. 81–100; see also J. Bruner, 'The Narrative Construction of Reality', *Critical Inquiry*, 18 (1991), 1–21.

Introduction

connections between social practice and perceptions of women's behaviour.[96] Scott argues that accounts of past events may appear straightforward, but their uncomplicated interpretation as experience can overlook the ways in which people are established as subjects. This also risks solidifying the identities of individuals and can 'locate resistance outside its discursive construction and reify agency as an inherent attribute'.[97] From this perspective, the notion of experience should be explored partly through its discursive composition.

Scholars of legal archives, both medieval and early modern, have applied various methods in analysing testimony. John Arnold emphasises the existence of multiple discourses that produce various selves, with language as 'the arena in which subjectivity is provoked, contained, and performed'.[98] Following Mikhail Bakhtin, Walker uses the theory of 'multivocality' to acknowledge the complexity of the discourses that men and women employed in legal cases.[99] Yet a reliance on 'discourse' as the sole analytic tool for analysing testimony can produce methodological problems. Tom Johnson underlines the intrinsic relationship between social and legal realms, whereby their depiction as dichotomous and an overreliance on the idea of discourse may not 'take seriously enough the legal framework in which the witness testimonies were produced'.[100] In church-court testimony, men and women demonstrated detailed knowledge of the workings of the law. Witnesses relied on language that suggests the dissemination of legal expertise in everyday conversation and through social networks, while the imagery arising from the discourses used emphasises the adaptation of their encounters to legal contexts.

Despite claims of the decline of experience as an analytic tool in social and cultural history, it has resurfaced in several areas, namely the field of memory studies, in relation to histories of the body, and in explorations of subjectivity.[101] Kathleen Canning identifies a reliance on experience in some works on the production and maintenance of ideologies, emphasising the fluidity and fragmentation to which this approach is attuned. A revised application of this term would accommodate both personal claims of experience and the circumstances of its production and representation. Two interrelated concepts, agency and subjectivity, will also be employed in this book to bridge

---

[96] K. Canning, 'Feminist History after the Linguistic Turn: Historicizing Discourse & Experience', in K. Canning, *Gender History in Practice: Historical Perspectives on Bodies, Class, and Citizenship* (Ithaca, NY, 2005), pp. 63–100, at p. 67.

[97] J. Scott, 'The Evidence of Experience', *Critical Inquiry*, 17 (1991), 773–97, at p. 777.

[98] Arnold, *Inquisition and Power*, p. 109.

[99] Walker, *Crime, Gender, and Social Order*, p. 7.

[100] T. Johnson, 'The Preconstruction of Witness Testimony: Law and Social Discourse in England before the Reformation', *Law and History Review*, 32 (2014), 127–47, at p. 139.

[101] K. Canning, 'Difficult Dichotomies: "Experience" between Narrativity and Materiality', in Canning, *Gender History in Practice*, pp. 101–20, at pp. 112–17.

the gap between experience and discourse.[102] As Canning remarks, subjectivity is a valuable methodological tool for mapping 'the subject positions assigned in and by discourses on the one hand, and the experience of those constructed, interpellated, or positioned by discourses on the other'.[103] The application of these terms ascribes to men and women the ability to engage with social structures and legal processes in meaningful ways. Chapter 1 focuses on the pastoral and interrogative impulses that shaped lay relations with the Church in confession and in the ecclesiastical courts, exploring how witnesses were produced as subjects through these experiences. An outline of the dynamics of canon law and court procedure provides the foundations for later discussions on the operation of gender and memory in legal testimony.

Theories of agency are especially instructive in considering how women and subaltern men operated within the strictures of patriarchy and the law. There are occasional limitations to their use, such as analytic imprecision and the implication of autonomy and independence despite constraints upon individual action. For example, Dana Wessell Lightfoot draws productively on Sherry B. Ortner's concept of 'agency of intentions' when exploring labouring-status women, marriage, and dowries in fifteenth-century Valencia. This refined version of agency aims to recognise the restrictions upon women's choices that patriarchal society entailed.[104] Judith Butler's notion of 'discursive agency' better accommodates the legal context of the church courts, where men and women were rendered as subjects through the interrogative process of examination. This kind of agency, as Butler emphasises, 'is not a property of the subject, an inherent will or freedom, but an effect of power, it is constrained but not determined in advance'.[105] Men and women were able to use language and its meanings in a variety of ways in their testimony, appropriating and deploying terms from different discourses of gender, sexuality, social position, and legal status that were current in their social worlds.

Scholars of gender have also turned to the history of the body or embodiment as a means of mapping experience, perhaps reacting against the discursive focus of the linguistic turn.[106] Materiality and embodiment can be traced in legal records not only through experiences like sex and reproduction where gender seems more overt, but also through practices of labour, the use of objects and textiles, and the effects of violence. Toril Moi, for instance,

---

[102] Canning, 'Feminist History after the Linguistic Turn', p.79; see also the discussion of gender, law, and agency in B. Kane and F. Williamson, 'Introduction', in Kane and Williamson, eds., *Women, Agency and the Law*, pp. 1–16, at pp. 2–3.

[103] Canning, 'Difficult Dichotomies', p. 117.

[104] D. W. Lightfoot, *Women, Dowries and Agency: Marriage in Fifteenth-Century Valencia* (Manchester, 2013), pp. 7–8.

[105] J. Butler, *Excitable Speech: A Politics of the Performative* (New York, 1997), p. 139.

[106] K. Canning, 'The Body as Method? Reflections on the Place of the Body in Gender History', in Canning, *Gender History in Practice*, pp. 168–88, at p. 168.

Introduction

notes that 'subjectivity is always embodied, but our bodies do not only bear the mark of sex'.[107] A growing interest in emotion from the perspective of legal history also offers another avenue for accommodating both the capacity to act as well as the constraints that men and women encountered. Legal experiences evoked and encouraged specific types of emotions and, as Chapters 3 and 4 demonstrate, these were often referenced alongside bodily proof.[108] This book draws on the gendered connections between experience, language, and subjectivity to identify more closely the relationship between memory and its use in legal testimony.

CONTEXT AND SETTING

The ecclesiastical courts in England emerged only gradually, with roots in earlier traditions of resolving disagreements. During the Anglo-Saxon period the Church relied upon the synod as the usual location for settling disputes, often through negotiation between parties, perhaps with the intermediary skill of the bishop or his representative.[109] For many reasons, including the frequent inability to conclude cases within the duration of a synod and the development of a literature on canon law, there existed a need and an impetus for a more delineated ecclesiastical forum for resolving conflict. The consistory courts, in the form which they were to assume for the rest of the medieval period, can only be identified from the mid-thirteenth century. Prior to this date, archdeacons and rural deaneries had tended to deal with transgressions which demanded the attention of the ecclesiastical authorities.[110] By the mid-thirteenth century, however, bishops were seeking to assert authority of their courts as places of appeal and of complaint in the first instance.[111]

The Church's jurisdiction in England was administered through the provinces of Canterbury and York, which comprised sets of courts that dealt with spiritual and moral matters at different levels of its hierarchy. Both Canterbury and York rendered judgement in a diocesan and provincial context, arbitrating in cases in the first instance and suits referred on appeal. The embryonic nature of the Church's legal system meant that ecclesiastical courts in a formal sense emerged only by the mid-thirteenth century. Records of judicial activities associated with the English Church, however, survive

---

[107] T. Moi, *What is a Woman? And Other Essays* (Oxford, 1999), p. 67.

[108] L. Kounine, 'Emotions, Mind, and Body on Trial: A Cross-Cultural Perspective', *Journal of Social History*, 51 (2017), 219–30; D. Lemmings, 'Law', in S. Broomhall, ed., *Early Modern Emotions: An Introduction* (Abingdon, 2017), pp. 192–5; B. Kane, 'Reading Emotion and Gender in the Later Medieval English Church Courts', *Frühneuzeit-Info*, 12 (2012), 53–63.

[109] Helmholz, *The Oxford History of the Laws of England*, p. 139.

[110] Helmholz, *The Oxford History of the Laws of England*, p. 134.

[111] Helmholz, *The Oxford History of the Laws of England*, p. 140.

Popular Memory and Gender in Medieval England

from as early as the mid-twelfth century. Charles Donahue notes that 'there were plenty of ecclesiastical proceedings, sometimes conducted by a bishop or a lesser ecclesiastical official, sometimes by the delegates of these persons, sometimes by delegates of the pope'.[112] Private suits between parties usually entailed legal representatives and the production of testimony, whereas prosecutions initiated by Church authorities, known as *ex officio* citations, were more laconic in format.

Cause papers and Act books are extant from only thirteen late medieval dioceses in England, but substantial records of private litigation survive from several ecclesiastical courts in this period.[113] This book draws primarily on the vast archive from York, in tandem with cases sent to Canterbury on appeal and suits brought in its diocesan court in the first instance. The archives of the consistory court in the diocese of London have already received ample attention from Shannon McSheffrey in a study of practices around marriage and sex in late medieval civic contexts.[114] Around six hundred instance cases remain from the courts of York for almost every year of the fourteenth and fifteenth centuries, in addition to deposition books from the dean and chapter of York. Earlier proceedings survive for Canterbury from the pontificate of Hubert Walter (1193–1205), alongside records from several archiepiscopal vacancies during the thirteenth century and deposition books dating from the fifteenth centuries.[115] The archive from York, particularly its vivid testimony, is regarded as perhaps the most extensive church-court material in western Europe for this period. For example, a register survives from Paris (1384–7) and several others are extant from the diocese of Cambrai during the mid-fifteenth century and Brussels for almost the same years. Only the sentences remain from the last two of these courts and the registers in general are less informative than the depositions from Canterbury and York.[116]

Witness statements from this litigation form the basis of this study, due to the focus on memory in the courts and in social practice within testimony rather than the operation of canon law per se. The book adopts a qualitative approach to the perceptions and experiences of memory among non-elite

---

[112] C. Donahue, Jr., 'Procedure in the Courts of the *Ius Commune*', in W. Hartmann and K. Pennington, eds., *The History of Courts and Procedure in Medieval Canon Law* (Washington, DC, 2016), pp. 74–124, at p. 100.

[113] *Select Cases on Defamation to 1600*, ed. R. H. Helmholz, Selden Society, 101 (London, 1985), p. xii; D. M. Smith, *Ecclesiastical Cause Papers at York: The Court of York, 1301–99* (York, 1988); D. M. Smith, *The Court of York, 1400–1499: A Handlist of the Cause Papers and an Index to the Archiepiscopal Court Books* (York, 2003).

[114] S. McSheffrey, *Marriage, Sex, and Civic Culture in Late Medieval London* (Philadelphia, 2006).

[115] B. L. Woodcock, *Medieval Ecclesiastical Courts in the Diocese of Canterbury* (Oxford, 1952).

[116] C. Donahue, Jr., *Law, Marriage, and Society in the Later Middle Ages: Arguments about Marriage from Five Courts* (Cambridge, 2007), pp. 9–10.

Introduction

men and women, by analysing the language and broader narratives used to describe past events. Although depositions from the church courts contain much narrative detail, the outcomes of suits are often unknown due to the patchy survival rate of sentences, while the legal rationale for judgements often went unrecorded.[117] A number of historians working on the English ecclesiastical courts in this period have produced statistical analyses of patterns of litigation, including cases in which women appeared as litigants and witnesses.[118] These findings inform the wider context of this book and demonstrate the prevalence of female parties in specific types of suits as well as the frequency with which women testified alongside men in these disputes.

Litigation relating to marriage and defamation has been the subject of numerous works on late medieval social and cultural life.[119] Disputes that developed from conflict over tithes, parochial rights, and related matters have produced a smaller body of scholarship that tends to explore records in their specific contexts. These initially seem confined to the machinery of these cases, although a number of works emphasise their significance in understanding a broader range of issues, including monastic history and the development of female Cistercian houses.[120] Parties in these cases articulated competing versions of the past expressed through accounts of local rights and custom. These disputes usually comprised different types of interactions, many of which occurred outside the remit of the law, with litigation merely representing their formal appearance in the courts.

Ecclesiastical courts in England relied upon a growing body of canon law and papal decrees, occasionally tempered by provincial legislation and the influence of customary and common law.[121] Procedures used in the ecclesiastical courts were followed in a flexible manner, privileging reasonable

---

[117] Helmholz, *Marriage Litigation*, pp. 20–1.

[118] See, for example, tables listed in Donahue, *Law, Marriage, and Society*, pp. viii–ix; Goldberg, 'Gender and Matrimonial Litigation', p. 47.

[119] M. M. Sheehan, *Marriage, Family and Law in Medieval Europe: Collected Studies*, ed. J. K. Farge (Toronto, 1996); Helmholz, *Marriage Litigation*; Goldberg, *Women, Work, and Life Cycle*; F. Pedersen, 'Demography in the Archives: Social and Geographical Factors in Fourteenth-Century York Cause Paper Litigation', *Continuity and Change*, 10 (1995), 405–36; P. J. P. Goldberg, 'Fiction in the Archives: The York Cause Papers as a Source for Later Medieval Social History', *Continuity and Change*, 12 (1997), 425–45; F. Pedersen, *Marriage Disputes in Medieval England* (London, 2000); Donahue, *Law, Marriage, and Society*.

[120] J. Burton, 'The Convent and the Community: Cause Papers as a Source for Monastic History', in P. Hoskin, C. Brooke, and B. Dobson, eds., *The Foundations of Medieval English Ecclesiastical History: Studies Presented to David Smith* (Woodbridge, 2005), pp. 63–76; E. Freeman, 'Cistercian Nuns, Cause Papers and the York Consistory Court in the Fourteenth and Fifteenth Centuries', *Australia and New Zealand Law and History E-Journal* (2006), 1–14.

[121] For a summary of the Stubbs–Maitland debate, see C. Donahue Jr., 'Roman Canon Law in the Medieval English Church: *Stubbs* vs. *Maitland* Re-Examined after 75 Years in

Popular Memory and Gender in Medieval England

outcomes rather than the precise application of legal rules.[122] Sessions dealing with instance litigation usually convened in the cathedral or its precincts, like the consistory courts of Canterbury and York, and dedicated courtrooms were occasionally established within these buildings.[123] A majority of litigants relied on the services of expert legal personnel, such as proctors or advocates, whose role in cases and level of education could vary considerably. Proctors were not required to gain formal legal degrees and, while some of these men perhaps spent time studying the law in the universities, practical experience in the courts represented the most common form of training. Advocates presented arguments to the Official and were available in several of the English church courts, including York and the Court of Arches, but in other places proctors discharged both sets of responsibilities.[124]

Instance suits began with citations that were delivered to defendants by apparitors, formal officers attached to the courts also referred to as summoners.[125] The premise of the case was then outlined in the libel, which contained points expanded into positions that were put to the opposing party. These points were reframed into articles that formed the basis for the examination of witnesses, alongside additional questions from the defendant known as interrogatories.[126] Legal theory dictated that witnesses should be examined separately and in private to prevent collusion and perjury, yet there were occasional exceptions to this practice.[127] The examination was conducted in the vernacular, with responses often recorded in note form before their translation into Latin, until the use of Middle English became more common towards the end of the fifteenth century.

The social background of witnesses and parties in the church courts suggests that, as Goldberg notes of the courts of York, the majority were 'neither persons of very high status nor persons at the lowest levels of the social hierarchy'.[128] Gentry and aristocratic families tended to settle disputes through other channels, turning to episcopal authorities in person rather than the courts, but they did initiate cases in small numbers, especially over the impediment of consanguinity within marriage and in relation to testamentary issues. Litigants were required to pay the costs which suits incurred, including

---

the Light of Some Records from the Church Courts', *Michigan Law Review*, 72 (1974), 647–716.

[122] Helmholz, *Marriage Litigation*, pp. 112–13.

[123] J. A. Brundage, *The Medieval Origins of the Legal Profession: Canonists, Civilians, and Courts* (Chicago, 2008), p. 423 n. 51.

[124] Helmholz, *Marriage Litigation*, pp. 148–9.

[125] Woodcock, *Medieval Ecclesiastical Courts*, pp. 45–9.

[126] Brundage, *The Medieval Origins of the Legal Profession*, p. 280.

[127] Helmholz, *The Oxford History of the Laws of England*, p. 339; J. A. Brundage, *Medieval Canon Law* (London and New York, 1995), p. 132.

[128] Goldberg, 'Fiction in the Archives', p. 429.

Introduction

those for the production of documents, the fees of proctors and advocates, and the expenses of witnesses. Many of these sums were sizeable, suggesting that parties were often more elevated in social background than deponents. Richard H. Helmholz notes a case from Lichfield in the late fifteenth century that came to the sum of 26*s.* 8*d.*, while other suits recorded even larger payments.[129] Many of the cases initiated in the consistory of York in the first instance involved litigants of moderate means, including the more affluent peasantry, but social status was higher among parties who resided further from the city.[130] A similar pattern is evident in the material from the courts of Canterbury, although a close study of the geographical origins and economic means of parties in these records has yet to be completed.[131]

This book concentrates in particular on the activities and testimony of lower-status men and women, especially the peasantry, labourers, servants, those alleged to be paupers, and the unfree. These social positions cannot be equated uniformly with lack of economic resources, nor was each of these groups in any way homogeneous in terms of members' social and financial situations. The poor were restricted in their ability to initiate suits due to their limited economic means. They also appeared as witnesses less frequently than men and women of low to middling status, as their marginality exposed them to attacks upon their reputations which could undermine the validity of their evidence. Although unfree persons were prohibited from testifying under canon law, in England their evidence was accepted and published, with opposing arguments against their depositions following afterwards.[132] Where serfs and the poor contributed to legal cases, their status or behaviour could become a source of contention as parties sought to construct their social position in competing terms.

Memory constituted a central 'modality' of medieval culture, and this study uses church-court testimony to address its characteristics in everyday life, especially among women whose contributions to more formal realms of remembrance were limited.[133] Chapter 1 focuses on the intersections of gender and testimony in relation to pastoral care and judicial inquiry. It traces the growing significance of memory in canon law in general, and the extent to which it influenced nascent methods of proof in litigation. Canon law developed through its use in litigation as much as through formal legal theory. During the twelfth century, for instance, English canonists collected decretals

---

[129] Helmholz, *Marriage Litigation*, p. 161.

[130] Donahue, *Law, Marriage, and Society*, p. 65; for a comprehensive study of York itself, see S. Rees Jones, *York: The Making of a City, 1068–1350* (Oxford, 2013).

[131] Woodcock, *Medieval Ecclesiastical Courts*, pp. 105–6.

[132] C. Donahue, Jr., 'Proof by Witnesses in the Church Courts of Medieval England: An Imperfect Reception of the Learned Law', in M. S. Arnold et al., eds., *On the Laws and Customs of Medieval England* (Chapel Hill, NC, 1981), pp. 129–32, at p. 143.

[133] Carruthers, *The Book of Memory*, p. 260.

Popular Memory and Gender in Medieval England

in large numbers, while legal judgements were more commonly recorded in lawyers' formularies during the fourteenth and fifteenth centuries. Attitudes towards women's mnemonic authority are explored in Chapter 2, by analysing critiques of their testimony which were often based on allegations of sexual promiscuity and poverty. Socio-cultural patterns associated with courtship and marriage produced competing accounts of premarital relationships told from male and female perspectives.

Bodies as sites of memory, and agents in its production and maintenance, provide the focus for the next two chapters, which explore embodied perceptions of the past through memories of physical characteristics and experiences. Chapter 3 examines the physical habits that offered materiality to men and women's everyday lives. Memories associated with work, clothing and other objects, and violence, death, and burial saw witnesses describe interactions with materials, surfaces, and other bodies. Sexuality and generation are addressed in Chapter 4, where gendered beliefs and depictions of men and women's reproductive pasts are analysed through memories of sex, childbirth, and parenting. Female bodies were seen to bear proof of sexual activity and birth in changes to the breasts and sexual organs. Men and women regarded practices around clothing, physical behaviour, and emotional responses as evidence of sexual and marital relationships and as confirmation of parental roles. Chapter 5 turns to memories of marriage and kinship in more detail, mapping the ways in which non-elite men and women interpreted and recalled their marital histories and those of neighbours and kin. Despite cultural associations that assigned mothers, wives, and female relatives greater responsibility for preserving family pasts, some men presented alternative accounts, especially in cases where kin groups were of less humble origins and the transfer of land was involved.

The two final chapters deal with memories of custom, writing, and the environment among non-elite men and women, considering the ways that gender and social hierarchy intersected with literacy and depictions of places and spaces. Men, and primarily churchmen, experienced the highest levels of literacy, especially towards the beginning of this period, albeit with varying degrees of expertise. Chapter 6 explores engagement with literate practices among women and non-elite men in legal and business transactions, aural and oral encounters with the written word, and local disputes over custom. Men and women contributed to the construction and maintenance of custom, drawing on gendered familiarity with the landscape to present complex histories of rights and uses in their communities. Memories of places, spatial mobility, and the agricultural landscape form the basis for Chapter 7. Gender relations and normative perceptions of men and women's roles produced diverging experiences of particular sites, spaces, and the worked land. Clerical and popular ideologies were inseparable in many realms of everyday life, yet non-elite women could circumvent and appropriate notional limits on their mobility. Manorial authority was also remembered through contact with the

Introduction

landscape, as men in particular clashed with seigneurial lords whose attempts to control their physical autonomy were recalled in suits concerning land.

The book aims to assess how men and women remembered the past in order to convey aspects of their personal identities and subjectivities, and thus ameliorate their circumstances through the law. It also offers an interpretation of how people below the level of the elite understood canon law and contributed to its development through their own use. Most significantly, it foregrounds women's legal encounters, suggesting how they employed memory, their own histories, and gender norms to negotiate patriarchal constraints upon their behaviour. Kate Crehan notes that hegemony, in part, consists of 'the power to determine the structuring rules within which such struggles are to be fought out'.[134] The law was not simply a site of domination, but instead a field in which subaltern people could, in some respects, contest the terms of their subordination. For all that testimony adhered to hegemonic values about gender, men and women could work to subvert these norms by telling the stories of their lives.

---

[134] K. Crehan, *Gramsci, Culture and Anthropology* (London, Sterling, and Virginia, 2002), p. 204.

1

PASTORAL CARE, CANON LAW, AND SOCIAL RELATIONS

Memory and introspection lay at the heart of the spiritual relationship between the clergy and laity in late medieval England, and this is best exemplified in confessional interrogation. In 1240, Walter de Cantilupe, bishop of Worcester, composed a *Summula* that counselled confessors on how to extract memories of sin from penitents. Later appended to the Statutes of Exeter in 1287, the tract interpreted biographical memory as a chronicle of past misdeeds. The penitent was instructed to 'return to the beginning of his life how he had been born, reflecting on all the years of his life that he can remember, and what he did in what years and on what days'.[1] Parish clergy with the cure of souls were ordered to hold a copy of the *Summula*, while those lacking a copy received a penalty of 1 mark. The *Summula* and similar treatises on virtues and vices embodied the Church's mounting interest in pastoral care, which intensified from the late twelfth century onwards. This programme gained formal confirmation in ecclesiastical councils and a raft of provincial and diocesan legislation, facilitating a growth in Latin and vernacular literature dedicated to pastoral duties.

This pastoral drive in the parishes coincided with the emergence of the ecclesiastical courts as a mechanism for detection and arbitration in medieval society. In theory and practice, the Church's pastoral and legal functions reflected similar concerns with the interior lives and moral behaviour of parishioners. As less rational forms of proof declined across Europe in the twelfth century, the more widespread use of witnesses generated written forms of evidence based on subjective depictions of past events.[2] Canonists already familiar with traditions from Roman law produced an increasing body of work

---

[1] *Councils and Synods*, II, p. 1071. Summula of Peter Quinel, bishop of Exeter (1287?): 'debet enim reverti in se ad exordium vite sue quomodo se gesserit, cogitans de omnibus annis vite sue qui possunt sue occurrere memorie, et sollicite quid quibus annis fecerit et diebus et in quibus locis, quia locus est principium memorie'; see also J. Goering and D. S. Taylor, '*Summulae* of Bishops Walter de Cantilupe (1240) and Peter Quinel (1287)', *Speculum*, 67 (1992), 576–94.

[2] R. Bartlett, *Trial by Fire and Water: The Medieval Judicial Ordeal* (Oxford, 1986), pp. 127–52.

on the examination of witnesses. From the late twelfth century onwards, both proceduralists and decretal law explored and attempted to reconcile agreed methods of weighing the value of witness testimony.[3] In common with the expansion of confessional practice, the 'routine of interrogation' provided the force behind these developments, fostering a novel emphasis on self-examination among penitents and canonical witnesses alike.[4] Theological teachings on conscience were framed in terms of its relationship to sin, while introspection in both penitential and legal terms was achieved through the remembrance of past behaviour.

These shifts in the pastoral and legal treatment of the laity occurred against a wider backdrop of developments in canon law and theology which debated central facets of lay experience, including sexuality, the condition of marriage, fertility, and conception.[5] Implicit in learned and clerical treatments of these subjects were gendered perceptions of human nature that accorded women ancillary social and procreative roles. The assumptions that marked misogynistic traditions pervaded works on pastoral care and canon-law treatises, although their force could be mitigated in social practice. The gender of penitents often influenced instructions on how to question sinners in manuals for confession, reflecting broader attitudes towards women which tended to reinforce misogynistic perceptions of their nature and social function. Canonists also identified restrictions on female testimony, asserting the superior authority of male witnesses, yet once again not every point of canon law in this area was observed in litigation.

By the thirteenth century, the Church was also developing novel mechanisms of control over the everyday lives of the laity, implementing sacramental and pastoral reforms through teachings in the parish and the expansion of its judicial remit. Memory and introspection permeated the laity's encounters with ecclesiastical authority. Confession and judicial interrogation differed in their immediate contexts and implications, yet both entailed similar sets of exchanges centred on concerns about 'truth', individual conscience, and the role of intention in describing the motivation for past behaviour. The production of this knowledge during confession, and in judicial testimony, demanded from parishioners a type of self-reflection that reinforced power relations related to the nature of ecclesiastical authority more generally. Foucault described confession as a 'ritual [of discourse] that unfolds within a power relationship', characterised by the unequal distribution of authority which resided primarily with the questioner, a figure with the capacity to

---

[3] Donahue, 'Proof by Witnesses', pp. 129–32.

[4] M. Curry Woods and R. Copeland, 'Classroom and Confession', in D. Wallace, ed., *The Cambridge History of Medieval English Literature* (Cambridge, 1999), pp. 376–406, at p. 377.

[5] I. Wei, *Intellectual Culture in Medieval Paris: Theologians and the University, c. 1100–1330* (Cambridge, 2012), pp. 247–92.

Pastoral Care, Canon Law, and Social Relations

'judge, punish, forgive, console and reconcile'.[6] Like acts of confession, the interrogation of parishioners during church-court litigation did not 'simply reflect or represent power relations but form[ed] part of these relations'.[7] Gender difference intensified the hierarchies that structured judicial testimony and the performance of sacramental confession, contributing an 'additional layer to these mechanisms of constraint' when clerical or priestly figures administered to the female laity.[8]

Historians of late medieval religion have emphasised the spiritual commitment that marked lay piety in the centuries before the Reformation.[9] A number of studies, in contrast, demonstrate the ways in which dominant patterns of conformity obscured more varied responses to institutional religion.[10] Many laypeople were no doubt committed to elements of local religion, cooperating with ecclesiastical authorities in maintaining social control through the regulation of moral behaviour. The dynamics of power emerged not from 'the primary existence of a central point', but were embedded in the social organisation of parish life which represented and reproduced uneven experiences with local authorities.[11] For example, while the Church investigated suspected crimes that came under its purview, their detection often depended on neighbours reporting behaviour that was seen as transgressive. Yet the experience of ecclesiastical authority during confessional and judicial interrogation was not entirely coercive in nature and, as Foucault argues, confessants responded to inquiries in 'perpetual spirals of power and pleasure'.[12] This conception of power overlooks the extent to which 'social categories [were] defined through domination and subordination', but these experiences provided opportunities for laypeople to examine their consciences and to expiate their sins in confession.[13] Power relations during interrogatory encounters were not inherently weighted towards clerical questioners, as Arnold notes, and could allocate 'power between the two

---

6   M. Foucault, *The History of Sexuality*, vol. 1: *An Introduction*, trans. R. Hurley (New York, 1990), pp. 61–2.

7   Arnold, *Inquisition and Power*, p. 8.

8   D. Elliot, 'Women and Confession: From Empowerment to Pathology', in M. C. Erler and M. Kowaleski, eds., *Gendering the Master Narrative: Women and Power in the Middle Ages* (Ithaca, NY, 2003), pp. 31–51, at p. 44.

9   E. Duffy, *The Stripping of the Altars: Traditional Religion in England, 1400–1580*, 2nd edition (New Haven and London, 2005); B. Kümin, *The Shaping of a Community: The Rise and Reformation of the English Parish, c. 1400–1560* (Aldershot, 1996).

10 R. Lutton, *Lollardy and Orthodox Religion in Pre-Reformation England* (Woodbridge, 2006), pp. 7–11; I. Forrest, *The Detection of Heresy in Late Medieval England* (Oxford, 2005).

11 Foucault, *The History of Sexuality*, vol. 1, p. 93.

12 Foucault, *The History of Sexuality*, vol. 1, p. 44.

13 S. D. Bernstein, *Confessional Subjects: Revelations of Gender and Power in Victorian Literature and Culture* (Chapel Hill, NC, and London, 1997), p. 20.

Popular Memory and Gender in Medieval England

people, constituting both as subjects within discourse'.[14] Indeed, the ability to act as deponents in the church courts offered laywomen in particular unusual access to situations in which they could articulate narratives that were socially and legally meaningful. Despite the simultaneous strengthening of ecclesiastical authority and its implications for the experience of authority, the Church's pastoral programme facilitated the transmission of the laity's memories.

This chapter initially addresses the relationship between pastoral literature and theological concepts of intention, contrition, and satisfaction in penitential discourse. Secular clergy of various levels of education were instructed on methods for confessing the laity, which included guidance on the examination of female penitents, whose supposed susceptibility towards sexual sin and its concealment complicated pastoral encounters. Pastoral texts were often produced in networks associated with the administration of canon law and the church courts. Intellectual circles centred on reforming bishops and higher clergy generated related texts on pastoral care, with a wealth of pastoral literature emerging during the fourteenth century from canonists and clerical administrators based in the diocese of York. The chapter then explores the development of examination procedures in the ecclesiastical courts, mapping the transition from earlier forms of proof to the interrogatory methods of witness testimony. Developments in pastoral theology informed the practical application of canon law in the courts, while the judicial format adopted in confession itself emerged from strands of legal theory.

PASTORALIA AND CONFESSION

The efforts of reforming popes and bishops in advancing theological and legal knowledge gathered momentum in the late twelfth and early thirteenth centuries. A vast amount of work emerged from clerical and legal circles, encompassing official injunctions, manuals for priests and confessors, as well as canon-law texts that guided procedure in the courts. The expansion of pastoral literature, focused especially on the laity's relationship with the clergy, was accorded legislative weight in formal assemblies, including the Third Lateran Council in 1179 and the Fourth Lateran Council of 1215.[15] Particular significance is often assigned to the latter meeting for the expansion of confessional practices. Yet Sarah Hamilton demonstrates the

---

[14] Arnold, *Inquisition and Power*, p. 93.

[15] *Decrees of the Ecumenical Councils*, ed. N. P. Tanner (London and Georgetown, 1990), vol. 1, pp. 230–71; M. Gibbs and J. Lang, *Bishops and Reform 1215–1272, with Special Reference to the Lateran Council of 1215* (Oxford, 1934), part III; H. Birkett, 'The Pastoral Application of the Lateran IV Reforms in the Northern Province, 1215–1348', *Northern History*, 43 (2006), 199–219; D. Summerlin, 'The Canons of the Third Lateran Council of 1179: Their Origins and Reception, ca. 1148–ca. 1191' (PhD thesis, University of Cambridge, 2012).

34

Pastoral Care, Canon Law, and Social Relations

prevalence of confession among the early medieval laity, depicting a world in which penitential practices pervaded many strands of religious life.[16] The laity confessed at least once a year before Lateran IV, but the canon *Omnis utriusque sexus* strengthened the directive for annual confession to a parish priest. In this sense, the Fourth Lateran Council 'certified an already existing concern with the sacrament of penance, and provided a substantial impetus to pastoral renewal'.[17] Its canons did, however, intensify two aspects of confession: namely, the desire for the laity to confess more often and the emphasis on the circumstances of sin.

As the stipulations of Lateran IV were disseminated in regional and diocesan legislation, there was a parallel growth in manuals aimed at the secular clergy. Such works sought to improve clerical knowledge of pastoral theology so as to better instruct the laity on the basic tenets of the Christian faith. The earlier guides developed in form and spirit during the twelfth century, but the thirteenth century saw the consolidation and expansion of literature on the *cura animarum*, with the appearance of a wider range of works on preaching and confession.[18] Leonard Boyle described this raft of related texts as *pastoralia*, a term that encompassed the breadth of the pastoral programme in a variety of media.[19] The education and levels of literacy among the parish clergy were central concerns from the late twelfth and thirteenth centuries, forming the basis for conciliar and synodal legislation that intended to improve their learning. Shortly after the Fourth Lateran Council, episcopal authorities in England began to formalise reforming ideas at the diocesan level. The Statutes of Salisbury, issued between 1217 and 1219 by Richard Poore, bishop of Salisbury, emphasised the need to educate the clergy better for their administration of pastoral care. Pastoral manuals and treatises of this kind acted as the 'vehicles by which the medieval church's doctrines and laws were taken from the schools and brought into parishes'.[20] These texts are also central to understanding the conjunction of clerical and lay attitudes towards confession and judicial interrogation.

The vernacular formed the principal language for the delivery of preaching and *exempla*, but the thirteenth and early fourteenth centuries saw the

---

[16] S. Hamilton, *The Practice of Penance, 900–1050* (Woodbridge, 2001).

[17] J. Goering and P. J. Payer, 'The "Summa Penitentie Fratrum Predicatorum": A Thirteenth-Century Confessional Formulary', *Mediaeval Studies*, 55 (1993), 1–50, at p. 1.

[18] L. Boyle, 'The Fourth Lateran Council and Manuals of Popular Theology', in T. J. Heffernan, ed., *The Popular Literature of Medieval England* (Knoxville, TN, 1985), pp. 30–43, at p. 33.

[19] L. Boyle, 'The Inter-Conciliar Period, 1179–1215, and the Beginnings of Pastoral Manuals', in F. Liotta, ed., *Miscellanea Rolando Bandinelli, Papa Alessandro III* (Siena, 1986), pp. 43–56, at p. 46; see also L. Boyle, 'A Study of the Works Attributed to William of Pagula: With Special Reference to the "Oculus sacerdotis" and "Summa summarum"' (DPhil thesis, University of Oxford, 1956).

[20] R. Helmholz, 'John de Burgh', *Ecclesiastical Law Journal*, 18 (2016), 67–72, at p. 69.

Popular Memory and Gender in Medieval England

production of pastoral works written primarily in Latin. Despite the language of composition, pastoral literature in Latin proved popular in clerical circles. William of Pagula's *Oculus Sacerdotis*, a manual completed between 1320 and 1327, survives in more than fifty manuscript copies. In the early 1380s, the *Oculus* was abstracted in the *Pupilla Oculi* of John de Burgh, a theologian educated at Cambridge University, who also gained practical legal experience as proctor and later chancellor of the university.[21] Both the *Oculus* and the *Pupilla* became popular guides, with the latter supplanting the former as the standard Latin pastoral manual for relatively well-educated priests. Although such texts were ostensibly aimed at the parish clergy in general, the structure and level of assumed knowledge implies that advanced Latin manuals tended to circulate mainly among graduates.[22]

Shorter catechetical texts in Latin also circulated among the parish clergy, often concentrating on the minimum requirements of Christian observance that parish priests communicated to the faithful.[23] Robert Grosseteste's *Templum Dei*, completed around 1225, included advice on confession and the spiritual needs of the laity, and spread widely among the more literate clergy, surviving in almost one hundred copies.[24] Despite variations in the education and competence in Latin enjoyed by parochial clergy, many of these texts appeared in parish libraries, whether through targeted acquisition or personal bequests from learned clerks and occasionally laymen.[25] Equally influential were injunctions and decrees that informed the clergy on the broader spiritual education of the laity.[26] Confessors were instructed to question penitents on the seven deadly sins, the commandments, and finally the five senses. In 1281, Archbishop Pecham promulgated *Ignorancia sacerdotum* that required the parish clergy to teach parishioners the tenets of faith outside the confessional. Priests were encouraged to communicate these articles to the laity several times a year in the vernacular.

---

[21] Helmholz, 'John de Burgh', p. 68.

[22] V. Gillespie, 'The Literary Form of the Middle English Pastoral Manual, with Particular Reference to the *Speculum Christiani* and Some Related Texts' (DPhil thesis, University of Oxford, 1981), p. 2.

[23] See C. Rider, 'Lay Religion and Pastoral Care in Thirteenth Century England: The Evidence of a Group of Short Confession Manuals', *Journal of Medieval History*, 36 (2010), 327–40.

[24] Robert Grosseteste, *Templum Dei*, ed. J. Goering and F. A. C. Mantello (Toronto, 1984), p. 14; for a recent dating of the *Templum Dei*, see J. Goering, 'When and Where did Grosseteste Study Theology?', in J. McEvoy, ed., *Robert Grosseteste: New Perspectives on his Thought and Scholarship* (Turnhout, 1995), pp. 17–51, at p. 29.

[25] S. Gee, 'Parochial Libraries in Pre-Reformation England', in Rees Jones, ed., *Learning and Literacy in Medieval England*, pp. 199–222.

[26] S. Powell, 'The Transmission and Circulation of *The Lay Folks' Catechism*', in A. J. Minnis, ed., *Late Medieval Religious Texts and their Transmission: Essays in Honour of A. I. Doyle* (Cambridge, 1994), pp. 67–84.

Pastoral Care, Canon Law, and Social Relations

Pastoral works in the vernacular began to appear, often in regional dialects, from the early fourteenth century in particular. The ecclesiastical centre of the southern province produced *Ayenbite of Inwit*, a translation of the *Somme le roi*, an influential thirteenth-century treatise on virtues and vices. Michael of Northgate, the author of *Ayenbite* and a monk of St Augustine's abbey in Canterbury, may have entered holy orders as a priest before his period in monastic life. Although the text was written in the 'Engliss of Kent' and aimed at 'lewede men', fathers, mothers, and their children, it was perhaps intended to be read aloud to reach a wider audience.[27] A version of Grosseteste's *Templum Dei* was composed in Middle English in the late fourteenth century, entitled *The Cleansyng of Man's Soule*.[28] Apparently aimed at the laity rather than Latin-literate parish clergy, only two copies survive, one of which was associated with the abbess of Barking abbey.[29] In 1357 a Latin catechism authored by John Thoresby, archbishop of York, directed archdeacons to inform local priests on the six tenets of the faith. Thoresby commissioned a vernacular translation of the text, known as *The Lay Folks' Catechism*, which recommended that the laity be examined on these points at Lent. These requirements were disseminated through rural deans who were expected to possess copies of decrees and understand their provisions.[30] Both the Latin and English versions were derived from the Lambeth Constitutions of 1281, promulgated by the archbishop of Canterbury, and three years later the clergy in the province of Canterbury received an almost identical directive.

Vernacular preaching communicated doctrine to the laity, achieved in part through the expansion of sermons and *exempla* as a genre from the mid-thirteenth century onwards. Theological and canon legal principles on marriage, for example, were circulated through discussions of consummation, adultery, remarriage, and the conjugal debt.[31] *Exempla* and preaching in general aimed to emphasise the grave importance of confession, ensuring that the laity understood the spiritual consequences of unprepared death and therefore discharged all sins from their conscience. Several *exempla* in John Mirk's *Festial* concentrated on confession, like the story of the three men who stole an abbot's ox, two of whom confessed while the third did not and died in a state of damnation.[32] Inducements to confess embodied clerical perceptions of gendered religious practices, which were situated in broader normative ideologies about men and women's behaviour.

---

[27] *Dan Michel's Ayenbite of Inwyt or Remorse of Conscience*, ed. R. Morris and P. Gradon (Oxford, 1979), p. 262.

[28] M. Rubin, *Corpus Christi: The Eucharist in Late Medieval Culture* (Cambridge, 1991), p. 87.

[29] S. Wood, *Conscience and the Composition of Piers Plowman* (Oxford, 2012), p. 52 n. 23.

[30] Powell, 'The Transmission and Circulation of *The Lay Folks' Catechism*', p. 67.

[31] D. L. d'Avray, *Medieval Marriage: Symbolism and Society* (Oxford, 2005), pp. 72–3.

[32] *John Mirk's Festial*, ed. S. Powell (Oxford, 2011), vol. 2, p. 252.

Popular Memory and Gender in Medieval England

Theological treatises occasionally accorded wives special influence over the moral and spiritual lives of their spouses, while women in general were seen to attend Church services and to confess more frequently than men.[33] Female agency in this area was nevertheless seen as limited and was often characterised in patriarchal terms. In his *Summa Confessorum*, composed around 1215, Thomas of Chobham acknowledged married women's authority over their husband's actions, but framed their interventions in primarily sexual and domestic terms.[34] Despite the autonomy attributed to laywomen in their patterns of worship, marital relationships could occasionally circumscribe their ability to confess. In 1434, Alice Barton recalled the response of John Mycholson to news that his wife had testified on behalf of the female plaintiff in a matrimonial suit, contradicting his own evidence for the male defendant. John swore that as soon as he returned home he would 'make his wife confess to the priest and receive penance for the perjury that she had incurred on her part'.[35] Although married women provided testimony on specific matters in the church court, husbands could discipline female speech in ways that diminished its authority in the later stages of legal actions, while reinforcing their own authority over household dependants.

Women's attendance at church services was also regarded with ambivalence in clerical circles. Mirk's *Festial* included an *exemplum* in which two women conversed with one another during Mass, only for the bishop to observe their misbehaviour, alongside a devil, known as Tutivillus, who recorded their words on a long scroll.[36] Completed sometime in the 1380s and written in Middle English, the *Festial* was intended for rural lay audiences and rapidly became the standard vernacular collection of sermons in late medieval England.[37] Sexual sin dominated treatments of female confession, as Jacqueline Murray notes, with moral theology often interpreting women's bodies as inferior to and weaker than men's, despite early Christian teachings on the 'sexless soul'.[38] Pastoral manuals warned clergy of the dangers inherent in hearing confession from women in particular. The early thirteenth-century Statutes of Salisbury instructed priests to administer

---

[33] A. Blamires, 'Beneath the Pulpit', in C. Dinshaw and D. Wallace, eds., *The Cambridge Companion to Medieval Women's Writing* (Cambridge, 2003), pp. 141–58, at p. 143.

[34] Thomas of Chobham, *Summa Confessorum*, ed. F. Broomfield (Paris, 1968), p. 375; quoted in S. Farmer, 'Persuasive Voices: Clerical Images of Medieval Wives', *Speculum*, 61 (1986), 517–43, at p. 517.

[35] BI CP.F.175. 'ipsam cito posset venire domum faceret dictam uxorem suam sacerdoti confiteri ac penitenciam recipere pro periurio quod in hac parte incurrebat'.

[36] *John Mirk's Festial*, ed. Powell, vol. 2, p. 250.

[37] For a useful study of Mirk's sermons, see J. A. Ford, *John Mirk's Festial: Orthodoxy, Lollardy and the Common People in Fourteenth-Century England* (Cambridge, 2006).

[38] J. Murray, 'Gendered Souls in Sexed Bodies: The Male Construction of Female Sexuality in Some Medieval Confessors' Manuals', in P. Biller and A. J. Minnis, eds., *Handling Sin: Confession in the Middle Ages* (York, 1998), pp. 79–93, at pp. 79–80.

Pastoral Care, Canon Law, and Social Relations

the sacrament to female penitents in open places where the pair could be seen but not overheard.[39]

Confession manuals emphasised the significance of memory in penitential discourse, and the internal structure of *pastoralia* was on occasion organised in order to aid the recall of their contexts. Ideas that were seen as central to pastoral texts were increasingly composed in rhyme or verse during the thirteenth century, with mnemonic passages appearing in popular handbooks the better to commit their contents to memory.[40] Diagrams and other schema were used in Grosseteste's *Templum Dei*, for example, both as a means of referencing particular points and to enhance understanding and recollection.[41] *Pastoralia* also advised clergy on the extraction of memories from penitents during auricular examination. The thirteenth-century formulary *Summa Penitentie Fratrum Predicatorum* noted the necessity to obtain more detail where accounts of past events seemed incomplete.[42] The *Summula* of Walter de Cantilupe emphasised the importance of actively encouraging penitents to remember their pasts, thus facilitating the detection of their sins. The text noted that 'we often bring back to memory that which we had given up to forgetfulness, and through this we are reminded of the number, that is to say of how many sins we committed which we should have confessed.'[43] Devotional works like the fifteenth-century regimen *Instructions for a Devout and Literate Layman* articulated an identical concern with examination of the conscience as analysis of the past was cast as a religious practice. Composed in Latin, the *Instructions* conclude with the counsel: 'when you are in bed, go back to the beginning of the day, and look diligently in your heart: if you have done any evil, and there be sorry'.[44] Sermon *exempla* depicted the concealment of sexual lapses during confession as a particularly feminine trait, relating tales of sinful women who failed to share memories of incest or adultery. The suppression of sexual sin induced great shame in the female penitents of these tales, while the sustained failure to confess past misdeeds led to death and damnation.[45]

The individual conscience was interpreted as the repository for memories of sin that confessors were required to examine in order to determine their

---

[39] B. A. Barr, *The Pastoral Care of Women in Late Medieval England* (Woodbridge, 2008), p. 13; *Councils and Synods*, I, p. 72. Statutes of Salisbury I (1217×1219).

[40] W. H. Campbell, *The Landscape of Pastoral Care in Thirteenth-Century England* (Cambridge, 2018), p. 158.

[41] Grosseteste, *Templum Dei*, ed. Goering and Mantello, p. 8.

[42] Goering and Payer, 'The "Summa Penitentie"', lines 58–63, p. 28.

[43] *Councils and Synods*, II, p. 1071. Summula of Peter Quinel, bishop of Exeter (1287?): 'reducimus sepe ad memoriam que tradidimus oblivioni, et per hoc recordabimur numerum, quotiens scilicet peccata que confitemur commiserimus'.

[44] W. A. Pantin, 'Instructions for a Devout and Literate Layman', in J. J. G. Alexander and M. T. Gibson, eds., *Medieval Learning and Literature* (Oxford, 1976), pp. 398–422, at p. 400.

[45] Barr, *The Pastoral Care of Women*, pp. 113–16.

Popular Memory and Gender in Medieval England

extent and magnitude. Early Christian interpretations of conscience depended on Greek traditions which emphasised the role of knowledge and self-examination in relation to personal behaviour.[46] By the twelfth century, handbooks on confession increasingly began to consider the conditions in which sin occurred, as more contemplative treatises on the character and behaviour of the sinner replaced older penitential manuals that consisted of lists of sins and their tariffs. Although contrition was a familiar concept in confessional thought by the eleventh century, reforms during the Gregorian period saw its wider reception in texts such as Gratian's *Decretum*, and the works of theologians like Peter Lombard and Thomas Aquinas.[47] Sermons preached to the laity similarly emphasised 'contricion of herte', 'schryfte of mowthe, and satisfaccion' for sinful deeds.[48] While the performance of penance continued to function as an outward form of expiation, the degree of contrition operated as a primary means of satisfaction and could mitigate the amount of penance awarded. Vernacular works such as *The Prick of Conscience*, composed in the mid-fourteenth century, urged the individual to 'ransak alle his lyf / And knawe whar of he sale hym schryf'. The confessional poem became widely popular in other English dioceses, as well as northern England where it was apparently produced.[49]

In lay contexts, sin and its expiation through confession was also understood in terms of the sinner's intention and contrition. In *The Book of Margery Kempe*, for example, Margery was depicted as keen to confess to her priest 'a thyng in conscynes whech sche had neuyr schewyd beforn that tyme in alle hyr lyfe'.[50] Before Margery could even articulate the sin, a misdeed that was perhaps sexual in nature, her confessor issued a rebuke and concluded the sacrament without its completion. Sermons and *exempla* on the confession of sexual sin developed gendered meaning for women. One story which circulated in different versions centred on a young woman whose incestuous relationship with her father, whom she later murdered, led to her entry into prostitution. When she heard a sermon on confession, she asked the priest to be shriven and he heard her sins but deferred the award of penance due to their gravity while he determined the appropriate amount. In the meantime, the young woman prayed to the Virgin Mary with such sorrow that her heart burst. Despite her death before receiving the sacrament in full, the woman's

---

[46] A. Murray, *Conscience and Authority in the Medieval Church* (Oxford, 2015), p. 189.

[47] S. Hamilton, 'Penance in the Age of Gregorian Reform', in K. Cooper and J. Gregory, eds., *Retribution, Repentance, and Reconciliation* (Woodbridge, 2004), pp. 47–73; T. N. Tentler, *Sin and Confession on the Eve of the Reformation* (Princeton, 1977), pp. 73–4.

[48] *John Mirk's Festial*, ed. Powell, vol. 2, p. 250.

[49] J. Hughes, 'The Administration of Confession in the Diocese of York in the Fourteenth Century', in D. M. Smith, ed., *Studies in Clergy and Ministry in Medieval England* (York, 1991), pp. 87–163, at pp. 95, 107.

[50] *The Book of Margery Kempe*, ed. B. Windeatt (Harlow, 2000), p. 51, lines 181–2.

Pastoral Care, Canon Law, and Social Relations

contrition afforded her a place in heaven.[51] Although promiscuity and its concealment were entwined with misogynistic tropes of female behaviour, women were depicted as striving for and receiving forgiveness in pastoral settings.

The growing significance of contrition led to an intensified interest in the circumstances of sin, an important way of determining penance in early medieval confession, as theologians and canonists considered the origins and contexts of sin in more detail.[52] This emphasis on the circumstances of sin in pastoral care and in the judicial activities of the Church relied on elements of classical legal theory as well as the work of Latin and Greek rhetoricians.[53] The doctrine of circumstances pervaded intellectual memory techniques, influencing advice on how events in general could be remembered more fully. Early medieval thought on confession had acknowledged the importance of circumstances for sin, yet these were understood in a localised fashion and were applied primarily to the allocation of penance. By the eleventh or early twelfth centuries, they were accorded especial importance, influencing works like the Pseudo-Augustinian *De vera et falsa poenitentia*, sections of which underpinned Peter Lombard's *Sentences* and the *Tractatus de penitentia* in Gratian's *Decretum*.[54] The degree of intention could thus be assessed with greater accuracy through the accretion of knowledge about sinful deeds.

During the late twelfth and early thirteenth centuries, theologians associated with Peter the Chanter's 'biblical-moral school' in Paris developed further questions relating to conscience and the circumstances of sin.[55] Peter, and the men surrounding him, interpreted pastoral care through its application in secular matters, including problems relating to marriage, infertility, and fornication.[56] Several notable works and legislation which dealt with confession emerged from figures attached to the Parisian circle, who in turn acted as conduits for the dissemination of these ideas in England during the thirteenth century. For example, Stephen Langton studied and taught at the faculty of theology in Paris until his election as archbishop of Canterbury in 1206, later assigning confession a central role in his diocesan statutes.[57]

---

51 *The Early English Versions of the Gesta Romanorum*, ed. S. J. H. Herrtage, EETS, extra series, 33 (London, 1879), pp. 390–2.

52 A. A. Larson, *Master of Penance: Gratian and the Development of Penitential Thought and Law in the Twelfth Century* (Washington, DC, 2014), pp. 206–9.

53 D. W. Robertson, 'A Note on the Classical Origin of "Circumstances" in the Medieval Confessional', *Studies in Philology*, 43 (1946), 6–14.

54 Larson, *Master of Penance*, p. 46 n. 33.

55 J. W. Baldwin, *Masters, Princes and Merchants: The Social Views of Peter the Chanter and his Circle*, 2 vols. (Princeton, 1970), vol. 1, p. 17.

56 P. Biller, *The Measure of Multitude: Population in Medieval Thought* (Oxford, 2000), pp. 31–3.

57 M. Haren, *Sin and Society in Fourteenth-Century England: A Study of the Memoriale Presbiterorum* (Oxford, 2000), p. 153.

Popular Memory and Gender in Medieval England

Instructions on the administration of confession in diocesan manuals included specific references to the circumstances of sin. Canon 20 of the *Summula* of Walter de Cantilupe, bishop of Worcester, written in 1240 and issued with the Statutes of Exeter in 1287, applied the following questions to the commission of sin, namely 'who, what, where, with what help, why, how, [and] when'.[58] Manuals for confessors noted that while the omission of these memories endangered the soul of the penitent, their remembrance might also lead to the confessor's sexual arousal.[59] This was recognised in canon 5 of the synodal statutes for the diocese of Exeter, where the confessor was instructed not to:

> ask about other unusual things except about their circumstances and from a distance, so that with this expertise their memory is refreshed; let the cause for confessing be given during that time, and to the inexperienced a chance to commit a crime may not be provided, while unknown things are kept hidden.[60]

Synodal decrees that emphasised the significance of circumstances in confession were published and reissued in English dioceses throughout the thirteenth and fourteenth centuries.

The novel import accorded to memories of sin initiated a process whereby penitents were encouraged to examine their consciences, while confessors simultaneously gauged the degrees of intention and contrition. This exchange relied on the assumed impact of clerical interrogation upon the subject, as Arnold notes, in which power 'primarily operates not from an exterior source "against" the individual's will and desires, but inculcates the notions of individuality, desire, and will, and shapes them in particular ways'.[61] The laity experienced their personal inner worlds in other ways during confession, since interrogatories produced for confessors from the late thirteenth and early fourteenth centuries acknowledged particular aspects of the penitent's identity, such as age, gender, and social status. The *Memoriale Presbiterorum*, a fourteenth-century English manual for confession, outlined the circumstances for sin before sets of questions aimed at specific groups and trades, to an extent mirroring the *ad status* sermons that developed on the Continent especially.[62] The *Memoriale* circulated less widely than more popular works

---

[58] *Councils and Synods*, II, p. 1069. Summula of Peter Quinel, bishop of Exeter (1287?): 'quis, quid, ubi, quibus auxiliis, cur, quomodo, quando'.

[59] H. C. Lea, *A History of Auricular Confession and Indulgences in the Latin Church*, vol. 1 (Philadelphia, 1896), p. 381.

[60] *Councils and Synods*, II, p. 994. Statutes of Exeter II (1287): 'de aliis inusitatis non requirat nisi per circumstantias et a longe, ut per hoc expertis, dum eorum recensetur memoria, detur materia confitendi, inexpertis, dum celantur incognita, occasio deliquendi non pandatur'.

[61] Arnold, *Inquisition and Power*, p. 92.

[62] Haren, *Sin and Society in Fourteenth-Century England*, p. 59.

Pastoral Care, Canon Law, and Social Relations

like the *Oculus Sacerdotis*, but it indicates the formulation of penitential identities, based on occupation, gender and status, which confessants could assume, reject, or negotiate.

The elevation of circumstances in confessional thought during the late twelfth and early thirteenth centuries coincided with the introduction of inquisitorial methods, in place of older, accusatorial forms of proof. These developments embodied an interrelated spiritual impulse towards the interrogation of consciences and the pursuit of truth in legal and penitential cultures. Joseph Goering notes the emergence of judicial metaphors in confession manuals where the examination of sin was framed as the 'penitential court'.[63] The primacy of introspection, combined with an emphasis on memory and circumstances, permeated the laity's relationship with Church authorities, shaping the way that misdeeds were understood in everyday settings. For example, sins were confessed in situations outside the auricular sacrament. In the church courts, witnesses in cases that involved marriage *sub pena nubendi* claimed that parties admitted continued sexual contact to friends, kin, and parish priests after swearing to renounce one another before local Church officials.[64] Memories of confession in legal testimony drew on gendered perceptions of sin, in particular tropes associated with its concealment, as well as the relationship between sexual behaviour, morality, and marriage.

PASTORALIA, CANON LAWYERS, AND GENDER

The language of introspection which saturated pastoral literature on confession extended to other areas of Church authority in late medieval England. Like the questioning of penitents during confession, the examination of witnesses under canon law was interrogative in nature, and in preparation men and women were urged to inspect their consciences. The networks of churchmen and canon lawyers overlapped in numerous areas. Sacramental and moral theology infused texts, such as Gratian's *Decretum*, that were integral to the curriculum for canon law at Cambridge and Oxford, despite their focus on the law's practical application.[65] The *Decretum* contained the *Tractatus de Penitentia*, which, as Atria A. Larson, notes was 'a foundational text on penitential theology in the twelfth century', shaping the concerns of later *summa confessorum*.[66] Embedded in the middle of a legal commentary on impotence as an impediment to marriage, the work concentrated on the

---

[63] J. Goering, 'The Summa of Master Serlo and Thirteenth-Century Penitential Literature', *Mediaeval Studies*, 40 (1978), 290–311, at p. 305.

[64] Helmholz, *Marriage Litigation*, pp. 172–81.

[65] Brundage, *The Medieval Origins of the Legal Profession*, p. 97; on the development of the *Decretum* and the role of additional scholars in its production, see A. Winroth, *The Making of Gratian's 'Decretum'* (Cambridge, 2000).

[66] Larson, *Master of Penance*, p. 496.

Popular Memory and Gender in Medieval England

nature of confession and its relationship with contrition and the forgiveness of sin.[67] A treatise central to studies on penance was thus contained in one of the most significant texts used in the application of canon law and legal procedure.

The libraries of canon lawyers and clerks employed in the ecclesiastical courts contained works on pastoral care as well as legal procedure. In 1414 John Neuton bequeathed an extensive collection of law books to York Minster as the foundations for a library and to the male descendants in his family, while Peterhouse in Cambridge also received a set of texts on theology and literature.[68] Aside from texts explicitly on the law, John's library held collections of sermons and contemplative works by Richard Rolle and Walter Hilton. During his clerical career, John served as an advocate in Ely's consistory court, later acting as vicar-general in the church-court administration in York. Canon lawyers also held copies of official constitutions that contributed to the transmission of legislative reforms, some of which appeared in texts alongside legal formularies.[69] Dorothy M. Owen described these collections as 'essentially the compilations of notaries learning their trade' early in their careers, neither wholly direct law reports nor entirely focused on canon law.[70] Conciliar and provincial legislation also influenced the arguments which underpinned suits and the final judgements rendered. Michael M. Sheehan noted the use of the canon *Humana concupiscientia* from the council of London in 1342 to underpin rulings in marriage suits at the consistory court of Ely.[71] Statutes confirming older customs whereby witnesses attended betrothals informed testimony in the courts. Men and women alike recalled invitations to these agreements, echoing stipulations in formal legislation that signalled prior intent and further implied the couple's consent.[72]

Contemporary theologians understood the intimate connections between the *cura animarum* and the application of canon law. In 1196 Peter the Chanter was himself elected papal judge delegate in a marriage dispute between Philip II of France and his wife, Ingeborg of Denmark.[73] Pastoral care was also

---

[67] Larson, *Master of Penance*, pp. 37–8.

[68] YMA L2 (4), fols. 168v–170r; see also J. A. Brundage, 'Neuton, John (c. 1350–1414)', *Oxford Dictionary of National Biography* (Oxford, 2004).

[69] I. Forrest, 'English Provincial Constitutions and Inquisition into Lollardy', in M. C. Flannery and K. C. Walter, eds., *The Culture of Inquisition in Medieval England* (Cambridge, 2013), pp. 45–59, at p. 52.

[70] D. M. Owen, 'The Canonists' Formularies', in D. M. Owen, *The Medieval Canon Law: Teaching, Literature and Transmission* (Cambridge, 1990), pp. 30–42, at p. 42.

[71] M. M. Sheehan, 'The Formation and Stability of Marriage in Fourteenth-Century England', in Sheehan, *Marriage, Family and Law*, pp. 38–76, at pp. 51–2.

[72] M. M. Sheehan, 'Marriage Theory and Practice in the Conciliar Legislation and Diocesan Statutes of Medieval England', in Sheehan, *Marriage, Family and Law*, pp. 118–76, at pp. 137–8.

[73] J. Bradbury, *Philip Augustus: King of France, 1180–1223* (New York, 1998), p. 181.

Pastoral Care, Canon Law, and Social Relations

entwined with canon law through the production of *pastoralia* by clerical men involved in ecclesiastical governance. Thomas of Chobham, sub-dean of Salisbury cathedral, finished his *Summa Confessorum* around 1215, after spending more than a decade of his earlier education in Peter the Chanter's school of theology in Paris.[74] Thomas's *Summa* was a manual for parish priests which addressed the nature and treatment of sin in tandem with impediments to marriage and discipline in the parish more generally. Alongside his pastoral works, Thomas acted as *officialis* to the bishop of Salisbury, holding judicial responsibility over moral and spiritual behaviour in the diocese. Memory underpinned a section of the *Summa*, where it was noted that all earlier sins should not be recounted on every occasion, except with a new priest to whom each misdeed should be confessed.[75] Other texts emerged from non-clerical men engaged in diocesan service, such as the mid-thirteenth-century *Manuel des péchés*, a penitential manual composed by William Waddington, a lawyer in the administration of Walter Gray, archbishop of York. A Middle English version of the text, *Handlyng Synne*, appeared in the early fourteenth century, with both versions demonstrating a preoccupation with conscience and the circumstances of sin.[76]

From the 1320s, a group of men trained in canon law at Cambridge and Oxford were engaged in pastoral and administrative activities both in the archiepiscopal see of York and the diocese of Exeter. William of Pagula, born near Hull and Oxford-educated, authored the *Oculus Sacerdotis* in this decade, a confession manual which found particular reception in Yorkshire.[77] Boyle described William of Pagula as a 'rare but ideal combination of canonist, theologian and parish priest'.[78] William was trained in canon law and developed an understanding of penitential thought during his appointment as confessor and penitentiary in the diocese of Salisbury. The centrality of confession and penance in pastoral writing during this period owed much to the patronage and influence of John Grandisson, bishop of Exeter after a stint as archdeacon of Nottingham. A prominent work associated with this network was the *Speculum Vitae*, a penitential vernacular verse composed in Yorkshire

---

[74] A. Reeves, *Religious Education in Thirteenth-Century England: The Creed and Articles of Faith* (Leiden, 2015), p. 20; see also F. Morenzoni, *Des écoles aux paroisses: Thomas de Chobham et la promotion de la prédication au début du XIIIe siècle* (Paris, 1995); Baldwin, *Masters, Princes and Merchants*, vol. 1, pp. 34–6.

[75] J. Goering, 'Thomas of Chobham', *Oxford Dictionary of National Biography* (Oxford, 2004); Thomas of Chobham, *Summa Confessorum*, ed. Broomfield, p. 239.

[76] Hughes, 'The Administration of Confession', pp. 90–2; *Robert of Brunne's Handlyng Synne*, ed. F. J. Furnivall, EETS, original series, 119, 123 (London, 1901, 1903; repr. Millwood, 1975).

[77] Hughes, 'The Administration of Confession', pp. 90–3.

[78] L. E. Boyle, 'The "Oculus Sacerdotis" and Some Other Works of William of Pagula: The Alexander Prize Essay', *Transactions of the Royal Historical Society*, 5th series, 5 (1955), 81–110, at p. 102.

Popular Memory and Gender in Medieval England

between 1349 and 1375, often ascribed to William Nassington, a canon lawyer employed as a proctor and Official at the court of York in the 1340s. William was active in the circle of John Grandisson, later working in the church courts of Exeter from 1332 as auditor of causes. Ralph Hanna has cast doubts on this identification, however Nassington can be identified as the author of *The Bande of Lovynge*, a poem that meditates on the redemption offered by the life of Jesus.[79]

Other English canonists and theologians associated with the ecclesiastical courts produced pastoral works with an emphasis on confession. William Doune, archdeacon of Leicester, has been identified as the author of the *Memoriale Presbiterorum*, a tract on penitential practice that appeared in the mid-1340s, probably composed in Grandisson's network.[80] Another contemporary pastoral treatise, John Acton's *Septuplum*, completed in 1346, was written in the same tradition of confessional estates commentary. John spent several years in the household of Richard Bury, the bishop of Durham from 1334 to 1345, later serving as Official in the court of York.[81] The pastoral text *Septuplum* followed more than others in the tradition of the *Memoriale* in its consideration of the social status of penitents. Composed in Latin, the *Septuplum* was probably not widely read among the parish clergy, despite its introductory claim to aid their efforts in administering the *cura animarum*.[82] The first half of the manual concentrates on the vices and virtues, while the second treats a range of topics that touched on the spiritual and sexual lives of lay men and women, including confession, baptism, and virginity.

Clerical ideas about gender often defined the milieu in which works on pastoral care and canon law were produced. Despite the anxieties of reforming churchmen about clerical concubinage, and the ability of clergy in minor orders to marry, universities and diocesan administrations were masculine cultures. Patricia Cullum has analysed the activities of the secular clergy in late medieval England, noting their participation in transgressive activities, such as fornication and violent disorder, which constituted deliberate breaches of constraints on their behaviour.[83] Although many of the men employed in the church courts and the upper levels of diocesan administration had entered major orders, vows of chastity were not required of the minor clergy who comprised sections of its legal counsel. Proctors in the ecclesiastical courts often spent periods of time in the universities, yet these men were seldom graduates, instead receiving their training in practical

---

[79] *Speculum vitae: A Reading Edition*, ed. R. Hanna, 2 vols. (Oxford, 2008).

[80] M. Haren, 'Confession, Social Ethics and Social Discipline in the *Memoriale presbiterorum*', in Biller and Minnis, eds., *Handling Sin*, pp. 109–22, at p. 109.

[81] Hughes, 'The Administration of Confession', pp. 96–7.

[82] Haren, *Sin and Society in Fourteenth-Century England*, p. 80.

[83] P. H. Cullum, 'Clergy, Masculinity and Transgression in Late Medieval England', in D. M. Hadley, ed., *Masculinity in Medieval Europe* (London, 1999), pp. 178–96.

Pastoral Care, Canon Law, and Social Relations

judicial spheres.[84] Intellectual theories on sex difference which circulated within the schools tended to reassert hierarchies of gender that depicted female bodies as sinful and inferior. Patterns of sociability between male students and masters reinforced these attitudes. Alexandra Shepard observes similar habits among young men studying at the University of Cambridge in the early modern period, where violence and sexual exploits operated as a form of male bonding.[85] Pastoral literature embedded clerical perceptions of women in commentaries on their social behaviour. Manuals on confession interpreted the sinner as male by default, with women usually appearing as a 'marked category, a signal of difference, exception or emphasis'.[86]

The varied status of secular clergy in the courts and the parish ensured that notional boundaries between clerical and lay experiences blurred in the realms of work, legal knowledge, and marital status. Proctors and advocates could marry provided they did not enter the priesthood, but the ambiguity of their marital status facilitated their engagement in transitory sexual relationships. Clerical men involved in diocesan and provincial administration could become defendants in marriage suits. In 1390, Joan Fossard brought a suit to enforce her alleged marriage to William Calthorne, a proctor-general of the church court of York. Neither the judgement in the case nor testimony from Joan's witnesses is extant, but William's deponents emphasised her poverty, while also claiming his absence on family matters related to his late father's estate.[87] A handful of other cases involving proctors and advocates from the courts survive, and these underscore the gendered implications of their legal knowledge when it was applied to their sexual and marital relationships.[88]

Clerical men read and perhaps authored other texts too, aside from pastoral manuals, and these circulated in the educational milieu in which canon lawyers, advocates, and proctors were trained. They were invariably imbued with gendered meanings. One such genre was the 'betrayed maidens' lament', which typically described the seduction, pregnancy, and abandonment of young lower-status women, occasionally servants, by clerical suitors. These lyrics appeared in a fifteenth-century miscellany, alongside model legal records which apparently belonged to a student, perhaps training in the law. Another formed part of a parish manuscript probably owned by a local priest, which included a practical manual for the clergy, sermon *exempla*, theological texts in Latin and the vernacular, and a secular romance. Ballads and lyrics

---

[84] Helmholz, *Marriage Litigation*, p. 149.

[85] A. Shepard, *Meanings of Manhood in Early Modern England* (Oxford, 2003), pp. 93–126.

[86] Murray, 'Gendered Souls in Sexed Bodies', p. 81.

[87] BI CP.E.175.

[88] See also Donahue, *Law, Marriage, and Society*, pp. 182–5; P. J. P. Goldberg, 'John Skathelok's Dick: Voyeurism and "Pornography" in Late Medieval England', in N. McDonald, ed., *Medieval Obscenities* (York, 2006), pp. 105–23, at p. 121. For comparable cases, see BI CP.F.63 and CP.F.129.

Popular Memory and Gender in Medieval England

were perhaps used and performed in pastoral settings, as Kim Phillips suggests, in order to teach young women about the dangers of premarital sex with men whose marital status was poorly defined.[89] The presence of these texts alongside works that dwelled more explicitly on the administration of the *cura animarum* alludes to the ways in which clerical perceptions of gender, pastoral care, and sexual behaviour overlapped in the parish.

Although *pastoralia* produced in these contexts circulated more readily between male readers, vernacular works reached women reading in private and communal settings. The Anglo-Norman *Manuel des péchés* has been associated with several female owners or patrons, probably mercantile or noble in origin. Female readers also possessed copies of texts imbued with pastoral concerns, like the fourteenth-century Middle English poem *Piers Plowman*, which contained a treatment of conscience.[90] Jocelyn Wogan-Browne demonstrates the prevalence of francophone pastoral texts among female readers in thirteenth- and fourteenth-century England, a pattern replicated with visionary works written in the vernacular.[91]

Non-elite men and women, including peasants, town-dwellers, servants, and other labourers, absorbed these ideas through channels which often had their origins in the written word. For example, the mid-fourteenth-century northern poem *The Prick of Conscience* formed the basis for a stained-glass window depicting the section on the Last Judgement in All Saints Church in York.[92] Misogynistic tropes that pervaded confessional discourse infused the fabric of parish life. Tutivillus, the demon depicted as the recorder of female gossip, appeared in mystery plays like the Towneley cycle that were performed in public spaces, and adorned the walls and misericords of churches. Several devils accompanied a group of gossiping women in a wall-painting in the parish church of St Margaret and St Remigius in Seething, Norfolk. While images of this kind illustrated motifs from pastoral thought, local communities were active in selecting their contents, and it was primarily male parishioners at the forefront of these commissions, the misogynistic bent of these paintings emerging from lay masculine contexts.[93] Parishioners were exposed to central

---

[89] For details on both of these manuscripts, see K. Phillips, *Medieval Maidens: Young Women and Gender in England, c. 1270–1540* (Manchester, 2003), pp. 95–6.

[90] K. A. Murchison, 'The Readers of the *Manuel des Péchés* Revisited', *Philological Quarterly*, 95 (2016), 161–99, at p. 187.

[91] J. Wogan-Browne, '"Cest livres liseez … chescun jour": Women and Reading c. 1230–1430', in J. Wogan-Browne et al., eds., *Language and Culture in Medieval Britain: The French of England, c. 1100–c. 1500* (York, 2009), pp. 239–53; K. Kerby-Fulton, '*Piers Plowman*', in Wallace, ed., *The Cambridge History of Medieval English Literature*, pp. 513–38, at p. 529.

[92] E. A. Gee, 'The Painted Glass of All Saints' Church, North Street, York', *Archaeologia*, 102 (1969), 151–202.

[93] Bardsley, *Venomous Tongues*, pp. 55–7; M. Jennings, 'Tutivillus: The Literary Career of the Recording Demon', *Studies in Philology*, 74 (1977), 1–95.

Pastoral Care, Canon Law, and Social Relations

strands of pastoral theology, but they also contributed to the formation and adaptation of these gendered attitudes. Yet, although gender ideologies were often interpreted as fixed and dichotomous in the moralistic environment of the parish, the practicalities of marital and domestic life no doubt tempered their tone and the force of their application.

MEMORY AND PROOF

Gender influenced the focus and content of canon law, initially affording husbands greater authority over wives, but it also extended certain protections to married women. Marital rights that applied to both spouses included the need to render the marital debt, the prevention of remarriage unless widowed, and the requirement to seek acquiescence if one partner wished to leave the union.[94] Canon law intersected more fully with procedure in the church courts through rules and practices on the provision of testimony. The twelfth and early thirteenth centuries saw the gradual transition from methods such as compurgation and sworn inquests to the more widespread use of witness depositions. Canonists who composed treatises on procedure in the church courts identified several groups whose status was seen to remove their legal capacity to act as deponents. Written around 1140, Gratian's *Decretum* expressed ambivalence towards female testimony through references to St Augustine, who stated that women should not act as witnesses.[95] Elsewhere, the *Decretum* acknowledged the admissibility of female testimony in contexts where women's expertise was assumed to be more extensive than their male counterparts', particularly cases involving marriage, sex and reproduction, and knowledge of family ancestries.[96] Gratian's *Decretum* was disseminated widely in the decades immediately after its completion, rapidly becoming a central textbook for the instruction of canon law in the schools. Canonists included women alongside other sections of society from whom the provision of legal evidence was seen to be irregular. Tancred, in his *Ordo iudiciarius*, written sometime after 1215, noted the unfree, children, and the poor as persons whose testimony was unacceptable, while women's evidence was described as prohibited in cases involving criminal matters or testaments.[97] Hostiensis, writing in the thirteenth century, similarly stated that witnesses could be

---

94 S. McDougall, 'Women and Gender in Canon Law', in J. M. Bennett and R. M. Karras, eds., *The Oxford Handbook of Women and Gender in Medieval Europe* (Oxford, 2013), pp. 163–78, at p. 170.

95 J. A. Brundage, 'Juridical Space: Female Witnesses in Canon Law', *Dumbarton Oaks Papers*, 52 (1998), 147–56, at p. 148.

96 C. 33 q. 5 c. 17; C. 27 q. 2 c. 29; C. 35 q. 6 c. 2. See also Brundage, 'Juridical Space', pp. 148–9.

97 *Pilii, Tancredi, Gratiae, Libri de iudiciorum ordine*, ed. F. Bergmann (Gottingen, 1842) (hereafter Tancred, *Ordo*), 3.6; for further discussion of Tancred's *Ordo*, see Donahue, 'Proof by Witnesses', pp. 130–1; for a detailed study of the origins of *ordines iudiciarii*,

Popular Memory and Gender in Medieval England

disqualified on grounds of 'condition, gender, age, discretion, reputation, fortune, and truthfulness'.[98]

Procedural manuals and treatises on canon law debated the relative worth of men and women's legal testimony. According to canon law, two witnesses were required to fulfil the criteria of proof, with the maximum number of deponents given as forty. Cases concerning tithes and parochial rights involved large numbers of witnesses up to the canonical limit, while suits over marriage, defamation, and testamentary issues often entailed between two and five since fewer people usually saw these events, and parties were required to pay for deponents' expenses.[99] Where the evidence of witnesses was in conflict, Tancred argued that men's testimony should be privileged over women's.[100] Formal restrictions of this kind were seldom observed in practice, although attitudes towards female witnesses were marked by patterns of selection and perceptions of inconsistency that did not apply to male deponents.

The provisions made by canon law were highly gendered, but it was through their application in the courts that patriarchal hierarchies were reinforced in practice. Donahue interprets the outcome of judgements in the late medieval court of York as an indication that the church courts favoured male rather than female parties.[101] As Goldberg notes, however, these trends reflected shifts in the types of cases which men and women pursued, while the courts upheld claims of marriage more frequently than suits to dissolve them.[102] Donahue comments, for instance, that 'marriage litigation in the court of York in the fourteenth century was an activity that women initiated', a pattern that was sustained in suits from the fifteenth century though with less of a gendered disparity.[103] In essence, female plaintiffs were more prevalent than male acting parties, particularly in earlier matrimonial suits and in litigation related to the enforcement of marriage contracts.

Social attitudes among the laity influenced the selection of deponents, producing gendered patterns that shaped men and women's participation in the courts both as parties and as witnesses. By the end of the fifteenth

---

see L. Fowler-Magerl, *Ordo iudiciorum vel ordo iudiciarius: Begriff und Literaturgattung* (Frankfurt, 1984).

[98] Helmholz, *The Oxford History of the Laws of England*, pp. 339–40; K. Pennington, 'Henricus de Segusio (Hostiensis)', in K. Pennington, *Popes, Canonists and Texts, 1150–1550* (Aldershot, 1993), no. 16, pp. 1–12.

[99] Helmholz, *Marriage Litigation*, p. 154.

[100] Tancred, *Ordo*, 3.12.

[101] C. Donahue Jr., 'Female Plaintiffs in Marriage Cases in the Court of York in the Later Middle Ages: What Can We Learn from the Numbers?', in S. Sheridan Walker, ed., *Wife and Widow in Medieval England* (Ann Arbor, 1993), pp. 183–213; Pedersen, 'Demography in the Archives', p. 420.

[102] Goldberg, 'Gender and Matrimonial Litigation', p. 52.

[103] Donahue, *Law, Marriage, and Society*, p. 77.

Pastoral Care, Canon Law, and Social Relations

century, the numbers of women providing testimony had waned as men appeared more often, even in disputes over marriage where female witnesses had been commonly employed. Although women enlisted female deponents in larger proportions than did male parties, especially where suits originated in urban areas, rural litigants of both sexes relied on male testimony to a greater degree.[104] Women appeared most often as witnesses in disputes relating to marriage breakdown, defamation, and breach of promise, spheres of activity that embodied normative assumptions about female behaviour. Male witnesses, in contrast, were prevalent in a range of suits and predominated in litigation dealing with parish customs, ecclesiastical rights, and tithes. The ideological perceptions that associated women with marital and domestic matters situated men's expertise in the areas of local history and land use, despite the occasional reliance of male witnesses on female sources of knowledge.

As procedures became more developed in manuals and statutes, proctors and advocates trained in the learned law instructed examiners on how to gather testimony from men and women. Practices of examination were increasingly seen to influence the content and extent of witness depositions. In a number of cases, clerical scribes recorded evidence from later witnesses by omitting the majority of their testimony and noting simply that they 'said the same in every respect' as the previous deponent.[105] Other statements were described as identical to the depositions which preceded them, with examiners only recording sections which differed in content.[106] The practice of summarising evidence was more common in the southern province, although the earliest suits from the diocese and province of York only survive from the first decade of the fourteenth century when court systems generally followed more developed legal processes.[107]

There were anomalies even in the later material from York, which suggest that methods of examination at times failed to replicate gender norms when recording testimony. In late medieval society, non-elite women were usually described as 'daughter of' or 'wife of' their male relations, signalling the way in which kinsmen were used to define female identity. Legal processes did not simply reproduce patriarchal nomenclature on every occasion. When a married couple testified together in 1394, Agnes Yonger gave evidence first while John, described as 'husband of Agnes Yonger', deposed after her. In addition, John's testimony was much shorter than Agnes's, noting merely that he agreed with his wife on every point, while on the second and third

---

[104] Goldberg, 'Gender and Matrimonial Litigation', p. 46.

[105] CCA E.S. Roll 40v; *Select Cases*, p. 30; see also CCA E.S. Roll 151ii; *Select Cases*, pp. 574–5.

[106] CCA E.S. Roll 265; *Select Cases*, pp. 546–9.

[107] Donahue, 'Proof by Witnesses', p. 138.

Popular Memory and Gender in Medieval England

articles he stated 'briefly' that he did not know how to depose.[108] The clerk perhaps condensed John's account since Agnes had included all the relevant information in her deposition. Yet this was an unusual format in cases where both spouses testified together and implies an anomalous power dynamic between the couple, perhaps indicating the wife's greater social or economic standing.[109]

The legal personnel staffing the courts attempted to remedy the problem of clerks summarising the words of witnesses, encouraging colleagues in charge of examinations to record evidence from witnesses in full. In 1270, a dispute between the prioress and sub-prioress of the Benedictine house of Higham in Kent reached the court of Canterbury on appeal. Examiners were instructed to note whether deponents 'spoke constantly or wavered', and to record their responses meticulously rather than merely stating that witnesses agreed with the previous deponent.[110] In another case from the late thirteenth century, the personnel of the court were urged to question deponents carefully on every article and to determine the origins of their knowledge.[111] Proctors and advocates also acknowledged the need for examiners to apply initiative in probing the memories of deponents beyond the questions composed in advance, depending on the content and implications of the evidence given. Interrogatories in a suit referred from the court of common pleas to the bishop of Lincoln in 1293 encouraged the identification of additional areas of inquiry. The questions concluded with the directive to inquire into the cause of the deponents' knowledge, after which the proctor noted that 'the diligence of the examiner may provide others, because you may be able to know more'.[112] In other early cases from Canterbury, scribes introduced internal referencing systems that made evidence easier to revisit, understand, and identify, serving to summarise testimony in a coherent and efficient way.[113]

The ability to remember past events was integral to Church teachings on legal testimony as treatises and manuals debated the most effective methods to secure evidence from witnesses. Memories of past events developed especial significance in proceedings from the province of Canterbury throughout

---

[108] BI C.P.E.210. 'Johannes Yonger maritus Agnetis Yonger ... item idem requisitus de secundo et tercio articulis dicit breviter quod nescit deponere'.

[109] This was the case on the manor of Badbury in Wiltshire during the fourteenth century: M. Müller, 'Peasant Women, Agency and Status in Mid-Thirteenth to Late Fourteenth-Century England: Some Reconsiderations', in C. Beattie and M. F. Stevens, eds., *Married Women and the Law in Premodern Northwest Europe* (Woodbridge, 2013), pp. 91–113, at p. 108.

[110] CCA E.S. Roll 333b; *Select Cases*, p. 164. 'Item si constanter vel vacillanter loquantur dicti testes'.

[111] CCA E.S. Roll 4i; *Select Cases*, p. 269.

[112] CCA E.S. Roll 231; *Select Cases*, p. 617. 'Item de causa sciencie diligenter inquiratur. Cetera supleat industria examinantis quia tu magis scire potes'.

[113] CCA E.S. Roll 4ii, 4iii; for a discussion of this case, see *Select Cases*, p. 311 n. 1.

Pastoral Care, Canon Law, and Social Relations

the thirteenth century. As early as 1200, witnesses in cases were asked about the time of the incidents they recalled, as well as the circumstances of their occurrence.[114] By the late thirteenth century, examiners questioned deponents specifically on how they recalled the events they described after the passage of so much time (*qualiter recolit de tanto tempore elapso*).[115] This phrase recurs in suits over marriage, and other cases that required the location of specific dates, in records from the provinces of Canterbury and York, with men and women remembering dates using personal, local, and sometimes political events. In the early decades of its use, witnesses were occasionally slow to recognise the intentions behind questions about their memory and answered in a tautological fashion. In a late thirteenth-century case from Canterbury, for instance, William Brun of Bekton stated that he recalled the events which he described by calculating and counting the years and the days that followed.[116]

The conditions surrounding the memories of witnesses formed a central strand of testimony as clerks were directed to 'inquire diligently about other circumstances' according to the examiner's discretion.[117] In many senses, the experience of examination in the church courts resonated with the format and purpose of auricular confession, including the use of circumstances as a way of extracting memories. Witnesses were examined individually and in private, and efforts were made to ensure that litigants did not coerce or coach deponents. During their examination, witnesses were often asked not only how they remembered a past event, but where it had occurred, whether it was a fair day, and who was present. If the dispute concerned a contract of marriage, they were asked what the parties had worn, were they sitting or standing and, on occasion, whether they had eaten fish or meat. Confessional manuals counselled penitents to examine their souls for memories of their wrong-doings, while witnesses were also instructed to consider their consciences before providing evidence.

By the mid-thirteenth century, practices in the church courts increasingly adopted the central tenets of canon law on the examination of witnesses. Inquisitorial methods also began to penetrate some areas of common law, such as proofs of age in which memories were gathered from local men to determine the ages of heirs and heiresses. Earlier inquests took the form of empanelled juries, but these groups were later examined like canonical witnesses and their accounts were explored through questions similar to those used in the church courts.[118] Yet common-law procedures also influenced the application of canon law. Despite the introduction of written testimony in the ecclesiastical courts, Donahue observes 'jurylike characteristics' in

---

[114] For example, CCA E.S. Roll 40ii and 40iii.

[115] See, for instance, CCA E.S. Roll 36, and other cases throughout this study.

[116] CCA E.S. Roll 265.

[117] CCA E.S. Roll 333; *Select Cases*, p. 164. 'de ceteris circumstanciis diligenter interrogentur'.

[118] Bedell, 'Memory and Proof of Age', pp. 6–7.

Popular Memory and Gender in Medieval England

cases from the administration of Hubert Walter, emphasising that these cases are 'as much the ancestor of the canonical witness as ... the ancestor of the secular jury'.[119] Witnesses who functioned akin to jurors appeared in cases where larger sections of the local community were involved, and the content and form of their statements closely resembled the responses in proof-of-age inquests. In 1270, Thomas de Waldingsend approached the archdeacon of Huntingdon, seeking to enforce his marriage contract with Cecilia, daughter of Bartholomew of Swynewelle.[120] Thomas requested that the cause be transmitted to the provincial court of Canterbury. Over seventy witnesses from a cluster of villages in north Hertfordshire, the majority of whom were women, testified on Cecilia's age at the time of the marriage, drawing on the births of their own children as a method of calculation. Despite restrictions on female testimony in proofs of age under common law, women were called to testify on the births of children in the church courts. In cases of this kind, men and women's evidence concentrated on one event to which witnesses testified in short, almost identical statements.

The precise question as to why people recalled events became less common as a direct query in the church courts towards the end of this period. It does not appear in the testimony in a range of suits from Canterbury in the early fifteenth century, marking a shift from practices in the *curia* and officiality of Canterbury two centuries before.[121] In York during the 1420s it was still used as a means to elicit information, appearing in several sets of depositions in suits concerning marriage.[122] As late as 1433, men giving evidence in a matrimonial suit were asked how they recalled the marriage contract they described, to which they responded with accounts of their own activities around the time.[123] Few witnesses were required to explicitly locate past events after this point, although men and women were still asked a series of segmented questions to structure the circumstances surrounding the events they claimed to have occurred.[124]

Clerical attitudes towards the *cura animarum* and confession had undergone a series of changes since the early programme of pastoral reform in the late twelfth and thirteenth centuries. Confession was theologically tied to other religious habits and sacraments, occupying a crucial role in relation to the instruction and worship of the Christian faithful. Miri Rubin describes the vitality and multivalence of the 'eucharistic symbolic system', from its dynamic expansion in the mid-eleventh century to the growing support for a feast centred on the body of Christ. This addition to the liturgical calendar had its

---

[119] Donahue, 'Proof by Witnesses', p. 136.
[120] CCA E.S. Roll 10.
[121] For example, depositions in KALHS X.10.1.
[122] See, for instance, BI CP.F.133 and 152.
[123] BI CP.F.49.
[124] For example, see witness statements in BI CP.F.279, 280, 347, and 351.

Pastoral Care, Canon Law, and Social Relations

origins in the affective spirituality of the beguines, the Cistercian order, and the mendicant friars based in the Low Countries during the early thirteenth century.[125] Confession became less central to pastoral care in the parishes by the end of the fourteenth century as writers on spiritual life accorded greater weight to contrition and the sacrament itself was progressively seen as internal and private.[126] The Mass had attained a new significance by the early fifteenth century, through the elevation of the Eucharist, and while confession remained crucial to Christian life, it 'became essentially a form of preparation for communion … [that] dignified people and prepared them for Eucharistic reception'.[127] The secular clergy were increasingly regarded as channels for the delivery of the Mass, and this perhaps caused a declining interest in the examination of the laity's consciences in texts authored by canon lawyers and learned churchmen.

Other methods accompanied explicit questions about memory in legal evidence, and memories and experiences were incorporated through their citation as sources of knowledge, primarily in the form of hearsay. The Church's attitude towards eye-witness testimony shifted from the gradual emergence of the courts in the early thirteenth century. The Fourth Lateran Council increased the level of proof needed in marriage suits involving close kinship or affinity, with hearsay evidence no longer accepted as valid testimony and to be replaced by personal knowledge.[128] Although the Church attempted to curtail its use, hearsay continued to appear in testimony as witnesses cited conversations and everyday encounters as evidence.

Men and women often gained knowledge of events because they had heard it from relatives, friends, or elderly members of their community. In a fourteenth-century suit from York, Eleanor de Barton knew of the dispensation sought by her sister and John Hildyard, senior, for their marriage as 'she heard it reported to her by a certain helpful woman'.[129] Where men predominated as witnesses, in cases over tithes and parish rights, women were still occasionally referenced as sources, albeit not as frequently as men. After witnesses gave the central core of their evidence, a statement that the testimony given was *publica vox et fama* usually followed. In another case from Yorkshire brought in 1362, John Feraunt claimed that he knew little of the exception made against a witness but 'he knows well that it is a common subject of discussion in Craven and roundabout'.[130] Gossip and other forms of speech held a social utility, facilitating the formation of relationships and

---

[125] Rubin, *Corpus Christi*, pp. 164–96.

[126] Hughes, 'The Administration of Confession', pp. 149–63.

[127] Rubin, *Corpus Christi*, p. 84.

[128] Helmholz, *Marriage Litigation*, p. 81.

[129] BI CP.E.108. 'audivit sibi referri per quadam mulierem auxiatricem'.

[130] BI CP.E.170. 'bene scit quod est communis lucutio in partibus de Craven et locis vicinis'.

the development of groups.[131] By the late fifteenth century, phrases in the vernacular, especially reported speech, were used increasingly throughout depositions. Although canon law operated alongside social attitudes to constrain women's ability to testify in the same way as men, the circulation and formation of social memory nevertheless accommodated their perspectives on a regular basis.

CONCLUSION

The enhanced importance assigned to memory, contrition, and the inspection of conscience in pastoral theology permeated the secular clergy's delivery of the *cura animarum*. Misogynistic stereotypes of women's moral and sexual behaviour were embedded in normative perceptions of gender, which in turn solidified the association of femininity with memory, forgetting, and the concealment of sin. The growth of *pastoralia* and its prevalence in parochial society also shaped the application of canon law in the ecclesiastical courts, as well as the development of new procedures for eliciting testimony. The employment of authors and translators of pastoral texts in Church administration generated a greater concern with memory and confession from a judicial perspective.

Men and women could testify in a range of cases, despite conflicting opinions among canonists on the legal position of female witnesses. Yet the capacity for women to give evidence was often limited to specific types of cases associated with stereotypically feminine activity. The clerical men of the courts were also well versed in canon law and pastoral theology, perhaps embedding normative perceptions of gender further in their work within the courts. There is evidence that some of these clerical men exploited their legal knowledge in their own personal lives, while misogynistic tropes appeared in ballads and lyrics, as well as in pastoral literature in general, all of which can be associated with clerical audiences.

Memory accrued introspective meaning through the Church's judicial and confessional activities, but parishioners remembered the past in a variety of everyday situations. One of the most significant areas of contestation for men and women in this period was marriage, and witnesses for opposing parties offering contrasting versions of the past during legal suits. The next chapter traces the treatment of women's testimony in case material, analysing how gender intersected with attitudes towards the authority of witnesses. It also explores the ways in which men and women used memory to produce plausible histories of their sexual and romantic relationships.

---

[131] C. Wickham, 'Gossip and Resistance among the Medieval Peasantry', *Past & Present*, 160 (1998), 3–24.

2

GENDER, NARRATIVE, AND TESTIMONY

In the *Wife of Bath's Prologue*, Alison criticised the misogynistic tales told in the 'book of wikked wyves' from which Jankyn, her husband, read every night. Central to the Wife's complaint was the extent of clerical control over the production of widely known depictions of women, exemplified in her reference to Aesop's fabled argument between the lion and the man. Drawing on this analogy, the Wife challenged misogynistic representations of women in her rhetorical question, 'who peyntede the leon, tel me who?', noting that female accounts of men's deeds would contain more wickedness 'than al the mark of Adam may redresse'.[1] Commonly cited in studies of medieval gender relations, Alison's commentary emphasises clerical authority over written narratives about women, as well as the extent to which men dictated the contemporary cultural memory of women in formal histories. Numerous works on literary practices, however, demonstrate female involvement in areas beyond reading and writing, including book ownership, patronage, and other literate activities that often occurred in family settings and within other social networks.[2] Indeed, the eponymous Wife undermined her husband's control over stories about women, ripping pages from his book and inducing him to burn it in the fire after his brutal attack upon her. Memories of her previous marriages also acted as a form of counter-memory, ostensibly narrated from the female position but in practice ventriloquized through Chaucer himself.

Perceptions of the comparative reliability of men and women's testimony in the church courts reflected broader gendered attitudes towards memory and speech, as well as assumptions about gendered areas of expertise. Male fantasies of the dangers of women's collective talk shaped portrayals of female testimony. Communal gatherings of women could be associated with the conspiratorial intent to fabricate evidence, in keeping with their supposed innate habit of dissimulation. The choice of witness in legal suits was influenced by gendered assumptions about trustworthiness which coalesced with expectations about the spheres of activity in which men and women more commonly acted. Cases concerning parish rights and tithes, for instance,

---

[1] *The Riverside Chaucer*, ed. L. D. Benson, 3rd edition (Boston, 1987), p. 114, lines 692–6.
[2] R. Krug, *Reading Families: Women's Literate Practices in Late Medieval England* (Ithaca, NY, and London, 2002), pp. 3–5.

Popular Memory and Gender in Medieval England

usually relied upon male rather than female testimony. Men and women tended to give testimony alongside each other in suits concerning marriage and defamation, which often turned on issues of sexuality and desire in ways that mattered more to the reputations of young unmarried women.

Men and women referred to and adapted culturally specific narratives and discourses in legal testimony, signalling their own personal 'memories, actions and intentions' and imbuing these with wider social meaning.[3] Witnesses and litigants were able to exercise agency during legal processes, arranging temporal and spatial referents into accounts in which they adopted specific subject positions that conveyed elements of their personal identities. The ability to depose in legal suits provided non-elite women with opportunities to communicate their memories and experiences in a meaningful fashion. As Laura Gowing notes, 'telling stories gave women both a formal cultural agency – a time in which their words were written down – and a way of putting themselves, as actors, at centre stage.'[4] Legal testimony and trial records more generally also included a variety of other influences, Walker notes, as narratives comprised multiple 'voices' and positions, including social perceptions and elements of the law.[5] While depositions provide evidence of gendered discourses and language, they were also produced at the intersection of everyday social practice and legal experience. The oral nature of witness testimony thus functioned as a conduit for women's experiences and narratives, often marginalised in everyday life and in other legal settings.

As noted in Chapter 1, men and women engaged in a variety of interrogative encounters through their experiences with the Church which imbued the experience of testifying with spiritual and introspective meaning. Later chapters will explore the boundaries of narrative, discourse, and experience where the dynamics of memory and gender were assigned specific importance in daily life. This chapter analyses the gendered use of narratives in the church courts, exploring the relationship between the requirements of canon law and the discourses that witnesses used to communicate elements of social relations. Women witnesses negotiated numerous constraints upon their testimony during litigation, including attacks on their reputations from male parties and deponents, as well as formal exceptions against the production of their evidence. The language of marginality was applied to testimony from poor and servile men and women, often depicting their gender identities in negative terms. Matrimonial disputes in particular foregrounded the sexual and marital histories of parties, producing sets of cases that allow comparison of the narratives common among young men and women of marriageable

---

[3]   J. D. Y. Peel, 'For who hath despised the day of small things? Missionary Narratives and Historical Anthropology', *Comparative Studies in Society and History*, 37 (1995), 581–607, at p. 582.

[4]   Gowing, *Domestic Dangers*, p. 234.

[5]   Walker, *Crime, Gender and Social Order*, pp. 7–8.

Gender, Narrative, and Testimony

age. Female litigants in particular used the existence of illegitimate children to press claims of valid marriages. A distinctly masculine youth subculture underpinned testimony in suits where women sought to enforce marriage contracts, expressed through nostalgic language which constructed collective male pasts. In both types of evidence, male and female witnesses drew on gendered language and imagery to depict varied emotional and sexual histories.

GENDER, TESTIMONY, AND PATRIARCHAL CONTROL

Patriarchal attitudes towards men and women's social roles, and the gender ideologies that underpinned social relations and structures more broadly, played a role in fashioning many of the narratives depicted in legal evidence. The types of memories which men and women recalled depended on gendered patterns of witness selection. Although some canonists debated the reliability of testimony from women, their evidence was on the whole accepted as valid. Yet despite the breadth of subject matter adjudicated in the church courts, female parties and witnesses were usually active only in cases concerning marriage and defamation. Perceptions of women's social value meant that matters relating to marriage and childbirth in particular became female areas of expertise. Outside the ecclesiastical courts, laywomen were empanelled as members of juries solely in relation to the examination of women's bodies for signs of pregnancy, for example, during criminal prosecutions in which the maternal state could affect sentences.[6] This gendered association also extended to marriage suits where details of kinship were required, and to cases involving male impotence initiated in the church courts.

There were limitations in certain circumstances, however, as depositions from mothers of female parties in marriage cases were open to criticisms of conspiracy and perjury in canon law and in practice.[7] More explicit suspicions of women gathering in groups to concoct testimony were also manifest in accusations made against female witnesses from opposing parties and deponents. In 1390 Joan Fossard initiated a suit in the court of York against William Calthorne and his de facto wife, Katherine, daughter of Roger de Wele. Several men who testified for William described Joan's witnesses as women of 'ill fame, dishonest conversation and fickle opinion', whose testimony had been fabricated during the course of the dispute.[8] Patrick de Newham reported that the women had been seen meeting in a room in the house of Richard Cosyn, a local vendor of ale, where they had 'invented the

---

6 H. M. Jewell, *Women in Medieval England* (Manchester, 1996), p. 74.

7 X 2.20.22.

8 BI CP.E.175. See, for instance, the deposition of Patrick de Newham: 'male fame, conversacionis inhoneste et levis opinionis'.

Popular Memory and Gender in Medieval England

content of their depositions'.[9] Several witnesses claimed that the women made up their evidence as they were William's enemies since he had spurned Joan and wed another. The absence of the women's husbands emphasised a lack of patriarchal authority over their speech and behaviour, while the fact of their meeting in an ale house alluded to moral anxieties over women's disorderly potential.

The motif of garrulous women meeting in ale houses or taverns to engage in disruptive talk appeared in poems and satires, forming the basis for the gossips' genre which grew in popularity from the fifteenth century onwards. These misogynistic fantasies of female speech were usually composed by clerical men, and characterized the content of women's conversation as trivial but simultaneously dangerous to the social order. Female talk was imagined as unsettling to patriarchal structures not only among city fathers, but also at the granular level of the household as it could be seen to play consciously on male anxieties. In one fifteenth-century poem, *A Talk of Ten Wives on their Husbands' Wares*, for example, the conversation of a group of married women is situated in the tavern, where their husbands' genitalia and sexual performance become the subject of detailed discussion and ridicule.[10] Depictions of women's legal testimony, like the characterisations in the case between Joan Fossard and William Calthorne, drew on the popular imagery and motifs which underlay this poetic genre. These legal narratives also acknowledged the gendered treatment of female speech in other jurisdictions. A growing concern with female speech generated increased prosecutions for scolding, barratry, and public insult in manorial, borough, and ecclesiastical courts from the late fourteenth and early fifteenth centuries onwards.[11] In *ex officio* actions within the church courts, for example, women were accused of defamation more often than men, appearing most often in citations involving sexual insult against other women.[12] The characterisation of female testimony as fabricated and possessing the capacity to erode male social power and undermine men's sexual reputations thus emerged from interlinked cultural perceptions of women's talk.

Female testimony was uniformly regarded as valid in the course of litigation, but both men and women's evidence was liable to objections, which in the English church courts occurred after witness statements were accepted.[13] Instead of excluding witnesses from testifying in the opening stages of suits, the courts permitted deponents to give evidence to which

---

9   BI CP.E.175. 'imaginerunt materiam in disposicionibus eorum'.
10   *A Talk of Ten Wives on their Husbands' Ware [in] Jyl of Breyntford's testament ... and Other Short Pieces*, ed. F. J. Furnivall (London, 1871), pp. 29–33.
11   Bardsley, *Venomous Tongues*, p. 82.
12   L. R. Poos, 'Sex, Lies, and the Church Courts of Pre-Reformation England', *Journal of Interdisciplinary History*, 25 (1995), 585–607, at p. 606.
13   Donahue, 'Proof by Witnesses', p. 143.

opposing parties responded in the form of exceptions. These could centre on aspects of the witness's person, such as their character or social status, or more indirect exceptions that presented an alternative series of events to imply their perjury.[14] The former objection produced depositions from both parties which constructed men and women's reputations in particular ways, effectively offering summaries of their *fama* based on memories of their behaviour, legal status, and economic worth. These statements aimed to determine the value and weight which the Official assigned to testimony, ultimately influencing decisions in the final sentence.

Exceptions against witnesses embodied normative attitudes towards gender relations, replicating patterns found in legal and cultural treatments of men and women's reputations elsewhere. Explicit allegations of sexual misconduct, namely prostitution or fornication, against witnesses were rare in instance suits, appearing primarily as insults against women, and occasionally the clergy, in cases of defamation.[15] Such accusations could emanate from personal antagonisms accumulated over years or decades of conflict, perhaps interspersed with periods of coexistence and mutual toleration. In a late fourteenth-century marriage suit, Alice de Bridelyngton's former master deposed on her character, stating that he had known her for fifteen years and that during that time she had fornicated with many men.[16] Witnesses occasionally constructed women's activities as suspicious by framing their alleged activities in relation to temporal and spatial norms. During a marriage case initiated in Canterbury in the early fifteenth century, Thomas Strete and Robert Rikedon claimed that Agnes Hacchys, a deponent for the female party, gave unreliable testimony due to her ill fame in the local community. Both men depicted Agnes's relationships as illicit and Agnes as promiscuous, alleging that she was known to leave her house at night to visit these men, on one occasion accidentally falling into a ditch filled with water outside the defendant's home.[17] Nocturnal behaviour that subverted moral values of respectability was expressed through the organisation of time and references to night-time habits that could be cast as night-walking.[18]

Oblique objections that implied female promiscuity were more frequent, perhaps because overt claims of sexual misconduct could provoke instance proceedings against the accuser or *ex officio* citations for fornication or scolding. In a case that reached appeal in 1270 Matilda de la Leye sought to enforce a marriage contract with Adam Attebury, enlisting two female deponents who recalled the couple's union. Adam lodged an exception against

---

[14] Donahue, 'Procedure in the Courts', pp. 84, 110.

[15] For allegations of fornication against a female plaintiff, see BI CP.F.139.

[16] BI CP.E.102; see also BI CP.F.104.

[17] KALHS X.10.1 fol. 16r.

[18] For a study of night-time from the mid-fifteenth century onwards, see C. Koslofsky, *Evening's Empire: A History of the Night in Early Modern Europe* (Cambridge, 2011).

Popular Memory and Gender in Medieval England

evidence from one of the women, Lucy, wife of Richard the ploughman, based on her 'ill fame, suspect life, and opinion', as well as her poverty that, he argued, made her testimony dubious.[19] Composite allegations like this were often rather generalised, referencing several aspects of the witness's character simultaneously, but their allusive quality aimed to foster suspicion around the individual's reputation. Applied to women's evidence, claims of 'ill fame' and 'suspect behaviour' cast doubts over their sexual histories, with connotations so expansive as to include a host of deviant practices like fornication, prostitution, and running a brothel. When the Official in this case nevertheless quashed the exception and upheld the couple's marriage, Adam appealed against the judgement. In the next set of depositions, Robert Crips testified that the ruling should be overturned as Matilda's sister, who also deposed in the case, was a soothsayer, thief, and prostitute. Since exceptions could fail if they were too broad in basis, the men located socially peripheral and criminal identities that were more specific in nature. The boundaries of these categories overlapped, suggesting marginality and emphasising the moral and sexual laxity of the plaintiff's social network, while ultimately aiming to undermine the reliability of her witnesses.

Allegations of poverty were the most prevalent form of objection to witnesses' testimony. During the late Middle Ages, clerical attitudes towards work situated lower-status and destitute men at the bottom of the social hierarchy.[20] Men's reputations were often refracted through the lens of economic expertise and honesty, to the extent that the fulfilment of these masculine ideals was central to their gender identities. The language of poverty was applied to exceptions against male witnesses, and could intersect with other conditions, such as itinerancy and begging. William Bridsall testified in a late fourteenth-century suit between Alice Redyng and John Boton, supporting Alice's account of the couple's marriage. William described himself as having nothing in goods and surviving upon the goodwill of neighbours and through seasonal labour as a harvest worker. Witnesses for the opposing party claimed that William's lifestyle undermined his ability to give reliable testimony, stating that he was reputed to be 'more stupid than wise', a drunkard, and a pauper who begged for bread from door to door.[21] Poverty was seen as a moral as much as an economic or physical condition, operating as a reflection of poor character and judgement. The practice of begging also carried gendered inferences since, as Sharon Farmer argues, male beggars 'were, in many ways, perceived as not masculine' because they relied on the labour of others.[22]

---

[19] CCA E.S. Roll 35; *Select Cases*, p. 122. 'est male fame suspecte vite et opinionis'.

[20] S. Farmer, *Surviving Poverty in Medieval Paris: Gender, Ideology, and the Daily Lives of the Poor* (Ithaca, NY, 2002), pp. 44–5.

[21] BI C.P.E.92. 'reputat eum pocius stultum quam sapientem'.

[22] Farmer, *Surviving Poverty*, p. 43.

Gender, Narrative, and Testimony

While accusations of poverty and economic vulnerability influenced depictions of witnesses' manliness, these claims were used more often to invalidate women's legal suits and their testimony. In one sense, female parties chose witnesses from their own social networks and kin groups, ensuring that higher numbers of women appeared in marriage cases. The fragmented nature of female work patterns also contributed to higher levels of financial precarity among lower-status women. The material conditions of female witnesses cannot be determined from exceptions, or testimony in general, but these characterisations were formulated in ways that recalled strands of social and legal experience. In one mid-fourteenth-century suit from York, Robert de Popilton described a poor female witness as unreliable due to her history of performing piece-meal work for neighbours and her reliance on their charity. Robert told the court that it was commonly reported in the area that in return 'for a small amount, she is willing to conceal the truth and speak falsehoods'.[23] Misogynistic tropes of female guile and concealment were framed in the material context of perjury for financial rewards as poverty was seen to render women's memories mutable.

The language of poverty was applied to female parties in cases where economic need was cast as motivation for their choice of spouse. During a suit initiated in 1419, men testifying in a marriage case from Pontefract described Isabella Foxholes, plaintiff against John Lyttster, as a 'base pauper and abject person, having nothing or little in goods'.[24] Robert Bower reported that Isabella was employed, but had 'nothing at all in goods', except the wool she used for spinning and carding which allowed her to buy food and clothing.[25] This kind of work was both low status and poorly paid, employing large numbers of impoverished single women as well as serving to supplement married women's income.[26] Such patterns of employment left female workers vulnerable to additional forms of exploitative labour, including prostitution, which was itself associated with poor women's survival strategies. Although male witnesses labelled Alice de Bridelyngton as promiscuous, she described herself as an unmarried spinster of wool, while her fellow witness, Joan del Hill, another spinster, was said to have left her husband's household.[27] Claims of poverty made against women deponents alluded to this structural and economic relationship, simultaneously implying their evasion of patriarchal control. Other legal cases saw female witnesses presented as industrious, engaged in remunerative work, and behaving like virtuous married

---

23 BI CP.E.82. 'pro modico vult tacere verum et dicere falsum'.

24 BI CP.F.81. 'pauperem vilem et obiectam personam ac nichil vel modicum in bonis habentem'.

25 BI CP.F.81. 'nichil penitus habet in bonis'.

26 P. J. P. Goldberg, 'Women', in R. Horrox, ed., *Fifteenth-Century Attitudes: Perceptions of Society in Late Medieval England* (Cambridge, 1994), pp. 112–31, at p. 116.

27 BI CP.E.102.

Popular Memory and Gender in Medieval England

women. As Cordelia Beattie observes, respectable female identities were thus constructed in relation to their marital status and employment.[28] Allegations of poverty and assertions of honour through work, however, existed on the same continuum that assessed the worth of women's words in terms of their sexual activity and marital ties.

The moral associations between poverty and perjury, or generalized poor character, meant that modest means were seldom equated with expertise in remembering past events. The ability to testify without receiving gifts or money from parties was regarded as crucial in legal evidence to avoid accusations of perjury. Poverty and lower socio-economic status, however, were not seen as entirely incompatible with the provision of accurate testimony. In 1451 exceptions were made against the evidence of two witnesses who testified on behalf of Lady Alice Hoghton in a case brought in York. Roger Shirburn claimed that William Eukeston and Alice Huntyngton were unfit to depose as they were poor and held land from Alice's son. Lady Alice responded that 'although paupers or tenants of Sir Richard Hoghton, [they] are faithful persons', noting that both 'are prudent and have orderly and clever memories, natural discretion, and integrity of mind and a record of the actions which they saw and understood in the few years preceding'.[29] Alice noted further that William and Alice were 'endowed with their own property, from which they might adequately thrive, continually free and immune from all tenure of the said Sir Richard'.[30] A defence based on the witnesses' ability to remember was unusual, as was its explicit framing in relation to economic worth, legal status, and land tenure. Although male testimony was generally regarded as more authoritative under the law, the memories of both witnesses were described in equivalent terms. Descended from gentry stock, Lady Alice Hoghton was married to a knight, and described as 'gentil woman' in the case. The family's position in the social hierarchy perhaps placed it in greater proximity to learned discourses as the defence appears to replicate the language of treatises on formal memory practice. The *ars memorativa*, a genre for training memory, advised readers to organize their memory so that recollections could be retrieved with greater ease.[31] Ordered memory formed the bedrock of classical and late medieval memory techniques through the separation of memory

---

[28] C. Beattie, 'The Problem of Women's Work Identities in Post Black Death England', in J. Bothwell, P. J. P. Goldberg, and W. M. Ormrod, eds., *The Problem of Labour in Fourteenth-Century England* (York, 2000), pp. 1–19, at pp. 12–13.

[29] BI CP.F.187. 'licet pauperes vel tenentes domini Ricardi Hoghton dicantur fideles … sunt et discreti et ordinatam ac ingeniosam habent memoriam et discrecionem naturalem et sunt in eis integritas sensum et recordacio actionum quos annis parum precedentibus viderunt et intellexerunt'.

[30] BI CP.F.187. 'sunt eciam in bonis propriis dotati unde competente valeant se sustentari et ab omni tenura dicti domini Ricardi liberi continue et immunes'.

[31] Carruthers, *The Book of Memory*, pp. 129–30.

images into manageable pieces.[32] William and Alice were also described as possessing 'natural discretion', with the word 'discretio' meaning prudence or understanding.[33] The exceptions not only served to restore their reputations and emphasise the value of their memory, but ascribed to them a high level of knowledge of the events that had occurred.

Exceptions based on poverty were not the only way that witnesses' testimony could be undermined by reference to their social position. Parties also objected to evidence based on their legal status, as well as that of their ancestors and kin. Canon law barred unfree men and women from providing evidence, but the local application of this rule in England saw their testimony admitted and presented to the other party for their exceptions. By the late fourteenth century, serfdom as a social system was in decline, persisting into the fifteenth century in some regions, often with alterations to seigneurial demands. In a number of manors, unfree tenures were changed into leasehold tenancies to offset declining numbers of tenants.[34] It was perhaps this type of landholding that Lady Alice's witnesses possessed, and which exempted them from claims of serfdom as well as of poverty.

Even where serfs secured manumission and gained freedom, their natal origin and former status persisted in local memory and could be deployed in suits to undermine the basis of legal arguments. These recollections appeared more often in cases where male parties and witnesses alleged disparities in wealth and social background between women seeking to enforce marriage contracts and the men resisting these claims. In the suit between Alice Redyng and John Boton, George Rayneson stated that, while Alice's father was a serf, she was later manumitted by a certain Clemence, seneschal of the Latimer family on the manor of Scampston in North Yorkshire. Witnesses were also asked whether Alice had paid the fine of leyrwite previously, underlining the sexual organisation of manorial control over unfree women's bodies. Another witness told how Alice had an illegitimate child with her manorial lord, during service in his household, but that her suitor knew about this at the time of their marriage.[35] Communal attitudes towards female sexual activity could be unforgiving when women lacked the resources to support offspring out of wedlock. Leyrwite and related fines were seen as an 'offence of the female poor', and allegations of serfdom embodied gendered perceptions that linked women's poverty with their sexuality.[36]

---

[32] Carruthers, *The Book of Memory*, pp. 7–9.

[33] R. E. Latham, ed., *Revised Medieval Latin Wordlist from British and Irish Sources* (Oxford, 1965; repr. with supplement, 1999), p. 149.

[34] M. Bailey, *The Decline of Serfdom in Late Medieval England: From Bondage to Freedom* (Woodbridge, 2014), p. 24.

[35] BI CP.E.92.

[36] Bennett, 'Writing Fornication', p. 154.

Popular Memory and Gender in Medieval England

Despite the gradual decay of serfdom, local memories of its existence in earlier generations were also cited in marriage cases. In the suit between Isabella Foxholes and John Lyttster, the latter's deponents described Isabella's father as servile in status, in comparison to John's family, which included Sir John Sayvell, a custodian of Pontefract castle, and the gentry Lockwood family on his mother's side.[37] The two family ancestries were depicted in oppositional terms, in which the descent of each kin group held inverse relationships with manorial authority. Allegations of serfdom against women, in the context of marriage cases, were perhaps also intended to raise doubts about their moral character as well as their socio-economic standing.

Social status permitted the female gentry and nobility to circumvent the constraints of traditional gender hierarchies in ways that were unavailable to non-elite women. In a late thirteenth-century dispute involving the church of Ratley in Warwickshire, Lady Eleanor Bassett gave evidence in an *ex officio* investigation of the alleged marriage between her sister and a claimant for the benefice of the chapel of Ratley. William Brun of Weldon, described as *illiteratus*, later stated that the Official of the bishop of Lincoln had written to Lady Eleanor asking her to 'send the deponents who knew best about these matters'.[38] In response to this request, Lady Eleanor selected witnesses to provide the most informed evidence. This level of consultation by church-court authorities appears to have occurred only in cases of aristocratic and gentry women, who were higher in social and economic status than most female litigants in the Courts Christian. The legal agency exercised by Lady Eleanor reflects the 'extra-curial' practices detected among gentry women in common-law disputes.[39] As with other areas of late medieval society, social hierarchy mattered more than gender in the church courts, and where the latter gained more prominence it tended to intersect with socio-economic status, particularly in relation to women's testimony.

The language of social description was used to invalidate legal suits and testimony from non-elite men and women in ways that referenced and reified normative perceptions and hierarchies. Women were more vulnerable in general to claims that undermined the authority of their speech, but the language of patriarchal norms was also used to challenge the reliability of evidence from men in dependent and marginal positions. The confinement of female parties and witnesses to specific types of cases meant that litigation involving both men and women usually centred on cases to enforce or annul marriages. The mechanisms that eroded evidence from these groups

---

[37] BI CP.F.81.

[38] CCA E.S. Roll 88; see also *Select Cases*, p. 555. 'ipsa faceret huc venire testes qui melius deponere scirent de facto isto'.

[39] E. Hawkes, '"[S]he will ... protect and defend her rights boldly by law and reason": Women's Knowledge of Common Law and Equity Courts in Late-Medieval England', in Menuge, ed., *Medieval Women and the Law*, pp. 145–61, at pp. 157–61.

Gender, Narrative, and Testimony

therefore operated alongside broader gendered narratives that touched on the overlapping borders of marriage, courtship, and sexual desire.

COURTSHIP, PREGNANCY, AND MARRIAGE

The centrality of marriage to the dynamics of everyday life and the progression of the life cycle ensured that its formation and breakdown were ubiquitous and often contested through the law. Marital status was usually the primary means of social description for women, while the theory of coverture absorbed wives' legal identities into their husbands'. In social practice, however, its use and force could be mitigated through the maintenance of certain rights and the existence of trading categories like *femme sole*, where married women could assume greater economic and legal autonomy from their spouses.[40] Writing of early modern London, for example, Gowing notes that the bond of matrimony 'defined women's status, their economic lives, and their social contacts'.[41] Despite hierarchical interpretations of women's marital status, this rite had a potent influence on both male and female identities, shaping perceptions of men's gender roles as well as their performance and subjective experience.

The dynamics of courtship could transform non-elite women into passive figures in the business of marriage-making, in contrast to the greater agency that men and wealthier widows experienced in choosing spouses and fulfilling promises of marriage.[42] Marital breakdown was sometimes managed outside the courts through informal decisions to separate, but where conflicts were complex, involving spousal disagreement with the decision, formalisation under the law was required. Marriage cases made up a large part of the regular activity of the English church courts, and, as Helmholz notes, more than three-quarters of those marital disputes involved the enforcement of contracts, greatly outnumbering suits to annul marriages.[43] During the fourteenth and early fifteenth centuries, women appeared as plaintiffs in matrimonial suits in higher numbers than men, and cases to enforce marriage contracts were more likely to be initiated by female plaintiffs. This pattern perhaps related to the greater cultural value of marriage to women in this period, a value which also left women vulnerable to temporary sexual relationships and premarital pregnancy.[44] Courtship did not always end in marriage for young women, with male suitors prone to depicting gifts as payment for sexual intercourse

---

[40] Müller, 'Peasant Women, Agency and Status', p. 94; M. K. McIntosh, 'The Benefits and Drawbacks of *Femme Sole* Status in England, 1300–1630', *Journal of British Studies*, 44 (2005), 410–38.

[41] Gowing, *Domestic Dangers*, p. 7.

[42] McSheffrey, *Marriage, Sex, and Civic Culture*, pp. 48–9.

[43] Donahue, *Law, Marriage, and Society*, p. 70.

[44] Goldberg, 'Gender and Matrimonial Litigation', p. 45; Donahue, *Law, Marriage, and Society*, pp. 78–9.

rather than tokens of betrothal or marriage.[45] The gendered politics of courtship influenced the shape of men and women's memories, as witnesses framed their evidence in a wider social context where male suitors could resist the marital bond.

Narratives that reflected women's interests usually proffered accounts of love, commitment, and domestic stability which were depicted as amounting to the mutual intention to marry. Witnesses in these cases occasionally claimed that unions were committed to their memory from the outset, citing deliberate acts of recollection in the dispute that followed. This type of explicit and active form of memory appears more often in testimony in support of female parties. In 1372, Christina de Man testified on behalf of a female plaintiff that she remembered the marriage ceremony since she was in attendance and committed it well to her memory.[46] Other witnesses associated marriage with memory more overtly, emphasizing the need to provide reliable testimony should litigation follow. In 1442, Christopher Twyselton, a skinner in the city of York, recalled that the female plaintiff asked those present during the couple's marriage to hold the contract in their memories in case she needed witnesses in the future.[47] Deponents aligned the need for women to remember contracts with the tendency of some male suitors to reject their wives, producing narratives in which female plaintiffs and witnesses created memories of marriages for future purposes. In a marriage suit from York in 1419, Margaret Carow remembered her niece's marriage to John Lyttster because 'she often returned the said contract to her memory lest the said John should wish [to be] false by denying the contract in the future'.[48] The cultural trope of young women embedding marriage contracts in their memory was still recognisable in late medieval England, and held such narrative force that it was also adopted by opposing parties. In 1490, for instance, Alice Cant remembered the female defendant telling the groom 'we wilbe handfast here a fore thies folk at they may beyr reccord theropon'.[49]

Considered acts of remembering could imply the female party's intention to marry, demonstrating the good faith with which they approached relationships, yet their necessity acknowledged socio-cultural patterns where female parties sought to enforce unions more often than men. These claims perhaps represented a subject position that female witnesses could adopt retrospectively, informed by the proliferation of cases in which women pursued recalcitrant men. Although the ability to use memory as a form of proof

---

45 Bennett, 'Writing Fornication', pp. 155–8.

46 BI CP.E.121. 'interrogatus qualiter recolit de lapsu temporis quia bene scit quod ita fuit et factum bene memorie commendavit'.

47 BI CP.F.262.

48 BI CP.F.81. 'sepius reduxit memorie sue dictum contractum ne forte in futurum dictus Johannes vellet [esse?] falsus huiusmodi contractum negando'.

49 BI CP.F.280.

Gender, Narrative, and Testimony

permitted women greater agency in asserting the existence of marriages, its deployment underlined the instability inherent in certain relationships. These instances also indicate an awareness among young women that sexual relationships could be construed as concubinage rather than legitimate marriages.[50] In terms of cohabitation, childbearing and childrearing, both concubinage and marriage could manifest themselves in comparable domestic practices. This was evident in a mid-fourteenth-century case from York in which Robert de Harwod claimed that he 'never heard tell of any marriage [between the couple] … but only of concubinage'.[51] The resemblance between the markers of marriage and concubinage prevented their conclusive categorisation and made their elision possible.

In order to counter claims of transitory sexual ties or concubinage, complex domestic and conjugal histories of couples were cited, based on memories of cohabitation, love, and childbearing. Couples whose relationships had already produced children occasionally cohabited, but were not necessarily engaged in courtship that would lead to marriage. Cultural expectations associated with courtship and childbearing provided the moral framework for legal arguments and testimony, alongside the influence of gendered models of behaviour and the weight of canon law. In 1392, for instance, a suit was initiated between Margaret Hobbedoghter and William Beveridge, a couple whose relationship had already attracted the interest of the ecclesiastical authorities in the East Riding of Yorkshire.[52] The pair had lived together in the parish of Skipsea for several years, during which time two children were born, but the couple had not committed to marriage in formal terms. Following the birth of their second child, Margaret and William were compelled to exchange conditional vows *sub pena nubendi* in the parish church of Skipsea before the dean and chapter of Holderness. A valid marriage would therefore exist if the couple had sex with each other again. In the 1392 case, Margaret was claiming that they had.

Witnesses in marriage suits often provided testimony of sex between the parties, but cohabitation was also cited as evidence of a couple's conjugal bond. In the case between Margaret and William, John Selow, the god-father of one of their children, testified that the couple had cohabited for a period both before and after the abjuration, which he knew from many visits to their home. John's relationship with Margaret and William symbolised a role of trust and intimacy that connoted an everyday familiarity with the couple's domestic life, imbuing his evidence with greater authority. Testimony from a god-parent underscored the moral obligations owed to the child by their

---

[50] R. M. Karras, *Unmarriages: Women, Men, and Sexual Unions in the Middle Ages* (Philadelphia, 2012), p. 201.

[51] BI CP.E.82. The English translation follows *Women in England, c. 1275–1525: Documentary Sources*, ed. and trans. P. J. P. Goldberg (Manchester, 1995), p. 159.

[52] BI CP.E.202.

kinsmen, which contrasted with the absence of the child's alleged father. While John was god-father to one of the couple's children, he also formed part of Margaret's support network and was her kinsman, invoking bonds that opposing witnesses cast as prejudicial to his impartiality. Other deponents claimed that John Selow colluded with Margaret on the nature of his evidence, before intimidating neighbours who supported William in the case. The testimony from Margaret's deponents underlined the longevity and established nature of their relationship, including their cohabitation and offspring, which their contract *sub pena nubendi* merely confirmed. The practices associated with marriage and childbearing thus operated as a substitute for evidence of sexual contact in suits of this kind.

Legal narratives that centred on sexual relations and marriage incorporated recognisable patterns and images that were used to render various types of sexual behaviour explicable. Allusions to sexual promiscuity could be used more precisely in suits where pregnancy and issues of paternity accompanied narratives of courtship. In 1269, Johanna de Clopton brought suit against Richard de Bosco in the consistory court of Salisbury to have their relationship confirmed as a marriage.[53] The couple had been lovers over a period of several years, to which several deponents attested and the pair themselves agreed. Several years previously, Johanna and Richard had abjured each other *sub pena nubendi* before the archdeacon of Berkshire, meaning that any further sexual intercourse would confirm their marriage. In this suit, however, Richard claimed that he had no intention of marrying Johanna, despite her argument that she and Richard had sex after their abjuration, which her deponents said they had witnessed in person.

As part of Richard's defence, witnesses not only denied that the encounter had ever occurred, but also alleged a previous sexual relationship with another woman, Matilda Goderhele, who was related to Johanna in the third degree of consanguinity. Richard's liaison with Matilda created an impediment of affinity if their relationship was proven. The argument for both parties focused on the construction of their sexuality, through gendered attitudes towards premarital sex and multiple partners. The female witnesses who testified on Johanna's behalf provided detailed evidence on the couple's alleged sexual relationship after their abjuration in the court. Johanna's apparent promiscuity was emphasised in the testimony of Petronilla, wife of Richard Syward, who told the court that Johanna was also accused of sexual relations with a servant from a neighbouring village. Johanna's witnesses drew on the language of secrecy and concealment to describe her encounter with Richard, which they claimed had occurred at night-time in a field, following an evening of ale. While Johanna's deponents emphasised her sexual promiscuity, this perception was used to frame her legal claim of consummation. The pair's

---

[53] CCA E.S. Roll 310; see also *Select Cases*, pp. 96–103.

Gender, Narrative, and Testimony

illicit sexual activity was also cited in an attempt to formalise her relationship with the child's father.

A comparable discourse appeared in testimony from Richard's witnesses, who told how Richard had also had sex with Johanna's kinswoman, an encounter that they claimed had similarly occurred in a field ten years earlier. Communication between witnesses outside the court in the form of gossip and rumour presumably allowed details of legal strategies to circulate via social networks. Richard's witnesses characterised him as a young man who was involved in a series of transient relationships outside the bonds of marriage. Illicit liaisons with both women implied that these encounters took place in a limited context of sexual desire rather than within the broader context of courtship and in the expectation of marriage.

The transitory nature of sexual relationships for young men in particular was emphasised in popular ballads and lyrics that circulated among the laity. A recurrent cultural motif that embodied this belief warned single women that sexual relationships could end in pregnancy and public shame rather than marriage. Lyrics and poems, such as *The Serving Maid's Holiday*, satirised the sexual desires of a young female servant whose dalliances with her suitor led to her pregnancy. In one early Middle English pastourelle, *In a fryht as Y con fare fremede*, the character of the maiden initially rejects the sexual advances of her suitor with the prediction that his affections would wander once he had satisfied his desire.[54] The maiden considers the consequences of a brief sexual liaison, but associates it with extramarital pregnancy and the fear of social marginalisation, poverty, hunger, and shame.[55] This depiction chimed with the counsel of churchmen that male passion could wane, as many promiscuous young men promised marriage only in order to initiate sex.[56] The prevalence of this stereotype, however, meant that male defendants could render different kinds of sexual relationships indistinguishable from one another in legal narratives.

Childbearing was central to the narrative construction of sexual and marital relationships, although the existence of children served primarily as evidence of sex and retained little significance under canon law. In the suit between Johanna de Clopton and Richard de Bosco, both Johanna and her kinswoman, Matilda, became pregnant during their involvement with

---

[54] 'In a fryht as Y con fare fremede', in *The Complete Harley 2253 Manuscript*, ed. S. Greer Fein, with D. Raybin and J. Ziolkowski (Kalamazoo, MI, 2014), vol. 2, pp. 150–1, lines 17–18; for a treatment of single women and pastoral attitudes towards female sexuality, see Beattie, *Medieval Single Women*, pp. 39–61.

[55] 'In a fryht as Y con fare fremede', pp. 150–1, lines 33–6. For a discussion of premarital childbearing in lyrics and ballads, see N. Cartlidge, '"Alas, I go with chylde": Representations of Extra-Marital Pregnancy in the Middle English Lyric', *English Studies*, 79 (1998), 395–414.

[56] Bennett, 'Writing Fornication', pp. 146–7.

Popular Memory and Gender in Medieval England

Richard, whom they identified as the father. Although he failed to recognize his child with Johanna, his paternity was confirmed through an inquisition of sworn women of the neighbourhood. Richard's witnesses, conversely, claimed that he acknowledged his offspring with Matilda, supporting and clothing the child as his own. The treatment of his alleged paternity in this instance implied that he did recognise and support his children, suggesting that another man had fathered Johanna's child and undermining her claims of sex. The existence of illegitimate offspring was also cited to undercut the reliability of women's testimony and sometimes to validate narratives of men's sexual activities. In the early fifteenth century, Thomas Copyn alleged that Agnes Hacchys, a witness for Juliana Prat, had fornicated with three men in the last few years, bearing an illegitimate child with each one.[57] Thomas stated that Agnes was said to be a concubine of William Rede, the defendant, thus depicting her as sexually immoral and William as engaged in a series of sexual relationships.

Domestic stability over long periods was used to rehabilitate female virtue and reputation in these kinds of suits. In 1453, deponents in a case from York testified in a multi-party suit which Agnes Vavasour initiated against William Warthill following a sexual relationship of several years duration.[58] Witnesses who deposed on William's behalf told the court of his recent marriage to Joan Kirkby during which the couple exchanged words of present consent before family and friends. Two deponents reported on William's earlier and more established relationship with Agnes Vavasour, the other female plaintiff in the case. These witnesses claimed that several years before, while they laboured with William in the fields, they had questioned him on why he had not married Agnes, whom he had held as his concubine for a long time. Another witness, William Mathew, challenged William Warthill more directly, asking why he did not care to marry Agnes since he had held her for so long from her virginity and had thus prevented her lawful marriage. Although William said that he wished to formalise their union and would marry her shortly, he also commented that he wished to consider the matter further. After the men confronted William, the couple had a child together and Agnes was pregnant again while the dispute ran in court. The relationship had many markings of a marriage, yet the deponents admitted that no contract could be proven between the pair. While William's hesitance and desire to deliberate further signalled his inconstancy, the couple's relationship was depicted as more established than mere concubinage. The birth of children was significant, yet greater emphasis was placed upon Agnes's conduct, which was marked by a monogamous commitment from her virginity to a bond that she viewed as stable and a precursor to marriage.

[57] KALHS X.10.1. fol. 16r.
[58] BI CP.F.191.

Gender, Narrative, and Testimony

Narratives of commitment and affection intersected with canon law on marriage as deponents attempted to emphasise the emotional authenticity of parties exchanging vows. Statements of love mattered little in legal terms, but the concept of intention was central to the evaluation of actions from a theological perspective and under canon law.[59] The sexual nature of many premarital relationships meant that the intentions of couples who claimed to have married could be contrasted with those of opposing parties. This kind of comparison was particularly significant in cases where the defendant claimed that the union was invalid due to a prior contract of marriage. The language associated with courtship was therefore imbued with emotions that drew on cultural expectations of behaviour during courtship. In this situation, pregnancy and the existence of children might only signify a previous sexual relationship rather than consent to marriage. For example, a number of suits to enforce contracts were judged unproven despite the birth of offspring within the relationship.[60] Yet the discursive overlap between concubinage and extended courtship was emphasised through the intentions and actions of young male suitors.

The gendered associations of courtship practices in late medieval England produced a range of subject positions that could be adapted to accommodate narratives surrounding the birth of children. The use of abjuration *sub pena nubendi* to formalise sexual relationships into marriages waned by the end of the fourteenth century.[61] Even after its decline, however, female plaintiffs could draw on entrenched gendered narratives of illicit sex, its meaning, and spatial location. Young women could appropriate and reconfigure cultural models that were hostile to female sexual activity in order to advance claims of marriage over the fathers of their children. Instead of tarnishing women's sexual reputations, these narratives could be used to fulfil the requirements of canon law after the couple had already appeared before the courts accused of fornication. Under canon law on marriage, childbearing had little influence on the outcome of matrimonial suits and in the earlier fourteenth century often served only to demonstrate that a couple had sex after their abjuration. In broader social practice, however, the birth of children mattered for women as their sexual activities could be cast as a stage in the couple's relationship after which marriage was expected to follow. Cohabitation and domestic stability were used to connote the established nature of these bonds while underscoring affective attachments between couples, particularly from the perspective of female plaintiffs.

---

[59] For a treatment of intention in relation to marriage and marital sex, see Wei, *Intellectual Culture*, pp. 266–7.

[60] Helmholz, *Marriage Litigation*, p. 132.

[61] R. H. Helmholz, 'Abjuration *sub pena nubendi*', *The Jurist*, 32 (1972), 80–90.

Popular Memory and Gender in Medieval England

MARRIAGE, MASCULINITY, AND MEMORY

Men's testimony in cases where women sought to enforce marriage depended on a variety of defences, from exceptions to witnesses to claims of consanguinity between the two parties.[62] In some suits, male parties sought to undermine the female plaintiff's argument through claims of their absence from the union, creating an alternative set of memories that placed the defendant elsewhere at the time of the alleged contract. Defences of absence functioned as alibis and acted as implicit accusations of perjury, since witnesses on both sides were questioned on the party's whereabouts.[63] Men initiated a small number of suits to enforce marriage contracts, in which women did occasionally use claims of absence, but these were fewer in number and failed to produce the same gendered patterns as alibis among male defendants. Donahue observes that the defence of absence relied on common 'story-patterns' where plaintiffs, usually women, alleged their good faith in marrying the defendant, whose witnesses often highlighted the latter's elevated social status.[64] At the level of proof, memories of absence often worked to extricate men from unwanted marriages, and by the fifteenth century judges increasingly accepted these defences by deciding in favour of defendants. Although only emerging in this format because of the rules of canon law, these arguments emphasised the interdependence of social and legal experience, providing glimpses of gendered attitudes towards courtship that anticipated and accommodated judicial processes.

Men's memories in these suits had their foundations in markers of youthful masculinity, and witnesses drew on perceptions of homosocial relations alongside recognisable forms of male sociability. These practices were integral to the gender identities of young men, and unruly masculine behaviour on occasion served as 'potent inversions of normative meanings of manhood'.[65] In marriage disputes, narratives of this kind served as the basis for the social memory of the men involved in the case, recalling their actions in ways that cast them as antithetical to the processes of courtship and marriage itself. Superficially, this allowed the men to reject the female plaintiff's case, but shared memories also functioned to represent the moral and social worth of defendants and witnesses through the use of gendered language and rituals.

Narratives of local and parish responsibility, usually founded on exclusively male company, were one method that young men used to underpin

---

[62] For a table and analysis of men's defences in fourteenth-century suits from York, see Donahue, *Law, Marriage, and Society*, p. 71.

[63] Helmholz, *Marriage Litigation*, pp. 156–7. See, for example, BI C.P.F.104, 113, 137, and 186.

[64] For a detailed exploration of these patterns, see Donahue, *Law, Marriage, and Society*, pp. 90–217.

[65] Shepard, *Meanings of Manhood*, p. 94.

Gender, Narrative, and Testimony

their legal defences. In 1269 Emma Prudfoot approached the archdeacon of Buckingham, requesting that the chapter recognise Robert Norman as her husband after their alleged marriage in the cellar of one of her witnesses.[66] Robert responded with claims of his absence, which eight men corroborated with statements that he had instead attended a meeting of a men's guild on the day of the supposed union. The witnesses described gathering at the house of Simon le Got, where they drank together all day until nightfall, without any of the men leaving to travel elsewhere. The alibi achieved greater substance with the claim that Robert not only attended the guild feast but also served as steward of the celebration. In 1271 several friends of Alice Dolling recalled her marriage contract with William Smith two years earlier on the feast of St Stephen.[67] Cecilia, daughter of Richard Long, remembered the union, including the clothing the couple had worn, but when asked why William had visited that day, she stated 'in order to have sex with Alice, if he could'.[68] William admitted that the pair had sex in the six months before she initiated the suit, but his witnesses supported his denial of marrying her, claiming that he was absent that day at the feast of a fraternal parish guild in Bulford (Wiltshire), where he had served as butler. When asked to testify once more, William's witnesses had either died or gone on pilgrimage.

The male identities depicted in these cases were inseparable from the positions of responsibility which they claimed to hold and were embedded in the fraternal networks through which these men associated. Katherine French demonstrates that on occasion women rose to become wardens of parish guilds, while others participated in 'maidens' guilds' and other activities to generate income for the parish church.[69] In general, though, men tended to dominate higher parochial offices, which in turn offered preparation for other forms of local governance. In many instances, men's testimony embodied the ideals of normative male behaviour, epitomising the markers of local responsibility and indicating their trustworthiness within the wider community.[70] John Chapelayn, for example, identified the guild brothers attending the parish feast with William Smith as all of the better men of the parish.[71] The composition of this group was no doubt intended to overlap with the comparably anonymous, and usually male, *boni homines* and *fidedigni* of the

---

[66] CCA E.S. Rolls 12, 21, and 39; *Select Cases*, pp. 102–12.

[67] CCA E.S. Roll 36; *Select Cases*, pp. 127–37.

[68] CCA E.S. Roll 36; *Select Cases*, p. 129. 'dicit quod ut haberet carnalem copulam cum illa si posset'.

[69] K. French, 'Maidens' Lights and Wives' Stores: Women's Parish Guilds in Late Medieval England', *Sixteenth-Century Journal*, 29 (1998), 399–425.

[70] S. McSheffrey, 'Jurors, Respectable Masculinity, and Christian Morality: A Comment on Marjorie McIntosh's *Controlling Misbehavior*', *The Journal of British Studies*, 37.3: *Controlling (Mis)Behavior: Medieval and Early Modern Perspectives* (1998), 269–78, at p. 269.

[71] CCA E.S. Roll 36; Select Cases, p. 131.

Popular Memory and Gender in Medieval England

local community. These kinds of men were regarded as reliable, substantial, and trustworthy, and their standing often saw their appointment to official roles on legal inquests and visitations. Social and economic status increasingly dictated the selection of this group from the thirteenth century onwards, as Ian Forrest argues, with economic pressures and rising prices producing deeper poverty at the lower end of the social hierarchy.[72] Although the criteria used to identify these men were more stringently applied during the late Middle Ages, integration within the community was a crucial marker throughout this period, and this was connoted through landholding and taxation.[73] References to this group evoked a more official type of social memory which implied gendered forms of respectability and responsibility available only to men in local communities.

Personal piety was also highlighted in claims of absence during marriage suits as other witnesses recalled seeing male defendants engaged in parish worship at the time of the disputed union, usually in churches situated in another village. In 1418 deponents in a matrimonial case from York told the examiner that John Kydde spent the weekend in which he was alleged to have wed Alice Walker several miles away with friends in the Yorkshire villages of Sicklinghall and Kirkby Overblow. During their time together the men had attended Mass together with John Kydde, staying in the village until after the raising of the Eucharist.[74] Witnesses for Thomas Bower told a similar story during a marriage case in which he was the defendant in 1424, claiming that Thomas had spent the day in the village of Pocklington, ten miles away from the city of York. Robert Barbour remembered seeing Thomas in the parish church where they both attended Mass and vespers, later joining other men in the village to socialise together.[75] The presumption of good character and reputation was encoded in the men's alibis which centred on guild offices and regular attendance at Mass, confirming the social and moral worth of the male defendant.

Although assaults on the character of female parties and witnesses served to convey their marginal status, the alleged socio-economic differences between parties were also outlined in more explicit terms. Memories of men's absences could emphasise the position of male defendants in local hierarchies in ways that referred to their economic standing and wider social relationships. Several witnesses recalled events that implied the male defendant's good standing through connections with neighbouring religious houses. In 1456, two monks of Selby abbey in North Yorkshire testified that both Thomas Nesse and his mother had spent the day of the alleged marriage with

[72] I. Forrest, *Trustworthy Men: How Inequality and Faith Made the Medieval Church* (Princeton, 2018), pp. 95–111, 202–9; see also Forrest, *The Detection of Heresy*, pp. 70–6.

[73] Forrest, *Trustworthy Men*, pp. 141–55.

[74] BI CP.F.79.

[75] BI CP.F.152.

Gender, Narrative, and Testimony

them at the monastery, where they shared dinner and socialised together.[76] In 1390, William Calthorne, a proctor-general of the court of York, brought witnesses to support his absence in a village miles from York on the day of the alleged marriage contract, where he was settling his father's estate following his death.[77] The men emphasised William's social and economic status in the village of Cawthorne, noting that his brother paid 5 marks annually to him for lands which he held, while a member of Monk Bretton priory had rendered him an animal that year as a payment. Male witnesses also recalled defendants' absences in relation to specific legal and business matters. In 1464, the men who testified for Nicholas Danby deposed that on the day of the alleged marriage they had gathered to eat and drink together, before Nicholas had a written bond drawn up in the house of a local scribe. The men then went to the house of John Gysburgh, the receiver of the archiepiscopal exchequer in York, where the document was sealed and signed. In contrast, William Ball recalled hearing from 'several honest and trustworthy men' that Margaret Barley had paid her witnesses to testify for her in the suit.[78] Men's testimony could thus draw on practices that were inaccessible to large numbers of laywomen, like the production of writing and legal documents, underlining the seemingly oral and ephemeral nature of women's memory.

Male witnesses also produced alibis that drew on normative tropes of youthful masculinity, which depicted men socialising in exclusively male groups from which women were usually absent. Like memories of local responsibility, these narratives depended on homosocial bonds that underscored men's immersion in spheres of public activity and sociability. The consumption of alcohol in groups was one of the central memories that young men used in narratives of absence from marriages. Robert Barbour described an evening drinking with Thomas Bower and other friends in the homes of 'many honest and faithful men'.[79] Nicholas Danby's witnesses reported a similar night where several men gathered at William Ball's house in the Fossgate area of York, drinking and socializing together until Nicholas and a friend left to conduct business before returning to the group later in the day.[80] Memories of drinking and socializing often coincided with other pursuits that depicted men as engaged in public and collective activities. Thomas Bower's witnesses told the court that at the time of the alleged marriage the men were practicing archery, and spent the rest of the day drinking in the homes of various men in Pocklington.[81] Similar stories of young men engaged in outdoor pursuits underpinned the memories of young men in other cases. In the case between Alice Walker and John Kydde

---

[76] BI CP.F.196.

[77] BI CP.E.175.

[78] BI CP.F.203.

[79] BI CP.F.152. 'a nonnullis honestis et fidedignis viris'.

[80] BI CP.F.203.

[81] BI CP.F.152.

Popular Memory and Gender in Medieval England

two women testified that one weekend two years earlier they had overheard the pair contract marriage in a barn in Stockhill.[82] John's friends offered a different narrative in which the men were miles away that day. After attending Mass, they spent the day fishing before returning to John's father's house where they joked and drank into the middle of the night, leaving only when berated by John's sleepless father. This type of male behaviour may have been recognized as particularly common among young, unmarried males, and implied that the men inhabited an earlier stage of the male life cycle. As Shepard notes, 'the collective consumption of excessive quantities of alcohol was an intrinsic part of male youth culture and one of the rites of passage into manhood'.[83] Memories of this kind not only established the defendant's absence from the alleged contract, but also constructed an identity based on conduct that was construed as particularly resistant to marriage.

Narratives of male bonding were also articulated through the language of embodiment in which men's bodies and feelings functioned as additional forms of proof. These memories emphasized the proximity of men's bodies in these periods of absence, during which they engaged in activities that underlined the affective nature of homosocial relations. Bed-sharing was occasionally used as testimony to the defendant's location on the evening of an alleged contract. Hugh Meriot claimed that he shared a bed with William Smith at his mother's house, while Thomas Calthorne recalled sleeping beside his brother on the evening when the latter was accused of wedding Joan Fossard.[84] Memories of men's sociability could be imbued with emotion which conveyed pleasure in same-sex company, and the shared remembrance of these times acted further to solidify male bonding. In the suit between Alice Walker and John Kydde, witnesses were explicit in designating the group of men testifying as friends, while Christopher Gyll described the trip as the 'finest recreation' the men had ever had. Other male witnesses in the case stated that they had talked about the day often since the event 'as young men do', a phrase that aimed to depict the men's behaviour as a gendered and natural stage of the male life cycle.[85] Men's conversation about past events was also presented as licit in their legal testimony, in contrast to women's collective speech that was more often denigrated as perjury and the fabrication of evidence.[86]

Memories of exclusively male company distanced men, both physically and ideologically, from the locations in which marriages were usually contracted. The omission of women from alibis reflected a particular type of masculinity

---

[82] BI CP.F.79.

[83] Shepard, *Meanings of Manhood*, p. 103.

[84] CCA E.S. Roll 36; *Select Cases*, pp. 131–2; see also BI CP.E.175.

[85] BI CP.F.79. 'fuit optimum solacium quod ipse iuratus dictus Johannes Kyd et alii consocii sui [damaged] et contestes simul habuerunt'; 'ut iuvenes viri volunt'.

[86] Wickham, 'Gossip and Resistance', pp. 15–16.

Gender, Narrative, and Testimony

associated with young, unmarried men, many of whom were servants and dependants.[87] Marriage was intimately connected with the creation of a household, as married men were granted a new social status as head of an independent household. While husbandly status permitted the exercise of patriarchal control, it also carried sets of behavioural expectations that reflected the differing gender ideologies of each social group. The formation of a new conjugal household often ensued after the conclusion of apprenticeships, while the postponement of marriage during periods of training chimed with stereotypes of male reluctance to wed. In a late fourteenth-century suit, for example, witnesses claimed that Thomas Baxter had asked Joan de Brerelay to wait for their union until the end of his apprenticeship.[88] Alibis of absence aligned the activities of young men with singleness, using gendered tropes of drinking and sociability that seemed to proscribe marriage and the creation of independent households.

CONCLUSION

The credibility of women's testimony was often undermined through subtle as well as more explicit critiques of their motivations, which depended on misogynistic tropes of promiscuity, poverty, and deceit to gradually erode female authority. Vulnerable to attacks on their honour and accusations of perjury in return for payment, women witnesses formulated strategies that endowed their claims with greater authenticity, for instance by recognising the value of memory in supporting other female parties in marriage cases. Patriarchal expectations relating to adult masculinity were used to diminish the worth of testimony from male deponents as well, where poor, servile, and marginal men were depicted as wanting in integrity and reliability. While poverty was a hindrance for both male and female witnesses, it was tied more fundamentally to the suspicion of women's sexual immorality.

Under the guidance of advocates and proctors, young men produced narratives of absence founded on moments of homosociality during which the world of marriage and domestic responsibility seemed implausible and distant. Misogynistic attitudes towards female testimony operated in tandem with these alibis in marriage cases, functioning as an inversion of women's communal memories of marriage, birth and baptism. These crucial life events were usually embedded in female patterns of kinship and sociability, where women offered material and emotional support that extended to legal suits that might arise in the future.

The evidence of the church courts suggests that higher-status men had the cultural resources to construct chronological and causal narratives which

---

[87] P. J. P. Goldberg, 'Masters and Men in Later Medieval England', in Hadley, ed., *Masculinity in Medieval Europe*, pp. 56–70.

[88] BI CP.E.255.

Popular Memory and Gender in Medieval England

firmly underpinned their claims of absence from alleged marriage agreements. Due to their elevated social position, male parties were able to frame the past in ways that echoed with broader official versions of history. In affirming their absence through reference to respectable and stereotypical masculine behaviour, these men could create stable historical narratives which aimed to convince the court of their interpretation of events. John Kydde, for instance, located his account in the public environment of the Mass, conferring legitimacy upon his claims. Other men drew on homosocial activities, again in public settings, which were not open to women in their local communities to the same extent. In contrast, Alice Dolling's witnesses could only affirm the couple's intentions and good faith, but these assertions were met with a denial that William Smith was present on that day as he was working elsewhere, to which many witnesses would attest. Put simply, these men were able to control narratives through testimony that reflected patriarchal representations of the past. While women could depend on affective networks to support their versions of the past, men could root their accounts with reference to a range of public experiences. Male temporalities depended on the linear isolation of specific events in ways that justified dominant power relations, and differed from women's synchronic organisation of time.

3

BODILY PRACTICES

Men and women framed the past using narratives and symbols centred on physical experiences and practices accumulated over long periods. Existing works on memory and the body in medieval culture, however, focus more on their interrelation in learned rather than non-elite contexts. For instance, the intellectual tradition of the *ars memoria* emphasised synaesthesia and embodiment in the formation of memory.[1] The human heart was itself interpreted as the storehouse for memory in ancient and medieval thought, and was often used as a metaphor for remembrance in literary and religious texts.[2] A number of studies on mystical texts similarly note how the body became a site of contemplation and mortification as men and women channelled affective responses to Christ and his suffering.[3] By the mid-fourteenth century, the Passion was itself enshrined in devotional lyrics in the form of the literary Charters of Christ, in which legalistic language and structures were applied to the metaphor of Christ's crucified body.[4] Likewise, pain was inflicted upon young bodies in both pedagogic and everyday settings, especially in cases concerning proof of land ownership, demonstrating a belief that physical chastisement could help imprint memories of past events.[5]

Such work highlights the embodied nature of remembrance, particularly in religious settings, yet the relationship between memory and the body in lay contexts remains underexplored. A constellation of practices underpinned the formation of memory in everyday life as embodied pasts were recalled in accounts that centred on the body and its affective states. This included fields of behaviour where the role of gender seems more overt, like sexual activity and childbirth, as well as areas such as work and physical violence, where gender initially appears less central but on closer analysis exerted a

---

[1] Carruthers, *The Book of Memory*; J. Coleman, *Ancient and Medieval Memories: Studies in the Reconstruction of the Past* (Cambridge, 2005).

[2] Carruthers, *The Book of Memory*, pp. 48–9.

[3] S. Beckwith, *Christ's Body: Identity, Culture and Society in Late Medieval Writings* (New York, 1993); Rubin, *Corpus Christi*.

[4] On the Charters of Christ as a literary and devotional genre, see E. Steiner, *Documentary Culture and the Making of Medieval English Literature* (Cambridge, 2003), pp. 193–226.

[5] For a study of the relationship between memory and violence, see J. Enders, *The Medieval Theater of Cruelty: Rhetoric, Memory, Violence* (Ithaca, NY, 1999).

Popular Memory and Gender in Medieval England

constitutive force. Popular memories thus developed in bodies that bore meaning in the present, by accommodating individual and collective notions from the past. This chapter explores the use and formulation of physical forms of memory in everyday contexts, while sexual and reproductive histories are addressed separately in Chapter 4.

Memories associated with the body and its practices represented attempts to stabilise physical behaviour into coherent testimony. A range of discourses were embedded in these narratives, an observation that does not reduce embodied memories to linguistic abstractions, but instead amplifies the role of cultural norms, motifs, and symbols in their production. Gowing identifies a similar process in early modern culture where expressions of the corporeal were both social and discursive.[6] Legal proof was established through accounts of bodily practice in which the language of embodiment conveyed frameworks of experience that were far from monolithic in meaning or representation. As noted in the previous chapter, motifs related to work could vary depending on the social and gendered connotations attached to specific kinds of labour, signifying moral worth in relation to poverty, trustworthiness, and sexual reputation.

The performative and discursive aspects of remembered bodies underlined the contingent nature of identity and the extent to which identities were constructed through memory.[7] Memories situated in the body, Pierre Bourdieu observed, incorporate gestures, emotions, and practices that represent specific subjectivities as well as entire cultural systems.[8] Despite the force of patriarchal social structures, institutions, and hierarchies, men and women could exert some control over the bodily memory expressed in their depositions. Moi emphasises the Beauvoirian notion of the 'body as situation' in which embodiment includes perspectives that were ideological as much as physical and subjective, a theoretical approach that eschews flat depictions of behaviour.[9] In a similar vein, Nick Crossley underlines the 'corporeal basis of agency' which encompasses 'human perception, emotion and desire'.[10] The ability to shape past events in testimony extended to representations of embodiment itself, as emotional experience and discourse coalesced to produce personalised versions of the past that were felt in affective and material ways.

Physical behaviour could become ingrained in body memory through 'incorporative practices' which marked material acts. Connerton describes this process of accretion as a 'mnemonics of the body' whereby body parts stored

---

[6] Gowing, *Common Bodies*, p. 4.

[7] Canning, 'The Body as Method?', p. 175.

[8] P. Bourdieu, *The Logic of Practice*, trans. R. Nice (Stanford, CA, 1990), p. 53.

[9] Moi, *What is a Woman?*, pp. 63–8.

[10] N. Crossley, *The Social Body: Habit, Identity and Desire* (London, 2001), p. 3.

Bodily Practices

knowledge and recalled habits.[11] This chapter focuses on the meaning and use of physical memory, exploring the central ways in which the laity recalled everyday bodily experiences. Memories of work, for instance, emerged from the repetition of labour, while tasks that accompanied specific trades accrued gendered and hierarchical meaning. Embodied pasts were also recalled through clothing, its worn use, and proximity to the skin, transforming textiles and mundane objects into repositories for active and emotional histories. Violence or the death of neighbours and kin produced memories that resonated at a physical level, with the former marking bodies and the latter entailing bereavement and burial. As with other forms of representing the past, embodied remembrance intersected with patriarchal attitudes and social institutions through routines that shaped personal and social memory.

BODIES AND MEMORY

The language of corporeality provided a principal way of interpreting and conceptualising everyday experience in late medieval culture. In religious thought, teachings on resurrection and bodily sin coincided with the theological importance of the Eucharist in cultural referents saturated with somatic imagery, some of which were gendered in essence.[12] Religious motifs centred on the body were communicated to the laity in orthodox terms, yet these could be reformulated in other contexts that subverted Church doctrine. Civic guilds adopted the symbolism of Christ's body in Corpus Christi rituals that undercut formal ecclesiastical structures dominated by the clergy.[13] Lay audiences reiterated and adapted teachings from sermons and *exempla*, quali-fying clerical beliefs that sought to situate bodies within moral and gendered systems. The spiritual and commemorative significance of the body was thus understood in a variety of interrelated discourses, not only in clerical and learned spheres, but also in more popular and secular contexts. Contact between these strands of thought allowed the laity to contribute to theological constructions of the body, which in turn were adapted and used outside the formal Church.

Learned treatises on remembrance emphasised its embodied nature, by allocating sensory perception an integral role in the formation of memories. Theologians and natural philosophers identified a close relationship between remembrance and the human body, above all in the form of the 'phantasmata', the physical imprint of memory on the brain.[14] In the Aristotelian tradition

---

[11] Connerton, *How Societies Remember*, pp. 72–4, 95.

[12] Rubin, *Corpus Christi*; C. W. Bynum, 'The Female Body and Religious Practice in the Later Middle Ages', in C. W. Bynum, *Fragmentation and Redemption: Essays on Gender and the Human Body in Medieval Religion* (New York, 1991), pp. 181–238.

[13] Beckwith, *Christ's Body*, pp. 22–40.

[14] Carruthers, *The Book of Memory*, p. 17.

Popular Memory and Gender in Medieval England

that exerted great influence on the revival of the *ars memoria*, memories were formulated not merely in the mind or the soul but also in physiological terms.[15] Emotion and physical experience merged to produce memories that were affective in nature.[16] This relationship underpinned the way in which theologians such as Thomas Aquinas understood perception and the intellect. In his *Summa Theologiae*, for instance, Aquinas eschewed the dualism of Neo-Platonist thought, arguing for the unitary nature of human experience in which the body and soul together generated sensory perception.[17] The senses of the body facilitated the production of memory, in particular sight, which generated the strongest impressions. Treatises on remembrance advocated synaesthesia in the creation of memories, a process in which a range of sensory markers coincided to produce 'simultaneous and "unsorted" sensory perceptions'.[18]

The significance of bodily habits and action in remembering past events was also emphasised in learned works on memory. In a short text composed around 1130 for school students, Hugh of St Victor outlined the methods that should be followed to remember pedagogic instruction on biblical history.[19] Physical experience was fundamental in composing memory-images, as Hugh of St Victor noted, not only those related to individual perception but also those recording the embodied behaviour of others. Thus, the preface explained that students should attend 'carefully to those circumstances of things which can occur accidentally and externally'. In order to anchor memories further, Hugh urged readers to 'recall also the face and habits of the people from whom we learned this and that, and, if there are any, the things that accompany the performance of a certain activity'.[20] When applied to daily contexts for remembrance, the doctrine of circumstances could be extended to incorporate bodily practice and expression, imbuing memories of past events with an embodied tone.

The association between memory and the human body was similarly profound in legal and administrative practices, despite the transition from the judicial ordeal to oral and written proof in the late twelfth and early thirteenth centuries.[21] Trial by ordeal depended on the perceived intervention of the

---

[15] Coleman, *Ancient and Medieval Memories*, p. 20.

[16] Carruthers, *The Book of Memory*, pp. 67–8.

[17] R. Pasnau, *Thomas Aquinas on Human Nature: A Philosophical Study of Summa Theologiae, 1a 75–89* (Cambridge, 2002), pp. 73–87.

[18] Carruthers, *The Book of Memory*, p. 78.

[19] W. M. Green, 'Hugo of St. Victor: *De tribus maximis circumstantiis gestorum*', *Speculum*, 18 (1943), 484–93, at p. 486; *The Medieval Craft of Memory: An Anthology of Texts and Pictures*, ed. M. Carruthers and J. M. Ziolkowski (Philadelphia, 2002), pp. 32–40.

[20] *The Medieval Craft of Memory*, ed. Carruthers and Ziolkowski, p. 38.

[21] For an outline of these developments, see K. Pennington, *The Prince and the Law, 1200–1600: Sovereignty and Rights in the Western Legal Tradition* (Berkeley, 1993), pp. 132–5.

Bodily Practices

divine, which enacted changes upon physical matter to produce legal judgements. In tests of this kind, legal proof was derived from the human body's interaction with the natural elements which indicated either innocence or guilt.[22] By the early thirteenth century, the arguments of proceduralists as well as the rejection of the ordeal at Lateran IV signalled a move towards proof by testimony. Despite these shifts, physical forms of evidence retained significance in ecclesiastical jurisdiction, comprising an integral part of legal memory even as testimony from witnesses was increasingly favoured.[23] The continued relevance of embodied forms of proof stemmed not from the persistence of elements of the ordeal, but from the resonance of the body and senses in learned tracts on memory, combined with ongoing efforts to substantiate evidence in the courts. Theologians simultaneously advocated the use of the doctrine of circumstances, which drew on embodied referents to provide the descriptive language for past events.

By the late thirteenth century, this classical tradition formed the backbone of penitential discourse, serving as an organisational framework for memories of past transgressions. One of the most popular confession manuals to employ this doctrine was the short verse treatise *Peniteas cito*, composed by William de Montibus around 1200, which became a basic text in the early instruction of grammar and theology during the fourteenth and fifteenth centuries.[24] According to the *Peniteas*, confession was intended to examine 'ages, senses, places, times and members', a version of circumstances which aligned memories of past events with the life cycle, sensory experience, and the sins of the body. Affective and embodied remembrance overlapped in a schema that interpreted the central components of memory as profoundly physiological and emotional in nature. In the apparatus of early ecclesiastical suits, examiners were instructed to investigate memories of past events with reference to the 'circumstances' in which they occurred. The use of this term in courts not only referred to immediate contexts, but also related to the doctrine's connotations in penitential discourse and juridical thought. In the church courts, the interrogative impulse that marked confessional traditions in manuals and *pastoralia* coincided with the inquisitorial practice of proof by testimony. In its most expansive and prevalent form, the doctrine of circumstances adopted a version of examination that elevated embodied experience as the primary means of remembering the past. Such interpretations could circulate widely through overlapping networks of learning and pastoral care, contributing to perceptions of memory among the secular clergy. The *Peniteas cito*, with its focus on somatic memory, was one of the 'mainstays' of

---

[22] Bartlett, *Trial by Fire and Water*, p. 89.

[23] Bartlett, *Trial by Fire and Water*, p. 127; Donahue, 'Proof by Witnesses', pp. 128–9.

[24] Woods and Copeland, 'Classroom and Confession', p. 385; see also J. Goering, *William de Montibus (c. 1140–1213): The Schools and the Literature of Pastoral Care* (Toronto, 1992).

Popular Memory and Gender in Medieval England

instruction in later medieval schools, as Goering notes, and represented one of the most popular confessional texts at this level.[25]

A central element of legal proof under canon law was the need for witnesses claiming personal knowledge of events to have seen or heard the events described. In the influential *Liber Extra*, the value of testimony was assessed through the language of corporeality, as the credibility of arguments and evidence was examined through sight of the bodies of witnesses or parties.[26] This method of proof extended to marriage cases, where the *Liber Extra* emphasised that consummation was proven only if the deponent had seen the couple having intercourse.[27] Witnesses reported the words exchanged between parties, such as Alice, wife of Robert Burges, who testified to the validity of a marriage contract in the late fifteenth century 'because on a certain feast day that she could not recall, this witness was in the home of her husband in Davygate in York and she saw and heard the couple talk and exchange words of consent'.[28] Men and women often described seeing the couple 'solus cum sola nudus cum nuda' ('alone together and naked'), while the phrase 'vidit et audivit' was the primary way of describing eye-witness testimony.[29] Auditory evidence was admissible when a deponent had not actually seen the marriage take place. In a fifteenth-century marriage case the testimony of a female witness was allowed despite an exception made against her on the grounds that she was blind and mentally impaired. The judge stated that although her sight was impaired 'she could perfectly well hear a contract to marry'.[30] Emphasis was placed upon the words of present consent during contracts, yet sexual activity could also be recalled through auditory memory. In December 1364, Alice de Rouclif, a young heiress, was alleged to have married John Marrays.[31] The abbot of St Mary's, York, claimed that he knew of the marriage's consummation from a young girl who 'heard a noise from them like they were making love together, and how two or three times Alice silently complained at the force on account of John's labour as if she had been hurt then as a result of this'.[32] In this context, the noise was intended to signify Alice's virginity as much as consummation. Physical forms of evidence in testimony incorporated bodily practices into oral accounts, transforming them into acceptable forms of legal memory.

Principles of canon law were applied to memories that highlighted physical appearance, corporeality, and affective experience, among both parties and

---

[25] Goering, *William de Montibus*, p. 107.

[26] See, for example, X 4.15.1; X 4.2.6.

[27] X 2.20.27

[28] BI CP.F.208.

[29] BI CP.E.103. Goldberg, 'Voyeurism and "Pornography"', pp. 108–9.

[30] Helmholz, *The Oxford History of the Laws of England*, p. 340.

[31] BI CP.E.89.

[32] *Women in England*, ed. and trans. Goldberg, p. 62.

Bodily Practices

witnesses, with legal rulings and precedent informing the language that deponents used to recall the past. From the early thirteenth century, litigants and witnesses in defamation suits were required to provide evidence of the defendant's malicious intent, according to the fifth canon of the Council of Oxford (1222).[33] In practice, narratives of insult in the courts depended on a broader base of behaviour than the claims of malice enshrined in canon law. Testimony depended not only on the language used and precise forms of speech, but also on the emotional state of the accused signalled through descriptions of facial expressions in particular. Deponents in a defamation dispute initiated in York in 1432, for example, claimed that the defendant made an accusation of adultery against one Agnes Langdale in a loud voice with an angry and spiteful expression.[34] Memories of bodies and physical behaviour thus operated to support legal claims while accommodating clerical and more popular understandings of embodied experience.

The narratives of witnesses occasionally drew on memories of bodily appearance to verify evidence, with witnesses required to account for their knowledge of parties and other deponents. Gender differences operated to influence these descriptions of physicality. Women were categorised more often in relation to reproductive capacities, or within the broader framework of feminine virtue, using language that drew on moral and patriarchal expectations of sexual behaviour, while age was the recurrent primary descriptor applied to men's bodies. Sexualised language also influenced the way in which male bodies were constructed, albeit with less frequency, although it pervaded testimony in marriage suits involving the examination of the husband's genitalia during impotence tests.[35] In general, however, age was an integral way of classifying male parties and witnesses. In suits relating to customary disputes and parish boundaries, for example, older men were selected as deponents due to the authority which their gender and senior status was seen to confer. Although age was the most significant physical identifier for men, other attributes could supplement descriptions in witness testimony where appearance was the court's chief concern. In 1430, for instance, three men who testified in a marriage case from the court of York were identified based on their physical characteristics. Richard Thoresby described the group according to their comparative ages, but John Tailour deposed that one of men, Thomas Northeby, was 'darker in colour' than the other two men, and aged around fifty or sixty, whereas William Wade and William Hill were both aged no more than thirty. Despite the disparity in age and complexion, John Tailour noted that the men 'did not differ greatly in respect of their persons'. John

---

[33] *Select Cases*, p. 94

[34] BI CP.F.95.

[35] J. Murray, 'On the Origins and Role of "Wise Women" in Causes for Annulment on the Grounds of Male Impotence', *Journal of Medieval History*, 16 (1990), 235–51; B. Kane, *Impotence and Virginity in the Late Medieval Ecclesiastical Court of York* (York, 2008).

Popular Memory and Gender in Medieval England

Willyamson, a resident of Ripon, described the men as aged around thirty, of common stature rather than fat or slender, and of fair enough complexion, neither pale nor dark.[36] Memories of the men's appearances provided more detail than the usual judicial focus on age or legal status as a means to identify deponents. Perceptions of physicality could thus be articulated using approximations based on body shape and comparative skin colour.

MEMORY AND WORK

Work was the most recurrent physical experience recalled by men and women in their testimony. Moments of routine labour or its disruption formed the basis for the everyday memories of witnesses in urban and rural areas. The gendered organisation of labour in late medieval culture ensured that past experiences of work retained different meanings for men and women. A growing number of studies emphasise the complexity of women's economic agency, yet among the lower to middling peasantry and in urban contexts, female labour was often regarded as inferior in status, paid less well than men's work, and was seen to be supplementary to the household economy.[37] Women's recollections of work and the identities they described were in many senses more complex than men's, reflecting the multiple roles which women adopted to make ends meet. Yet both men and women's testimony conveyed the embodied nature of work, through accounts of its manual tone, the materials used, and its spatial context. These memories were both practical and symbolic in function, acting to provide narratives with ideological value and gendered meaning.

The embryonic nature of examination in early proceedings from Canterbury produced from men and women more extensive self-descriptions of work than in later suits where one occupational term was usually preferred. This approach encouraged witnesses to consider and categorise aspects of their identity, creating subjectivities formed in relation to social expectations as well as legal processes and the nature of the suit itself. In 1294, a clerical scribe detailed forms of employment through comparison with the previous deponent, rather than references to their sole occupation. Geoffrey le Brewere was described as 'a brewer, living on his labour and his service', while Felicia de Wodeham, whose testimony followed, was 'not a brewer, but lived from her manual work making silk caps and breeches'.[38] The occupations of later

---

[36] BI C.P.F.113. 'dictus Thomas Northeby nigrioris est coloris quam alii duo … Thomas Northeby Willelmus Till et Willelmus Wade multum differunt et discrepant inter se non in respectu personarum'.

[37] Goldberg, *Women, Work, and Life Cycle*; Bennett, *Ale, Beer, and Brewsters*; B. A. Hanawalt, ed., *Women and Work in Preindustrial Europe* (Bloomington, IN, 1986); Beattie, 'The Problem of Women's Work Identities', pp. 1–19.

[38] CCA E.S. Roll 239. 'est iste iuratus pandaxator et vivit ex operibus et servicio suo';

Bodily Practices

witnesses in the case were again contrasted with the deponent who preceded them. Mabila de Wimel described herself as living from diverse industries and works, and the next deponent, Avice de Croydon, stated that she worked as a brewer, supporting herself from her service. This method of recording occupations evidently prompted some degree of self-reflection among witnesses, particularly women, on their patterns of work. Each of them associated their labour directly with economic survival and autonomy, and several expressed their work in language that conveyed their manual and physical activities.[39] The relationship between the forms of work cited remains obscure, but it likely reflected the piece-meal composition of labour practices among non-elite women in this period.

Working identities were an integral part of men and women's labour histories, and formed a transitional stage in their biographical memory. Entry into employment represented a key phase for large numbers of young people, and acted as a significant temporal marker in the life cycle. Service was a significant form of employment for young men and women in this period, many of whom left their natal homes to work before marriage in a demographic pattern often referred to as 'life-cycle servanthood'. Goldberg's analysis of poll-tax returns and court evidence demonstrates that higher numbers of women migrated to York from its environs for temporary labour in the decades after the plague.[40] Accounts of service were common in female testimony, particularly in the more full records from York. In a marriage dispute from 1430, Alice, wife of Robert Dalton, recalled the alleged union, telling the court that she entered into service in Aldwark in the city of York, where she worked for a year in the household of William Lemyng. In the same case, Robert Dalton remembered a marriage because he entered Robert Ketill's service around that time, where he remained for three years.[41] Although servants and apprentices usually resided in their masters' households, this work provided adolescents with some degree of independence to earn wages, accrue skills, socialise, and engage in courtship, while living outside their parental home for the first time.[42] Stages of courtship overlapped with service, functioning in many cases as a prelude to marriage and licit sexual activity. The social, economic, and emotional implications of these early adult years for men and women's identities and daily experiences were no doubt profound.

Some forms of training, especially among young men, were concerned with integration into trade networks that would provide social and economic

---

'ista iurata non est pandaxitrix set vivit ex opera suo manuali facienda tenas et bricas sericales ut dicit'.

[39] For early modern social description, see Shepard, *Accounting for Oneself*, pp. 6–8.
[40] Goldberg, 'Female Labour, Service and Marriage'.
[41] BI CP.F.201.
[42] Riddy, 'Mother Knows Best', pp. 66–86.

Popular Memory and Gender in Medieval England

advancement, yet these experiences were associated with feelings of apprehension as much as excitement. In 1372, for instance, William Tayliour, a resident of Coney Street in York, testified in a marriage suit that he recalled the union because he was made free of his craft around that time, as a result of which he was 'rather anxious'.[43] In the context of skilled crafts, the completion of an apprenticeship offered occupational and domestic independence, signalling the fulfilment of the initial stages of adult masculinity.[44] Male workers were incorporated into the upper social echelons, while the ability to marry and establish a household and workshop underscored their new role in the patriarchal order. Apart from several notable exceptions, young female workers were excluded from formal apprenticeships.[45] Memories of integration into trade communities were therefore rooted in peculiarly masculine experiences of economic and social inclusion.

The dynamics of social and legal hierarchy could determine the administrative positions that men recalled alongside their regular labour. In manorial contexts, elected and appointed officers carried out the management and organisation of everyday tasks. These men were usually selected from their own communities and from specific status groups, with many of these positions having implications for social cohesion and internal politics on the manor. In 1425 Thomas Gyselay remembered Katherine Northefolk's birth because he had then been elected constable of Gate Fulford, in the suburbs of York.[46] The local constable held responsibility for keeping the peace, enforcing the lord's authority, and detecting misbehaviour. Although women were ineligible for the majority of local offices, the election of these figures represented important knowledge about the local area, and female villagers had contact with them on numerous occasions. Women were perhaps present when male relatives and neighbours discussed a variety of issues, and remembered these appointments for a long time afterwards. In the case involving Katherine Northefolk, Margaret, wife of Hugh Tailour, recalled her husband's selection as reeve in his community around the same time as the girl's birth.[47] The daily management of the manor depended on the reeve, including the collection of rents, the rendering of accounts, and the administration of the demesne.[48] While election to this role could confirm a place among the

---

[43] BI CP.E.121. 'fuit magis solicitus illo die [missing] quam aliqua die festivale precedente fuit pro vestibus consuendum et liberandum magistris suis ad festum pentecoste'.

[44] R. M. Karras, *From Boys to Men: Formations of Masculinity in Late Medieval Europe* (Philadelphia, 2003), p. 126.

[45] M. Kowaleski and J. M. Bennett, 'Crafts, Gilds, and Women in the Middle Ages: Fifty Years after Marian K. Dale', in J. M. Bennett et al., eds., *Sisters and Workers in the Middle Ages* (Chicago, 1989), pp. 11–38.

[46] BI CP.F.89.

[47] BI CP.F.89.

[48] D. Stone, 'The Reeve', in S. H. Rigby, with A. J. Minnis, ed., *Historians on Chaucer: The 'General Prologue' to the Canterbury Tales* (Oxford, 2014), pp. 399–420, at pp. 400–1.

Bodily Practices

'better part' of the village, some of these administrative duties were onerous and became more contentious towards the end of the fourteenth century, when growing tensions focused on officials as representatives of manorial authority.[49] Appointments to these offices were significant moments for the identity and social standing of families and individuals, whether for good or ill, and carried a host of consequences for their future relationships with others in the local community.

Memories of work focused not only on transitional phases, but also on the bodily habits and practices that marked particular trades. The skills that underpinned labour were accrued over extended periods, and inculcated through the repetition of actions. These embodied aspects of work represented a 'complex of customs and activities involving practical know-how and ongoing calculations of physical and social kinds'.[50] Testimony that described the everyday practices of work tended to refer to the physical materials and processes which these trades entailed. In 1356, Mariona, wife of John Helis, recalled the presence in her home of one William Theker, who spent the day covering the roof of her house with straw.[51] Men also recalled the purchase of supplies in order to complete their work. In a case initiated in 1430, Thomas Catryk remembered a marriage contract because of his employment as a plumber for the abbot of Bardenay in Lincoln. While travelling to Scarborough to buy coloured glass for the church choir upon which he was working, Thomas had heard from an acquaintance that the couple involved in the case had wed.[52] Manual work on the church building offered physical proof of his evidence, which was exemplified further in his description of the glass used in the choir. Memories of this kind drew on the minutiae of skilled labour, outlining the regular activities that surrounded crafts and trades and enabled their completion.

Women also referred to the processes associated with their work, including the materials which they handled in the daily context of their trades. This was more characteristic in suits where female witnesses worked in the production of textiles and provided memories of the different stages of cloth-making. Katherine Lorymer and Alice Burton testified alongside Thomas Catryk in the case initiated in 1431, deposing on the absence of Agnes Schilbottil, the female defendant and their employer, from an alleged marriage contract. Both women told of their visit with Agnes to the house of William Goddeshelp, a weaver in Scarborough, to whom they brought a skein of white woollen thread which the women helped to weigh before its preparation for weaving. The women drank there for several hours with Agnes and a number of men who

---

[49] C. Dyer, *Everyday Life in Medieval England* (London, 1994), pp. 7, 211.

[50] A. R. Jones and P. Stallybrass, *Renaissance Clothing and the Materials of Memory* (Cambridge, 2000), p. 105.

[51] BI CP.E.70.

[52] BI CP.F.113.

Popular Memory and Gender in Medieval England

later gave evidence for the opposing party, which her witnesses claimed to be perjured due to their presence in the weaver's house.[53] The defence of absence was based upon testimony that reflected common female work patterns, as well as the sociability that accompanied the different stages of this kind of labour. Although Katherine and Alice were described as Agnes's servants, both appear to have worked as spinsters as part of their service contract, an often unstable and poorly remunerated form of employment that attracted large numbers of young unmarried women.[54]

The embodied practices that marked particular trades acted as additional forms of proof, with narratives structured through memories of shared physical habits and spaces. In a mid-fifteenth-century suit, John Selybarn recalled a marriage contract 'because he was a servant at the time of the contract and, lying in bed, he saw and heard' the couple exchange words of consent.[55] In rural areas, memories of work were often tied to the agrarian cycle, where the production of grain and animal husbandry occurred at specific places and times. In 1372, for instance, deponents claimed that Hugh Stry worked in the fields from sunrise until dusk gathering his master's corn on the day that Cecilia, daughter of William Routh, alleged that they appeared in the chapter over their sexual relationship.[56] Several other local men supported these claims, including his master, William Tykton, who remembered Hugh stopping for lunch before returning to the fields. Meal-times were interspersed throughout agricultural time both for workers and employers, and routines associated with agricultural work punctuated rural temporalities, coexisting with other labour practices that shaped the movements of workers' bodies.

Memories of work accrued particular meaning in cases where the spatial dynamics of duties conflicted with normative gendered practices. In 1394, Walter de Mellerby testified that the plaintiff, Margery Spuret, was absent on harvest work at the time of her alleged contract with Thomas de Hornby, junior.[57] This departure of servants was an annual disruption to the domestic rhythm of the household, during which daily duties were reassigned to other servants. Walter remembered Margery's absence as he 'carried a jug with water from the River Ouse to his master's house for the whole of the aforesaid time, which duty Margery was wont to do when she was present in the city of York'.[58] Although women were exposed to a range of processes in trades and workshops, gender continued to influence many aspects of the division of labour, with female servants usually allocated domestic tasks that included the

---

53 BI CP.F.113.

54 Goldberg, *Women, Work, and Life Cycle*, pp. 144–5.

55 BI CP.F.189.

56 BI CP.E.114.

57 BI CP.E.159. Depositions from this case are translated in *Women in England*, ed. and trans. Goldberg, pp. 103–9.

58 BI CP.E.159; *Women in England*, ed. and trans. Goldberg, p. 105.

Bodily Practices

carrying of water. Female servants congregated at the river daily to fetch water and wash clothes in an environment that was demarcated by gender.[59] Gender influenced the construction of work identities as specific tasks were assigned according to hierarchical and often gendered assumptions.

Memories of labour were similarly organised through references to physical habits that both reflected and produced distinctive gender ideologies. Such details could inform the subjective identities that witnesses sought to construct through their testimony. Perceptions of women's sexual virtue depended in part on their labour activities and marital status, strands of female identity that underpinned judgements on respectability and trustworthiness.[60] The possession of materials involved in textile production could signify gendered aspects of women's reputations at a local level. In 1366, Walter Waryner testified in the suit between Alice Redyng and John Boton, noting that despite uncertainty around the pair's union and the common access the couple had to each other's chambers, Alice often brought different goods with her, 'namely wool and thread for making clothes'.[61] She was a woman of 'good industry', Walter claimed, and was wealthy enough that others had already urged John Boton to marry her before the pair were alleged to have wed. The wool and thread, and their conversion into clothes, underpinned a narrative in which Alice's labours in their chambers implied not only the honesty of her work, but also the apparent permanency of their bond. The bedchamber became a place of industry, akin to a workshop, rather than simply a site of premarital sex, while her activities signified an intention to marry since their relationship was not founded solely on sexual desire and replicated several facets of shared domestic life. In this context, men and women could incorporate aspects of labour identities into their testimony, producing subject positions that depended in part upon their skill in particular trades.

CLOTHING AND OBJECTS

Memories that centred on bodily experience were prompted by practices relating to material objects: their use, exchange, and reuse. Physical things imbued narratives with meaning and goods were assigned import through their relationship with legal processes, forming part of the material of memory in depositions. The categorisation of things in judicial settings, as Johnson notes, was achieved through their naming and the characteristics attributed to them. In this way, the nature and operation of law can be interpreted 'as

---

[59]   H. Graham, '"A woman's work ...": Labour and Gender in the Late Medieval Countryside', in P. J. P. Goldberg, ed., *Woman is a Worthy Wight: Women in English Society, c. 1200–1500* (Stroud, 1992), pp. 126–48, at p. 136.

[60]   Beattie, 'The Problem of Women's Work Identities', pp. 1–19.

[61]   BI CP.E.92.

Popular Memory and Gender in Medieval England

a quality that can inhabit physical stuff'.[62] In the church courts, these details were part of the circumstances of past events about which examiners inquired. Learned treatises on memory emphasised its embodied tone, with some texts including dress as informal variations on circumstances.[63] Memories of clothing not only carried ideological connotations, but also acted as proof in the courts, with witnesses in marriage cases often questioned on the dress worn by parties during alleged marriage contracts. The clothes that people wore were so intimately attached to their body that they embodied identities, acting as a proxy for more complete sight of the face. In 1269, Petronilla, wife of Richard Syward, was asked in her testimony how she recognised a couple having sex in a nearby field, to which she responded that it was by the clothing that they wore at the time.[64] Forms of dress were interpreted as markers that could make men and women distinguishable to their neighbours even when privacy was sought for illicit encounters.

Objects were also used to constitute the places and spaces that men and women inhabited in their testimony. Events that took place in domestic environments were remembered through references to the things that denoted the function of rooms and spaces. Marriages were often situated in places that emphasised the sexual and domestic potential of the couple's relationship, while simultaneously underlining their premarital chastity. In 1335, witnesses recalled a union made with the couple sitting upon a wooden bench, called 'le dees', next to a bed in the cellar.[65] The spatial location of furniture could act as additional proof in testimony of marriages formed in domestic spaces. In 1394, Alice de Stodlay recalled an alleged marriage that was made at the foot of her bed as she lay in child-bed at her marital home, her impending maternity perhaps used to imply the procreative intent behind the couple's contract.[66]

Objects not only evoked past events, but also provided a material way for 'meanings and social relations [to be] literally embodied'.[67] Marilyn Strathern observes the dynamic nature of material goods, which accrued histories beyond the oppositional binaries often applied to the relationship between agents and objects.[68] Identities were made and articulated through the exchange and gifting of objects, often items that were produced and circulated in everyday contexts.

---

[62] T. Johnson, 'Medieval Law and Materiality: Shipwrecks, Finders, and Property on the Suffolk Coast, ca. 1380–1410', *American Historical Review*, 120 (2015), 407–32, at p. 410.

[63] Carruthers, *The Book of Memory*, p. 125.

[64] CCA E.S. Roll 310; *Select Cases*, p. 98.

[65] BI CP.E.28.

[66] BI CP.E.198.

[67] Jones and Stallybrass, *Renaissance Clothing*, p. 8. C. Richardson, '"Havying nothing upon hym saving onely his sherte": Event, Narrative and Material Culture in Early Modern England', in C. Richardson, ed., *Clothing Culture, 1350–1650* (Aldershot, 2004), pp. 209–22.

[68] M. Strathern, *The Gender of the Gift: Problems with Women and Problems with Society in Melanesia* (Berkley, 1988).

Bodily Practices

The ability to exercise agency was not confined to individuals as subjects, with objects regarded as retaining considerable power and meaning to influence present and future events. In 1425, Alice, wife of John Jakson, remembered sending an 'agnus dei' charm to Agnes Northefolk, who 'laboured tirelessly in the birth of [her daughter] Katherine'.[69] The item recalled the intimate relationship between materials and the body, as Alice described it hanging around her own neck before she passed it to Agnes. Its proximity to Alice's skin and its use in earlier births acted as a kind of disembodied female memory, detached from its previous wearers but imbued with their past experiences.

The use and transmission of everyday goods and textiles depended on practices that reflected the nexus of memory, gender, and materiality. For example, parishioners with sufficient goods made bequests to the Church, and female testators left domestic items to their parishes in greater numbers and with specific instructions on their use. Gender relations were therefore 'manifested through the performance of exchange' which embedded relationships in meaningful narratives.[70] Physical objects were also cited to exemplify intimate ties of friendship and love. In periods of courtship and during the formation of marriage contracts, love tokens including rings and gloves were cited as signs of the couple's intention to marry. In an early fifteenth-century suit, Thomas Aslowe remembered John Thorp entrusting him with a ring and a letter to deliver to Agnes Schilbotill in Scarborough, shortly before Christmas.[71] Memories of gifts and tokens were more common in support of female plaintiffs in suits to enforce marriage contracts, and on rare occasions objects associated with courtship and love were submitted to the court in parties' apparatus. In an appeal case from 1423, Christina de Acle produced two silver rings, a purse, and a letter from William Thornburgh as proof of their relationship and union.[72] Objects associated with courtship were rich with emotions and memories and could provide enduring evidence of relationships, even where these were contested.

Cloth was understood as a tangible form of memory, possessing durable qualities that could incorporate and withstand its use and reuse over extended periods. Fabric served not only as a kind of material proof under the law, but also signified the structure of social bonds and hierarchies in narrative terms. The possession of goods acted as an indicator of social and economic standing, operating as a shorthand for the credibility of a deponent's legal evidence, while paupers were described as having no goods and living on the charity of others. Parental roles were reflected in memories centred on the provision of clothing for children, with gifts of garments operating as

---

[69] BI C.P.F.89. 'in partu dicti Katherine assidue laboranti'.

[70] E. Campbell, *Medieval Saints' Lives: The Gift, Kinship and Community in Old French Hagiography* (Cambridge, 2008), p. 53.

[71] BI C.P.F.113.

[72] BI C.P.F.139.

proof of parenthood for men in particular. In 1269, Adam le Waleys testified on the alleged marriage between Richard de Bosco and Johanna de Clopton. Witnesses claimed that the relationship produced a child, whom Richard had recognised as his own through the provision of clothing and other necessaries that signified his paternity. Adam recalled that he had also given Richard an old russet tunic to be reworked into clothes for the child.[73] Clothing and its biographies could be refashioned, serving practical purposes at the same time as it encoded bonds of friendship. When men and women testified on children's ages in legal suits, textiles used in childrearing practices were recalled to verify memories of parents caring for their children. Robert Souman remembered the time of Katherine Northefolk's birth in various ways, but also described seeing the infant wrapped in a swaddling cloth and carried to the parish church for baptism.[74] Emotional relationships were in many senses worked into the very fabric of clothing through their regular use and the affective bonds which they represented.

Domestic goods were regarded as part of the marital household in late medieval England, with the majority of goods and property belonging to the husband, apart from the wife's everyday clothing. The remembered function of clothing could prove crucial to their use in the future, as items of dress were seen to carry the identity of the previous wearer.[75] In a marriage case initiated in the London consistory in 1487, a gift of clothing was used to establish proof of the putative groom's intentions. John Robert recalled how the defendant, John Ely, had tried to allay the fears of Agnes Whitingdon, who was concerned that he intended to marry another. Inviting the witness and his wife for dinner, John Ely brought Agnes and the married couple into his bedchamber, in order to give her a set of wedding gifts to be worn on the day of their nuptials. Presenting the bed and bedding to Agnes and his friends, John also laid out the embroidered girdles and gowns that belonged to his first wife, by then deceased. The spousal role of their previous wearer ensured that the clothing functioned as proof of John Ely's intention to marry Agnes, embodying an affective and material bond that strengthened her position as John's rightful wife. His attempts to assimilate Agnes into the pre-existing category of wife, both symbolically and materially, underscored the patriarchal dynamics of the marital household, where the role of wife could become an apparently transferable identity. The provision of clothes for their wives by more prosperous husbands also alluded to the domestic instability that women could experience as dependants of their spouse. Memories of women's clothing in cases concerning spousal cruelty signified the disciplinary force of patriarchal control over female bodies and dress. In 1348, deponents in a

---

[73] CCA E.S. Roll 310; *Select Cases*, p. 102.

[74] BI CP.F.89.

[75] P. Stallybrass, 'Worn Worlds: Clothes, Mourning, and the Life of Things', *Yale Review*, 81 (1993), 35–50, at p. 38.

Bodily Practices

marriage suit from Newcastle-upon-Tyne recalled how Margery de Devoine fled her husband's household injured and wearing only her chemise, following one of several severe attacks. Torn clothing and the inversion of marital and domestic intimacy thus underscored the extent of physical and emotional abuse in women's legal arguments.[76]

BODIES AND VIOLENCE

Memories of violence and death foregrounded bodily movement as an explicit part of their organisational framework, drawing on a wide range of discourses centred on the body. Chastisement and force were used to imprint knowledge on the body and mind, with violence forming a primary way of committing knowledge to memory in learned treatises. The foundation myth of the classical *ars memoria*, for instance, emerged from the story of Simonides, a Greek poet who remembered the identities of the otherwise unrecognisable dead so their families could claim their bodies.[77] The prevalence of this imagery, as Jody Enders notes, ensured that 'violence often lay at the architectural and epistemological foundations of classical and Christian mnemotechnics'.[78] Its critical role in the production and maintenance of memory was acknowledged outside the schools and legal circles. In local contexts, the corporeal punishment of young boys reinforced territorial boundaries at a somatic and emotional level. This practice embedded customs in the memories of a social group whose youth could ensure the legacy of communal memory after older inhabitants had died.[79] Physical force was integral to the formal application of the law in several jurisdictions, with violence underpinning inquisitorial justice despite the decline of the ordeal as a method of proof.[80] Representations of violence similarly appeared in pastoral literature aimed at the laity as sermons and *exempla* told of sinners wounded or struck down in didactic tales of divine punishment. Discourses on physical force from different literary and religious genres were also interrelated, as Hannah Skoda has recently observed in the context of thirteenth-century France.[81] Narrative representations of physical force and trauma in legal testimony depended on traditions and symbolic meanings that were closely associated in a variety of ways.

When violent incidents were cited in evidence, they were often situated in public settings, perhaps to offer greater veracity to the claims of witnesses.

---

[76] BI CP.E.257.

[77] Enders, *The Medieval Theater of Cruelty*, pp. 63–4.

[78] Enders, *The Medieval Theater of Cruelty*, p. 66.

[79] van Houts, 'Gender and Authority', pp. 206–7.

[80] Bartlett, *Trial by Fire and Water*, pp. 140–1.

[81] H. Skoda, *Medieval Violence: Physical Brutality in Northern France, 1270–1330* (Oxford, 2013), p. 19.

In a case from York, for instance, one deponent recalled the execution of the archbishop of York, an event that was performed publicly outside the walls of the city, attracting a large group of onlookers.[82] Men's bodies could similarly function as corporeal evidence of trauma, primarily in relation to work accidents and bodily violence. Bedell observes that injuries in proofs of age under the common law became 'stock memories', yet their remembrance in ecclesiastical testimony suggests a greater emphasis on their physical consequences.[83] In a marriage case initiated in 1269, Hugh, son of William de Bolendene, remembered a guild feast which the defendant and his friends attended due to an accident that befell him; six years earlier, Hugh had injured his own hand with an axe, around the same time as the feast and the alleged marriage.[84] Bodily injuries occurred in contexts that conformed to gendered perceptions of men's social and economic activity. Aside from temporary or prolonged impairment, physical injuries could disrupt work patterns and increase vulnerability to poverty, with memories of accidents perhaps recalling periods of financial instability.[85] Serious injuries were also inscribed on the body in ways that supplemented oral memory. In 1294, Robert Scot testified in a marriage case, recalling the period due to an accident in which he fell from his horse and injured his head, causing a 'fracture [that] was still apparent on his head'.[86] Disfigurement of this kind could act as material proof visible to court officials, authenticating personal memories as well as adding veracity to broader legal narratives.

Memories of physical injury were prevalent in stories of interpersonal conflict between men, with the language of male violence integral to these narratives.[87] In a marriage case initiated in 1365, John de Gertham remembered a dispute with one Thomas Chapman, over the repayment of a debt.[88] After John paid the sum owed, Thomas demanded a further 3*d.* which John refused to pay, leading to a public brawl between the men in a local tavern the next evening. John recalled how Thomas had 'pulled many hairs from his beard' before John retaliated, attacking him with a chair until he fell to the ground. The violence intensified after the beard-pulling, although several intermediaries reconciled the pair, who then bought one another ale which they drank together until sunrise. Despite this resolution, John was initially still aggrieved with Thomas, perhaps for publicly assaulting the most visible emblem of his manhood.[89]

---

[82] BI CP.F.201.

[83] Bedell, 'Memory and Proof of Age', pp. 10–12.

[84] CCA E.S. Roll 12; *Select Cases*, pp. 106–7.

[85] Farmer, *Surviving Poverty*, p. 33.

[86] CCA E.S. Roll 113i. 'fregit capud suum que quidem fractura adhuc apparet in eodem'.

[87] Walker, *Crime, Gender and Social Order*, p. 33.

[88] BI CP.E.102.

[89] D. G. Neal, *The Masculine Self in Late Medieval England* (Chicago, 2008), p. 128.

Bodily Practices

Memories of men's violence shaped perceptions of the past beyond the narrative construction of gendered behaviour among the laity. Disputes erupted involving the clergy as much as parishioners, despite the protection conferred by clerical status and injunctions against clerical involvement in violence more generally, a prohibition that was occasionally breached in practice.[90] Cullum suggests that conflict could emerge from the perceived vulnerability of clerical manliness, based on the eschewal of sexual intercourse and violence, the markers of lay masculinity.[91] In the church courts, however, cases involving the clergy could centre on jurisdictional disputes over benefices and church rights as well as interpersonal conflict. Clerical bodies were characterised as extensions of the physical church; indeed, violence against a priest was tantamount to an offence against the Church itself. Witnesses remembered attacks with reference to religious rites and sacraments in ways that underlined the clergy's spiritual function. In a case initiated in the diocese of Lincoln, dating from around 1200, deponents recalled how a layman had thrown Alan de Carlton, a parson, to the ground following the celebration of Mass shortly after Pentecost.[92] Memories of violence against the clergy were characterised as inseparable from the rites which they administered, while assaults were situated in sacramental time.

Sporadic violence involving the clergy could become part of local memory as disputes had the capacity to disrupt lay religious practices. In 1293, for instance, a suit was initiated over possession of the prebend of Thame in Oxfordshire, initially granted to Thomas de Sutton, archdeacon of Northampton. Several knights attacked the church of Thame on behalf of Edward de St John, a rival claimant, assaulting clerks and shedding blood in the church building. Witnesses testified to Thomas de Sutton's rightful claim, depicting Edward de St John's men as assailants who desecrated holy ground with practical religious implications. Hugh de Estrafford told how he sustained a serious injury in the attack, which polluted the high altar and the church itself, while other deponents similarly emphasised the 'effusion of blood' from his wound.[93] Religious texts forbade the spilling of blood on consecrated ground, an act that polluted churches and ensured the suspension of services until reconsecration. Despite this prohibition, witnesses claimed that Edward de St John's men continued to celebrate services in the church, incurring sentences of excommunication from the bishop of Lincoln. The men's narratives emphasised the consequences of the assault and seizure of the church, which prevented the celebration of sacraments in the parish and interfered with the regular provision of pastoral care. John de Clipston, a clerk associated with Thomas de Sutton, testified that the men's occupation meant

---

[90] H. M. Thomas, *The Secular Clergy in England, 1066–1216* (Oxford, 2014), p. 213.

[91] Cullum, 'Clergy, Masculinity and Transgression', pp. 178–96.

[92] CCA E.S. Roll 40ii; *Select Cases*, p. 31.

[93] CCA E.S. Rolls 79 and 152; *Select Cases*, pp. 567–611.

Popular Memory and Gender in Medieval England

that a female parishioner received the rite of purification from the chapel of Thame rather than the church where it was usually performed. Violence against clerical bodies could alter established religious worship, with these variations contributing to local memories of parish customs.

The functional role of violence in the maintenance of memory was also articulated in explicitly gendered terms. Violence against women occurred in anti-feminist traditions that associated unruly female speech with the disruptive force of women's memory. Physical punishment of the female body was seen to ensure male mastery of woman's disorderly nature.[94] In an early thirteenth-century tract, the *Rhetorica novissima*, Boncompagno da Signa noted that '[w]omen, of course, remember those who beat them and afflict them through mistreatment, and forget those others who cherish them and honour them'.[95] Misogynistic tropes of female fickleness cast the formation of female remembrance in brutal imagery. While Boncompagno attributed active properties to the feminine faculty of memory, depictions of women's remembrance conformed to essentialised patterns of female faithlessness and passivity. From this perspective, men's violence was viewed as fostering female remembrance through acts of physical and emotional abuse.

Male brutality formed the principal focus of legal suits involving violence against women in the church courts. Female bodies were vulnerable both at home and in the streets, yet incidents of violence were particularly prevalent in cases for separation *a mensa et thoro* on the grounds of spousal cruelty. The domestic contexts in which many of these acts occurred made eye-witness testimony difficult to obtain, with deponents providing evidence that echoed identifiable narrative patterns. Sara Butler notes that accounts of spousal abuse could integrate elements from religious and pastoral discourses familiar to the laity. The recurrence of eye injuries in depositions perhaps reflected motifs drawn from female saints' lives, in particular the ocular torture of St Lucy.[96] Memories of spousal violence represented embodied versions of the past that depended on gendered motifs, principles of canon law, and the expectations of the Church. The language of bodily violence thus replicated past abuse at a narrative level. While claims of cruelty were downplayed in evidence for defendants, memories of violence dominated testimony for the plaintiff, with assaults upon female body-parts punctuating accounts of abuse.

Memories were constructed in ways that recalled the embodied experience of brutal attacks, evoking blows that ruptured skin, drew blood, and broke

---

[94] J. Enders, 'Cutting off the Memory of Women', in C. Mason Sutherland and R. Sutcliffe, eds., *The Changing Tradition: Women in the History of Rhetoric* (Calgary, 1999), pp. 47–55.

[95] Boncompagno da Signa, 'On Memory', in *The Medieval Craft of Memory*, ed. Carruthers and Ziolkowski, pp. 103–17, at p. 115.

[96] Butler, *The Language of Abuse*, p. 177.

Bodily Practices

bones. Accounts were thus organised in a narrative order in which attacks grew in severity. In 1345, for instance, Simon de Munkton's alleged abuse of Agnes Huntington culminated in an incident where blood was described as flowing from her ears and nose.[97] Deponents also emphasised the emotional suffering that accompanied physical violence. In 1410, witnesses in a suit from York claimed that Henry Wyvell's cruelty towards his wife, Cecilia, almost forced her to jump from a window into the river Ouse due to her distress and 'other fears' concerning her husband. Her attempts only failed because her mother and her servants intervened. Deponents recalled how Cecilia acted 'as a woman out of her mind', underlining her psychological trauma while attributing her behaviour to routine and cumulative abuse.[98] Prevalent in the secular courts, the defence of insanity was used more commonly in cases involving women, perhaps referencing popular and legal discourses of female instability and mental vulnerability.[99]

Memories of domestic violence underscored its embodied nature in accounts that emphasised the use of objects in attacks as well as its physical and mental effects. Although clerical writers tended to characterise husbandly violence as a necessary form of patriarchal discipline, the use of weapons and the endangerment of life were seen to constitute excessive abuse.[100] In a late fourteenth-century marriage suit between Margery Nesfeld and her husband, Thomas, witnesses recalled his attacks that involved a club and later a dagger, during which her arm was wounded and broken.[101] Vulnerable and passive female bodies were juxtaposed with solid material objects that signified and enacted male violence, marking the surfaces of skin and fracturing bones. Witnesses described Henry Wyvell's extreme brutality towards Cecilia, whom he beat 'with a certain short staff called a wardrer'.[102] Such objects implied the deliberate use of a weapon that men more commonly drew in armed altercations, rather than chance recourse to a household item during a heated domestic dispute. The language of gendered agency structured defendants' narratives as bodies and weapons performed mnemonic functions in stories of violence.

DEATH AND MEMORY

Memories of death and bereavement were similarly expressed in ways that underlined their embodied and affective nature. The remembrance of the dead was a central strand of Christian doctrine, from the commemoration

[97] BI CP.E.248.
[98] BI CP.F.56.
[99] Butler, *The Language of Abuse*, p. 116.
[100] Skoda, *Medieval Violence*, p. 214.
[101] BI CP.E.221.
[102] BI CP.F.56

Popular Memory and Gender in Medieval England

of Christ's death and resurrection to the use of intercessory prayer for the salvation of the deceased.[103] Accounts of loss punctuated memories of past events, and the deaths of kin were especially common mnemonic strategies. Married couples rarely cited the death of spouses, perhaps due to the preference for childbirth and marriage as primary referents. In cases where older men testified, local uses of the land were the central focus of their evidence, rather than events which formed part of their own personal histories.

Both mothers and fathers recalled the deaths of children as memories of childbirth became embedded in accounts of parental grief. Women in particular associated the physical experience of birth with the child's subsequent death. In 1425, Alice, wife of Robert Bolton, remembered that she had given birth to twins who would have been fourteen years old had they survived.[104] Isabel, wife of John Croxton, in a suit from York initiated in 1430, recalled a marriage sixteen years before from the birth of her daughter 'named Johanna, who died many years past, and would have been sixteen at the feast of St Martin last past if she had lived'.[105] Maternal memories of deceased infants often included their age should they have lived into childhood, a characteristic that implies reflection on their survival and suggests that mothers perhaps imagined their deceased children's lives. Calculation of a child's age in this manner was more common in female accounts of birth and infant death, a pattern that relates to the prevalence of birth memories within female testimony in general.[106] Mothers also remembered giving birth to children who survived infancy but died later in childhood. Agnes, wife of John Ingram, recalled that she was pregnant herself when Katherine Northefolk was born, with a girl named Johanna, who 'lived for almost ten years and died at the feast of St Michael ... three years ago'.[107] Some unfortunate parents suffered multiple bereavements, and the loss of several children in a row shaped their memories of birth and maternity. In 1294 Mabila de Wimel, then aged thirty, told the examiner that she recalled the alleged contract as she had three children die in succession after that time.[108] The trauma of bereavement perhaps intensified memories of labour and birth, and the provision of further details on the birth and projected age of deceased children could allow women

---

[103] P. Geary, *Living with the Dead in the Middle Ages* (Ithaca, NY, and London, 1994); Geary, *Phantoms of Remembrance.*

[104] BI CP.F.89.

[105] BI CP.F.201. 'ipsamet iurata peperit de utero suo unam filiam Johannam nominatam pluribus annis elapsis defunctis que si vixisset ad festum sancti martini ultimo preteritum fuisset etate xvi annorum'.

[106] Rosenthal, *Telling Tales*, p. 20.

[107] BI CP.F.89. 'peperit in hunc mundum et ipsa filia sua vocabatur Johannam et vixit fere per decem annos ac moriebatur ad festum sancti michaelis ... ad tres annos'.

[108] CCA E.S. Roll 239.

Bodily Practices

to express maternal identities and to convey the trauma and sense of unful-filment resulting from child death.

Parental memories of child loss elicited feelings of culpability and led to repentance. In the suit concerning Katherine Northefolk, Alice, wife of John Jakson, testified on the girl's age, recalling her own son's birth and early death as an infant. Alice told the court that she recalled Katherine's birth thirteen years before since 'on the same Monday, she was lying in childbirth after the birth of William, her son, who died of [*subito oppressionis*] on the Monday immediately following in May, and because of whose death this witness and her husband carried out public penance'.[109] The precise meaning of the phrase *subito oppressionis* is uncertain, but it had connotations of a sudden pressing down, a crush, or a seizure. Pastoral manuals including the *Memoriale Presbiterorum* addressed parental care, yet confessors were urged to question women in particular on sins relating to child neglect, such as whether they had 'knowingly or unknowingly' overlain their own child.[110] Despite clerical concerns over infanticide, evidence from the coroners' rolls suggests that most child deaths – when not of diseases – were accidental, occurring in and around the household.[111] The allocation of penance in this case indicates that Church authorities regarded both parents to be responsible for the child's death. In his early thirteenth-century *Liber Poenitentialis*, for instance, Robert of Flamborough advised penance of seven years in cases where infanticide had occurred but where the mother's poverty acted as mitigation.[112] Although pastoral writers usually associated infanticide and suffocation with maternal care, evidence from the fifteenth-century church courts of Canterbury and Rochester indicates that fathers and spousal couples were cited almost as often as mothers.[113] In her testimony, Alice rejected cultural assumptions of

---

[109] BI CP.F.89. 'dicit quod eadem die lune iacebat ipsa iurata in puerperio post partum Willelmi filii sui qui obiit subito oppressionis in mense maii dictum diem lune immediate sequentem racione cuius mortis et subite oppressionis ipsa iurata et dictus maritus suus egerunt publicam penitentiam'. See also Helmholz, *Marriage Litigation*, p. 99 n. 93.

[110] M. Haren, 'The Interrogatories for Officials, Lawyers and Secular Estates of the *Memoriale Presbiterorum*', in Biller and Minnis, eds., *Handling Sin*, pp. 123–63, at p. 161. In other penitential contexts, both spouses were held responsible for sin, such as sexual intercourse prior to the wife's purification after childbirth. Barr, *The Pastoral Care of Women*, p. 82.

[111] B. A. Hanawalt, *The Ties that Bound: Peasant Families in Medieval England* (Oxford, 1986), p. 102; G. Walker, 'Just Stories: Telling Tales of Infant Death in Early Modern England', in M. Mikesell and A. Seeff, eds., *Culture and Change: Attending to Early Modern Women* (Newwark, NJ, 2003), pp. 98–115.

[112] Robert of Flamborough, *Liber Poenitentialis*, ed. J. J. Francis Frith (Toronto, 1971), p. 222.

[113] R. H. Helmholz, 'Infanticide in the Province of Canterbury during the Fifteenth Century', *History of Childhood Quarterly*, 2 (1975), 379–90; Jones, *Gender and Petty Crime*, pp. 88–90.

Popular Memory and Gender in Medieval England

sole maternal guilt, deposing that both she and her husband had been found culpable for the child's death and assigned penance. The emphasis on the conjugal bond underlined Alice's identity as a married woman rather than a single woman destroying evidence of premarital sex. Infant death not only produced memories that were inherently physical and affective, but also generated accounts of postnatal care and parental guilt where legal authorities deemed their behaviour to have been suspect.

Men and women recalled the deaths of kin, referring most frequently to the demise of nuclear family members. Richard de York, a clerk and witness in a late thirteenth-century marriage case, remembered a marriage contract that occurred two years earlier, due to the arrival of a merchant from York who carried news of his brother's death.[114] Memories of grief were embedded in a wider nexus of meaning, encompassing other more pragmatic experiences that intersected with emotional loss. In a late fourteenth-century marriage case from York, for instance, several deponents testified that their brother had not wed the plaintiff at that time since the men had travelled to another village where they divided the goods of their late father.[115] Men's memories of absence referred to the more mundane routines that accompanied bereavement, such as the dissolution of a family member's household, legal responsibilities that more often fell upon male rather than female kin. More official modes of commemoration influenced the ways in which deceased kin were remembered. In a case initiated in 1386, Thomas de Myton, a webster of York, recalled a marriage contract that took place on the same day as an anniversary Mass held in a Dominican friary for Katherine, his father's wife.[116] Whether Thomas's father had already died is unknown, but Thomas himself remained involved in the formal commemoration of his stepmother for some time after her death.

Women's memories of deceased relatives generally extended further beyond the nuclear family than did men's recollections, and they included the deaths of a wider circle of kin. In 1270, for example, a marriage suit came before the archdeacon of Huntingdon in which primarily female witnesses from a cluster of villages in north Hertfordshire deposed on the female defendant's age when the contract was made.[117] Despite the prevalence of childbirth memories among female deponents in testimony more generally, only eight women recalled the births of children twelve years before, while fourteen remembered the death of family members, mostly parents, aunts, and uncles. This over-representation could reflect early practices in suits involving the ages of children where memories of death were regarded as more affecting than those of childbirth. Yet in 1257–8, when these deaths occurred, poor weather

---

[114] CCA E.S. Roll 69; *Select Cases*, p. 356.
[115] BI CP.E.175.
[116] BI CP.E.138.
[117] CCA E.S. Roll 10.

Bodily Practices

had caused a series of famines, high grain prices, and pestilence. This in turn produced high mortality rates in rural areas of England as well as London, perhaps accounting for the clustering of family deaths in memories of this period.[118]

Women's recollections of loss tended to centre on their children, but death appeared in men's memories more often when it retained implications for the local community. Their testimony was especially prominent in cases where deaths held legal importance or related to parish rights and Church appointments. In a late fourteenth-century suit, Thomas Forster, a layman, stated that Walter Flemyng, rector of the parish of Appleton-le-Street in the North Riding, made his testament on his deathbed as friends prayed for his soul and held him in their memories.[119] The men's recollections later functioned as legal proof of the testator's sound mind, while the language of commemoration connoted bonds of friendship and emotional loss. The embodied nature of death influenced the content of other memories, with some deponents referring specifically to the corpse of the deceased. One deponent in a case from 1294 recalled the death of his sister-in-law, remembering that her body was given over for burial the day after a neighbour's marriage contract was solemnised.[120] The transferral of her corpse from her close kin group to the churchyard perhaps engendered an emotional response that was more memorable than her death or the burial itself.

References to corpses appeared as forms of proof in men's evidence where the deaths of individuals were regarded as particularly significant, such as in disputes over patronage or appointments to benefices. During a suit from the late thirteenth century, John de Kent stated that he served Master William de Meriden, an earlier claimant to the benefice, until William's death, when he had purchased the items needed for his burial and 'placed his corpse in the tomb with his own hands'.[121] John's claims were underscored by his personal involvement in William's interment, with his physical actions serving as both material proof and a form of manual inspection. In 1368, in a dispute over a benefice, John de Gylton testified on the death of the vicar of Preston, the previous incumbent, whose body he saw lying covered with a cloth in the hallway of the vicarage.[122] John testified that he had viewed the vicar's body and knew it to be him, stating that the deceased's identity was commonly

---

[118] R. B. Stothers, 'Climatic and Demographic Consequences of the Massive Volcanic Eruption of 1258', *Climatic Change*, 45 (2000), 361–74.

[119] BI CP.E.169; M. M. Sheehan, *The Will in Medieval England from the Conversion of the Anglo-Saxons to the Thirteenth Century* (Toronto, 1963).

[120] CCA E.S. Roll 131i.

[121] CCA E.S. Roll 349; *Select Cases*, p. 259: 'propriis manibus posuit corpus eiusdem in sepulchro'.

[122] BI CP.E.100; on burial rights and their meaning in parishes, see Forrest, *Trustworthy Men*, pp. 299–306.

acknowledged in the local area. Women were no doubt aware of the deaths of important local figures and provided essential physical and post-mortem care for neighbours and kin. Yet men's memories of contact with – or the sight of – corpses were framed in communal or public settings and assigned greater worth in some types of cases. The ideological alignment of women with birth and family life translated into a preference for female memories only in settings that reinforced normative perceptions of gendered behaviour.

The death of neighbours and kin formed part of the memorial fabric of local communities. Burial rights were integral to funeral practices, and acted as an indicator of a church's status. In a suit between the chapel of Sutton and the church of Wawne in Yorkshire during the early fifteenth century, the burials of forty-four parishioners in the surrounding areas of Sutton, Stoneferry, and Lopholme were listed in the positions of the suit.[123] The men who testified in the case remembered the names of neighbours and kin buried in the disputed cemetery, recalling social bonds based on shared histories in the local area. Collective and personal experiences could structure memories of death in relation to endemic disease, particularly the plague that reached England in 1348. Despite its occasional use as a temporal marker, personal memories of the epidemic were rare in depositions, with emotional trauma perhaps influencing the extent to which these events were remembered.[124] Deponents in some cases referred to the plague, albeit in general terms, describing events that occurred in the 'time of the great pestilence'. In 1367, Adam de Shorwode recalled his employment as servant of the prior and convent of Durham during the 'great pestilence' when he aided in the collection of tithes as well as mortuary fees.[125] Such references compressed the disruption that marked daily life during the plague, acting as a temporal shorthand for the shifts which it brought, while simultaneously offering distance from its emotional effects.

Memories of the plague reflected the social dislocation that accompanied its progress as 'the bond between land and family was thus broken, to be replaced by a new mobility'.[126] High mortality rates re-shaped families significantly and the deaths of close relatives brought greater reliance on the extended kin group. In 1357, one witness recalled how during the epidemic William Aunger had entered into the custody of his nearest male relative, after his mother and grandfather perished in the pestilence, his father having

---

[123] YMA M2 (3)c.

[124] P. J. P. Goldberg, *Communal Discord, Child Abduction, and Rape in the Later Middle Ages* (New York, 2007), p. 96.

[125] BI CP.E.96. See also, B.I. CP.E.201. In the latter case from 1392, William del Pole stated that the vicar of Helmsley (N. Yorks) collected tithes in that area at the 'time of the great pestilence'.

[126] J. Bolton, '"The world upside down": Plague as an Agent of Economic and Social Change', in W. M. Ormrod and Phillip Lindley, eds., *The Black Death in England* (Stamford, 1996), pp. 17–78, at p. 51.

Bodily Practices

died before William was born.[127] Settlements in many regions declined in size as high death rates brought personal relationships between neighbours to an abrupt end. In a late fourteenth-century suit, witnesses recalled the deaths of several neighbours during the plague, describing how their corpses lay in their houses before their transferral to a local cemetery.[128] Memories of death and violence thus evoked personal responses that focused on embodied loss, while alluding to its wider social consequences.

CONCLUSION

This chapter has demonstrated the broad resonance of bodily experience in the recollections of men and women who gave testimony to the church courts. While men were able to dominate traditional legal narratives in support of their claims, physical forms of memory were more accessible to women and non-elite men as they depended on the rhythms of daily life rather than masculine ideals of respectability and claims of social capital. Chapter 2 illustrated that men could tie their testimony to a specific public recollection of the past, but this chapter has argued that a more expansive residual memory existed that was constructed and sustained through embodied experience. There were, however, differences in the types of embodied memory which men and women recalled. Female memories of the rupture and marking of their bodies centred on domestic violence and birth. In contrast, men's bodies were described as altered through memories of work and journeys which fractured bones and scarred tissue.

Both men and women could draw upon this type of remembrance, yet women were more likely to present elements of this residual memory in their evidence. This is for two reasons. Firstly, traditional patriarchal narratives were more exclusively aligned with the perceived parameters of male experience, while the mnemonic traces of physical pain, emotions, and trauma were less rigorously policed. Secondly, in many ways this type of sensory recall was associated with normative perceptions of female social experience. This seems to have lent women's embodied memories greater legitimacy than men's in legal evidence within the courts. This chapter has discussed the general role of physicality in broadening our understanding of effective testimony, a theme that will be revisited in Chapter 7, which addresses memory in the material environment. In the interim, Chapter 4 extends the analysis of bodily experience to consider the use of sexual and reproductive memories in negotiating the boundaries between legal discourse and subjectivity.

[127] BI CP.E.76.
[128] BI CP.E.101.

4

SEXUALITY AND GENERATION

In 1269, Alice de Mordon testified on the birth of Cecilia, daughter of Bartholomew of Scuynewell, twelve years earlier in the village of Ashwell in Hertfordshire. Alice told the court that she remembered when Cecilia was born 'because she was her wet nurse, and nursed her for two years', and her own son had been born in the same year.[1] Initiated in the archdeaconry of Huntingdon, the suit concentrated on Cecilia's age at marriage, which her family claimed had fallen short of the legal requirement of twelve for girls, hence fitting the impediment of nonage.[2] Other women in the same case also based their testimony on memories of childbirth and nurture. One Matilda de Hinteworth recalled that she had travelled late in her pregnancy to give birth in the village of Ashwell, where Cecilia's mother brought her alms during her time in child-bed. Similar in function to men's evidence in proof-of-age inquests, testimony of this kind instead foregrounds women's memories of birth and highlights their ability to navigate both social norms and legal expectations.

Pregnancy and childbirth were common motifs in women's narratives and, as evidence like Alice's suggests, birth and early maternity offered a set of recognisable rhythms by which the past could be described. Current interpretations of the relationship between gender and memory, however, flatten the complexities of men and women's engagement with corporeal and reproductive memory. Existing works associate memories of childbirth with women in particular, characterising female remembrance as attuned to the reproductive life cycle and the home.[3] Several studies explore male experiences of the birth-chamber and acknowledge the extent to which women's memories informed men's evidence in legal fora where female testimony was prohibited.[4] A narrow focus on birth alone, as well as the slant of such sources, nevertheless reinforces gendered assumptions that align men's memories with

---

[1] CCA, E.S. Roll 10. 'quia eius nutrix fuit et eam nutrivit per biennium'.
[2] Helmholz, *Marriage Litigation*, pp. 98–100.
[3] Goldberg, 'Gender and Matrimonial Litigation', pp. 49–50.
[4] Harris-Stoertz, 'Remembering Birth', pp. 45–59; for perceptions of birth in the early modern period, see U. Rublack, 'Pregnancy, Childbirth and the Female Body in Early Modern Germany', *Past & Present*, 150 (1996), 84–110.

the 'public' sphere and women's with the domestic. By addressing memories of sexuality and generation more squarely, the complex ways in which gender intersected with embodiment emerge in greater detail. The use of a broader framework also contributes to a more detailed understanding of the patriarchal and often judicial power structures that shaped legal encounters related to sex and generation.

As we saw in Chapter 2, testimony in the church courts represented an amalgamation of overlapping discourses that accommodated various legal arguments and ideological positions. Intellectual and more popular ways of thinking about corporeality and memory were integral to clerical perceptions of the past. The association of femininity and women's memory with the body was ubiquitous in legal, clerical, and more popular discourses, mirroring gendered dichotomies prevalent in intellectual and medical spheres. Learned thought linked female remembrance with the traits of passivity and longevity, producing depictions that were not entirely negative. Lay attitudes towards women's embodied memories were similarly complex, so that female speech was endowed with authority in certain contexts but denigrated in others, revealing the adaptable nature and application of patriarchal power.

The memories of witnesses condensed a range of embodied habits that complicated binary oppositions and allude to the way in which gender operated in everyday practice. The language of gender influenced the construction of men and women's positions in the world, through memories of sexuality, reproduction, and conjugality. These gendered subjectivities similarly provide glimpses of the identities that mattered in everyday life, and were translatable in judicial and clerical settings. Canon law and methods of proof in the courts also influenced the content of witness testimony, as did the prevalence of gendered cultural tropes. Yet the contingent nature of deponents' memories illustrates how men and women remembered the past in ways that occasionally conveyed personal feelings of love, desire, pain, and loss. Female parties and witnesses made adjustments to gendered, and often misogynistic, narratives and subject positions to communicate other facets of their identities. Memories of embodiment thus provided a significant source of agency for men and women as they negotiated aspects of the law. This chapter explores the ways in which sexual and reproductive memory operated, charting its meaning and function in these contexts. The first section focuses on learned and clerical perceptions of the relationship between sex, gender, and memory; discussion then turns to memories of sexual embodiment and desire in legal testimony. Memories of childbirth, nursing, and parenting form the basis for the final section of the chapter. Despite the persistence of gendered motifs, the relationship between embodiment and popular memory was not static throughout this period. Patterns in the courts coupled with socio-economic shifts produced new types of narratives centred on the body, alluding to changes in gender relations and the articulation of embodied identities that depended only partly on gender.

Sexuality and Generation

SEXED BODIES AND MEMORY

Attitudes towards gender relations and sexuality were inscribed in bodily practices that reinforced the patriarchal order. Binary ways of interpreting gender roles imbued the language of sex with the connotation that men were active agents while women were passive. The human soul was regarded as sexless in early Church thought, but secular and learned perceptions of women's social roles influenced depictions in pastoral literature, infusing sermons, *exempla*, and confession manuals with a misogynistic dualism.[5] This dichotomy replicated and solidified wider perceptions of masculine and feminine identities in their ideal form. Alongside the passivity attributed to female nature in general, women were aligned with the body in male scholarly discourses and represented as particularly sexual in disposition. The fundamental role of sexual virtue in exemplary versions of femininity meant that women were often defined through their marital status and as legal dependants in relation to fathers or husbands. In social practice, however, both the prevalence of singleness and the limits of coverture mitigated the language of female passivity and the elevation of marriage.[6]

Despite the alignment of women with sexuality and the demands of the body in theological treatises, clerical writers were troubled by male embodiment, evident in their attempts to reconcile the attributes of ideal manhood with the social experience of maleness.[7] Peasant men, in particular, were associated with bodily pleasure in popular and clerical discourses; yet, as Paul H. Freedman notes, these depictions centred on the digestive system, in contrast to the sexualisation of peasant women and their objectification as the focus of elite male desire.[8] Taxonomic systems that applied to the body in medieval culture, more generally, privileged male experience. One of the most prevalent models for organising physiological progression was the 'ages of man' schema, which divided the life cycle into phases of ageing.[9] This system focused primarily on male development and the stages of men's lives, although intersections between the female body and ageing occurred in other contexts, including within didactic and hagiographic texts. 'Maidenhood' was depicted as the ideal age for women in these works, as Phillips argues, with purity and reproductive fertility coinciding in a phase that was seen to epitomise ideals

---

[5] Murray, 'Gendered Souls in Sexed Bodies', pp. 85–6.

[6] See essays in Beattie and Stevens, eds., *Married Women and the Law*.

[7] J. Murray, "'The law of sin that is in my members": The Problem of Male Embodiment', in S. J. E. Riches and S. Salih, eds., *Gender and Holiness: Men, Women and Saints in Late Medieval Europe* (Abingdon, 2002), pp. 9–22.

[8] P. H. Freedman, *Images of the Medieval Peasant* (Stanford, 1999), p. 169.

[9] J. A. Burrow, *The Ages of Man: A Study in Medieval Writing and Thought* (Oxford, 1996).

Popular Memory and Gender in Medieval England

of femininity.[10] This schema of the female life cycle exerted similar power in historiographical traditions associated with medieval women, temporality, and gender. Studies of female experience emphasise the centrality of marital status in women's lives, and cyclical phases such as childbirth and marriage must indeed have structured memory over extended periods. Female experience could still be homogenised within this type of framework, as Patricia Skinner notes, but the variability of women's actions retained the power to qualify and unsettle its borders.[11]

Intellectual traditions codified elements of memory practice in gendered terms, through metaphors and imagery that aligned femininity and masculinity with specific traits. Joan Cadden notes, for instance, that the characteristics attributed to each gender 'bear with them medieval concepts of behaviours, temperaments, and social roles understood to be typical of women and men'.[12] Aristotelian thought promoted an idea of the feminine that was increasingly dualistic, interpreting the female form as an incomplete male. Despite limits on this logic in social practice, the relationship between gender and memory was understood within this dichotomy. In his *History of Animals*, for instance, Aristotle noted that:

> [w]oman is more compassionate than man, more easily moved to tears, at the same time is more jealous, more querulous, more apt to scold and to strike. She is, furthermore, more prone to despondency and less hopeful than the man, more void of shame or self-respect, more false of speech, more deceptive and of more retentive memory.[13]

Volatile in temperament and shameless in manner, woman's only laudable traits here are compassion and good memory. Such praise was perhaps surprising since *memoria* formed one of the five principles of rhetoric and acted as a signifier of intellect in classical and medieval thought. In his *De Memoria*, however, Aristotle noted a further distinction between memory and recollection based on ideas from natural philosophy: 'the persons who possess a retentive memory are not identical with those who excel in power of recollection … [and] as a rule, slow people have a better memory, whereas those who are quick-witted and clever are better at recollecting'.[14] In Aristotelian

---

10 K. Phillips, 'Maidenhood as the Perfect Age of a Woman's Life', in K. J. Lewis, N. J. Menuge and K. M. Phillips, eds., *Young Medieval Women* (Stroud, 1999), pp. 1–24.

11 P. Skinner, 'The Pitfalls of Linear Time: Using the Medieval Female Life Cycle as an Organising Strategy', in Cox, McAvoy, and Magnani, eds., *Reconsidering Gender, Time and Memory*, pp. 13–28, at p. 16.

12 J. Cadden, *Meanings of Sex Difference in the Middle Ages: Medicine, Science, and Culture* (Cambridge, 1993), p. 169.

13 Aristotle, *History of Animals*, 608b, in *The Complete Works of Aristotle: The Revised Oxford Translation*, ed. J. Barnes (Princeton, 1984), vol. 1, p. 949.

14 Aristotle, *De Memoria*, 449b, in *The Complete Works of Aristotle*, ed. Barnes, vol. 1, p. 714.

Sexuality and Generation

thought, women's skill in remembering was thus also associated with sluggish intellect.[15]

Perceptions of gender roles fused with learned ideas of feminine and masculine traits in treatises on natural philosophy. The distinctive physiological tone of female remembrance in these traditions extended to the reception of memory, with the supposed vagaries of female nature acting to shape its retention. In his *De Amore*, composed during the late 1180s in a courtly context, Andreas Capellanus described women as 'like melting wax, always ready to assume fresh shape and to be moulded to the imprint of anyone's seal'.[16] The motif of the 'seal in wax' was an established metaphor for the formation of memory from the classical period onwards, but it could develop misogynistic meanings of submissiveness when applied to women.[17] Writing in the mid-thirteenth century, Albertus Magnus noted that '[w]oman's complexion is more humid than man's. [The nature] of the humid receives an impression easily but retains it poorly'.[18] The gendered attributes associated with sex difference were seen to influence the preservation of experience, with female memory often characterised as passive and pliant. In the context of female remembrance, this imagery also drew on humoral and reproductive theory that interpreted women's bodies and feminine nature generally as receptacles of implicitly male memories.

Treatises such as these circulated widely in the schools and formed part of the curricula in the arts and scholastic philosophy. For instance, although prohibited in the early thirteenth century, the study of Aristotle's works in the Parisian schools was formally reintroduced in 1255 when his texts were accorded central place in the university's faculty of arts.[19] These stipulations also set aside two weeks for close analysis of his *De Memoria*, the same amount of time allocated to his work on the spirit and the soul.[20] Latin glosses on the works of Aristotle were popular in scholastic contexts, such that Albertus Magnus and Thomas Aquinas both produced commentaries on his *De Memoria* in the latter half of the thirteenth century.[21] Similarly, the only

---

[15] D. Bloch, *Aristotle on Memory and Recollection: Text, Translation, Interpretation and Reception in Western Scholasticism* (Leiden, 2007), p. 72 n. 82.

[16] Enders, *The Medieval Theater of Cruelty*, p. 97.

[17] Carruthers, *The Book of Memory*, p. 21.

[18] *Alberti Magni opera omnia*, vol. 12: *Quaestiones super De Animalibus*, ed. E. Filthaut (Münster, 1955), XV, q. 11, p. 265; 'Complexio enim feminae magis est humida quam maris, sed humidi est de facili recipere et male retinere'. Cited in Cadden, *Meanings of Sex Difference*, p. 185.

[19] Wei, *Intellectual Culture*, p. 162.

[20] *The Medieval Craft of Memory*, ed. Carruthers and Ziolkowski, p. 155.

[21] C. H. Lohr, *Latin Aristotle Commentaries*, vol. 5: *Bibliography of Secondary Literature* (Florence, 2005).

named texts that Chaucer's Clerk, a student of philosophy at Oxford, desired by his bedside were the works of Aristotle.[22]

The supposedly feminine inability to retain memories appeared outside Latin texts in allegorical poems and treatises written in the vernacular. In the Anglo-Norman *Mirour de l'Omme*, composed in the late fourteenth century, John Gower described female memory as 'written in the wind', while women were portrayed as incapable of keeping the counsel imparted to them.[23] Both Andreas Capellanus and Gower attributed a lack of consistency to women's memories, which were also characterised as fluid and inconstant. Misogynistic tropes of female vacillation and infidelity were reiterated through claims that women apparently forgot the influence and advice of men, in particular. Intellectual traditions thus associated women uniquely with memory, just as with the flesh, even while their capacity and rationale for remembering were maligned. Such motifs acted to maintain patriarchal interests through the reassertion of gendered norms, undermining the value of women's versions of the past and entrenching binary perceptions of gender. Tensions of this kind perhaps represented intellectual efforts to reconcile misogynistic attitudes with the memorial roles apportioned to women in social practice.

EMBODIMENT AND DESIRE

A tale that exemplified and enshrined gendered associations between memory and sexuality underpinned the procedure for examining ecclesiastical witnesses in the church courts. The biblical story of Susanna and the Elders recounted a charge of adultery which two male accusers levelled against her as a married woman. The truth of their testimony was only challenged when the young Daniel conducted their interrogation, separately and in private, revealing inconsistencies in their memories and, in turn, preventing her execution. This tale formed the proof-text that instructed canon lawyers on the proper interrogation of deponents, entailing the examination of at least two witnesses and comparison of their evidence.[24] Although the charge against Susanna was refuted and her innocence restored, the patriarchal regulation of female sexuality was used to exemplify the relationship between memory and proof. The story worked to reinforce tropes of feminine lust and deceit, while simultaneously asserting the idealised characteristics of fidelity and passivity. Oral discussion of Susanna's honour occurred between men, and the gendered nature of the inquiry reinforced male control over the construction of her

---

[22] *The Riverside Chaucer*, ed. Benson, p. 28, lines 294–5.

[23] J. Gower, *Mirour de l'Omme*, trans. W. Burton Wilson, rev. N. Wilson Van Baak (East Lansing, 1992), p. 242, lines 17653–64.

[24] Helmholz, *The Oxford History of the Laws of England*, pp. 340–1; R. H. Helmholz , 'The Bible in the Service of the Canon Law', *Chicago-Kent Law Review*, 70 (1995), 1557–81, at p. 1557.

Sexuality and Generation

sexual history. Goldberg notes that gendered prejudices which influenced testimony originated with lay deponents and clerical personnel rather than the application of canon law.[25] From the twelfth century onwards, however, legal procedure on examination adopted as a precedent an exemplar that consolidated perceptions of gendered authority and female sexuality.

The relationship between memory and sexual desire also informed other learned discourses on remembrance. Scholarly treatments of desire assigned great significance to the faculties of memory and imagination with the remembrance of pleasure regarded as the inspiration for sexual impulses. Cadden observes, for instance, that 'the idea or memory of pleasure was widely held to be the motive cause of arousal, seed production, and, ultimately, pleasure itself'.[26] One anonymous English master writing in the late twelfth century alluded to the intersection of memory, sexuality, and femininity, noting that 'men differ from other animals in that animals only have a knowledge of the present; but men have a knowledge of the present, memory of the past and the capacity to conjecture about the future. Therefore, when a woman remembers past delights she desires the same again'.[27] Sexual desire, then, emerged from the human ability to remember, a skill that the English master believed animals lacked. Desire and memory were entwined with womanhood to such an extent that the perceived attributes of female remembrance were used to explain the nature of sexual memory. The recall of desire was also characterised by repetition and cast as recidivism, a behaviour that was often associated with sexual sin. Women's remembrance of sexual pleasure was thus seen to persist even when divorced from the reproductive work of childbirth. Moral commentators linked female sexuality with memory more explicitly, depicting women as culpable for the arousal of male desire. In a sermon delivered to scholars in Paris in 1140, Bernard of Clairvaux emphasised the habitual tone of sexual memory, but associated sexual activity with the creation of impure memories of desire. The remembrance of these sins, according to Bernard, impressed on male memory 'certain bitter marks' in the form of 'filthy traces'.[28] Implicit in this interpretation was the alignment of female lust with the provocation of male desire, a relationship that was seen to produce memories of sexual sins in the present.

A complex set of assumptions governed the remembrance of sexual sin in pastoral literature, the channel of communication with which the

---

[25] Goldberg, 'Gender and Matrimonial Litigation', p. 55.

[26] Cadden, *Meanings of Sex Difference*, p. 138.

[27] *The Prose Salernitan Questions: Edited from a Bodleian MS (Auct. F.3.10), an Anonymous Collection Dealing with Science and Medicine Written by an Englishman c. 1200*, ed. B. Lawn (Oxford, 1979), pp. 13–14, as cited in Cadden, *Meanings of Sex Difference*, p. 98.

[28] Bernard of Clairvaux, 'Ad clericos de conversione', in *Sancti Bernardi Opera Omnia*, vol. 4, ed. J. Leclercq and H. M. Rochais (Rome, 1966), p. 75, as cited in Enders, *The Medieval Theater of Cruelty*, p. 89.

Popular Memory and Gender in Medieval England

parish clergy, and laypeople, were more familiar. In these texts, confession involved the examination of penitents' transgressions, particularly their sexual histories, and this level of scrutiny was compounded by gender. Caution was urged where the questions used to guide confession exceeded the extent of the penitent's sins. Writing in the early thirteenth century, Robert of Flamborough instructed priests to ask only general questions to avoid introducing men and women to new forms of sin.[29] Probing the sinner's sexual past was believed to fire the erotic imagination of priest and penitent alike, yet it was essential for the process of confession and penance.

Memories of sexual activity were common forms of legal proof in ecclesiastical suits, especially disputes relating to marriage and defamation. The language used to describe sex depended on the type of case and the legal points argued. The law in tandem with widely held perceptions of sexual behaviour provided the discursive frameworks through which these memories were expressed. In cases where the principal concern was the consummation of marriage, proof of sexual activity acted as the focus for witness testimony. Following the advancement of theories on the doctrine of marriage under Pope Alexander III (1159–81), words of consent were increasingly regarded as fundamental to the creation of a lawful union, although consummation was still seen as its final ratification.[30] Memories of sexual encounters accrued especial value in suits that attempted to validate marriages after abjuration *sub pena nubendi*. The significance of sex, both licit and illicit, in matrimonial cases meant that detailed stories of eye-witness accounts were developed to explain these encounters. Witnesses incorporated tropes and motifs drawn from popular culture, as well as narrative models from *pastoralia* and their own knowledge of canon law. Memories of sex depended on the accumulation of legal, religious, and popular meanings that produced new narratives and rendered them familiar to clerical audiences.

Sexual practices were reconstructed in church-court evidence as witnesses advanced testimony that was plausible and admissible under canon law. In a number of cases, deponents provided eye-witness accounts of nudity and bed-sharing to establish circumstantial proof of sexual activity. The incidental observation of sexual acts through shared spaces, open doors, and thin walls, operated as versions of the 'keyhole testimony' associated with later legal trials.[31] While popular ideas of extra-marital sex exerted considerable narrative force, the interrogative nature of examinations also influenced the content of legal evidence. Procedures for establishing proof in the early

---

[29] Robert of Flamborough, *Liber Poenitentialis*, ed. Frith, p. 196.

[30] J. A. Brundage, *Law, Sex, and Christian Society in Medieval Europe* (Chicago, 1987), p. 334.

[31] G. E. Haggerty, 'Keyhole Testimony: Witnessing Sodomy in the Eighteenth Century', *Eighteenth Century: Theory and Interpretation*, 44 (2003), 167–82; Gowing, *Common Bodies*, p. 30.

Sexuality and Generation

Canterbury cases generated extended narratives of sexual encounters as examiners presented deponents with detailed questions. In 1269, for example, witnesses in the case between Johanna de Clopton and Richard de Bosco reported seeing the couple having sex in a croft during the previous year.[32] The examiners requested further details from the deponents, asking how they knew that Richard was having sex with her, whether Johanna's knees were bare, as well as information on their sexual position. In later suits that survive from York, the phrase 'solus cum sola nudus cum nuda' ('alone together and naked') was used instead, which worked to compress the lengthier evidence of consummation found in earlier cases.[33]

Parts of the body were referenced in ways that evoked genital proximity and operated as a proxy for genital contact itself. In 1294, John le Longe testified that he had witnessed William de Eldenham 'lying upon the belly' of Alice, daughter of Robert de Schyltelye.[34] The noun 'venter' not only connoted the area of the body above the genitals, but also retained the additional gynaeco-logical meaning of the womb in medical discourse. Sexual acts were similarly signified through the exposure of body parts that were usually clothed. In the case involving Richard de Bosco, one witness claimed to recall the sight of Matilda Goderhele's 'naked flesh' as Richard 'pulled his trousers back up' after the pair finished having sex. Nicholas, a fisherman from Clapton in Berkshire, provided similar testimony, but claimed that he also glimpsed 'the man's member in the member of the woman'.[35] The positioning of clothing on specific areas of the body was significant in these narratives, and was used to convey sexual contact. In the suit from 1294, for instance, witnesses noted that William's trousers were lowered to his calves, while Alice's shift was 'raised to her navel'.[36] Other cases referred to the raising of women's apparel to the 'girdle' or 'belt', an item of clothing associated with chastity in many contexts, but also the vagina, nuptiality, and pregnancy. Belts and girdles operated as general symbols of female sexuality and fecundity, serving as a signifier of women's genitalia in particular. The movement of clothing by both parties alluded to the sex act, while the exposure of skin before and after emphasised the intimate nature of encounters.

Memories that depended on the simulation of affective states, such as sexual passion or desire, were an integral part of these accounts. The language of embodiment was combined with descriptions of emotional

---

32 CCA E.S. Roll 310a–c; see also CCA E.S. Roll 292; *Select Cases*, pp. 96–102.

33 Goldberg, 'Voyeurism and "Pornography"', p. 108.

34 CCA E.S. Roll 181. 'vidit ipsum Willelmum iacentem super ventrem dicte Alicie'.

35 CCA E.S. Roll 310a–c; *Select Cases*, p. 101. Roger le Cannevere: 'vidit nudam carnem mulieris et virum tractantem braccas suas quando surrexit'; Nicholas, a fisherman of Clopton: 'vidit membrum viri in membro mulieris'.

36 CCA E.S. Roll 181. Henry Wollemelk: 'camisia dicte mulieris sursum elevata usque ad umbilicum'.

Popular Memory and Gender in Medieval England

experiences, operating in tandem to further authenticate witnesses' narratives. In a marriage case from 1269, Phillip, son of Richard, remembered his own sexual encounter with his uncle's wife. When the examiner questioned Phillip about whether the door and window of the room where the couple had sex had been open or closed at the time, he replied that both were open as he cared little at the time.[37] In this context, the memory of passion focused on the affective nature of sex, signalled in a loss of inhibition and an apparent indifference to material surroundings. Sexual acts were also signified through other bodily markers, such as affective states that were visible in facial expressions. In 1362, Robert Thomeson initiated a suit against Alice, daughter of Thomas Belamy, to enforce an alleged contract of marriage. Deponents who testified for Robert attempted to prove both the contract and its consummation through descriptions of the couple's behaviour that concentrated on Alice's appearance. Thomas Tailour reported that several witnesses stood near a barn and overheard the couple 'behaving riotously together ... [while] the said Alice [was] very red in the face'.[38] Witnesses asked Alice about this time alone with Robert, using the Latin phrase 'sola cum solo' that echoed the legal term 'solus cum sola nudus cum nuda' and implied an illicit sexual encounter. Alice replied that 'she had no shame because the same Robert was her husband'.[39] The marital bond authorised the couple's sexual relationship. Facial reddening was portrayed as evidence of sexual activity, rather than a sign of female shame associated with premarital sex.

The gendered language of sex relied on binary perceptions that associated men with the active sexual role, while women were ascribed a passive position. In the suit concerning Richard de Bosco, several men described his sexual encounter with Matilda Goderhele, claiming that they 'saw him lying between her legs, doing with her what a man does with a woman'.[40] This depiction replicated wider social norms relating to sexual roles, and the functional role of women in general was cast as primarily sexual and reproductive. In order to establish a legal exception to his marriage, based on the close kinship of two women with whom Richard had sex, witnesses also cast his sexual history as promiscuous and marked by multiple partners. This language reinforced the idea that male extra-marital sex represented the natural order of gender relations. Gendered dichotomies that operated at a discursive level were manipulated to characterise sexual activity as an essential part of masculine behaviour. In the case from 1269, one deponent

---

[37] CCA E.S. Roll 11.

[38] BI CP.E.85. 'dicta Alicie valde rubicunda facie'.

[39] BI CP.E.85. 'Interrogata a predicto Thoma conteste sua quid ipsa ibidem fecerat sola cum solo predicto Roberto in predicto loco ... inde non habere pudorem eo quod idem Robertus fuerat maritus suus'.

[40] CCA E.S. Roll 310; *Select Cases*, pp. 100–1: William le Muner: 'vidit virum iacentem supra mulierem inter crura mulieris et facientem secundum quod vir facit cum muliere'.

Sexuality and Generation

remembered that Phillip, son of Richard, was 'moving manfully' during the sexual encounter that he claimed to have witnessed.[41] The phrase depicted sex as a series of male bodily movements, and inscribed them in a framework that associated masculinity with the active sexual role. The language of men's sexual behaviour reproduced normative hierarchies of gender in miniature, alluding to the solidification of gender roles in everyday life.

Memories of sexed bodies drew on gendered meanings that were available in the social environment and embedded in canon law. Physical examination of the body was enshrined in legal principles that sought to establish proof of sexual abilities in the church courts. This type of evidence was common in marriage suits that focused on spousal impotence as well as those dealing with the age of parties at their union. In cases to annul marriages on the grounds of impotence, deponents emphasised the bodily markers of maleness through the language of sexuality and marital sex. In 1434, witnesses examined William Barton to establish evidence of his sexual capacities in a marriage suit that centred on the impediment of impotence. Testimony from deponents for both parties concentrated on the signs of male sexual desire which they described in narratives of physical intimacy and genital touch. The sexual and reproductive histories of married female witnesses imbued claims of William's virility with additional authority. Emmota Garde, a widow aged forty, told the court that William had testicles and other marks of manliness 'just as this witness's husband had when still living, to whom she had borne seven children'.[42] Although a widow, Emmota based her judgement on memories of her husband's genitalia as well as their sex life and childbearing. Female deponents drew on the language of conjugality to foreground marital identities in ways that allowed them to comment on genital size without damage to their sexual virtue. The daily intimacy of married life, coupled with the everyday familiarity that marked marital coexistence, offered further authenticity to the women's comparisons. Female testimony in suits involving impotence drew not only on marital identities, but also on discourses of paternity that equated genital size with the ability to father children. Women were therefore able to adopt subject positions that legitimised the discussion of sexual histories through the language of marital sex and parenthood.

Male deponents employed similar methods to convey the virility of the husbands under examination. In the case concerning William Barton, several married men who provided testimony on his inspection compared their own genitals with those of the male defendant. William Gretehed deposed that William Barton 'had, and has, large and fit testicles, and all the other manly signs to achieve sexual intercourse, just as this witness ever had or better'.[43]

---

[41] CCA E.S. Roll 11. 'vidit ipsum viriliter de moventem'.

[42] BI CP.F.175. 'sicut maritus ipsius iurate cui peperit septem proles dum vixit'.

[43] BI CP.F.175. 'habuitque et habet idem Willelmus testiculos magnos et habiles ac omnia

Popular Memory and Gender in Medieval England

Another deponent, named John de Metelay, reported that 'at the time of seeing and touching the aforesaid rod, William's yard was longer and larger than the rod of this witness ever was'. The experience of marriage and generation also framed John's evidence in his claim that 'he has a wife, still living, with whom he had begotten ten children'.[44] Married men who testified could assume similar subject positions to wives, incorporating elements of gender identities that were relevant to the suit. Gendered expertise was also derived from the patriarchal authority attributed to married male heads of households at an ideological level, as well as the sexual experience associated with biological maleness and the conjugal role. The comparison of genital size between men, who were often friends and acquaintances of the defendant, implies that male sexual identity was not based solely on genital size. It was aligned with virility, more generally, as well as the ability to impregnate one's wife and father children.

Witnesses also referred to their own body parts in other ways to recall the physical dimensions of male genitalia. Male and female witnesses quantified William Barton's member with reference to judgements that were based on manual inspection and intimate touch. William Gretehed, for example, reported that the defendant's member was 'at least as long as two of this witness's fingers'.[45] This type of comparative measurement recalled the moment of palpation, which could perhaps be recreated in oral examinations through gestures that demonstrated the organ's approximate size. The physical appearance of sexed bodies was also referenced to signify sexual dysfunction. In 1441, Joan Savage recalled the appearance of John Marche's member, which was marked by 'white, dead, empty skin down to its end'.[46] Descriptions of John's organ, particularly the colour and tone of the skin, implied the absence of male heat, as well as a lack of blood or sperm that was needed to allow sexual activity. In contemporary works on natural philosophy, the production of semen depended on the circulation of blood in the male body and the ability to sustain an erection relied on this physical process.[47] Popular discourses on genital health in legal testimony acknowledged the significance of heat in male virility, as witnesses sought to encourage its movement. In a number

---

alia signa virilia pro carnali copula perficiendum tam bona sicut ipse iuratus unquam habuit vel melior'.

[44] BI CP.F.175. 'tempore visionis et palpacionis supradicti virge predicti Willelmi fuit melioris quantitatis in longitudinis et grossitudinis quam virga ipsius iurati unquam fuit … ipsemet iuratus habet uxorem viventem cum qua habuit decem proles inter ipsis procrearunt'.

[45] BI CP.F.175. 'predicta virga temporibus quibus stetit … fuit longitudinis duorum maniplorum ipsius iurati ad minus'.

[46] BI CP.F.40. 'se erigere nec stare potuit sed semper propter debilitatem tanquam pellis alba mortua et vacua finem suum deorsum'.

[47] D. Jacquart and C. Thomasset, *Sexuality and Medicine in the Middle Ages*, trans. M. Adamson (Cambridge, 1988), p. 54.

Sexuality and Generation

of suits, men and women engaged in activities that were presumably aimed at increasing blood flow around the genitals, providing warming victuals for male defendants and ensuring that fires were set to heat their organs.[48]

Female bodies were seen to retain the physical imprint of intercourse as a form of embodied memory that signified sexual corruption. Medical works such as the Pseudo-Albertus *De Secretis Mulierum* outlined a number of markers that were used to detect past sexual activity. Moral conduct was exemplified in emotional states such as shame and modesty that were gauged from physical behaviour. Physiological signs associated with sex organs were more common points of reference, however, including the intactness of the hymen, and the appearance of breasts, the vagina, and urine.[49] Although *De Secretis* had a limited transmission in England, Monica Green observes a regional resonance with the Continental tradition, 'both in the interest in generation and in the use of the terminology of "women's secrets".[50] Virginity tests occurred in canon law, vernacular romances, and medical writing, yet across these genres there was interaction between discourses on proof of female virginity.[51] Inspections in the church courts did draw on elements of the law, but the application of these principles saw their reformulation alongside lay ideas of sex and virginity.

Female sexual experience was detected in physical examinations that scrutinised women's bodies for evidence of intercourse. In marriage cases concerning impotence in the English church courts, husbands rather than wives were usually examined but other methods of proof were also available. The *Liber Extra* admitted the physical examination of female plaintiffs through the use of married women regarded as 'experts in marital matters', trustworthy, and of good reputation.[52] In the case involving William Barton, female deponents inspected the plaintiff, Katherine Barlay, for signs of intercourse to determine whether the marriage had been consummated. The women's testimony incorporated lay notions of sexual experience, detailing perceived physiological differences between the body of a virgin and that of a sexually experienced woman. Joan, wife of Robert Ireby, told the court that if Katherine was a virgin 'certain marks that are present on women's breasts, called "kirnells" in English, would have appeared round and whole at the time

---

[48] Murray, 'On the Origins and Role of "Wise Women", pp. 235–51; Kane, *Impotence and Virginity*.

[49] *Women's Secrets: A Translation of Pseudo-Albertus Magnus's De Secretis Mulierum with Commentaries*, ed. H. Rodnite Lemay (Albany, 1992), pp. 128–9.

[50] M. Green, *Making Women's Medicine Masculine: The Rise of Male Authority in Pre-Modern Gynaecology* (Oxford, 2008), p. 228.

[51] On virginity tests in general, see K. C. Kelly, *Performing Virginity and Testing Chastity in the Middle Ages* (London, 2001).

[52] X. 4.15.7. 'Vos vero, ne id forte confiterentur in fraudem, a matronis bonae opinionis, fide dignis ac expertis in opere nuptiali, dictam fecistis inspici mulierem, quae perhibuerunt testimonium, ipsam adhuc virginem permanere'.

Popular Memory and Gender in Medieval England

of this palpation'.[53] The Middle English term 'kirnel' referred to the 'teat' or 'pap' and can be interpreted as the nipple and the surrounding area of glands.[54] Lay understandings of female sexuality thus associated the absence of sexual experience with the structural integrity of the breast. Skin surrounding the breast was also seen to record the memory of multiple sexual encounters, as Katherine was judged to be 'corrupt' and 'known carnally on many occasions' because of marks which the women called 'sulekornes'.[55] This vernacular term incorporated the connotations of two separate words, with 'sule' meaning 'dirty' or 'befouled', while 'corne' referred to a 'horny growth'. In their general appearance, Katherine's breasts were described as 'soft and broken' rather than 'hard, whole and healthy'.[56] The language of female sexuality aligned healthy tissue with virginity, while sexual experience was seen to produce bodily changes that undermined the integrity of the breasts. The absence of virginity was not uniformly interpreted as evidence of pregnancy and only one witness identified the marks on Katherine's breasts as proof of conception.[57]

Descriptions of women's bodies depended on and also worked to reinforce patriarchal ideas about gender and sexuality, yet female knowledge also contributed to the language and criteria used in these tests. Women's expertise in gynaecological and reproductive matters was drawn from communal and personal experience that accrued over generations into shared cultural memory. In the suit involving Katherine Barlay, Joan, wife of Robert Ireby, interpreted the marks on her body as signs of corruption, 'just as it is commonly said and reputed among women'.[58] This kind of gendered memory depended on the oral transmission of sexual and reproductive knowledge beyond the immediate contexts of birth and bodily regulation.

Along with changes in the texture and appearance of sexual organs across the generative life cycle, female bodies were seen to retain the memory of sex in other ways, particularly in the genitals themselves. The women attempted to inspect Katherine's 'secret parts', but she refused to consent to their request. As Gowing notes for early modern England, marital status formed part of the 'politics of touch' such that single women's bodies were more vulnerable to uninvited intrusion due to the precarity of their social and economic

---

53 BI CP.F.175. 'si predicta Katerina tempore huiusmodi palpacionis fuisset virgo quoddam signum in mamillis mulierum existens anglice vocatam kirnell in mamillis dicte Katerine apparuisset rotundum durum et integrum'.

54 *MED*, 'kirnel'.

55 BI CP.F.175. The term is employed in the depositions of three female witnesses: Matilda, wife of John Leek; Joan, wife of John Rychereson; and Joan, wife of Robert Ireby.

56 *MED*, 'sule'; 'corne'. BI CP.F.175. Alice, wife of William Gretehed: 'si dicta Katerina virgo fuisset durum et integrum et sanum apparuisset de certa sua sciencia dicit'.

57 BI CP.F.175. Joan, wife of John Rycherson: 'in virtute iuramenti sui quod predicta Katerine de certa sua sciencia est mulier corrupta ac prout credit pro firmo pregnans'.

58 BI CP.F.175. 'prout inter mulieres communiter dicitur et reputatur'.

Sexuality and Generation

standing.[59] Although Katherine and William had contracted marriage, the nature of the case, including Katherine's claims of spousal impotence, placed her in a marginal sexual and social position. The authority of the women inspecting her was derived from marital identities that were more distinct and which, in turn, underpinned their regulatory role in the examination. Much of the inspection concentrated on Katherine's breasts, but in medical commentaries the state of the vagina and hymen were regarded as particular evidence of virginity. The alignment of genital examination with conclusive proof of corruption may have encouraged Katherine to ensure that her sexual past was unintelligible to further inquiry. The bodily act of resisting vaginal inspection allowed Katherine to mediate a subject position based on sexual corruption and promiscuity, and to exercise agency over the construction of her legal and moral identity.

Social memory retained in communities included knowledge of other people's sexual relationships, which circulated in the same networks that transmitted local information such as customs and parish rights. Discussion between neighbours and kin ensured that rumours concerning sexual behaviour often solidified into 'common fame'.[60] In a case initiated in 1357, witnesses recalled the consummation of a marriage between William Aunger and Johanna Malcake several years after a contract was formed, when the pair were under the canonical age of marriage. William Raynald recalled that after encouragement from Johanna's friends, William Aunger had entered her chamber and the pair had lain together 'to the interest of certain neighbours in the area', just as he heard from others.[61] Conversations about the sexual histories of others occurred in family contexts, and between generations of the same kin group. In 1269, the consistory court of Salisbury ordered an inquest into the paternity of Johanna de Clopton's illegitimate child, which found that Richard de Bosco was the father according to common fame in the area. Public knowledge of the couple's relationship facilitated Johanna's claims of further sexual involvement after their abjuration *sub pena nubendi*. Nicholas, a witness in the case, testified that Richard also had sex with one of Johanna's kinswomen, which he claimed to have witnessed in a nearby croft. When asked how he remembered these events, Nicholas told how he related the incident to his father when he returned from the tavern, the latter of whom 'counted the years' while the case proceeded in court.[62] The corroborative memory of an older male family member endowed Nicholas's evidence with greater authority. Memories of custom and parish rights relied on similar

---

59 Gowing, *Common Bodies*, p. 73.

60 For an analysis of *fama*, see C. Wickham, '*Fama* and the Law in Twelfth-Century Tuscany', in T. Fenster and D. Lord Smail, eds., *Fama: The Politics of Talk and Reputation in Medieval Europe* (Ithaca, NY, and London, 2003), pp. 15–26, at pp. 16–17.

61 BI CP.E.76. 'ad excitationem quorundam vicinorum dicte ville'.

62 CCA E.S. Roll 310; *Select Cases*, p. 101. 'pater suus computavit annos'.

Popular Memory and Gender in Medieval England

processes of oral transmission, with older men communicating local history over generations. Discussion of Richard's relationships in male conversation thus transformed memories of local sexual activities from informal rumour into reliable sexual history relevant to the church courts.

The sexual relationships of neighbours were embedded in networks of communication that overlapped with informal channels used to identify and police immorality. In a defamation case initiated in 1474, William Palmer of Newland in Yorkshire claimed that his wife referred to the suspected relationship between his sister and a local priest only 'to avoid the sclander and diffame yat was like to rise and grew betweene tham amang ye people of ye pyrshyn'.[63] The detection of illicit sex served as a conduit for the dissemination of sexual histories and coincided with their discussion within the parish. Memories of proceedings in the lower church courts also under-pinned testimony in earlier cases where plaintiffs asserted sexual contact after abjuration. In 1293, Anabilla Daly remembered the abjuration of William Lytesone and Isabella Daly which she heard 'from the report of neighbours who were then present in the church'.[64] Despite clerical anxieties that penitential memories might arouse the sexual imagination, Church author-ities relied on local knowledge of sexual activity to monitor lay behaviour and supplement the legal memory of punishment through the courts.

Sexual histories in testimony were often constructed to undermine the reputations of female parties and deponents, and claims of promiscuity acted to undercut women's legal standing. The suggestion that lower-status women engaged in prostitution, or sexual relationships for which they received recompense, was a common motif in legal narratives, reflecting wider tropes that associated female poverty with promiscuity and material gain.[65] Women's sexual pasts were depicted as varied in other subtle ways, particularly through the language of ambiguity that was used to present their histories as uncertain. In 1363, deponents in a defamation suit from York attempted to mitigate the damage to Margaret de Pickworthe's reputation, claiming that she was 'in her virginity' before the sexual relationship that led to her pregnancy.[66] Robert de Berlay, her father's servant with whom she had the affair, also provided evidence, recalling that she was 'then a virgin' when their relationship began. The positions drawn up for Margaret's father, plaintiff in the suit, similarly noted her virginity, but the legal counsel for the defence capitalised on the promiscuity that her pregnancy was seen to imply. In their response, proctors for the defence acknowledged that Robert no doubt 'knew her carnally', but stated that the identity of the man who deflowered her was unknown.

---

[63] BI CP.F.256.
[64] CCA SVSB III, no. 55.
[65] Bennett, 'Writing Fornication', pp. 156–8.
[66] BI CP.E.249.

Sexuality and Generation

Sexual pasts were adapted in other ways as relationships were rendered obscure to ecclesiastical officials. In 1292, rumours circulated in the Kent town of Faversham regarding the paternity of Matilda Sparuwe's child, following the infant's birth and her citation before the archdeacon of Canterbury.[67] Although Matilda answered a charge of fornication alongside one James de Brenlay in a case that followed, neighbours testified that Richard Everard, a local man who feared his father would disinherit him, had asked James to acknowledge the child as his instead. Several men who gave witness for Richard Everard attempted to conceal the infant's paternity further through claims that Richard's brother, Stephen, had in fact fathered the child. The discourse of paternal uncertainty was used to suggest Matilda's promiscuous past and kinship between two of the men was claimed to form a pre-emptive legal exception that prevented either of the men from marrying her. Sexual histories were mutable for both men and women, but the visibility of the maternal role meant that women like Matilda were unable to avoid detection by ecclesiastical authorities and neighbours. In contrast, paternal identities were more flexible and were depicted as less definitive than unmarried motherhood. Gendered motifs associated with fornication and illegitimate parenthood appear to have allowed men greater agency in the construction of past relationships. The Church's judicial role could be construed as reinforcing patriarchal power relations and penalising women for their alleged sexual pasts. Yet where citations and relationships developed into instance suits, ecclesiastical testimony permitted the development of alternative narratives of reproduction from female perspectives.

CHILDBIRTH, GENERATION, AND MEMORY

Maternity imbued women's evidence with greater authority as the embodied nature of birth provided female deponents with physical proof of past events. The reproductive female body similarly functioned as a site of memory outside the ecclesiastical courts in clerical and theological writings. Learned treatises cast the womb itself as a container for memories. In his *De Philosophia Mundi*, Honorius Augustodunensis emphasised its passive nature, noting that 'the womb, indeed, is certainly the receptacle of the semen; it is lined within with villi to retain it better, and is composed of seven cells with the shape of a man stamped on them as if on a coin'.[68] Patriarchal authority was seen to pervade even the internal organs of the female body at a generative level. The language of memory embodied and reified the dichotomy of male agency and female passivity. Metaphors of generation reproduced the creational logic of *memoria*

---

[67] CCA E.S. Roll 89.
[68] Enders, *The Medieval Theater of Cruelty*, p. 86.

Popular Memory and Gender in Medieval England

in learned works as the production of masculine knowledge was interpreted as a form of intellectual birth.[69] In this classical tradition, the language of birth coincided with the 'creational violence of rhetorical invention'.[70] The English theologian, scholar, and preacher Thomas Bradwardine produced one such treatise, *De Memoria Artificiali*, written in the 1330s, in which a pregnant woman gives birth painfully to a crab that splits her stomach as it emerges.[71] In intellectual culture, memory itself was framed in a generative discourse of violence and female bodily rupture.

In a more pragmatic sense, the value assigned to women's reproductive systems centred on the functional role of the menses and birth, both of which were recognised as occurring at temporal intervals during the female life cycle. Medical texts that circulated among the literate laity observed the cyclical nature of women's reproductive lives. These treatises assigned particular importance to menstruation in the removal of excess humours, and works including the *Trotula* observed that it should appear at the 'appropriate time and with suitable regularity'.[72] In practice, the cyclical elements of birth meant that women could locate past events through the order of their children. Female deponents were therefore regarded as expert witnesses in legal cases where memories of children's births formed the central means of proof.[73] Recurrent childbirth and periods of nurture resulted in the repetition of life stages for many women, a pattern that Skinner describes as the 'suspension of linear time'.[74] Despite the potential for homogeneity and routine, personal birth stories alluded to diverse experiences of labour and maternity. In ecclesiastical testimony, women relied not only on generic tropes of birth, but also on discourses of corporeality and emotion that provided the gendered agency through which subjective identities could be expressed. Childlessness was similarly framed in temporal frameworks that referred to the past and the future in narratives of frustrated parenthood. Female plaintiffs in impotence cases, for instance, used the language of unfulfilled motherhood to convey a

---

[69] D. D. Leitao, *The Pregnant Male as Myth and Metaphor in Classical Greek Literature* (Cambridge, 2012); E. Fantham, 'The Concept of Nature and Human Nature in Quintilian's Psychology and Theory of Instruction', *Rhetorica: A Journal of the History of Rhetoric*, 13 (1995), 125–36, at p. 35.

[70] Enders, *The Medieval Theater of Cruelty*, p. 84.

[71] Carruthers, *The Book of Memory*, p. 134; Enders, *The Medieval Theater of Cruelty*, pp. 82–3.

[72] *The Trotula: A Medieval Compendium of Women's Medicine*, ed. and trans. M. Green (Philadelphia, 2001), p. 73.

[73] Goldberg, 'Gender and Matrimonial Litigation', p. 49; P. Skinner, 'Gender and Memory in Medieval Italy', in van Houts, ed., *Medieval Memories*, pp. 36–52, at p. 47.

[74] Skinner, 'The Pitfalls of Linear Time', p. 22. Skinner bases her discussion of the life cycle and female temporality on Bettina Bildhauer's argument that widowhood could result in the 'gendered stagnation of time'.

Sexuality and Generation

maternal desire for children.[75] The failure to achieve this role at some point in reproductive life represented the inability to attain the embodiment of married femininity. The marital and emotional pasts of these female plaintiffs were imbued with the absence of longed-for children, and annulment was thus sought in order to begin new marriages that could produce children in the future.

The affective and embodied nature of birth solidified its literal and metaphorical association with memory. The emotional trauma and physical danger that accompanied labour functioned as an additional mnemonic to birth itself. Pastoral literature of various kinds acknowledged the strain of childbirth. Written in Middle English probably around 1400, Mirk's *Instructions for Parish Priests* advised on the spiritual care of pregnant women before labour to prepare them for the dangers of birth 'for drede of perele that may be-falle in here trauelynge that come schalle'.[76] Church authorities recognised its mortal risk by encouraging women to receive confession before labour.[77] The statutes of the diocese of Salisbury (1217–19), for example, directed priests to administer confession due to the 'imminent peril' which pregnant women faced during birth.[78] Later statutes, aimed at midwives, female kin, or neighbours, provided guidance on maternal death, noting that live infants should be removed from deceased mothers and baptised.[79] Appeals to the saints in miracle stories depicted divine caesarean sections on pregnant women whose lives were endangered during arduous labours.[80] Neither was the safe delivery of infants guaranteed. In a late fourteenth-century suit, Alice Sharpe, a widow, recalled that one Simon de Folifayt had revived the newborn infant of Maud de Herthill.[81] The women who attended Maud's labour remembered the incident because another local child was born around the same time. The frequent physical and psychological trauma of childbirth could thus ensure its recollection over extended periods. Fear of death during labour was managed partly through the cultural memory on which women relied before and during birth, composed of collective practices and personal experience accrued over lifetimes and generations. After successful births, the ritual elements of lying-in and purification functioned as gendered rites that

---

75 See, for instance, BI CP.E.105, BI CP.E.259, and BI CP.F.40. For a detailed treatment of suits concerning impotence, see Kane, *Impotence and Virginity*.

76 *John Mirk's Instructions for Parish Priests*, ed. G. Kristensson, Lund Studies in English, 49 (Lund, 1974), pp. 71–2.

77 Barr, *The Pastoral Care of Women*, p. 82.

78 *Councils and Synods*, I, p. 89. Salisbury I (1217×1219), canon 88.

79 *Councils and Synods*, I, p. 183. 'Constitutiones cuiusdam episcopi' (1225×1230?), canon 4.

80 K. Quirk, 'Men, Women and Miracles in Normandy, 1000–1150', in van Houts, ed., *Medieval Memories*, pp. 53–71, at pp. 59–60.

81 BI CP.E.89.

Popular Memory and Gender in Medieval England

incorporated mothers back into society after a dangerous physical experience.[82] In both clerical culture and female experience, birth and postnatal care represented a period of gendered rupture in which the mother became dislocated from normative communal time.

Aside from the temporal implications of birth, these experiences allowed the female body to be seen as bearing memory that was deemed useful in church-court testimony. The embodied experience of birth meant that the maternal body was no longer a virginal *tabula rasa*, but could be interpreted for its moral state. In judicial contexts, postnatal changes to the female body provided proof of intercourse and signalled guilt during inquiries initiated by ecclesiastical authorities.[83] In 1434, the women who examined Katherine Barlay interpreted the markings on her breasts as evidence of sexual activity. The absence of a newborn might also be inferred from the physical state of the newly maternal body. In 1517, Alice Rydyng was found guilty of infanticide during an *ex officio* action in the diocese of Lincoln, but denied giving birth despite the suspicions of local women who raised questions about the shape of her stomach. After the incident, the matrons seized her and 'inspected her belly and her breasts by which they knew for certain that she had given birth'.[84] The female form was perceived to be altered and inscribed at a material level through intercourse and childbirth. Several women in a late thirteenth-century marriage suit noted that one Agnes, pregnant by Thomas de Derby, was 'near birth'.[85] Women's proximity to labour was established through sight of their bodies which was in turn interpreted as proof of sexual relationships.

Maternal remembrance depended in part on the physical experience of childbirth, with female deponents drawing on embodied language to construct a kind of uterine memory. In 1430 during a marriage suit in the court of York, Isabel, wife of John Croxton, remembered the birth of her child 'from her womb', a phrase that appears in other narratives of childbirth.[86] The act of giving birth also served as proof of claims to maternity in cases where female witnesses testified on the ages of one or both parties. In 1425, Johanna, wife of William Wighton, recalled the birth of Agnes Northefolk's daughter, thirteen years before, referencing the birth of her own child 'from her own womb' that same year.[87] These descriptions were framed in somatic terms

---

[82] G. McMurray Gibson, 'Blessing from Sun and Moon: Churching as Women's Theater', in B. A. Hanawalt and D. Wallace, eds., *Bodies and Disciplines: Intersections of Literature and History in Fifteenth-Century England* (Minneapolis, 1996), pp. 139–54.

[83] Gowing, *Common Bodies*, pp. 43–6.

[84] *Women in England*, ed. and trans. Goldberg, pp. 119–20.

[85] CCA E.S. Roll 293. Matilda de Rossa, wife of John le Barbur: 'Agnes est pregnans de eodem Thoma et proxima partui'.

[86] BI CP.F.201.

[87] BI CP.F.89. 'de utero suo propio peperit unam filiam Johannam'.

Sexuality and Generation

that conveyed the activity of labour, as well as the physical experience of birth itself. Women also remembered their pregnancies as significant periods in their lives. In 1294, witnesses deposed on the alleged marriage between Walter de Heyndon and Johanna Hunte.[88] Both Alice Atehide and Matilda Atehulle stated that they remembered the couple's marriage based on the children they carried during that period.

Memories of childbirth emphasised the practical and emotional implications of labour. In the suit that sought to establish Katherine Northefolk's age, a number of women recalled the births of their children within a year or two of each other, suggesting networks of mutual support composed of local women, their kin, friends, and neighbours. The physical care that childbirth and postnatal recovery entailed both reflected and reinforced intimate bonds of dependence and trust between mothers and attendants. After Katherine Northefolk's birth, Joan, wife of Robert Souman, told her neighbours with whom she travelled on pilgrimage to Bridlington, that 'she greatly wished to be with' Agnes Northefolk and her newborn daughter.[89] Joan and her husband, Robert, had provided pre- and postnatal care for Agnes, preparing food and proffering support after the child was born. Multiple births within a community in the same period meant that women remembered the labours of friends and kin in temporal frameworks that emphasised their conflicting demands. Another friend of Agnes Northefolk, one Joan, wife of Thomas Nayler, recalled Katherine Northefolk's birth despite her absence from the delivery, stating that 'she would have travelled with Katherine More, her fellow witness and god-mother of Katherine Northefolk, on the same Monday if she had not been nearing the birth of her own son, Richard Neleson, now deceased'.[90]

Feelings of disappointment accompanied memories of birth where women were deemed to have failed in their responsibilities to one another.[91] In 1422, Agnes, wife of John Bacon, recalled a marriage she had attended thirteen years earlier because her friend Alice, wife of John Towton, was in labour that day. Agnes told the examiner that her failure to attend the birth had caused Alice to be 'annoyed and troubled with this witness for a long time'.[92] Alice's response to her friend's absence drew on expectations of close friendship

---

[88] CCA E.S. Roll 307.

[89] BI CP.F.89.

[90] BI CP.F.89. 'ipsa iurata eodem die lune transmisset cum Katerine de More conteste sua commatre eiusdem Katerine Northefolk si non fuisset prope partum cuiusdam Ricardi Neleson fili sui iam defuncti'.

[91] On women's responsibilities related to birth, see D. Cressy, 'Purification, Thanksgiving and the Churching of Women', in D. Cressy, *Birth, Marriage and Death: Ritual, Religion and the Life-Cycle in Tudor and Stuart England* (Oxford, 1997), pp. 197–228, at pp. 201–3.

[92] BI CP.F.133. 'diu fuit molestata et gravata cum illa iurata'.

Popular Memory and Gender in Medieval England

that included support in labour and provoked displeasure when these were not met. While their friendship eventually recovered, Agnes told the examiner that Alice often counted the years since her son's birth, a context in which Agnes's absence may have surfaced in conversation once more. The emotional rift remained in both women's memories for a long period, and acted as an additional mnemonic closely associated with labour and birth.

Men remembered past events with reference to childbirth in their testimony, but with less frequency than female witnesses. In some instances, as Ulinka Rublack found in early modern Germany, husbands were present during miscarriages or witnessed the delivery of their children. The everyday physical needs that accompanied pregnancy and birth affected domestic routines, and in households where wives contributed to their husbands' craft these bodily states might also entail the reallocation of their work.[93] Despite the involvement of fathers in these activities, men's memories of their own children tended to focus on their comparative age to the parties involved in the suit, rather than the birth itself. In a case from York initiated in 1332, Hugh Wodecok stated that he knew the defendant, William Crane, was underage because his own son was the same age.[94] In 1348, Adam de Helay and Richard de Helay both testified that they each had a child the same age as the plaintiff, William Hopton, who had been nine years old when he married the defendant.[95] Paternal accounts of birth could structure the testimony of male witnesses, but men's memories often focused on the social contexts of birth. In 1431 John Tailour recalled a marriage contract from the birth of his son, William, because after the birth he had asked William Rosyn to be god-father.[96] John then celebrated with his son's god-father and other male friends, eating and drinking with them. The general exclusion of men from the birthing room may have caused fathers, male kin, and neighbours to associate memories of birth with the only traditions and practices available to them. Celebrations after the birth of local children were often mixed sex, yet female witnesses drew on a broader range of events attached to birth. Female testimony also focused on on physical rituals that went beyond labour itself, imbuing memories with more public forms of social and communal meaning. In 1425 Margaret, wife of John Galt, remembered her purification following the birth of her son, John, who had died ten years before. Several female deponents in the same suit had acted as god-mother for another child, recalling how they had raised the infant from the font during her baptism.[97] Temporal markers associated with birth were more multifaceted and embodied for mothers, and women in general.

---

[93] Rublack, 'Pregnancy, Childbirth and the Female Body', pp. 98–9.
[94] BI CP.E.23.
[95] BI CP.E.62.
[96] BI CP.F.113.
[97] BI CP.F.89.

Sexuality and Generation

Female witnesses depicted the movement of women between friends and kin as an integral part of their reproductive life cycle, but men's memories of labour and postnatal care differed from these experiences. In 1425 Robert Souman deposed on the postnatal care of Agnes Northefolk, his wife's niece, noting their provision of her care during her labour and for a long time afterwards.[98] Robert recalled that the women who were present at the birth stayed at his home both for the labour itself and the subsequent baptism. Joan Souman, Robert's wife and Agnes's aunt, also remembered the child's birth, but omitted the arrival of the women, their stay, and Agnes's postnatal care, perhaps interpreting these birth practices as routine rather than memorable. Although male kin and neighbours were confined to other areas of the house, they could aid their wives in caring for parturient women, and in domestic contexts both men and women were engaged in the provision of care during and after birth. In temporal terms, however, male engagement with the routine and bodily elements of birth occurred from a gendered physical distance.

Beyond the household contexts of births, local men relied on oral reports that female birth attendants and god-mothers communicated to neighbours and kin. In 1332, John de Draycote testified on the ages of William Crane and Alice, daughter of Richard de Draycote, who had married prior to their canonical majorities.[99] John testified that the girl's mother and the boy's god-mother had informed him of their ages. Nicholas Symson stated that several women who were present at the delivery told him about Katherine Northefolk's birth, as well as the 'wife of a certain man of Fulford Gate'.[100] Harris-Stoertz notes that despite the reliance on male jurors in proof-of-age inquiries, female experiences of birth contributed to the 'collective memory' of surrounding communities.[101] Women's testimony in church courts, however, shows how female networks drove the transmission of these kinds of knowledge. The influence of gender on birth practices, as well as local relationships and modes of communication, shaped the formation of social memory through the incorporation of reproductive pasts.

Despite the greater frequency of maternal memory in testimony, birth accounts occasionally differed between spouses. In the case involving Katherine Northefolk, men and women testified on her birth to prove that she had been old enough to profess as a nun in a convent in Nottinghamshire.[102] Johanna, wife of William Wighton, remembered the birth of her daughter that same year, while William, her husband, recalled the couple's relocation to

---

[98] BI CP.F.89.

[99] BI CP.E.23.

[100] BI CP.F.89. 'uxoris cuisdam viri de Fulford Galt'.

[101] Harris-Stoertz, 'Remembering Birth', p. 52.

[102] For a discussion of the case more generally, see S. H. Wright, 'Women in the Northern Courts: Interpreting Legal Records of Familial Conflict in Early Fifteenth-Century Yorkshire', *Florilegium*, 19 (2002), 27–48.

Popular Memory and Gender in Medieval England

the village of Water Fulford. When Alice, wife of Robert Bolton, remembered that she had given birth to twins who would have been fourteen years old had they lived, her husband failed to mention the birth of these children and referenced instead his period of service with Katherine More.[103] The association of singleness with life-cycle servanthood perhaps meant that Robert was Alice's second husband, and the children she recalled were from an earlier marriage.[104] In the same suit, Joan Souman remembered that her son John, who had died aged one and a half, was born the same year as Katherine Northefolk. Robert Souman, her husband, failed to mention their son's birth or death in his deposition, locating Katherine's birth using a list of his tenants over the preceding thirteen years thirteen years.[105] Conjugal memories of children's births were far from uniform in content. Married couples discussed their own personal histories, as well as those of their neighbours, yet the production of these memories occurred in situations where emotions and perceptions differed between spouses.

Parental disagreement extended to the details of when children were born. John Norton and his wife, Joan, recalled the name of their daughter differently, with Joan referring to her as Alice and John remembering her as Matilda. Despite the discrepancy in their memories, perhaps a scribal error, both John and Joan told how she was born fourteen years earlier and, if she had lived, would have been fourteen at the time of the case.[106] Multiple births may have confused spousal memories surrounding their order, yet disagreement also emerged over the exact age of children. In 1355, Maud Katersouth, a resident of the city of York, testified on the age of her son, Robert, due to his proximity to the male age limit of fourteen for ecclesiastical witnesses. Maud deposed that 'her son was aged fourteen years, coming up fifteen years' when he was examined in the case. Robert, however, deposed that he was 'fifteen years and more as he heard his father, who is living still, swear and firmly assert'.[107] Regarded locally as a poor woman of little means, Maud lived apart from Robert's father which perhaps explained aspects of the parental conflict.[108] The reliance on paternal memory also reflected lay perceptions that men provided more trustworthy testimony, as well as gendered hierarchies that accorded male opinion greater value.[109] Popular perceptions of male authority could allow men's memories to supplant women's embodied experiences of birth.

---

[103] BI C.P.F.89.

[104] Goldberg, 'Masters and Men', p. 58.

[105] BI C.P.F.89.

[106] BI C.P.F.89.

[107] BI C.P.E.82. Maud Katersouth: 'fuit etatis xiiii annos et attingens xv annum'; Robert, son of Maud Katersouth: 'xv annorum et amplius prout audivit patrem suum qui ad huc superstites est iurare et firmiter asserere'.

[108] BI C.P.E.82.

[109] Goldberg, 'Gender and Matrimonial Litigation', p. 46.

Sexuality and Generation

Memories that focused on parenting emphasised the smaller acts that sustained parent–child relationships and generated accounts of the emotional and physical care given during the early years of nurture.[110] Deponents emphasised the maternal bond in memories of material support that sought to prove the relationship between mother and child. Witnesses not only remembered Katherine Northefolk's birth, for example, but also aspects of the care provided during her infancy. Thomas Gyselay, a constable from the neighbouring village of Gate Fulford, remembered visiting the house in which Agnes had given birth, where he saw her holding Katherine in her arms. Margery, wife of John Carbot, remembered seeing Katherine breastfeeding on Agnes's bosom. The physical nature of nursing underlined the relationship between Agnes and her daughter, founded on gendered bodily practices which developed into a form of maternal habit memory.

Memories of breastfeeding evoked the emotional bond between mother and child, as well as the physical contact of skin that echoed their biological bond. Disruptions to the supply of maternal breast milk could also underpin postnatal memory. Johanna, wife of William Wighton, told the examiner that she breastfed Katherine in her mother's absence, while Agnes Northefolk nursed her daughter when Johanna could not.[111] Female friends and neighbours were engaged in exchanges that involved the nurture of each other's children, with maternal habits used to nurse infants outside the nuclear family. Women who were unable to breastfeed their children, for instance, due to infant death, were occasionally hired as wet nurses. The inability to breastfeed one's child was in many ways associated with its death or failure to thrive. In 1365, one witness recalled that she had refused to act as wet nurse to Ellen de Rouclif's child as 'she loved her son just as much as Ellen loved hers and consequently she could not allow her son to perish on account of Ellen's'.[112] Mothers understood the early stages of parenting not simply as a duty of care, but as a form of love that was founded on and bore evidence of the bond between mother and child.

Memories of parenting evoked other kinds of responsibilities that accompanied the parental role. In marriage suits where the relationship had produced children, for example, witnesses referred to the alleged father's provision of clothing for their offspring. This kind of testimony offered an alternative memory of the couple's sexual history, cast otherwise as temporary and casual, and also acted as evidence of paternity. Parties and witnesses drew on other expectations of parental care in personal disputes. In 1418, for instance, the court was told how John Gamell had called at Margaret Whytell's

---

[110] For an important study of parenting in Georgian England, see J. Bailey, *Parenting in England, 1760–1830: Emotion, Identity, and Generation* (Oxford, 2012).

[111] BI CP.F.89.

[112] BI CP.E.89. 'bene dilexit filium suum sicut ipsa Elena dilexit suum et ideo noluit tollerare filium suum proprium perire propter filium dicte Elene'.

door late at night, with a group of armed men, on the suspicion that she was having a premarital relationship with John Bewmond. John Gamell gained entry to her house by shouting that his daughter was gravely ill and requesting that she open her door 'for the love of God'.[113] When Margaret admitted John Gamell, the men found John Bewmond lying naked in her bed and forced the pair to marry. The men appropriated behaviour that characterised ideals of parental care in periods of child illness, including seeking support from neighbours and the use of emotionally charged and urgent language.

Witnesses' memories could also convey the exercise of parental authority, the foundations of which were rooted in patriarchal family structures.[114] Marriage suits involving the betrothal of children before they reached the canonical age of consent noted the early histories of these unions, while parents and other kin were implicated in marriages where parties claimed that patri- archal force had elided their consent.[115] In 1362, Richard Bellamy testified on his involvement in the marriage of his great-niece, Alice, daughter of Thomas Belamy, to Robert Thomeson several years earlier. Richard recalled that he had intimidated Alice, threatening to throw her down her down the household well, causing her to weep and plead on her knees for time to consider the union further.[116] Although Richard claimed to have been instrumental in the marriage's formation, his narrative supported an argument of 'force and fear' that centred on the absence of consent and aimed to extricate Alice from the union. The past behaviour of parents and senior kin was depicted in different ways depending on the subject positions that they chose to adopt, and which witnesses and the opposing party attributed to them. In some instances, however, the acceptance of parental versions of the past was characterised as unproblematic. Cases concerning tithes and parish rights depended on the transmission of memories of custom to children and younger kin. Deponents recalled conversations where parents and older relatives imparted details of local histories that represented a form of generational memory. Memories of this kind were depicted as authoritative and any traces of conflict over their veracity were omitted from witnesses' accounts.

CONCLUSION

Memory was embedded deeply in the gendered experience of reproduction in late medieval culture. Learned texts identified a close relationship between women's memory and the perceived feminine traits of passivity, fickleness,

---

[113] BI CP.F.75. Deposition of Richard Bryg: 'pro amore dei'.

[114] For an important discussion of paternal authority in late medieval English texts, see R. E. Moss, *Fatherhood and its Representations in Middle English Texts* (York, 2013), pp. 187–8.

[115] Helmholz, *Marriage Litigation*, pp. 98–9.

[116] BI CP.E.85.

Sexuality and Generation

and sexual voracity, although cultural expectations acknowledged women's expertise in remembering and interpreted their bodies as sites of memory. Sexual and reproductive histories were central strands of a village's or neighbourhood's past, supplementing other types of knowledge about local inhabitants. Gender influenced memories of sex and generation in discourses that referenced bodily movement, affective responses, and physical appearance, including descriptions of sexual organs. These accounts highlight the resources and mechanisms that sustained gendered power relationships in social practice. Memories of early nurture and parenting alluded to the emotional and physical intimacy of care, drawing on routines and habits that were culturally recognisable and crucial to witnesses' personal histories.

Women encountered a range of events that marked their bodies in physical and emotional terms, such that birth represented only one aspect of the embodiment of their sexual and reproductive memory. Birth and nurture were more prominent in women's legal narratives, and depictions of sexual histories tended to interpret female behaviour as promiscuous and men's as merely the fulfilment of adult masculinity. These patterns replicated gender binaries prevalent in clerical and popular contexts, suggesting that men and women reshaped their evidence to incorporate familiar models and motifs. Narratives of this kind demonstrate the extent to which embodied depictions of women, often expressed through patriarchal language, pervaded male and female testimony. Women, in particular, sought to mediate essentialised and restrictive subject positions, exercising agency through memories that rejected, articulated, or appropriated embodied identities and behaviour. Memories of sex, birth, and parenting enabled the partial articulation of identities that were governed by cultural expectations, but might also be internalised at a personal level. Embodied forms of memory thus operated as a particularly feminine source of agency that allowed women to negotiate social and legal expectations, and at the same time voice aspects of their own gendered pasts.

5

MARRIAGE, KINSHIP, AND WIDOWHOOD

In the preface to his *Polychronicon*, Ranulph Higden observed that 'shortness of life, dullness of perception, numbness of the soul, weakness of memory and fruitless occupations prevent us from knowing many things, and forgetfulness is ever the stepmother and enemy of memory'.[1] The capacity to remember was thus described through discourses of gender and kinship, emphasising the significant yet precarious role of women in preserving family memory. Higden's highly popular fourteenth-century history found its principal audience in the clergy and religious, with a smaller lay readership among the aristocracy and gentry.[2] By the late fourteenth century, John Trevisa's vernacular translation of the *Polychronicon* widened its circulation among the mercantile and bourgeois classes, with a prologue that once more described 'forȝetingnes' as the 'craft of a stepdamme'.[3] The figurative alignment of stepmothers with the neglect of memory, while its preservation was associated with motherhood, not only embodied the concerns of lay elites, but also referenced wider social attitudes and fears of memorial rupture after widowhood.[4]

This perceived role of female kin as guardians of memory emerged from the correlation of remembrance with practices deemed to be feminine. Mothers were characterized as responsible for the socialization of children and the everyday household, and this association extended to female relatives who were regarded as carers for the sick and dying, and as accountable for

---

[1] *Polychronicon Ranulphi Higden monachi Cestrensis; Together with the English Translations of John Trevisa and of an Unknown Writer of the Fifteenth Century*, ed. C. Babington, Rolls Series, 41 (London, 1865), vol. 1, p 4, cited in Given-Wilson, *Chronicles*, p. 59. 'Siquidem vita brevis, sensus hebes, animus torpens, memoria labens, inutilis demum occupatio nos impediunt multa scire, novercante semper oblivione memoriae inimica'. I have used Given-Wilson's translation.

[2] A. Gransden, *Historical Writing in England*, vol. 2: *c. 1307 to the Early Sixteenth Century*, 2nd edition (London, 1996), p. 44; R. Radulescu, 'Literature', in R. Radulescu and A. Truelove, eds., *Gentry Culture in Late Medieval England* (Manchester, 2005), pp. 100–18, at p. 111.

[3] *Polychronicon Ranulphi Higden*, ed. Babington, p. 5.

[4] C. Klapisch-Zuber, 'The "Cruel Mother": Maternity, Widowhood, and Dowry in Florence in the Fourteenth and Fifteenth Centuries', in L. Hutson, ed., *Feminism and Renaissance Studies* (Oxford, 1999), pp. 186–202, at p. 193.

Popular Memory and Gender in Medieval England

the commemoration of late husbands and other male kin.[5] Yet perceptions of female remembrance did not always reflect the relationship between gender and memory in social practice. The mental categories that organized memorial roles were both socially constructed and ideological, influenced by gendered attitudes that shaped the maintenance of family history.[6] The depiction of kin-group memory as feminine, for instance, embodied assumptions about gendered roles, the nature of unwritten memory, and the operation of the patriarchal household, while simultaneously occluding the contributions of husbands and fathers in the transmission of these histories. Male kin from gentry and aristocratic stock were intimately involved in the preservation of family memory through written histories, often relying on heraldic conventions to preserve their genealogies. Oral accounts of births, marriages, and bonds of kinship circulated among men and women at every social level.[7] There were, nevertheless, profound differences in the way that gender influenced family memory, from the circulation of knowledge about ancestry to gendered perceptions of kinship, and from the organisation of family histories to encounters with the law.

In the church courts, marriage suits were initiated in order to annul unions made within forbidden degrees of kinship or affinity, encoding in writing oral ancestries of family histories from the peasantry to the lower gentry. Marriages, ancestry, and parentage were also inscribed in legal memory, providing women with the means to exercise agency in discursive terms, in both the construction of family memory and the use of canon law. Female kin were thus able to construct narratives that represented a familial form of social memory, articulated from a feminine perspective. Gendered perceptions of commemoration were also used to deprive widows of goods and property rights, and displace them from their marital genealogy. Concerns over memory and forgetting could underpin hostilities between female kin and their marital family. These issues were particularly prevalent in suits over testamentary rights and the validity of marriages in relation to property disputes, highlighting the extent to which family histories became sites of contest for male and female relatives.

Halbwachs identified the family as a specific kind of memory community in which 'relations of kinship' shaped perceptions of its past.[8] The family unit in medieval society was predominantly nuclear and co-resident, although in many manors and vills relationships with extended kin were maintained through social networks and support during legal actions. The extent of the household differed from the nuclear family due to the inclusion of servants,

---

5   R. E. Archer and B. E. Ferme, 'Testamentary Procedure with Special Reference to the Executrix', *Reading Medieval Studies*, 15 (1989), 3–34.

6   Geary, *Phantoms of Remembrance*, p. 52.

7   Lee, 'Men's Recollections of a Women's Rite', pp. 224–41.

8   Halbwachs, *On Collective Memory*, p. 63.

Marriage, Kinship, and Widowhood

apprentices and day labourers, especially in urban areas.[9] Dependent workers in households supplemented and absorbed family histories, ensuring that members of the nuclear family were not the only figures to influence its composition. Details of ancestries circulated outside the immediate kin group, providing local inhabitants with the knowledge to testify on the genealogies of neighbouring families. The social memory of the family thus stretched beyond its nuclear, household, and residential base, encompassing a range of customs and practices that embedded family memory in wider social relations. Family histories, and ties with kin, were not recalled solely as structural relationships before the courts. David Herlihy, for instance, identified emotional bonds as a distinctive element in the construction of the medieval family, alongside its composition and form.[10] Thus, while legal evidence tended to focus on specific relations of kinship, everyday encounters within kin groups and between families in the wider community fostered an affective familiarity that accommodated a range of emotions.

Aside from family structure, social gradation qualified the involvement of men and women in the production of family memory, with gendered roles imagined and enacted differently across the status groups. The commemoration of kin through writing and material culture was more prevalent among the gentry and nobility, while remembrance has been closely associated with oral communication in non-elite families. Memory formation and transmission were more complicated in practice, however, with intricate patterns evident below the level of the aristocracy, among the lesser gentry, town-dwellers, and peasantry. Those of middling status and below understood the power of the written word in constructing family histories. In judicial contexts, non-elite memories of kinship intersected with the written record where inheritance, ownership of land, and blood ties were central points of dispute. Oral traditions similarly underpinned many aspects of memory in late medieval culture, regardless of social standing. The socialization of children was secured through the transmission of tales and objects, some of which were associated with stages of a family's past that preceded written records and settled into formal accounts only over generations.[11] This chapter will explore the intersections between marriage and memory in the courts, before turning to ancestries in matrimonial disputes concerning close kinship.

---

9   M. Kowaleski and P. J. P. Goldberg, 'Introduction. Medieval Domesticity: Home, Housing and Household', in M. Kowaleski and P. J. P. Goldberg, eds., *Medieval Domesticity: Home, Housing and Household in Medieval England* (Cambridge, 2008), pp. 1–13, at p. 2.

10   D. Herlihy, 'The Making of the Medieval Family: Symmetry, Structure, and Sentiment', *Journal of Family History*, 8 (1983), 116–30, at p. 117.

11   M. Innes, 'Keeping it in the Family: Women and Aristocratic Memory, 700–1200', in van Houts, ed., *Medieval Memories*, pp. 17–35, at p. 30; D. R. Woolf, 'A Feminine Past? Gender, Genre, and Historical Knowledge in England, 1500–1800', *American Historical Review*, 102 (1997), 645–79, at pp. 654–5.

Popular Memory and Gender in Medieval England

The final section deals with the ways in which memory was used and appropriated in suits between widows and their marital families.

MARRIAGE AND MEMORY

Parentage was the cornerstone of kinship under canon law, but the foundations of family memory at a generational level lay in the conjugal bond that in turn ensured the transfer of ancestral histories. Marriage patterns varied according to status group, locale, and region, yet patriarchal authority over kin and household was widely assumed, even while coverture was perhaps less relevant in social practice. Despite the visibility of formal histories in elite contexts, marriage impinged on the conjugal couple's experiences across the social strata, producing memories that evoked shared domestic, social, and economic pasts. In a similar vein, among the aristocracy and gentry, the female commemorative role shifted upon marriage, with women regarded as responsible for the continuation of their marital family's genealogy.

Memories of the marital bond formed the basis of proof in matrimonial suits, with two witnesses needed to provide evidence of a contract. While canonists emphasized the importance of the marriage contract itself, other forms of evidence were needed where words of consent were absent or regarded as insufficient. The courts tended to follow the advice of canonists, requiring proof that the couple cohabited over a long period, as well as public fame of the marriage, and additional detail to corroborate the union.[12] Cohabitation outside of wedlock was not uncommon, but it was regarded as a central marker of marriage and used as proof of the couple's marital treatment of one another. In an early thirteenth-century case initiated in London, a number of witnesses described how John the blacksmith cohabited with Alice 'in a marital fashion', sharing the same bed, and 'returned to her as a wife'.[13] This testimony acknowledged the existence of other kinds of sexual ties, including temporary relationships that might involve co-residence but were more transitory in nature. Marriage was conceptualized in opposition to these kinds of bonds, through the language of permanence, stability, and daily routine that underscored its everyday practice. Witnesses also noted instances where couples lived together but did not share a marital bed, as one witness described in a case from York in 1370.[14] The couple's failure to sleep together was offered as evidence that the pair were aware of their close kinship which would have nullified the union.

---

[12] Helmholz, *Marriage Litigation*, pp. 45–7.

[13] CCA E.S. Roll 40iii; *Select Cases*, pp. 26–7. Evelina, wife of Edmund: 'more maritali'; Aeldrita, widow of Ralph, the baker: 'dicit quod Johannes Aliciam exhibuit diu in domo sua et ad eam rediit sicut ad uxorem'.

[14] BI CP.E.108.

Marriage, Kinship, and Widowhood

Local knowledge underpinned memories of sexual relationships and marriages, and the public and shared nature of 'common fame' transformed gossip into testimony that was admissible as proof.[15] Despite the use of *fama* as evidence of marriage, it was often challenging to establish as the reading of banns was increasingly encouraged to identify potential impediments to unions, including earlier contracts made in other parishes.[16] The Fourth Lateran Council required the publication of banns before unions were solemnized, and local legislation, such as the mandate published in the diocese of York in 1238, reinforced their importance for inquiries into the histories of couples wishing to marry.[17] In 1329, the Council of London issued a canon instructing parish priests to advise the laity in the vernacular on the reading of banns.[18] The dissemination of teachings on banns encouraged parishioners to remember in detail the personal histories of betrothed couples, and objections made during the reading of banns drew on these memories. The practical significance of banns under canon law, however, could also provide deponents with a convenient form of proof. Witnesses frequently described the reading of banns before the contract to characterise a union as valid and canonically sound, such as in the case of the marriage of Katherine Blayke and Roger Nebb, which reached the court of York in 1449.[19] Other couples were accused of attempting to limit the publication of banns to prevent their past unions impeding the marriage.

Marital histories of neighbours were outlined in extensive detail, offering evidence that these relationships were well known in the local area and beyond. In one late thirteenth-century suit from the court of Canterbury, a seventy-year-old witness described how his father had been present at the contract in question and had told him that the marriage was widely known and notorious in the area during his own childhood.[20] Neighbours used residential proximity to explain their knowledge of the couple's marriage, citing memories of visits to the conjugal home where the pair were observed living as a married couple. The celebration of marriages through parties and feasts underscored their common fame in the community, embedding unions in the social memory of the area through accounts of shared festivities. Deponents also associated personal memories of gift-giving with their

---

15 Wickham, '*Fama* and the Law', pp. 15–26.

16 T. Kuehn, '*Fama* as a Legal Status in Renaissance Florence', in Fenster and Smail, eds., *Fama: The Politics of Talk and Reputation*, pp. 27–46, at p. 28.

17 *Councils and Synods*, I, pp. 259–60. Mandate against neglect of marriage-banns in the diocese of York (1238).

18 *Concilia Magnae Britanniae et Hiberniae, 446–1718*, ed. D. Wilkins (London, 1737; repr. Brussels, 1964), vol. 2, p. 554; for a discussion of Church legislation on banns, see Sheehan, 'Marriage Theory and Practice', pp. 152–3.

19 BI CP.F.184 and 185.

20 CCA E.S. Roll 231.

remembrance. In 1200, one Adam Tugge told the court that he recalled the marriage of a local couple, Edith and Fulk, because he saw his neighbour's wife making a gift to take to their nuptials.[21] Marriages were depicted as occurring within dense networks of personal relationships that were marked by friendship and exchange.

Aside from testimony on cohabitation and common fame, witnesses also drew on other less tangible markers of marriage, including the presence of affection within the relationship. Memories of the emotional bond between the couple, for example, were used to underline the validity of unions. In a suit from London, John the blacksmith abandoned his marriage to Alice, but later admitted their contract before witnesses in the church of St Mary of the Arches. John's public confession referred to the history of the couple's relationship, with one witness noting that he had acknowledged that 'so much had taken place between John and Alice that he was not able to wed any other while she lived'.[22] The performance of conjugal roles over a union's duration similarly emphasized their enduring nature, highlighting a lifetime of mutual support and the affective ties that could accompany marriage. In an early thirteenth-century suit, one deponent remembered visiting the house of Arnold de Thorley where he saw him honour Agnes de Parage and 'hold her dear, as his legitimate wife', emphasizing his love and affection for her.[23] In 1294, one witness described a couple 'living as married', which he noted separately from their cohabitating and raising children together.[24]

Marital histories similarly referred to periods of domestic discord and the absence of affection from unions. Established patterns of abuse formed part of the local memory of marriages, as much as cohabitation and childrearing. In 1333, one Alice, wife of Robert de Flixton, claimed to have witnessed Geoffrey de Brunne's violence towards his wife, behaviour that was said to be known in the area and was also commonly reported from others in the neighbourhood.[25] Routine cruelty was also emphasised where deponents attempted to depict husbands as habitual abusers. In 1410, one female witness told the court that Henry Wyvell maltreated his wife, Cecilia, often and on various occasions.[26] Regular abuse of this kind was integrated into the community's common fame, transforming rumour into accepted knowledge about husbands' physical treatment of their wives.

---

[21] CCA E.S. Roll 40.

[22] CCA E.S. Roll 40iii; *Select Cases*, p. 28. 'ipse intellexit per confessionem Johannis quod tantum inter Johannem et Aliciam factum fuit quod nullam aliam ducere potuit ea vivente'.

[23] CCA E.S. Roll 205; *Select Cases*, p. 22. 'caram habuit tanquam uxorem suam'.

[24] CCA E.S. Roll 231; *Select Cases*, p. 62. Richard de Bocton: 'matrimonialiter vivere'.

[25] BI CP.E.25.

[26] BI CP.F.56.

Marriage, Kinship, and Widowhood

Deponents used the notion of custom to underpin memories of marriage, depicting certain practices as long held and widely recognized. References to custom not only provided proof of the intentions of both parties to contract a marriage, but also offered lay perspectives on marriage beyond its canonical validity. In 1200, one witness in a case from Canterbury recalled that a penny was placed upon a book during the contract, stating explicitly that this was a custom used during marriages.[27] A similar practice of the betrothed couple each offering oblations of a penny or halfpenny during the ceremony was noted in early thirteenth-century London.[28] Local customs concerning marriage were used to draw distinctions between different kinds of relationships, and could be deployed to restrict the fiscal power of unmarried and sexually active women.[29] Laypeople also relied on custom to refine their understandings of marital and sexual histories and how these could be remembered. Custom was thus a principal component of non-elite memory more broadly, operating beyond agrarian practice in the more explicitly gendered areas of marriage and domestic life.

The use of marriage as a memory strategy was imbued with a host of practical and symbolic meanings that differed according to gender. Marital status acted as an indicator of sexual reputation for women in particular. In 1394, a male deponent in a marriage suit from York corroborated the evidence of two female witnesses, noting both their honest labour and their marital status as widows and wives.[30] Perceptions of female authority underwent a series of shifts after marriage, and the cultural capital and expertise associated with motherhood saw many married female deponents testify on issues concerning childbirth. Marriage functioned as a memory strategy for men and women at a personal level. Men and women recalled marriages more often than entering a trade or beginning service, with the domestic rearrangement associated with marriage perhaps representing a more lasting mnemonic than the temporary resettlement of life-cycle service. The practicalities of marriage and family life, as well as the established nature of these emotional bonds, ensured that an individual's marriage remained a more memorable event than others over time.[31] The subjective meaning of marriage and its visibility in the local community contributed to its prevalence in legal testimony.

The significance of marital status as a category extended to the social and economic roles allotted to men, and retained importance for male as much as female identities. Male witnesses relied upon memories of marriage to a

---

[27] CCA E.S. Roll 205; *Select Cases*, p. 22.

[28] CCA E.S. Roll 40iii; *Select Cases*, p. 27.

[29] For a useful discussion of custom and widowhood in early modern England, see Wood, *The Memory of the People*, p. 303.

[30] BI CP.E.159; Beattie, 'The Problem of Women's Work Identities', pp. 13–14.

[31] Rosenthal, *Telling Tales*, pp. 16–19.

Popular Memory and Gender in Medieval England

greater extent than women, who often preferred to focus their testimony on childbirth. In 1431, John Wyman remembered a marriage contract 'because on Sunday nearest after the feast of All Saints at the parish of St Wilfrid's, a marriage was solemnised between this witness and the said Cecilia, blood relative of John Elvyngton, thirty-nine years ago'. Other male witnesses in the suit married around the same time, but their wives had predeceased them, with the memory of their death used to verify the widowers' testimony. William Gudale, by then aged sixty-eight, remembered his marriage thirty-eight years before to Margaret Farman, who had died many years earlier, while William Kenlay remembered 'because of the marriage between himself and Alice, his wife, now dead'.[32] Marriage and, to a lesser extent, service, may have provided men with a convenient mnemonic reference in instances where memories of childbirth and nurture were not deeply embedded. The authority which the newly married *paterfamilias* exerted over servants and dependants represented social adulthood as it signalled freedom from dependence upon a father or employer.[33] This placed married men higher in the social and economic hierarchy than single men without similar domestic and financial independence. Marriage thus marked the attainment of one of the primary markers of lay masculinity, and facilitated several other stages of the male life cycle, including the formation of a separate household and entry into fatherhood.

The symbolic and practical importance of marriage in a wider sense meant that deponents remembered the unions of family, friends, and neighbours alongside their own nuptials. Mothers recalled their children's marriages as often as their own, particularly those of their daughters. In a case from York initiated in 1425, Margaret, wife of Hugh Tailour, remembered a birth because of its proximity to the marriage of her daughter, Agnes, to Nicholas Kyrkeby, another witness in the suit.[34] Male witnesses provided evidence on the marriages of younger female relatives, with memories often focused on their central roles during marital negotiations in the absence of fathers and masters. In 1418, for example, John Carow remembered the marriage of his niece, which took place in his home, while Thomas Northeby recalled his own niece's union, in a case begun in 1430, from his journey to Scarborough in order to discuss her marriage prospects.[35] Marriages from within the wider kin group acted as recognition of married men's patriarchal authority over other dependent family members.

---

[32] BI CP.F.101.

[33] P. J. P. Goldberg, 'Migration, Youth and Gender in Later Medieval England', in P. J. P. Goldberg and F. Riddy, eds., *Youth in the Middle Ages* (York, 2004), pp. 85–99, at pp. 95–6; on the male and female life cycle in relation to adulthood, see D. Youngs, *The Life Cycle in Western Europe, c. 1300–1500* (Manchester, 2006), pp. 136–8.

[34] BI CP.F.89.

[35] BI CP.F.81; BI CP.F.113.

Marriage, Kinship, and Widowhood

The complex associations between gender and patriarchal power were encoded in these memories, emphasizing the transformative influence of marriage on male identities in particular. Marriage also formed a central strand of the local community's social memory, with married couples unifying the pasts of different kin groups. From the perspective of the Church, however, marriage performed two specific functions: first, the generation of offspring, following the commandment to multiply; and second, the control of concupiscence, with marriage regarded as a remedy for illicit desire.[36] In its most exemplary and ubiquitous form, marriage produced children whose birth and socialization generated new memorial cultures based on the union of two distinct lines of descent. Each line contained histories that accumulated over generations, with the married couple representing a new stage in its development.

FAMILY MEMORY, MARRIAGE, AND GENDER

The Church promoted marriage as the fulfilment of Christian adulthood for the majority of its followers. While valid contracts were regarded as sacramentally binding under canon law, a series of impediments allowed for marriages to be annulled in certain circumstances.[37] The need for mutual consent was recognised in suits claiming force and fear, for example, and the role of consummation in making a valid marriage was reflected in the impediment of spousal impotence. Other restrictions centred on the identity and condition of marriage partners, whether free or unfree, Christian, or in solemn vows. It was the set of rules relating to kinship, however, that shaped the marital decisions of laypeople most often in everyday life. Canon law identified three kinds of kinship that acted as barriers to valid marriage. The first of these was consanguinity in the form of restrictions upon marriage with extended family. The second type of kinship, known as affinity, forbade unions with the kin of those connected through sexual relations or marriage to the same number of degrees as applied for consanguinity. The final category of spiritual affinity focused on bonds established during baptism, prohibiting marriage between god-parents and the immediate family of their spiritual charge.[38]

Although the early Church was concerned with incest, the period from the tenth to the late twelfth centuries witnessed additional restrictions on the number of degrees within which marriages could be formed. One argument for the intensification of kinship rules relates to an ecclesiastical desire to breach the lay monopoly on landed estates through the censure of endogamous

---

[36] Wei, *Intellectual Culture*, pp. 250–1.

[37] For a comprehensive outline of impediments, see S. Worby, *Law and Kinship in Thirteenth-Century England* (Woodbridge, 2010), p. 10.

[38] Helmholz, *Marriage Litigation*, pp. 77–8; F. Pollock and F. W. Maitland, *History of English Law*, 2nd edition (Cambridge, 1968), vol. 2, p. 389.

marriage.[39] Roman law on inheritance also shaped the kinship rules which extended to the seventh degree of kinship.[40] The Church sought to promote social inclusion through exogamous marriages, a function expounded in the work of theologians such as the eleventh-century reformer Peter Damian.[41] Acknowledging the difficulty with which the laity remembered their ancestry, the Fourth Lateran Council of 1215 restricted the number of forbidden degrees from seven to four.[42] With the relaxation of kinship rules, a new expectation arose that deponents should render more accurate testimony rather than repeat hearsay.[43]

Marriage suits dealing with consanguinity and affinity underscored the structural and symbolic relationship between ancestry, memory, and kinship. Both male and female deponents testified in these sets of suits, highlighting the influence that gender exerted on these modes of remembrance. Evidence in these cases generated oral accounts of family histories that were expressed in genealogical form, and witnesses traced lines of descent from the couple in question. Laypeople were not unacquainted with genealogy as a way of organizing relations of kinship. The most familiar genealogy at the level of the parish was divine – the Tree of Jesse which recorded the descent of Christ. While earlier versions focused on the Virgin and Child, depictions of this sacred ancestry became increasingly patrilineal and traced a descent that was profoundly masculine.[44] From the eleventh and twelfth centuries onwards genealogy was also a popular form for the expression of structural and symbolic relations of kinship. For example, elite families commissioned genealogies to record the deeds of their ancestors, with histories of this kind solidifying into a recognizable genre by the close of the twelfth century.[45] Family histories reported in the church courts demonstrate the circulation of ancestries further down the social scale, among lower-status families in particular. These genealogies were intended to record not the descent of land,

---

[39] Brundage, *Law, Sex, and Christian Society*, p. 88; C. N. L. Brooke, *The Medieval Idea of Marriage* (Oxford, 1989), p. 135.

[40] J. Goody, *The Development of the Family and Marriage in Europe* (Cambridge, 1983), p. 137.

[41] D. L. d'Avray, 'Peter Damian, Consanguinity and Church Property', in L. M. Smith and B. Ward, eds., *Intellectual Life in the Middle Ages: Essays Presented to Margaret Gibson* (London, 1992), pp. 71–80, pp. 74–9.

[42] *Decrees*, ed. Tanner, p. 258.

[43] E. Champeaux, '*Jus sanguinis*: Trois façons de calculer la parenté au Moyen Age', *Revue historique de droit francais et étranger*, 4th series, 12 (1933), 241–90, at p. 254; d'Avray, *Medieval Marriage*, pp. 105–6.

[44] P. Sheingorn, 'Appropriating the Holy Kinship: Gender and Family History', in C. Neel, ed., *Medieval Families: Perspectives on Marriage, Household and Children* (Toronto, 2004), pp. 273–301.

[45] G. M. Spiegel, 'Genealogy: Form and Function in Medieval Historiography', *History and Theory*, 22 (1983), 43–53; Rosenthal, *Telling Tales*, pp. 63–94.

Marriage, Kinship, and Widowhood

but relations between kin, although suits involving minor gentry families did exhibit concerns over inheritance and property rights. In manors and villages, the peasantry at various levels were often acutely aware of their family histories. The personal status of villeins derived in part from their ancestry, which was occasionally expressed in oral genealogies committed to writing in legal disputes with manorial lords.[46] While these cases dealt primarily with the status and ancestry of one individual, the extent of these genealogies implies a developed sense of family history in peasant communities, as accounts incorporated distant ancestors alongside extended family. Memories of marriage and kinship were embedded in variegated ways of understanding family histories that reached beyond the framework of canon law alone.

Suits to enforce contracts far outnumbered actions to annul marriages in the church courts. Donahue examined the defences used in cases from York during the fourteenth and fifteenth centuries, noting that consanguinity and kinship were central concerns in 12 percent and 7 percent of marriage cases, respectively.[47] Helmholz argues that the paucity of cases relates to the respect with which kinship rules were observed.[48] Few marriages were made openly within forbidden degrees in circles below the aristocracy, since the papal penitentiary was not liberal in granting dispensations. It has been suggested that the gentry and aristocracy might not appear before the church courts since their marriages were already allowed through dispensations.[49] Parties drawn from the lower ranks of the gentry, however, appear in several suits from the late medieval court of York. The greater tendency amongst the nobility and gentry to marry their kin does not mean that such unions were common or undertaken lightly.[50] Laypeople at every social level interpreted rules of kinship so strictly that a union within these degrees could be resisted by one party, opposed by parents, or annulled at a later date. Yet these rules were not observed uniformly, particularly at their boundaries. In 1394, deponents in a case from the North Riding of Yorkshire described the kinship of a couple alleged to be related in the fourth and fifth degrees. Agnes

---

[46] H. Cam, 'Pedigrees of Villeins and Freemen in the Thirteenth Century', in H. Cam, ed., *Liberties and Communities in Medieval England: Collected Studies in Local Administration and Topography* (London, 1963), pp. 124–35; S. Worby, 'Kinship: Canon Law and the Common Law in Thirteenth-Century England', *Historical Research*, 80 (2007), 443–68.

[47] Helmholz, *Marriage Litigation*, p. 25; for these statistics, see Donahue, *Law, Marriage, and Society*, p. 71; for a summary of these statistics in the context of kinship, see Worby, *Law and Kinship*, pp. 93–4.

[48] Helmholz, *Marriage Litigation*, p. 79.

[49] Helmholz, *Marriage Litigation*, pp. 86–7.

[50] S. L. Waugh, *The Lordship of England: Royal Wardships and Marriages in English Society and Politics, 1217–1327* (Princeton, 1998), pp. 36–7, 61. Gentry families most often married their children into neighbouring families of comparable social status. E. Acheson, *A Gentry Community: Leicestershire in the Fifteenth Century, c. 1422–c. 1485* (Cambridge, 1992), pp. 156–8.

Popular Memory and Gender in Medieval England

Yonger, their kinswoman, told how William Botry had said 'freely that he would marry Anabel Blakeden if the grades of kinship did not hinder them'.[51] The pair had already conceived a child together and Agnes's witnesses testified to their marriage. Marriages within the forbidden degrees were regarded as especially problematic, and were entered into only rarely. Those within the forbidden degrees of affinity appear to have been slightly more common, with the result that affinity appears more often than consanguinity in suits to annul or prevent the enforcement of contracts.[52] From the perspective of the Church, though, marriages made within forbidden degrees of any kind were regarded as endangering the consciences of married couples.

The commemoration of ancestors and kin was also associated with the expiation of this kind of sin. In 1370, John de Estthorp, a parish chaplain, recalled that John and Katherine Hildyard offered to 'give six marks to this witness every year during his life so that this witness should celebrate Mass thenceforward for the souls of the father, mother, and ancestors of the abovesaid John Hildyard'.[53] The language of penitence and its importance in repairing ruptures in family memory was used to demonstrate the couple's knowledge of their kinship. Yet even spiritual affinity, established through god-parenthood, was regarded as an impediment to marriage due to the bonds of kinship it created. In a late fifteenth-century suit from York, the defendant married her mother's god-son, to which her mother was said to have responded 'thow filth and harlot, why hast art thow handfast wit John Wystow – when thy fadre knowys it he wylle dynge [beat] the and myscheve the'.[54] If this was a fictive defence raised to dissolve a marriage, it was at least regarded as a plausible response to a union made within forbidden degrees.

Rules on kinship were communicated widely through provincial and diocesan legislation to the parish clergy and the laity. In 1102 the Council of London reiterated earlier regulations on the impediment of kinship, emphasizing the number of degrees to which it applied. New rules on the detection of unions were included, too, stating that kinship ties within these degrees were to be publicised and reported before the contracts were made.[55] As previously noted, the relationship between marriage practices and kinship was also addressed in larger ecclesiastical councils. These rules were disseminated through formal constitutions that passed from the higher echelons of the Church to the diocesan and parish level, ultimately instructing laypeople on changes to marriage law. Much of the earlier legislation governing

---

[51] BI CP.E.210.

[52] Worby, *Law and Kinship*, pp. 102–3.

[53] BI CP.E.108. 'darent isti iurati singulis annis durante vita sua sex marcas sterlingorum dii tum iste iuratus imposterum celebraret pro animabus patris matris et parentum johannis hildyard supradicti'.

[54] BI CP.F.280.

[55] Sheehan, 'Marriage Theory and Practice', p. 120.

Marriage, Kinship, and Widowhood

consanguinity was directed specifically towards men, although these rules evidently applied to kin of both sexes. Herlihy, for instance, emphasises the 'virilocal' nature of marriage in the high Middle Ages in which 'incest rules … primarily affected the movement of women between households'.[56]

By the early thirteenth century, however, parish priests were the principal channel through which ideas on marriage and close kinship were communicated to male and female parishioners. Advice against incest appeared in Mirk's *Instructions*, one of the most popular manuals on pastoral care, which was composed in mnemonic rhyme.[57] The *Instructions* included sexual relationships between kin under the sin of lechery, and priests receiving confession were encouraged to extract details from their charges. Laymen were questioned on sexual sin, and asked 'whether hyt were wyf or may, sybbe or fremde that thow by lay; and yef ho were syb to the'.[58] Manuals in general aimed their advice at male parishioners, although short subsections occasionally dealt with the female laity in particular.[59] The *Instructions*, for instance, inquired about women's sexual relations with 'syb' only in brief, alongside other categories of men with whom they might sin.[60] The degree of kinship noted in the final question influenced the allocation of penance, and pointed to the range of premarital sexual relationships that had the potential to end in consanguineous marriages. A short treatise on consanguinity was also included in one copy of Mirk's *Instructions* between a section on baptism and another on marriage.[61] Secular literature similarly addressed sexual relationships in the nuclear family, yet these related to incest between close kin rather than endogamous marriage within prohibited degrees. One late medieval ballad, the *Sheath and the Knife*, recounts the incestuous bond between a brother and sister, culminating in a pregnancy that leads to the latter's death alongside their child.[62]

The prohibition on unions within degrees of spiritual affinity was circulated through *pastoralia* in brief moral tales that acted as shorthand for the complexities of canon law. Robert Mannyng's early fourteenth-century confession manual, *Handlyng Synne*, contained an *exemplum* which recounted the fate of a god-father who began a sexual relationship with his god-daughter during Easter week.[63] After this occurred, the god-father visited his parish church but

---

56 D. Herlihy, *Women, Family and Society in Medieval Europe: Historical Essays, 1978–1991*, ed. A. Molho (Providence, RI, and Oxford, 1995), p. 105.

57 For a brief summary of the manual's context, see Barr, *The Pastoral Care of Women*, p. 32.

58 *John Mirk's Instructions*, ed. Kristensson, pp. 138–9, lines 1239–42.

59 Barr, *The Pastoral Care of Women*, p. 67.

60 *John Mirk's Instructions*, ed. Kristensson, p. 77, lines 1289–92.

61 Oxford, Bodleian Library, MS Douce 60 (SC 21634), fol. 50.

62 *English and Scottish Popular Ballads*, ed. F. J. Child (Boston, 1869), vol. 1, no. 16.

63 *Robert of Brunne's Handlyng Synne*, ed. Furnivall, pp. 304–6, lines 9719–86.

Popular Memory and Gender in Medieval England

did not receive confession, presuming that his sins had been overlooked. The tale concludes with his death a week later, and a fire subsequently a fire begins in his grave and consumes his corpse. Canon-law teachings on kinship were communicated in this way through the parish clergy, who in turn educated laypeople about these rules on a regular basis.

Judicial processes and the application of canon law shaped the way in which kinship was constructed in legal evidence to a greater extent than the cultural tropes prevalent in *pastoralia*. The focus of these suits, for instance, meant that the only relations of kinship examined were those between the conjugal couple. Following the redefinition of forbidden degrees in 1215, relatives who were named in suits before this date would no longer be included. Beyond the influence of canon law, the intervention of clerical scribes played a part in the format that memories of kinship assumed in testimony. Examiners questioned deponents on the alleged degree of kinship between the couple, generating sets of ancestries which the scribe recorded. The interrogatories used to question deponents fashioned their memories into narrative genealogies, a process of textualisation that transformed memories of ancestry into a stable written format. The standardized structure of the ancestries, providing evidence only on the alleged family relationship, suggests that the scribe reshaped these oral accounts. The genealogical tree as a representation of the family, for instance, was disrupted when deponents were asked about their personal knowledge of the relatives named in their accounts. Men and women usually supplied the names of several family members they had seen and known, who tended to be drawn from their own line or from the kin group of the party for whom they deposed. Although intended to substantiate the witness's report of the genealogy, a lack of knowledge of the other branch instead reinforced the structural difference between the lines.

Genealogies were occasionally verified with reference to the couple's shared ancestor. Canonists, such as Hostiensis, stated that deponents were expected to know the predecessor whom parties held in common, including their name or alias.[64] In 1476, Margery Goldesmyth remembered that the common ancestor of the parties in dispute, Sir John Booth, was also known as 'Jenkin Booth' 'to the end of his life'.[65] Sir John Booth fathered two future archbishops of York, William and Lawrence Booth, whose influence on the fifteenth-century Church was profound, particularly in the episcopal seat of York where the legal suit was heard.[66] When John Smelt, aged 'more than one hundred

---

[64] Hostiensis, *Lectura in Decretales (in primum ... librum decretalium commentaria)* (Venice, 1581; repr. Turin, 1965), X.2.20.47; see also Helmholz, *Marriage Litigation*, p. 83, and d'Avray, *Medieval Marriage*, p. 108.

[65] BI CP.F.257. 'alias ut terminis eorum vitam Jenkyn Booth'.

[66] A. C. Reeves, 'Lawrence Booth: Bishop of Durham (1457–76), Archbishop of York (1476–80)', in S. D. Michalove and A. C. Reeves, eds., *Estrangement, Enterprise and Education in Fifteenth-century England* (Stroud, 1998), pp. 63–88.

Marriage, Kinship, and Widowhood

years', was examined in 1462, he deposed that he had known John and Jak Kyghley, from whom the parties descended, more than eighty years ago. John described the pair as 'brothers in life as in death', alluding to a bond that was both fraternal and affective throughout their lifetime. The limits of generational memory were perceptible in some suits through a lack of knowledge of the common ancestor. Although he claimed to be familiar with the elderly brothers almost a century before, John Smelt noted that 'he did not see their father because John and Jak Kyghley were old men at this point and they had died seventy years before'.[67] Regardless of the canon-law requirement to name a shared ancestor, then, a family's origins could be lost or confused. In a case initiated in 1370, the absence of a common forebear from whom the couple descended led to the reconstruction and invention of the family's past. Richard Hildyard deposed that the ancestor 'was born in that part of the country called Essex', but could not identify the area. John Hildyard was unable to name the ancestor, but believed that he was born and had resided in 'South Essex' or Essex, while John de Sprottelay identified the village as 'Hildyard'. There were disparities, however, in the accounts that circulated about the Hildyard family in the local community. Another witness claimed to have heard from the couple at the centre of the suit that their common ancestor was 'born in the area of Holderness and was accustomed to live in the vill of Riston in Holderness'.[68] The two sons could have moved from their natal village in Essex to Holderness since migration was common enough in the thirteenth century.[69] Despite the absence of an agreed ancestry, the Hildyard family developed several origin myths that intersected with social patterns, such as migration and the use of toponymic surnames. While these explanations were probably apocryphal, the family remained uncertain where they came from, a lacuna in their history that became increasingly problematic as they accrued more lands and experienced an elevation in social and economic status.

The behaviour associated with kinship represented another form of proof, with deponents questioned not only on the identity of relatives and spiritual kin, but also on the nature of relationships within families. This interest in the habits and actions of kin derived from canon law. In his *Summa Aurea*, Hostiensis instructed that witnesses should state 'whether they had seen any of the persons whose degrees they had counted behaving as relatives'.[70]

---

[67] BI. CP.F.202. 'patrem eorum non vidit quia adtinus isti iidem Johannes et Jak Kyghley senes erant et moriebantur ad lxx annos ultimos elapsis'.

[68] BI CP.E.108. Richard Hildyard: 'ille stipes procreatus fuit in illa patria que dicitur Estsex'; John Hildyard: 'quod procreatus et natus in comitatu Southsexie vel Exsexie et ibidem morari communis consuevit prout audivit a suis senioribus dici'; John de Veer: 'natus fuit in partibus Holderness et in villa de Ryston in Holderness communis morari consuerit'.

[69] N. J. Miller, *Winestead and its Lords: A History of a Holderness Village* (Hull, 1933), pp. 74–5.

[70] Hostiensis, *Summa Aurea* (Venice, 1574), X.2.20.47. 'Duodecim, utrum viderint aliquas

Popular Memory and Gender in Medieval England

The majority of deponents answered that all the individuals named in their statement acted as relatives, although a smaller number framed their recollections in more expansive terms. In 1292, witnesses testified that two ancestors, Mariota and Alice, were sisters 'from public fame and the way they greeted each other'.[71] Another deponent, Matilda, wife of John Marescalle, provided the names of the sisters' parents, who were her grandparents and raised her for twelve years before their deaths. Memories of affection were used to prove the existence of kinship and affinity. In one suit from the diocese of Chichester in 1200, the mother of a child noted that his god-mother lifted her son from the sacred font and gave a gift in his name, and as the child grew older he 'always greeted her as god-mother, with a kiss'.[72] Close kinship between the pair was embodied in the kiss, which strengthened the association between spiritual and blood kin, and rendered their emotional bond distinct from those outside the kin group. The reliance on behaviour rather than mere statement of affinity or the blood tie indicates the extent to which cultural perceptions of conduct supplemented formal law. Memories such as these indicate how families and affines were supposed to behave in social practice, as well as the kinds of proof that would be accepted under canon law.

Evidence of kinship revolved around other more official types of behaviour that endowed families with identities that could appear more tangible under the law. In 1337 witnesses in a marriage case were asked how they knew that the Lascy family 'regarded themselves as relatives and acted as kin do'. This was common knowledge in the local area, according to their testimony, and several witnesses produced concrete examples. Margaret de Cloghton remembered that:

> a certain disagreement came about between some of the family of the lord of Newbiggin and those from the aforesaid kin. An agreement was reached between them at Brigholm in the manor of the lord of Brigholm where this witness saw the aforesaid family of Lascy act together on one side, just like relatives.[73]

Neither the nature of the dispute nor its mode of resolution was specified, but the reference to an 'agreement' rather than a legal action suggests their reliance on informal arbitration. The encounter referred to routine activities

---

de personis graduum quos computant pro consanguineis se habere'.

[71] CCA E.S. Roll 69; *Select Cases*, p. 360. John de Gildford: 'scivit fama referente et illis predictis mutuo se salutantibus adinvicem'.

[72] CCA SVSB II, p. 51. *Select Cases*, pp. 29–30. 'eam ut commatrem semper in osculo salutavit'.

[73] BI CP.E.33. 'quondam discordia fuerat mota inter aliquis de familia domini de Neubiggins et illos de consanguinitate predicta et concordia fuerat facta inter eos apud Brigholm in manerio domini de Brigholm ubi ipsa iurata vidit quod predicta de consanguinitate de Lascy simul tenuerunt ex una parte tanquam consanguinei'.

Marriage, Kinship, and Widowhood

involving kin groups that occurred at the margins of the law yet were not recorded in written legal memory. In terms of the family's own ancestral memory, the relationship articulated in Margaret's evidence was expressed by uniting both branches of the family and eliding bilateral bonds of kinship into one cohesive line.

The choice of deponent also influenced the construction of family memory. In the majority of cases, parties selected witnesses to outline their ancestries in order to prove or refute bonds of kinship. Treatises on canon law dealt with methods of proof, detailing rules on the production of deponents and occasionally limiting or excluding testimony from particular individuals or groups. The imperfect application of these rules in England, alongside seemingly infinite allowances, meant that those excluded in theory could sometimes testify in practice.[74] While Gratian's *Decretum* on one occasion prohibits family members, another canon states that 'moreover parents, brothers, and relatives of both sexes should be admitted to testify to a marriage of their relatives either to unite or separate them'. Members of the same kin group could be seen as particularly motivated to uncover their own family history. The *Decretum* further notes 'for that reason, parents especially and, if parents are wanting, the closest relatives are admitted because each one strives to know their genealogy with witnesses and documents, as well as from the testimony of their elders'.[75] Relatives were thus permitted to testify about their ancestries, although positions and articles were used to identify which witnesses were household members and kin. So, for example, four of the ten men produced on the side of Peter Hildyard in 1370 were family members: two uncles and two brothers.[76]

Gender exerted a central influence on the selection of witnesses in cases that concerned kinship. James Brundage notes that the position of women as 'repositories of genealogical lore' accorded female knowledge on matters of kinship more value.[77] The association of women with the oral transmission of family memory did not translate into a sustained preference for female rather than male testimony. The gender balance was uneven in matrimonial cases more generally, as Goldberg has calculated, with men selected as witnesses more often than women, especially in rural areas, to the ratio of around 3:1.[78]

---

[74] Donahue, 'Proof by Witnesses', p. 143.

[75] C. 35 q. 6 c. 2; 'Quod autem parentes, fratres et cognati utriusque sexus in testificationem suorum ad matrimonium coniungendum vel dirimendum admittantur, tam antiqua consuetudine quam legibus approbatur. Ideo enim maxime parentes, et, si defuerint parentes, proximiores admittuntur, quoniam unusquis que suam genealogiam cum testibus et chartis, tum etiam ex recitatione maiorum scire laborat'. For a reference to this canon, see Brundage, 'Juridical Space', p. 149 n. 18.

[76] BI CP.E.108.

[77] Brundage, 'Juridical Space', p. 151.

[78] Goldberg, 'Gender and Matrimonial Litigation', p. 46.

Popular Memory and Gender in Medieval England

This pattern appears to have been more marked in suits that related specifically to the longer histories of marriages and ancestries. A small number of cases, particularly those brought *ex officio*, saw groups of local residents appointed to conduct an inquisition into marriages where a child's legitimacy or a couple's ancestry were under scrutiny. These panels tended to be male in composition, and made up of 'trustworthy men' or the 'nearest relatives' of the parties.[79] All forty witnesses who reported as part of an inquiry into bastardy in 1294 were male, for example.[80] The choice of deponent in this case was contingent partly upon seniority, a relevant detail since the marriage was said to have occurred at least sixty years earlier and the couple had since died. Although only seven of the men were aged under forty, none of the older witnesses claimed attendance at the wedding, focusing instead on local knowledge of the marriage during the couple's lifetime and after their deaths. In another thirteenth-century case from the court of Canterbury, jurors were selected and 'sworn to inquire about the marriage' between Stephen de Bello and one Agnes. The inquisition concluded with the statement that 'the entire neigh-bourhood testifies to this, and it is well known to all'.[81] Evidence in these cases depended on local opinion as much as personal memory, with jurors apparently conducting inquiries in the wider community. This preference for male testimony resembles patterns in disputes over tithes and parish rights where men were chosen to articulate the social memory of the community. As with tithe cases, though, there were exceptions to the selection of male witnesses. While only four of the thirteen jurors in the inquiry into Agnes and Stephen's marriage were female, two of these women offered statements alongside the other male jurors. The presence of women in this group admitted both male and female versions of the past, reflecting more accurately the composition of local memory. Female jurors may have been enlisted in this instance due to the nature of the case, which centred on spiritual affinity, and both women gave testimony on the child's baptism, with one deposing as his god-mother.

Male deponents were also preferred in instance cases concerning kinship where panels of jurors were eschewed in favour of witness statements. Cases of this kind focused on family histories rather than the making of marriages themselves, producing chronologies that spanned several generations. Like inquiries with jurors, many of these suits relied on the testimony of older men

---

[79] For the reference to 'fidedignis', see CCA SVSB III, no. 124; the use of 'proximiores consanguinitati eorum' appears in CCA SVSB III, no. 129. For a further discussion of such cases, see Helmholz, *Marriage Litigation*, p. 82; for examples of 'trustworthy men' providing sworn evidence during the investigation of marriages, see Forrest, *Trustworthy Men*, pp. 124–5.

[80] CCA, E.S. Rolls 80, 184, 230 and 231.

[81] CCA SVSB II, p. 51; *Select Cases*, p. 29. 'Nomina iuratorum inquirendum de conjugio inter St. de Bello et Agnetem uxorem eius'; 'Idem attestatur tota vicinia et est omnibus notissimum'.

Marriage, Kinship, and Widowhood

who may have been drawn from neighbouring areas and families. In 1476, six witnesses in one suit were male, with only one woman providing evidence.[82] Five elderly inhabitants of the village of Apple Trewick testified in 1461 on the alleged consanguinity of Robert Kyghley and Isabel, daughter of Henry Yonge, both of the same village.[83] Gentry litigants employed female witnesses less often than parties of lower social status. Suits involving families from the lesser gentry, such as Hoghton *c.* Shirburn in 1451 and Townley *c.* Talbot in 1476, each employed only one female deponent, who testified on behalf of the female party.[84] This pattern emerges in cases limited to the area of ancestry, as well as those that examined kinship when inheritance was the underlying issue.

While there was a general preference for male testimony in these suits, women were occasionally selected to provide evidence. In the suit from Apple Trewick, the second-eldest witness was Margaret Hall, a widow more than eighty years old.[85] As the exception in an otherwise male group, Margaret's seniority and her marital status afforded her greater authority than younger women, and perhaps younger men, in the area. She thus testified as one of the oldest inhabitants with knowledge of the couple's ancestry. Although memories of kinship were frequently depicted as 'common fame', male witnesses often relied on reports from elderly locals, referred to as *senioribus*, whose gender was not recorded. Instances where deponents recalled discussions with mothers and aunts implies that these groups comprised both older men and women of the village. Younger women also testified in disputes over kinship. Two of the four deponents in a mid-fourteenth-century case from Doncaster were women, aged forty and forty-seven.[86] In 1476, Margery Goldesmyth, aged thirty-seven, was the only woman in a group of six witnesses and offered the most detailed evidence on the family's ancestry.[87] Married women deposed alongside their husbands on matters of kinship. In a late fourteenth-century suit from York, Agnes Yonger testified before her husband, with his evidence summarised and described as concurring with his wife's.[88] In this case, the examiner privileged female knowledge of ancestry notwithstanding the marital bond between the two witnesses. Despite the legal shift that women encountered upon marriage, the inversion of this descriptor alludes to the way in which female memory could mediate the force of patriarchal authority in social practice and under the law.

---

[82] BI CP.F.257.

[83] BI CP.F.202; see also Helmholz, *Marriage Litigation*, p. 83.

[84] BI CP.F.187; BI CP.F.257.

[85] BI CP.F.202.

[86] BI CP.E.69.

[87] BI CP.F.257.

[88] BI CP.E.210. 'Johannes Yonger maritus Agnetis Yonger … item idem requisitus de secundo et tercio articulis dicit breviter quod nescit deponere'.

Popular Memory and Gender in Medieval England

Gender influenced the genealogical structure of family memory itself, shaping ancestries and memories of kin in a variety of ways. Although genealogies followed particular lines of descent by necessity, these were articulated through language that carried assumptions about the gendered relations of kinship and generative agency. Deponents identified different family networks in ancestries, with genealogies often focused on kin of the same gender. In 1351, Peter le Bogher identified Sir John de Doncaster in his ancestry, despite the latter not forming part of the primary line of descent. Peter was also the only deponent who remembered that Stephen, Ellota's son and John de Doncaster's brother, was later killed in Doncaster.[89] Generational differences, as much as gender identification, may have motivated the inclusion of these additional details; Peter was sixty at his deposition and much closer in age to John and Stephen de Doncaster than the other witnesses. Female testimony similarly traced descent through other women more often than male relatives, a pattern more common among witnesses from non-elite backgrounds. In the same suit from 1351, the women who testified placed greater emphasis on female lines of descent.[90] Agnes Pykburn, for instance, structured her account of the family's history around a self-contained female network. Agnes, wife of William de Sprotburgh, included her own relationship to Joan, who was her grandmother. Women organised accounts of kinship around female relatives more often than male witnesses, with wives outside the line of descent included more often than husbands. Oral ancestries from non-elite women thus qualify the argument that genealogies became increasingly agnatic and patrilineal from the high Middle Ages.[91]

In contrast, the majority of male deponents downplayed the structural importance of wives in family descent, while others omitted them entirely. Female family members were often represented as adjuncts to their own genealogy, referenced through their relationships with male kin. In his genealogy of the Doncaster family Peter le Bogher identified Ellota, one of two descendants from the common ancestor, through her relationship with her husband and son, describing her as the wife of Adam Fykays and the mother of Sir John de Doncaster, knight.[92] The oral transmission of ancestries meant that same-sex ancestries could influence the evidence of other deponents. In the same case, Agnes, wife of William de Sprotburgh, named Peter le Bogher as one of the sources of her genealogical knowledge, since he had explained her grandfather's relationship to the other branch of the family. Agnes recounted Peter's description of these male ties, but this followed the main genealogy in a separate family tree. Female kin functioned

[89] BI CP.E.69. 'fuit interfectus in villa de Doncaster'.
[90] BI CP.E.69.
[91] G. Duby, 'Lineage, Nobility and Knighthood: The Mâconnais in the Twelfth Century – A Revision', in Duby, *The Chivalrous Society*, trans. C. Postan (London, 1977), pp. 59–80.
[92] BI CP.E.69.

Marriage, Kinship, and Widowhood

as 'grafts' elsewhere in medieval society, particularly in secular genealogies among social elites where they often acted as 'agent[s] of transmission'.[93] The mother's inclusion in the family tree was often seen to dilute the filial relationship between father and son; her exclusion ensured that their 'natural' kinship remained absolute.[94] Genealogies produced in cases with higher-status parties excluded wives more frequently than ancestries from non-elite families. The concern with land rights in these suits implies that common-law practices such as primogeniture and entail may have influenced the function and form of ancestries.[95] The exclusion of women from family histories such as these did not necessarily indicate a conscious preoccupation with patri-lineal genealogy. Rather these male-dominated lines of descent may reflect concerns with descent of land, compounded by socio-cultural norms which led parties of both genders to rely on male rather than female witnesses.

Where conjugal couples appeared in ancestries, male deponents usually assigned generative agency to the husband rather than the wife, even where the former had married into the family. The ascription of active sexual roles to men and the depiction of women in passive terms reflected normative perceptions of gender relations in medieval culture. In 1462, for instance, John Smelt testified on the kinship of two parties, outlining their paternal ancestry without reference to the male ancestors' wives. The only marriage described in the genealogy was that of Emmota Kyghley, the sole female ancestor, but generative agency was given to her husband John, who 'begat from Emma a son named Henry'.[96] While this dichotomy was more variable in social practice, it operated in tandem with a patrilineal kinship system to produce oral accounts that emphasized the centrality of male kin. This pattern was particularly marked among the gentry and male deponents in general, and in these instances female family members were consigned to the margins of genealogies. Alternative ancestries appeared in women's testimony where the generative agency of wives and mothers was emphasized through the language of birth. In the case from 1351, Agnes Pykburn named the grandfather of one party, but ascribed procreative power, and not simply the line of descent, to the grandmother, Joan, from whom Matilda, her daughter, was born.[97] Yet the matrilineal transmission of ancestry could occur beyond female networks

---

[93] Z. Stahuljak, *Bloodless Genealogies of the French Middle Ages: Translatio, Kinship and Metaphor* (Gainesville, FL, 2005), p. 118; C. Klapisch-Zuber, *Women, Family and Ritual in Renaissance Italy*, trans. L. Cochrane (Chicago and London, 1985), p. 118.

[94] Stahuljak, *Bloodless Genealogies*, pp. 138, 141; see also C. Klapisch-Zuber, *L'Ombre des ancêtres: Essai sur l'imaginaire médiéval de la parenté* (Paris, 2000).

[95] J. Biancalana, *The Fee Tail and the Common Recovery in Medieval England, 1176–1502* (Cambridge, 2002).

[96] BI CP.E.202. 'ex qua Emmota dictus Johannes Yonge procreavit unum filium vocatum Henricum Yonge'.

[97] BI CP.E.69.

Popular Memory and Gender in Medieval England

in evidence from male witnesses. In 1337, all four deponents, three female and one male, followed the descent of both branches of the family through the female line.[98] The only male deponent in this suit, Robert de Thweng, also deposed that 'from Joan came her daughter Elizabeth, and from the said Elizabeth came Joan, daughter of Peter'.[99] Although identified as the daughter of Peter de Acclum, Joan was nevertheless described as born from Elizabeth, with her father accorded no procreative responsibility for her birth.

One of the most prevalent genealogies that was likely to have shaped women's accounts of maternal descent was the 'peperit' prayer used during childbirth to aid delivery.[100] Usually written in simple Latin, the number of different versions, as well as instructions given in the vernacular, suggest their oral use. The repetition of phrases such as 'Maria genuit Christum' reinforced the generative bond between mother and child. Such prayers and charms could circulate outside elite groups where literacy, in Latin or the vernacular, was more common. In 1365, Anabilla Pynder recalled that late in her pregnancy a local gentry woman, herself recently churched, sent her 'some writing that was said to be good for pregnant women'.[101] Described only as free in status, Anabilla's surname suggests a familial association with the office of 'pinder', members of the middling peasantry in charge of the village pound.[102] Whether or not expectant mothers could read, birth charms and prayers were used for their talismanic properties, tied to the stomach during labour or recited with varying degrees of comprehension. Charms and prayers used for medicinal purposes tended to rely on internal motifs that acted as a mnemonic in order to aid their remembrance.[103] Their circulation indicates that collective practices surrounding birth could transcend social status and perhaps influence non-elite women's attitudes towards descent.

Ancestries that emphasised same-sex kin underscored the predominantly oral culture that sustained memories of kinship in everyday life. The Fourth Lateran Council had prohibited the use of hearsay evidence in marriage cases, favouring first-hand knowledge of common ancestry instead. Despite this change in canon law, witnesses still relied on the oral testimony of others to imbue memories with greater authority and to explain their source. The wider significance of local opinion in other ecclesiastical suits, and in marriage cases

---

[98] BI CP.E.33.

[99] BI CP.E.33. 'Ex alio vero latere videlicet de Johanna processit Elizabet filia sua carnale de dicta Elizabet processit Johanna filia Petri'.

[100] M. Elsakkers, '"In pain you shall bear children" [Gen. 3:16]: Medieval Prayers for a Safe Delivery', in A. Korte, ed., *Women and Miracle Stories: A Multidisciplinary Exploration* (Leiden, 2001), pp. 179–209, at p. 194.

[101] BI CP.E.89. 'unum brevem quod ut dicebatur fuit bonum pro impregnantibus'.

[102] P. L. Larson, *Conflict and Compromise in the Late Medieval Countryside: Lords and Peasants in Durham, 1349–1400* (New York, 2006), p. 61.

[103] L. T. Olsan, 'Charms in Medieval Memory', in J. Roper, ed., *Charms and Charming in Europe* (Basingstoke, 2004), pp. 62–3.

Marriage, Kinship, and Widowhood

where 'common fame' was invoked, may have underpinned its continued use. Ancestries were discussed on many occasions, at family gatherings and in personal conversations between neighbours. Deponents often relied on the testimony of faithful neighbours, termed *fidedigni*, but others depended on groups that were more clearly identified as male, comprised of 'good, truthful and honest men'.[104] Despite the emphasis on the word of 'honest men', the memories of female neighbours and relatives were included in a number of cases, even in suits where only male deponents testified. Young men also discussed their family's pasts with older female relatives, which produced a more representative version of the kin group's memory. In 1292, for instance, John le Ferrur deposed that he learned his ancestry from his mother, and 'talked often with Alice de Thorley in his youth, as with his mother's aunt'.[105] Memories of kinship drew on a wide range of sources from family and neighbours of both genders. For example, in the case from Doncaster, Agnes, wife of William de Sprotburgh, deposed that she had heard part of her family's history from her parents, two of her fellow witnesses, and 'many other elderly men and women of the vill of Doncaster, now deceased'.[106] The social standing of these groups was also emphasised to endow their word with additional authority. In 1476, George de Manchester deposed that he had heard of the kinship between the parties 'from Sir Thomas Pylkyngton, knight, Roger Pylkyngton and some others then in the vill of Lancaster at the time of the session last held in the same place in Sawly, Clitheroe, and other villages and surrounding places'.[107] The significance of social standing was exemplified not only in the noble status of witnesses and their friends, but also through associations with local governance and the enforcement of justice.

The oral form of ancestries reported in testimony contributed to their malleable nature, yet memories of kinship could be committed to writing in the course of judicial processes. Despite the existence of pragmatic literacy among the peasantry and labouring groups, the ability to read and write was more common among the clergy and social elites. The production of written documents relating to marriage thus occurred more commonly among the nobility and gentry. This section of society demonstrated greater concerns with ancestry as a form of self-representation and memorialisation, while also seeking *ex post facto* dispensations from the Church for marriages to kin

---

104 BI CP.F.187. 'aliis viris bonis veris et honeste'; Forrest, *Trustworthy Men*, pp. 100–2, 186–7.

105 CCA E.S. Roll 69; *Select Cases*, p. 363. 'quia frequencius in iuventute sua conversabatur cum … Alicia de Thorley tamquam cum amita matris sue'.

106 BI CP.E.69. 'aliis pluribus senioribus hominibus et mulieribus ville de Doncaster defunctis et de Petro le Bogher adhuc superstite'.

107 BI CP.F.257. 'a domino Thome Pylkyngton milite Rogero Pilkyngton et nonnullis aliis tam in villa Lancastr tempore cessionis ibidem ultimo tente quid in villa de Sawlay Clytherow ac aliis villis et locis circumvicinis'.

Popular Memory and Gender in Medieval England

in larger numbers than their non-elite neighbours.[108] In the case initiated in 1370, Katherine Hildyard's stepson sought to establish proof that she and his father had sent a priest to Rome, albeit in vain, for a dispensation to allow their marriage within forbidden degrees of kinship. John de Neuton, a public notary, testified that he saw a document recording the relationship between the couple, which he also described to the court.[109] A writ was sent from the *ex officio* personnel, and was included in the apparatus of the dispute, in reply to a request for information about the couple's marriage. The *ex officio* personnel inspected the rolls and registers relating to the year 1367 for information about John Hildyard, as well as any appearances before the archbishop. The archival search showed that John had been cited, but had not appeared on those occasions. Written records held in official archives could supplement lay memories of marriage when incorporated alongside oral testimony, but were not regarded as definitive proof despite their fixed nature.

Though gentry families commissioned and consumed written works that were imbued with genealogical concerns, relations of kinship were only rarely identified in testimony using the term 'genealogy'.[110] References of this kind were uncommon in general across the social strata, but gentry families demonstrated a greater familiarity with this genre, in comparison to non-elite ways of charting descent that were more reliant on oral memory. In 1451, for instance, during the course of a suit that involved gentry litigants and witnesses, Christopher Saylbury described the family relationship between the married couple as a 'genealogy'.[111] Christopher also stated that he learned of the couple's kinship from the report of 'Geoffrey Whalley, Richard Whalley [and] Thomas Syngleton of the parish of Preston, who better knew the genealogy and ancestry of the same'.[112] Despite the written format of many ancestries in this milieu, the family history to which Christopher referred was still preserved, at least in part, through speech networks. Oral memory continued to act as a conduit for memories of kinship even where literacy was more widespread.

Social hierarchies influenced discourses and practices relating to family memory in other ways too, most notably through the inclusion of kin beyond the primary lines of descent. Foucault observed that genealogy as a system of inquiry displayed both presence and absence, a dynamic evident in ancestries reported in church-court testimony.[113] Genealogies were a selective form

---

[108] BI CP.E.108. Helmholz, *Marriage Litigation*, pp. 85–7.

[109] BI CP.E.108.

[110] Radulescu, 'Literature', p. 113.

[111] BI CP.F.187.

[112] BI CP.F.187. 'Galfridi Whalley Ricardi Whalley Thome Syngleton de parochia de Preston qui melius sciverunt genelogiam et parentelam eorumdem'.

[113] M. Foucault, 'Nietzsche, Genealogy, History', in P. Rabinow, ed., *The Foucault Reader* (New York, 1984), pp. 76–100, at p. 76.

Marriage, Kinship, and Widowhood

of representation, since neither canon law nor the church courts required a comprehensive ancestry from witnesses. Despite the judicial focus on specific bonds of kinship, deponents occasionally included relatives whose presence augmented the family line. Gender determined the pattern of these additions as adjuncts to the main line of descent, the majority of whom were male, with daughters and sisters mentioned only where they contributed directly to the parties' kinship. In 1351, for example, two of four deponents remembered Sir John de Doncaster in their ancestries, although his presence was recorded outside the line of descent.[114] In 1476, Margery Goldesmyth was the only relative to include Lawrence Booth, archbishop of York, in her family's ancestry, despite his illegitimate birth and position outside the line of ancestry.[115] Outranked only by the archbishop of Canterbury in the hierarchy of the national Church, Booth was enthroned the same year the suit was initiated. Booth's inclusion also alluded to the extensive patronage network that he fostered in the decades before his appointment to the archiepiscopal see, perhaps attracting the interest of the clerical scribe who recorded the bond of kinship.[116] Additions to the main line of descent underline the ways in which ancestries functioned as 'mnemonics of social relationships', embodying the social memory of kin groups at specific moments in time.[117] The pragmatic genealogies embedded in testimony provide glimpses of ancestries that were generated against a legal backdrop to suit present needs.[118] Gender was evidently an integral and creative force in the articulation of memories of kinship across the social strata.

FAMILY MEMORY AND WIDOWHOOD

Socialised to care for the sick and dying and to pray for their souls, women and widows in medieval culture had long been regarded as memory specialists in the remembrance of the family's dead. The memorial role of married women intensified upon the death of a spouse. This shift in responsibility and cultural perception was more marked higher up the social scale, partly due to the need to disperse larger amounts of chattels and landed goods after spousal death. Despite such associations between female kin and memory practices, the commemorative responsibilities of women were perhaps challenged in the

---

[114] BI CP.E.69.

[115] BI CP.F.257.

[116] Reeves, 'Lawrence Booth', p. 84.

[117] J. Goody, ed., *Literacy in Traditional Societies* (Cambridge, 1968), pp. 32–3.

[118] This use of the term 'pragmatic' borrows its context from M. B. Parkes's notion of 'pragmatic literacy'. M. B. Parkes, 'The Literacy of the Laity', in M. B. Parkes, *Scribes, Scripts and Readers: Studies in the Communication, Presentation and Dissemination of Medieval Texts* (London, 1991), pp. 275–97, at pp. 278–9; see also R. H. Britnell, ed., *Pragmatic Literacy, East and West, 1200–1300* (Woodbridge, 1997).

Popular Memory and Gender in Medieval England

twelfth century when monasteries developed new archival mechanisms for the memorialisation of the dead.[119] Yet the relationship between monastic institutions and the laity in general was also marked by cooperation, with 'particular tasks set aside for men and women'.[120] Formal duties were occasionally assigned to other members of the kin group in this milieu, but widows could still seek to ensure that commemoration was enacted to their satisfaction. In 1471, for example, Margaret Paston wrote to her son John about the delay in providing a monument for his late father's grave, emphasising the public censure that surrounded its continued absence.[121]

Aside from concerns about commemoration, bereavement generated grief as well as reflection on the family's emotional history. The marriages of deceased relatives could become sites for a range of anxieties, embodying a nexus of personal and collective concerns related to the family's past and its perceived future. Such conflicts were often manifest in the wake of funerals and in response to the need for commemoration of the dead, and relationships on occasion deteriorated to the extent that only the law could resolve them. Property and material goods were interwoven with family memory and the preservation of the family line. In this context, the dispersal of household goods and land acted as a centripetal force, which encouraged the articulation of tensions between widows and their marital kin. The transfer of land after death came under the jurisdiction of the common law, but the ecclesiastical courts tended to deal with cases involving the recovery of chattels and other goods.[122] These issues could underpin both marriage cases concerning the validity of a couple's union and testamentary suits that touched more overtly on ownership of goods.

Personal items acted as everyday memory objects across the social strata and material goods were central to the maintenance and communication of many family histories.[123] There were socio-economic differences in how items were transferred to younger generations after death, which in turn shaped the material residue of family and parental memory. The prevalence of debts, money, and fine metal vessels in disputes over testaments, and the relative absence of lower-value chattels from these suits, imbue the goods of the peasantry and labourers with an ephemeral quality. Yet non-elite families owned a range of possessions with multiple functions and worth varying amounts depending on their prosperity. These items and tools related to domestic labour, farming, and other types of work, but there is some evidence of expenditure on textiles and pottery from the fourteenth century onwards.

---

[119] Geary, *Phantoms of Remembrance*, pp. 52–73; Jussen, 'Challenging the Culture of Memoria', pp. 229–30.

[120] van Houts, *Memory and Gender*, p. 14.

[121] Archer and Ferme, 'Testamentary Procedure', p. 14.

[122] Archer and Ferme, 'Testamentary Procedure', p. 15.

[123] van Houts, *Memory and Gender*, p. 93.

Marriage, Kinship, and Widowhood

Objects showed signs of wear and, as Christopher Dyer observes, peasant goods were 'kept in use as long as possible, so that inventories often describe items as old, worn or broken'.[124] Maintenance agreements that older men and women arranged with adult children, kin, and younger inhabitants of their communities emphasise the transition of objects and goods between generations.[125] Household items and tools at this social level were more often bequeathed or conferred upon children, acquiring physical traces of regular use and occasional repair as they passed through the hands of different owners.

In mercantile and gentry families, emotional tensions informed the tone of disputes over goods, with the perceived nature of relationships influencing concerns about the value and possession of these items. In a late thirteenth-century suit, Emma de Honilane, a remarried widow of a London merchant, defended herself against claims from her stepchildren's executors. The latter's argument focused on goods including clothing and jewellery which the children's mother, described as their father's 'faithful' wife, had bequeathed to them.[126] The language of fidelity and conjugality emphasised perceived differences in the function of the mother, casting the stepmother's role as transitory in relation to the wider family. In this context, Emma was depicted as undermining her stepchildren's attempts to remember their mother, and by extension their late father, through the family's material goods.

Conflict could arise in relation to objects that families held in particular regard higher up the social hierarchy, especially following the death of a relative or spouse. In 1382, Margaret, widow of Richard del Sandes, from the diocese of Carlisle, pursued her claim to possessions that her husband had bequeathed to her in a testamentary case against Richard's kinsman, Thomas del Sandes.[127] She alleged that Thomas obstructed her duties as co-executor, while William de Derham claimed that Thomas's efforts to hinder her administration were common knowledge in the city of Carlisle. In many contexts, widows could continue to hold and control their late husband's goods after the testament had been discharged but, despite Margaret's role as executrix, she had little control over the allocation of her late husband's goods. William de Derham testified to the executors' disposal of much of the couple's property, including 'various animals and household utensils'.[128]

---

[124] C. Dyer, *Standards of Living in the Later Middle Ages: Social Change in England, c. 1200–1520*, revised edition (Cambridge, 1998), pp. 169–75, quote at p. 174.

[125] On maintenance in old age, see E. Clark, 'Some Aspects of Social Security in Medieval England', *Journal of Family History*, 7 (1982), 307–20; E. Clark, 'Social Welfare and Mutual Aid in the Medieval Countryside', *Journal of British Studies*, 33 (1994), 381–406.

[126] CCA E.S. Roll 135, 147, 315, and 325; see also *Select Cases*, pp. 633–89.

[127] BI CP.E.139.

[128] BI CP.E.139. 'diversa animalia et utensilia domus vendita fuerant per dictos executores'.

Popular Memory and Gender in Medieval England

Aside from withholding Richard's goods and frustrating Margaret's activities as executrix, it was alleged that her husband had bequeathed a particular object to her, then in Thomas's possession. Margaret's proctor described the item in detail as 'a silver cup with a beautiful silver lid standing upon three silver lions on whose lid was a knob, on the top of which cover was painted the arms that the same Richard was accustomed to bear while he was living'.[129] Ownership of the object was disputed as Richard also left silver cups to each of his other executors, Thomas, and William, rector of the church of Bowness. The cup's location was confused further since Richard had allegedly mortgaged it to the abbey of Holmcultram for 10 marks prior to his death, although the house's abbot promised to release it to whoever paid him the amount. In contrast to non-elite family memory, gentry and noble families commissioned effigies and objects and had their heraldry emblazoned on household items – these heraldic devices were used to demonstrate status or act as evidence of a kin group's pedigree.[130]

The armorial cup in Richard del Sandes's possession was intended to function as a prompt for the commemoration of its original owner and his descendants. The arms and heraldic motto upon the knob encapsulated the family's desire to be remembered, providing a physical and symbolic representation of their noble past that served as a site of memory for the del Sandes family. Bequests to relatives were often mediated by gendered patterns and assumptions. Women left goods and household objects more often than men in late medieval England, yet male testators bequeathed dishes, plate, and items of higher value.[131] An ornate silver cup decorated with the family's arms was perhaps expected to pass to a male relative who would sustain the kin group's lineage. No children from the couple's marriage were acknowledged in the suit, nor were any included in Richard's will.[132] The absence of a direct male heir, coupled with the lack of clarity around Richard's bequests, may have strengthened Thomas's resolve to secure the cup through the courts. By 1382, Margaret had also remarried. John de Schilton recalled an occasion when Richard Orfevre, Margaret's second husband, intervened in the dispute, requesting that Thomas permit his wife to complete the administration of her late husband's possessions.[133]

---

[129] BI CP.E.139. 'unum ciphum argentum cum cooperculo argento pulcrum stante super tres leones parvos argentis in cuius cooperculi summitate fuerat unus nodus argentum in quo depingebatur arma que idem Ricardus dum vixerat portare solebat'.

[130] N. Saul, 'Bold as Brass: Secular Display in English Medieval Brasses', in P. Coss and M. Keen, eds., *Heraldry, Pageantry, and Social Display in Medieval England* (Woodbridge, 2002), pp. 169–94, at p. 181.

[131] K. L. French, *The Good Women of the Parish: Gender and Religion after the Black Death* (Philadelphia, 2007), pp. 41–2.

[132] A copy of Richard's testament survives alongside the other apparatus of the suit.

[133] BI CP.E.139.

Marriage, Kinship, and Widowhood

When widows remarried, often as a social and economic necessity, this could nonetheless isolate them from their former marital kin, and place them at a disadvantage when dowers and other bequests were yet to be settled. Cultural anxieties relating to the widow's role in the commemoration of her dead husband fixated on remarriage in the motif of the 'faithless widow', the corollary of whom was the exemplary widow of literature and sermons. The widow who failed to live only as the living embodiment of her deceased husband was seen to initiate a memorial rupture that enacted the symbolic execution of her late spouse and the obliteration of his memory.[134] In the context of this gendered motif, the passage of commemorative objects to childless and remarried widows would mean the alienation of part of the family's material past.

When the deceased's kin aimed to undermine his widow's position, the couple's marital past was constructed in ways that challenged the validity of their union. Testimony of this kind also appeared in cases that dealt with the status of marriages in relation to bastardy and rights of inheritance. In 1200 Richard de Melksham alleged the bastardy of Henry, son of Henry de Winchester, claiming that his parents were never lawfully married due to his mother's entry into religious orders.[135] The language of validity was particularly prevalent where widows acted as parties against their marital kin. In 1370, Katherine, the widow of John Hildyard, sought her dower in the court of common pleas after her late husband's sons frustrated her attempts to recover her portion of their father's lands.[136] When a widow was endowed an heir lost part of his lands, a concern that perhaps motivated Peter Hildyard's initial petition to prevent Katherine's access to dower.[137] Katherine answered his petition with a request for a third portion of landholdings in the East Riding of Yorkshire, simultaneously bringing suit in the church courts to prove her marriage, which Peter then challenged on the grounds of consanguinity. Principles from canon law informed the arguments used to underpin cases involving dower, as Paul Brand argues, and lawyers in both jurisdictions tended to be instructed in both common and canon law.[138] Peter's legal counsel claimed that Katherine and John were related in the third and fourth degree, creating a bond of kinship that would prohibit their union. A sentence

---

[134] Jussen, 'Challenging the Culture of *Memoria*', pp. 215–31.

[135] CCA Christ Church Letters II, no. 233; CCA SVSB III, no. 5, p. 2; CCA E.S. Roll 223i and ii; *Select Cases*, pp. 1–3.

[136] BI CP.E.108.

[137] S. S. Walker, 'Litigation as Personal Quest: Suing for Dower in the Royal Courts, circa 1272–1350', in Walker, ed., *Wife and Widow in Medieval England*, pp. 81–108, at p. 81. In the ecclesiastical suit associated with this action, Peter is described as John Hildyard's son and heir.

[138] P. Brand, '"Deserving" and "Undeserving" Wives: Earning and Forfeiting Dower in Medieval England', *Journal of Legal History*, 22 (2001), 1–20, at p. 8.

Popular Memory and Gender in Medieval England

that confirmed the validity of Katherine and John's marriage in the church courts was requested for Katherine to obtain her dower.[139] The pair's marital history was central to the narratives of both parties' witnesses, underpinning versions that depicted their relationship and knowledge of the couple's kinship in disparate ways.

Memories of marriages, as they appeared in ecclesiastical testimony, tended to focus on the contract itself, which usually occurred in front of witnesses who could later report its formation if necessary. Peter Hildyard's deponents, in contrast, depicted Katherine and John's marriage as clandestine, taking place in the darkness of night behind a closed church door. John de Sprottelay, a kinsman of Peter, told of his presence at the ceremony during which pieces of cloth were hung over the windows of the chapel.[140] Witnesses also attested to the suspension from office of the parish priest who oversaw the union for solemnization of an illegitimate and clandestine marriage. While parties in marriage suits occasionally testified on the reading of banns, they were not actually required in order to make a canonically valid marriage contract.[141] The language of secrecy, however, appeared to confirm local knowledge of the couple's kinship and to illustrate their own awareness of their bond, which they had sought to conceal from Church authorities. In a similar vein, the absence of banns implied that the pair had sought to prevent objections to their union, precluding its entry into local memory since existing histories of the family demonstrated their kinship. The couple's sexual history was also depicted differently in the context of their alleged kinship. Several deponents testified to the chaste nature of the couple's marriage after the exposure of their kinship. John Hildyard claimed that the archbishop banned them from sexual intercourse with one another, instructing them to 'regard each other as brother and sister'.[142] The issue was not that the Hildyards' marriage was invalid through lack of coitus, but that the couple acknowledged that they should not have intercourse since the bishop had made an injunction against them. For instance, one deponent stated that the couple accepted this judgement and no longer shared a marital bed, but John Colnvill, who testified on Katherine's behalf, claimed that the couple had lived together for many years as husband and wife.

Testimony that dealt with widows' claims also incorporated discourses on conjugality and motherhood that mattered little under formal canon law. Language of this kind could still influence characterisations of the couple's marriage and perceptions of the widow's reputation and behaviour. In the case involving the Hildyard family, John Colnvill told the court that Katherine had wept by her husband's deathbed, crying 'I have been too often a widow

---

[139] Walker, 'Litigation as Personal Quest', pp. 87–8.

[140] BI CP.E.108. 'fecerunt panes suspendi coram fenestris capelle de Riston'.

[141] Helmholz, *Marriage Litigation*, p. 27.

[142] BI CP.E.108. 'sed ut frater et soror se adinvicem haberent'.

Marriage, Kinship, and Widowhood

and I have many ungrateful sons'.[143] This depiction relied on a range of motifs associated with the idealised figure of the widow, including weeping and the provision of deathbed care, but it also elided the roles of widow and mother. The use of the possessive pronoun as well as references to the Hildyard men as 'sons' underscored the maternal aspects of Katherine's identity, although the sons to whom she referred were her stepchildren. John's children were similarly depicted as disrespectful towards their family's maternal figure and unappreciative of her motherly care. John Hildyard's response to the uncertainty of Katherine's position emphasised his own paternal authority which he attempted to extend beyond his own death: 'if any of my sons should do injury to you, so I give to them my malediction just as I begat them'.[144] John's conditional curse was aligned with the initial act of fathering his sons, a threat of paternal censure intended to operate after his death to disown the men from the point of their origin, subject to their treatment of Katherine.

Inheritance and the transfer of land through marriage provoked several suits involving gentry litigants and witnesses. The wider dispute between Katherine and Peter Hildyard centred not only on the validity of her marriage to Peter's father, but also on the inheritance of lands in relation to the pair's consanguinity. In a similar vein, witnesses in a case from 1476 described the abduction and assault of Alice Townley, a gentry landowner who resisted marriage to Roger Talbot, one of her kinsmen. Ralph Bryscow recalled the words of one of Roger's men during the attack: 'I shall ryd her for els sho will ryd us all of Sailebery'. Roger evidently believed that marriage to Alice would prevent the alienation of his family's lands in that area, in particular the manor of Salesbury in Lancashire.[145] Tensions could also arise in relation to the lands of kinswomen after their husbands' death. The estates listed in Katherine Hildyard's petition included Riston, a manor belonging to the Aumale fee, that had descended through her own branch of the Hildyard family rather than that of John Hildyard, her late husband. Following the death of their father, Katherine and her sister Elizabeth became heiresses in their own right.[146] By the fourteenth century, the branch of the Hildyard family from which John and Peter descended had also built up a collection of holdings in the surrounding areas, especially in the area of Arnold in the East Riding of Yorkshire.[147] Katherine thus sought her dower at a time when the Hildyard

---

[143] BI CP.E.108. 'ego nimis sepe fui vidua et habui plures filios ingratos'.

[144] BI CP.E.108. 'dixit si aliqui de filiis meis faciant tibi iniuriam ego do eis ita plene maledictionem meam sicut eos genaravi'.

[145] BI CP.F.257.

[146] *Chronica de Monasterii de Melsa a fundacione usque ad annum 1396*, ed. E. A. Bond, Rolls Series 43, 2 vols. (1866–88), vol. 2, pp. 292–3.

[147] G. H. R. Kent, ed., *VCH: A History of the County of York East Riding*, vol. 7: *Holderness Wapentake, Middle and North Divisions* (London, 2002), p. 344; W. P. Baildon and J. W. Walker, eds., *Notes on the Religious and Secular Houses of Yorkshire*, Yorkshire

Popular Memory and Gender in Medieval England

men were in the process of consolidating their holdings. By 1370 Katherine had wed Sir John Chaumon, another important landholder in the Riston area, in a union that consolidated her existing lands to which she could add her dower.[148] Gentry families were occasionally loath to share estates with widows who were perceived as a drain on the male heir's inheritance.[149] The dispute intensified by 1370 when the Hildyard men aimed to prevent the alienation of lands through Katherine's right to dower, and perhaps the transferral of family lands to her second husband. Cases relating to kinship and marital histories could thus carry significant financial consequences which family members debated through the language of memory and commemoration.

Male witnesses in these cases attempted the paradoxical task of excluding widows from their own family histories by invalidating their marriages, and this was achieved in part through a focus on male ancestry. In the Hildyard case, the men who testified on Peter's behalf emphasised male patterns of descent, claiming that the pair were related in the third and fourth degree. Several deponents traced the line from Peter, the second brother from whom the line descended, whose son was Robert, father of the recently deceased John Hildyard. John de Sprottelay, junior, and many of the other men who deposed also tracked the couple's relationship through the male line. The men heard accounts of the blood relationship from John Hildyard himself, Peter his uncle, and William Boy, an octogenarian, as well as elders of the village. Only male deponents narrated the family's genealogy, which contained few references to the ancestors' wives. John Helwysson told the court that he heard the genealogy from John Veer, John de Sprottelay, and Alice, John de Veer's wife, yet only the two men appeared as deponents.[150] The exclusion of female testimony in the Hildyard genealogy allowed interpretations of its history which placed emphasis on a male line. Marriages to high-status women were similarly omitted, such as Robert Hildyard's marriage to the mother of Sir John de Sutton, knight of Holderness. Despite its prestige, only Hugh Gilt, who was not a kinsman of the Hildyard family, included the union in his testimony. By tracing kinship through predominantly male ancestors, the Hildyard genealogies were thus patrilineal in a dispute involving dower and landed possessions.

In the context of inheritance disputes, ancestries that followed male descent implied an additional knowledge of inheritance patterns associated

---

Archaeological Society Record Series, 17 and 81, 2 vols. (London, 1895 [vol. 1] and Wakefield, 1931 [vol. 2]), vol. 1, p. 136.

[148] Kent, ed., *VCH: East Riding*, vol. 7, pp. 343–4. See also East Riding Archive Office, DDRI/22/33.

[149] S. M. Wright, *The Derbyshire Gentry in the Fifteenth Century* (Chesterfield, 1983), p. 34; C. Richmond, *The Paston Family in the Fifteenth Century: Fastolf's Will* (Cambridge, 1996), p. 8.

[150] BI CP.E.108.

Marriage, Kinship, and Widowhood

with primogeniture and entail. Sam Worby notes that civil and canon law influenced common-law ideas on kinship, while common-law treatises occasionally used canon law to calculate forbidden degrees.[151] Genealogies followed male and female descent, however, in suits where land and dower were not central concerns. Patrilineal genealogies were therefore not the norm in ecclesiastical testimony. While witnesses traced the Hildyard ancestries via male kin, with scant mention of wives and female relatives, a number of them could name the collateral line of cousins, providing additional information including Robert Hildyard's knighthood. Even where male lines of descent were followed, parties and deponents remained conscious of the bilateral kin group from which the other party originated.

CONCLUSION

Genealogies reported in the ecclesiastical courts were but partial representations of family memory, with testaments and disputes in other jurisdictions alluding to broader interpretations of kinship outside the remit of canon law.[152] Earlier work on women's memorial function in late medieval society suggests a relationship validated by domestic responsibilities, including the naturalised duty to remember family origins. Litigation relating to marriage, kinship, and dower demonstrates the extent to which the work of memory was contested in social practice, as gendered ideological assumptions influenced the allocation of roles and responsibilities.

Despite a marked preference for male witnesses in marriage cases, female relatives provided a more balanced ancestry when details of family lore were needed, sometimes remembering female ancestors and kin who were omitted from male accounts. In family contexts, memory and its incorporation into the legal record held consequences for male as much as female identities, since its articulation affirmed their position in their family network and provided the opportunity to engage in the more official production of their kin group's history. Here, the act of remembering underlined their place in legal and social hierarchies, and thus contributed to the performance of normative adult masculinity, just as it actively advanced male interests. It also allowed non-elite men and women to participate significantly in the legal formation of family memory.

The figure of the stepmother, widowed or otherwise, was characterised as the enemy of family cohesion in more elite kin groups. These depictions represented attempts to reinforce patriarchal interests and restore the normative gender order by manipulating the fault-lines in women's marital and maternal identities. Widows sometimes occupied liminal positions in relation to their

---

[151] Worby, 'Kinship: Canon Law and the Common Law', p. 453.

[152] D. Herlihy and C. Klapisch-Zuber, *Tuscans and their Families: A Study of the Florentine Catasto of 1427* (New Haven and London, 1985), p. 343.

Popular Memory and Gender in Medieval England

marital kin, and the obstruction of claims to dower undermined their practical and symbolic role as custodians of their husbands' memory. Suits that attempted to render marriages invalid deprived widows of their dower, but they also had the legal effect of erasing the couple's marital history and the wife's identity as widow. The role of litigant afforded married women and widows the practical and discursive space to adopt gendered subject positions, aspects of which appropriated patriarchal cultural motifs associated with their marital status. In many cases, litigation over testamentary and marriage issues did not eliminate wives and widows from the family histories of their marital kin, but instead emphasised their relationship to and position within the kin group.

6

ORALITY, WRITTEN MEMORY, AND CUSTOM

Memories of custom and legal experience were imbued with gendered meaning in later medieval England. In social practice and in the courts, men and women engaged with local histories in ways that exemplified their relationship to the land and to the wider community. The remembrance of custom and rights arose from the coalescence of legal statements and more popular accounts of the past, communicated primarily through male testimony.[1] In a late fifteenth-century dispute from Yorkshire over parochial rights, all forty-three witnesses from Kirkham Roo were men, producing a uniformly male version of parish history that was constituted by excluding others.[2] Women of the village were thus absent from many formal versions of parish and manorial histories.[3] Men's memories of local custom often omitted the role and agency of female neighbours and kin, due to ingrained perceptions of women's authority that encouraged their elision from legal accounts of the past.

Although greater formal significance was ascribed to men's evidence, women nevertheless contributed to the formation of parish and village pasts, by participating regularly in agrarian and communal practices that were conveyed across the generations. Personal experience operated alongside the remembrance of custom, gradually developing into a form of cultural memory that was passed down over generations. Male witnesses occasionally remembered local events and customs that were transmitted in accounts from mothers, aunts, and grandmothers as well as kinsmen. References to female relatives underlined the extent to which histories were recounted in mixed-sex family settings where women's memories were granted considerable authority even when men's stories were accorded more worth in the courts. Like other areas of memory, local histories of this kind were not straightforward accounts of past events, but were instead subjective interpretations of shared and collective histories, conveying elements of litigants' and witnesses' identities as well as the interests of sections of their community.

---

[1] On the use of men's evidence during custom disputes in early modern England, see Shepard, *Meanings of Manhood*, pp. 221–30.

[2] J. Burton, 'Priory and Parish: Kirkham and its Parishioners, 1496–7', in B. Thompson, ed., *Monasteries and Society in Medieval Britain* (Stamford, 1999), pp. 329–47, at p. 33.

[3] YMA, M2 (3)c.

Memory provided the foundations for several key features of manorial and parish society. The church building itself was the site in which Christ's Passion was re-enacted at the altar during Mass, and his life was recalled in the festive cycles of the liturgical calendar.[4] This culture of remembrance extended to the commemoration of the dead, who were remembered through their association with various objects, rituals, and places. Beyond the churchyard, accounts of the past were bolstered by memories of customs and the law. In peasant communities, agricultural activities retained a reciprocal relationship with customs claimed to be long held, based in the liturgical and agrarian calendars. Local governance depended on popular memories recounted during legal processes as much as the institutional archives that recorded court decisions.

Canon law accommodated a range of rights and customs related to the land and its produce, such as the payment of tithes which had its basis in scripture, as well as oblations and mortuary fees underpinned by custom itself.[5] The settlement of disputes centred on inhabitants recalling the nature and history of these practices. Legal suits over burial rights referred to memories of the deceased, both male and female, whose kin and neighbours remembered their deaths in relation to the customs surrounding their interment.[6] Tithes also functioned as 'part of an infrastructure of memory, continuity, and authority' which in turn sustained local pasts, operating beyond their primary purpose as sources of finance for the Church.[7] Matters of custom and rights were integral to other suits where the payment of tithes and dues was an ancillary concern, including issues relating to ecclesiastical offices and benefices where custom was cited to demonstrate earlier practice.[8]

The nature of custom and its relationship to manorial authority has been traced thoroughly by historians, in part due to the prevalence of peasant resistance during the fourteenth and fifteenth centuries. Steven Justice notes how sections of the peasantry sought to exert control over writing during the Peasants' Revolt of 1381 as 'documentary competence' became a symbol of political self-determination as much as a way to challenge seigneurial memory.[9] Likewise, Wood emphasises the importance of memory among peasant communities striving to minimise the extractive demands of lordly

---

4   J. Le Goff, *Histoire et mémoire* (Paris, 1988), pp. 130–48; Rubin, *Corpus Christi*, p. 105.
5   Helmholz, *The Oxford History of the Laws of England*, pp. 435–65.
6   On later medieval burial practices, see I. Forrest, 'The Politics of Burial in Late Medieval Hereford', *English Historical Review*, 125 (2010), 1110–38.
7   J. Eldevik, 'Driving the Chariot of the Lord: Siegfried I of Mainz (1060–1084) and Episcopal Identity in an Age of Transition', in J. S. Ott and A. Trubore Jones, eds., *The Bishop Reformed: Studies of Episcopal Power and Culture in the Central Middle Ages* (Aldershot, 2007), pp. 161–88, at p. 173.
8   Adams and Donahue, 'Introduction', *Select Cases*, pp. 72–80.
9   S. Justice, *Writing and Rebellion: England in 1381* (Berkeley, 1994), pp. 155–6.

governance through claims that centred on custom, agrarian practice, and tenurial rights.[10] Other studies demonstrate how non-elite men and women encountered the law through common social structures such as the family and household, tracing the regular engagement of peasant communities in legal institutions within the wider community.[11] While significant in mapping the peasantry's uses of manorial and customary law, these works devote less attention to their involvement in church-court suits or private litigation in general.[12]

Studies on the development and organisation of parochial society tend to overlook the roles of custom, memory, and orality in relation to non-elites, and women in particular.[13] Gendered elements of custom have been considered more thoroughly for the early modern period in initial studies that underscored women's apparent alienation from the application and use of customary law.[14] While women participated in the agrarian activities and local networks through which rights and traditions were forged, gendered assumptions and practices affected the visibility and treatment of their memories. The patriarchal nature of custom was embedded in both social experience and strands of the law. Practices relating to the ownership and inheritance of land could constrain women's presence in formal legal memory.[15] While customary land was occasionally transferred to female kin in peasant communities, and urban widows could extend their property rights according to local custom, the restrictions on women's access to land represented an 'important component of the patriarchal structure of late medieval England'.[16] These limits on landholding carried other implications in the parallel marginalisation of women's engagement with custom and rights under the law. Female perspectives on a variety of issues were seldom included in legal versions of parish and village custom, despite women's contributions to local histories and their efforts in maintaining them. For example, men were usually preferred in suits over tithes and parish rights, despite definitive evidence of female knowledge

---

[10] Wood, *The Memory of the People*, pp. 62–3.

[11] Musson, *Medieval Law in Context*, pp. 84–134.

[12] R. C. Palmer, *Selling the Church: The English Parish in Law, Commerce and Religion, 1350–1550* (Chapel Hill, NC, 2002), pp. 30–47.

[13] C. Burgess, 'Pre-Reformation Churchwardens' Accounts and Parish Government: Lessons from London and Bristol', *English Historical Review*, 471 (2002), 306–22; Kümin, *The Shaping of a Community*.

[14] A. Wood, 'The Place of Custom in Plebeian Political Culture: England, 1550–1800', *Social History*, 22 (1997), 46–60; A. Wood, *The Politics of Social Conflict: The Peak Country, 1520–1770* (Cambridge, 2004), pp. 132–3.

[15] For analysis of this exclusion in early modern society, see Wood, *The Memory of the People*, pp. 298–305.

[16] S. Bardsley, 'Peasant Women and Inheritance of Land in Fourteenth-Century England', *Continuity and Change*, 29 (2014), 297–324, at p. 300.

Popular Memory and Gender in Medieval England

in these areas. Oral and written versions of the past were also commonly vocalised in contexts that reflected patriarchal ideologies and practices.

Memories of custom could nevertheless function as a significant source of women's agency and authority. More recent analyses of customs and rights in early modern communities, for instance, emphasise female contributions to their everyday development. Patriarchal power relations set many of the parameters for gendered experiences in late medieval and early modern culture but, as Gowing notes, 'women drew on a set of other powers from the realms of custom, tradition and law'.[17] Whyte similarly argues that women's daily and seasonal work in late sixteenth- and seventeenth-century England was embedded in the customary experiences of the local community.[18] Customs and traditions were central to other spheres of women's activity from the thirteenth to the late fifteenth centuries. Although the gendered division of work often channelled women into occupations less specialised than those in which men predominated, female labour intersected with a wide range of trades and practices outside the household. In rural areas, women engaged in agrarian activities that varied regionally, but included tending livestock, dairying, gathering fuel, and gleaning as well as other forms of harvest work.[19]

Customs and duties associated with the late medieval parish also acted as a major outlet for women's organisational activities at an everyday level. French observes that activities such as churchkeeping, fundraising, and involvement in parish guilds provided laywomen with 'greater initiative and agency' than did other social structures and institutions.[20] In daily contexts, women dealt with a series of intertwined customs, from those associated with ecclesiastical tithes of goods and produce to manorial dues related to the use of mills and other resources. In towns and cities borough customs shaped how men and women interacted with local authorities, influencing their participation in commercial trade and giving substance to their wider economic standing. Restrictions remained upon some of these activities, and while in some regions, such as fifteenth-century Fordwich, female traders were afforded status as *femme sole*, incorporated into urban custumals, and permitted to engage in private litigation, they were treated less favourably in other contexts with many opting to remain *femme coverte* under the law.[21]

---

[17] L. Gowing, 'Language, Power and the Law: Women's Slander Litigation in Early Modern London', in J. Kermode and G. Walker, eds., *Women, Crime and the Courts in Early Modern England* (Chapel Hill, NC, and London, 1994), pp. 26–47, at pp. 30–1.

[18] Whyte, 'Custodians of Memory', pp. 153–73.

[19] Graham, '"A woman's work ...", pp. 116–19.

[20] French, *The Good Women of the Parish*, p. 21; see also K. French, '"To free them from binding": Women in the Late Medieval English Parish', *Journal of Interdisciplinary History*, 28 (1997), 387–412.

[21] McIntosh, 'The Benefits and Drawbacks of *Femme Sole* Status', pp. 410–38.

Orality, Written Memory, and Custom

Custom formed only one component of legal memory among non-elites since jurisdictions overlapped and operated simultaneously. Men and women possessed intricate notions of canon and common law which interacted with customary law and were formulated through use of the courts. Memories of these legal experiences developed in a nexus in which spoken and written ways of recalling the past coexisted. The growth of bureaucratic record-keeping from the twelfth century, coupled with the expansion of vernacular literacy during the fourteenth century, meant that the ability to read and write became increasingly common outside clerical and governmental circles.[22] Charters and other documents, however, were read most often among higher-status men, although the organisational machinery of the parish and manor fostered a range of literate abilities among administrative officials.[23] As literate practices proliferated in villages and manors, peasant communities engaged with documentary culture to maintain and record their legal rights and transactions. Poems and other literary texts indicate the extent to which the peasantry, including serfs in the thirteenth and fourteenth centuries, understood and used the law in a variety of ways. Gender, as much as social hierarchy, influenced the capacity to read and understand documentary records in this period. Women in particular were associated with patterns of vernacular reading that tended to centre on religious texts, both within formal orders and in more elite households.

Despite the extension of literacy, broadly defined, to an increasing range of legal situations, oral cultures were not supplanted wholesale but instead maintained a complex relationship with the written word.[24] Speech networks retained their significance in the wider remit of common and canon law. In church-court testimony, social and moral worth was established through oral accounts of 'common fame' – the measure of one's reputation in the community – which were often based on accumulated memories and personal experiences.[25] These perceptions were often accepted as character evidence from male and female witnesses, referencing judgements made daily between neighbours and transmitted verbally in these groups. Local knowledge was accrued in various ways, with deponents expressing their memories through the spoken word and via their contact with written records. The social memory of parishioners was thus rehearsed in church-court testimony, indicating the way in which perceptions of the past were formed and depicted in these communities.

Patriarchal assumptions and habits were integral to the overlapping treatment of local histories that circulated outside the courts and in legal

---

22 Musson, *Medieval Law in Context*, p. 120.

23 K. French, *The People of the Parish: Community Life in a Late Medieval English Diocese* (Philadelphia, 2001), pp. 48–58.

24 Clanchy, *From Memory to Written Record*, pp. 260–6.

25 Wickham, '*Fama* and the Law', pp. 15–26.

testimony. Despite these constraints, women remembered past events associated with parochial and manorial rights in a variety of ways, producing memories similar in content to men's recollections, as well as others that reflected more feminine experiences and concerns. This chapter opens with a treatment of orality and literacy, exploring the ways in which men and women interacted with documents, before addressing the nature and composition of custom and legal memory among non-elite men and women. The final section examines how women in particular harnessed local knowledge and traditions, and memories to underpin custom and navigate their legal experiences.

LITERACY, ORALITY, AND GENDER

A prominent metaphorical model for recording memories in learned thought related to the imprinting of images onto surfaces, usually either a writing tablet or a seal pressed upon wax. The process of remembering in intellectual and legal works centred on the interpretation of physical materials marked with specific shapes that aimed to record, adapt, or construct memories in concrete ways.[26] In contrast, perceptions of the past in pre-modern rural communities have been characterized as social, family-centred, and cyclical as opposed to official memory that generated linear, masculine, and often written national histories.[27] Foucault saw non-elites as alienated 'from writing, from producing their books themselves, [and] from drawing up their own historical accounts'.[28] This argument depends on two problematic assumptions: first, that literacy is unilaterally accepted as powerful regardless of the context, negating the potential authority of speech even in primarily literate cultures; and second, that oral and literate cultures exist in oppositional and monolithic form.[29] Ruth Finnegan challenges this 'Great Divide', arguing that '[i]n practice a *mixture* of media (oral and written) is far more typical than a reliance on just one, with writing being used for some purposes, oral forms for others'.[30] Few societies operate only through literate means, and the attributes associated with both categories are frequently shared.

Literacy rates are often depicted in a similarly teleological manner, increasing from the thirteenth and fourteenth centuries and extending beyond religious houses only to clerks, notaries, and the gentry. An increase in book production and ownership then met the needs of an increasingly literate lay

---

[26] On the materiality of late medieval texts, see Steiner, *Documentary Culture*, pp. 18–20.

[27] Fentress and Wickham, *Social Memory*, pp. 98–9.

[28] Misztal, *Theories of Social Remembering*, p. 62.

[29] For differences between orality and literacy, see W. Ong, *Orality and Literacy: The Technologizing of the Word* (London, 1982).

[30] R. Finnegan, *Literacy and Orality: Studies in the Technology of Communication* (Oxford, 1988), p. 141.

Orality, Written Memory, and Custom

population.[31] Consequently, literacy among the laity has meant their contact with vernacular rather than Latin texts and perhaps the ability to read more often than to write. Local officers, such as reeves and bailiffs, sometimes gained enough education to interact with records in English, French, and Latin. In Somerset and Exeter, for example, churchwardens' accounts were recorded in Latin with a 'reckoning' in English, suggesting that parishioners themselves, albeit those with positions in church governance, were involved in the production of this type of local memory.[32] Although M. B. Parkes described such a relationship to the written word as 'pragmatic literacy', this draws too firm a distinction between the capacity to read for interest and 'functional' literacy for administrative purposes.[33]

In the late Middle Ages, literacy usually connoted the ability to read and write in Latin, with *litteratus* referring to men of clerical status. In 1267, one William Freman confirmed this association, stating that 'since he is a layman and *illiteratus*' he knew little about the letters to appoint proctors in the case, except from the report of others.[34] Other witnesses identified fewer distinctions between these categories. In 1271, deponents testified in a dispute over the presentation of the church of Longborough in Gloucestershire. Denis de Aslebery remembered the arrival of letters of presentation appointing William de Meriden as the church's rector, at the same time describing himself as 'somewhat literate'.[35] The inability to understand or write in vernacular languages was overlooked within these categories, leaving skill in these areas unacknowledged. These classifications seldom applied to women, with the *litteratus/illiteratus* binary holding little relevance for female involvement with the written word and literacy in general.[36] Rebecca Krug uses the term 'literate practices' instead to characterise lay, and particularly women's, interaction with texts, a concept that extends to 'literary patronage, dictation, memorization, and recitation – as well as reading and writing' in household settings.[37]

Gendered patterns of literacy meant that gentry and mercantile women engaged with documentary culture more often in vernacular and mundane situations. Below these social levels, women interacted with written records in legal contexts where the language of composition could function as a potential barrier to understanding. Chaucer drew on this cultural motif in *The Friar's*

---

[31] J. C. Crick and A. Walsham, 'Introduction: Script, Print and History', in J. C. Crick and A. Walsham, eds., *The Uses of Script and Print, 1300–1700* (Cambridge, 2004), pp. 1–28, at p. 11.

[32] Musson, *Medieval Law in Context*, p. 121; French, *The People of the Parish*, p. 59.

[33] Parkes, 'The Literacy of the Laity', p. 555.

[34] CCA E.S. Roll 9i; *Select Cases*, p. 277. 'dicit quod cum ipse laicus et illiteratus'.

[35] CCA SVSB I, p. 95 and E.S. Roll 368; *Select Cases*, pp. 247–8. 'parum litteratus'.

[36] Phillips, *Medieval Maidens*, p. 63.

[37] Krug, *Reading Families*, p. 8.

Tale as the corrupt summoner attempted to extort money from an old widow, claiming that he possessed a writ citing her to appear in the archdeacon's court over undefined charges. In response, the widow requested a written copy of the summons in order to appoint a representative to answer the accusation in her place.[38] Levels of literacy among non-elite laywomen were lower than among men in general and women of higher social status, but competence in canon and common law, as well as local custom, could allow the circumvention of these constraints.

Ecclesiastical documents written in Latin were seen to embody local power relationships as much as the Church's judicial authority. During the fifteenth century, an officer of the consistory court of York attempted to deliver a citation to inhabitants of the North Yorkshire village of Stainburn, but a group of men attacked him as he reached the local chapel to enforce the document's contents.[39] The rural peasantry, and non-elites more broadly, were increasingly adept at dealing with documentary culture, as Justice reminds us, with many male and female tenants understanding the import of legal records, both in the prelude to revolt in 1381 and during its aftermath.[40]

Laypeople were not unfamiliar with complex and coexisting versions of the past, nor did they comprehend the past solely through reference to speech. In parishes, word and image were used to communicate biblical history to the laity in ways that supplemented the written word. Wall-paintings of scriptural teachings were primary channels for the education of parishioners, operating together with liturgy delivered orally from written texts and sermons.[41] The laity were taught basic prayers in their local churches, following pastoral legislation to improve religious understanding after Lateran IV.[42] Although the formal interaction of parishioners with books was intermittent and perhaps limited to judicial and liturgical contexts, the laity of both sexes recognised texts and documents as instruments of learning, knowledge, and institutional power. Documents were assigned symbolic value as physical objects that signified authority and could overshadow their contents.[43] In 1293, witnesses testified in a case over an annual pension from the church of Frankton in Warwickshire. Alexander de Eastleigh, a clerk, remembered seeing and inspecting the writ of prohibition which the opposing party initiated, a document that was included in the legal apparatus of the case.

---

[38] *The Riverside Chaucer*, ed. Benson, p. 127, lines 1586–97.

[39] BI CP.F.312.

[40] Justice, *Writing and Rebellion*, p. 36.

[41] On knowledge of the Bible among the laity, see E. Poleg, *Approaching the Bible in Medieval England* (Oxford, 2016), pp. 43–4, 63–5.

[42] N. Tanner and S. Watson, 'Least of the Laity: The Minimum Requirements for a Medieval Christian', *Journal of Medieval History*, 32 (2006), 395–423, at p. 401.

[43] A. Musson, 'Law and Text: Legal Authority and Judicial Accessibility in the Late Middle Ages', in Crick and Walsham, eds., *The Uses of Script and Print*, pp. 95–115, at p. 112.

Orality, Written Memory, and Custom

Robert de Marston, an 'unlettered' layman, stated in contrast that although he did not 'inspect' the bill, he saw it and its contents were explained to him in English.[44] Deponents in disputes over benefices and church rights were not uniformly literate in Latin, but testimony that referenced involvement in legal processes was treated as authoritative despite the person's inability to read documents directly. Memories that centred on witnessing legal records were far less common in women's testimony, though male deponents figured more often in benefice and rights cases from the outset.

Lay witnesses engaged in a variety of other literate practices including the production of written documents. Men in particular associated their memories with routine financial encounters, referencing records of payments and debts created in the course of these transactions. In 1431 John Billyng recalled the marriage under dispute since he was then visiting Scarborough to settle a debt owed to one Robert Awner. The amount was recorded in 'a certain bond', which John Billyng described alongside the money owed.[45] Memories that incorporated written documents, especially legal and financial records, featured more prominently in men's testimony, but also appeared as forms of proof in evidence from female witnesses on rare occasions. While gentry women were educated in practical household management, some of which necessitated the comprehension of written documents, their levels of literacy were limited despite their social status. Such constraints were alleviated to an extent as women often understood the contents of accounts and documents, whether through clerks or male kin summarising texts aloud or through their own varying abilities in reading and writing.[46] Female gentry occasionally dealt with documents related to landholding which referred to the tenure and lease of their estates. In a marriage case initiated in 1365, Lady Margery de Rouclif, a seventy-year-old widow, remembered a child's birth from the 'dates of certain writings and indentures by which she demised certain of her lands at farm'.[47] The intersection of social hierarchy and life cycle fostered different experiences of literacy among women. Female encounters with text also occurred in reproductive settings, where birth charms circulated between women of childbearing age. In the same dispute, another female witness recalled writings described as helpful in childbirth which a friend lent to her before labour, perhaps provided with oral instructions on their use.[48] Gendered literate practices usually associated with more elevated social status could filter outside this milieu through local networks of women, and mothers in particular.

---

[44] CCA E.S. Roll 54; *Select Cases*, p. 502.

[45] BI CP.F.113. 'quoddam scriptum obligatorem'.

[46] A. Truelove, 'Literacy', in Radulescu and Truelove, eds., *Gentry Culture in Late Medieval England*, pp. 84–99, at pp. 91–2.

[47] BI CP.E.89. Translation from *Women in England*, ed. and trans. Goldberg, p. 75.

[48] BI CP.E.89.

Popular Memory and Gender in Medieval England

Patterns of literacy intersected with gender beyond their alignment with social hierarchy through literacy's fundamental role in religious life and education. A basic level of literacy was a marker of clerical and monastic status as men taking these vows were required to demonstrate competence in key liturgical texts. Secular clergy, monks, and friars relied on written documents to support their memories much more often than the laity. Parish and institutional histories were referenced in evidence from men of clerical and monastic status, embodying their everyday contact with officially sanctioned forms of memory. In a fifteenth-century dispute over parochial rights, William Semanson, chaplain of the church of Sutton, remembered the date of the church's consecration as September 1349. In the aftermath of the plague and its high levels of mortality, emergency procedures had been implemented to facilitate the ordination of clergy and the consecration of parish churches, which the chaplain perhaps recalled.[49] In Sutton, the church's ceremony was recorded in 'ancient calendars' written in 'an old hand', which William often consulted in the parish church where they were stored with other books. The description of the hand in which the calendars were recorded underscored the authority of their antiquity and the passage of time.[50] Monastic houses also held comprehensive archives of their rights and privileges which served to memorialise institutional histories and acted as plausible written proof in legal disputes. In 1344, the prior of Malton, a house of Gilbertine canons, laid claim to tithes in the East Riding parish of Wressle from the areas of Brind, Loftsome, and Newsholme. Many of the local inhabitants deposed that the tithes were granted by Lord Eustace, known as de Vescy. When Eustace de Vescy sought a horse and money from the rector of Wressle, the latter refused to offer aid. The prior of Malton, however, responded to his appeal and met his request, later receiving a grant from de Vescy in gratitude. One canon of the priory, Brother William de Clifton, knew of the grant of tithes because it was preserved in the house's muniments.[51] In suits involving local parishes and religious houses, the apparent ubiquity of written records produced contexts in which parties could authenticate their spoken testimony with reference to documents.

The centrality of written texts to the institutional memory of religious houses meant that female monastic foundations also drew on textual sources to endorse their own histories. This group demonstrated greater involvement with written records and documentary culture in general. Networks of book ownership were not restricted to religious houses, however, and gentry and mercantile women participated alongside nuns and vowesses in reading subcultures that 'not only overlapped but were more or less indistinguishable'.[52] Although a broader range of literate practices centred on devotion and

[49] C. Daniell, *Death and Burial in Medieval England, 1066–1550* (London, 1997), p. 145.
[50] YMA, M2 (3)c.
[51] BI CP.E.49.
[52] F. Riddy, '"Women talking about the things of God": A Late Medieval Sub-Culture', in

180

Orality, Written Memory, and Custom

administrative matters were common in female religious houses, women's scribal activity was limited overall in late medieval society.[53] In spite of these constraints, female religious testified on matters associated with their houses in the practical context of legal disputes, occasionally referring to documents as forms of proof in suits over tithes and related rights.[54] In 1345, a dispute arose between the rectors of the church of Thwing and the prioress and convent of Wykeham in Yorkshire over the payment of tithes. Four female religious from Wykeham testified that they had seen and heard others read written documents that confirmed the house's Cistercian identity and its exemption from paying tithes. Emma de Wilton knew of the exemption 'because she saw and heard this many times in the privileges and bulls of the said monastery'.[55] Agnes de Wynerthorp, a fellow nun of Wykeham, also referred to these documents, stating that she had seen 'two papal bulls but could not recall the name of the pope who conceded this'.[56] Although the women remembered seeing and hearing the contents of the grants read aloud, none of them described reading the documents in person, while one nun told how she heard of the house's rights from her elders. As female religious, they were able to circumvent gendered patterns of literacy prevalent elsewhere in society, facilitating their contact with institutional records of various kinds. Yet even in monastic houses where documents were more commonplace, the patriarchal organisation of female orders in relation to neighbouring male houses and the more limited provision of education may have shaped women's contact with writing.

Parishioners could appropriate official documents produced during parochial administration, drawing on records of tithes and dues paid to the Church in order to supplement oral memory. In 1431 both Richard Sereby and John Thorp claimed to have married Agnes Schilbottil of Scarborough with all three parties appearing in a multi-party marriage suit.[57] John's witnesses stated that Agnes and John contracted marriage at her father's house the year before. Witnesses for the other party offered a different narrative in which Richard Sereby, rather than John Thorp, had married Agnes at her home in Scarborough, three years earlier around the feast of St John the Baptist.

C. M. Meale, ed., *Women and Literature in Britain, 1150–1500* (Cambridge, 1993), pp. 104–27, at p. 110.

[53] V. M. O'Mara, 'Female Scribal Ability and Scribal Activity in Late Medieval England: The Evidence?', *Leeds Studies in English*, new series, 27 (1996), 87–130; on reading in nunneries, see N. B. Warren, *Spiritual Economies: Female Monasticism in Later Medieval England* (Philadelphia, 2001), pp. 27–8.

[54] E. M. Makowski, *English Nuns and the Law in the Middle Ages: Cloistered Nuns and their Lawyers, 1293–1540* (Woodbridge, 2011), pp. 45–50.

[55] BI CP.E.52. 'quia hoc multotiens vidit et audivit in privilegiis et bullis dicti monasterii'.

[56] BI CP.E.52. 'quia vidit dua bullas papales scire hoc sed non recolit de nomine pope qui hoc concessit'.

[57] BI CP.F.113.

Popular Memory and Gender in Medieval England

Two witnesses, Thomas Cottesworth and John Thomeson, contradicted this account, stating that Richard Sereby had been in Calais for several weeks before and after the feast of St John the Baptist. Instead of conceding the men's account, Richard Sereby charged one of his witnesses, Robert Gaytenby, with the task of locating the men so their evidence could be examined further. Robert travelled first to the East Riding parish of Weel, inquiring about the two men locally before visiting Thomas Tollerton, the vicar of Weel, to request inspection of the parish tithe books for evidence of the men. The vicar examined tithe records for the previous sixteen years, but found no record of the men living in the parish during those years or at the time of the suit. Absence from tithe books did not preclude their residence in the parish, as it was possible that the men had indeed lived there, perhaps in transitory employment, but did not pay tithes. The need to consult parishioners as well as the local tithe books highlights the limitations of written forms of parochial history, yet records used to maintain and enforce custom in the parish could be deployed as a method of proof in other types of suits.

Although parishioners were seldom fully literate in Latin, memories of religious texts read aloud were integral to the laity's interaction with written documents. Aurality differed from other oral practices as it exhibited 'dependence on a written text as the source of the public reading'.[58] In mercantile and gentry circles, household manuscripts containing saints' lives, romances, and instructions on domestic management were often read orally, transforming texts into collective aural encounters for men and women. Below this social level, laypeople tended to encounter documentary culture in legal contexts, during suits or citations in the church or manorial courts. Male witnesses in particular remembered hearing legal apparatus read aloud in the course of legal business conducted in local churches and priories. Often, the men recalling these events were members of the clergy, monks, or personnel of the courts, like the clerical deponents who testified in a marriage suit in 1441. Both the official of the archdeaconry of Cleveland and the dean gave evidence in this case on inquiries into the alleged servility of two witnesses, and described the recording of *acta* in the case.[59]

Where laymen testified about hearing legal documents read aloud, their memories centred on their public description or recitation, usually involving translation from Latin into the vernacular. In a mid-fourteenth-century case over a pension which the priory of Blyth sought from the Nottinghamshire church of Elton, several laymen stated that they had seen and heard papal bulls and letters from the archbishop of York confirming this grant read aloud in English.[60] Laymen also claimed to be able to recognise liturgical phrases

---

[58] J. Coleman, *Public Reading and the Reading Public in Late Medieval England and France* (Cambridge, 1996), p. 28; see also Steiner, *Documentary Culture*, p. 26.

[59] BI CP.F.227.

[60] BI CP.E.86.

182

Orality, Written Memory, and Custom

as well as the words that accompanied specific religious ceremonies. In 1293, Reginald le Bolacer recalled the excommunication of the rival claimants to the prebend and church of Thame, during which the priest threw a candle to the ground while declaring 'so be it; so be it. Amen'. The other words were uttered in Latin and fellow witnesses identified them as the ritual of excommunication. Elias de Wycombe stated that he did not know who had been excommunicated during the ceremony, but remembered that the list of individuals began with the name 'John'.[61] Where the precise meaning of speech in Latin could not be discerned, witnesses relied on familiar words and phrases to describe their understanding and involvement in these events.

Laywomen beyond gentry circles rarely described memories that entailed seeing or hearing documents read aloud. Such instances were more likely to occur in cases over disputed testaments where female witnesses recalled the last will of the deceased. In 1390, John de Buttercram and Henry de Gudechilde, executors of William de Awne's testament, pursued John Clerk, cardmaker, in the court of York for non-payment of a debt of 13*s*.[62] Avice de Awne, William's widow, and Agnes, their daughter, testified that they had often seen his testament and heard it read before his death. In contrast to patterns typical in men's evidence, laywomen's experiences of aural memory were situated in domestic and familial settings, yet they could still participate in activities relating to legal matters outside the courts. Despite their limited competency in the archival language of the Church, the laity's memories depended on processes that emphasised the interplay of written records and speech.

Due to clerical and social attitudes towards female embodiment and the judicial function of female witnesses, and their perceived relationship with memory practice, women's legal evidence often centred on pregnancy and birth. These reproductive memories were communicated by oral means, circulating primarily through speech and dependent on personal experience. Written records and documentary discourse were much less pervasive in women's memories of pregnancy and labour, seldom featuring as a means of proof in the laity's testimony about birth in general. By 1200 genealogies, and occasionally the births of children, were recorded in the muniments of religious orders, especially within monastic houses, commemorating the lives, deaths, and family histories of patrons, donors, and deceased monks and nuns.[63] Chronicling the arrival of children in writing was much more common among aristocratic and gentry families where the precise age and ancestry of potential heirs was assigned central importance. The role of the religious orders in recording family memory began to recede by the late

---

[61]   CCA E.S. Roll 151i and 335; *Select Cases*, p. 585.

[62]   BI CP.E.174.

[63]   Geary, *Phantoms of Remembrance*, pp. 48–80.

Popular Memory and Gender in Medieval England

Middle Ages, but male jurors in proof-of-age inquiries noted a handful of occasions in which births were committed to monastic chronicles. Elite women remained integral to the written transmission of their family memory, and could request the entry of their children's births into monastic archives in cases where land and endowment formed the primary inheritance.[64]

Written records of children's births appeared in testimony from male religious on only one occasion in the church courts of Canterbury and York. The witnesses who deposed on the age of Katherine Northefolk in 1425 were doing so as part of a dispute over her profession into religious orders following her alleged abduction from the Benedictine house of Wallingwells in Nottinghamshire.[65] Men and women in the suit used memories of their children's births in order to establish Katherine's age at the time when she entered the religious house. Michael Dawnay, a friar at the Franciscan house of Doncaster, and Katherine's kinsman, remembered recording Katherine's birth in a small quire, alongside other births in his extended family. The friars were great owners and collectors of manuscripts, emerging in the late Middle Ages as the principal makers of service books. Franciscans and Dominicans carried portable quires and *vademecum*, small books that contained biblical, pastoral, and liturgical texts that embodied the friars' peripatetic and missionary work.[66] From the dates of the children's births, Michael described how he intended to calculate their 'lives and fates', based on the years, days, months, and hours of their births recorded in his quire.

References to the 'provisions, fates, and fortunes' of these infants indicate that Michael Dawnay was casting early nativity horoscopes.[67] Astrology was widely accepted as a way of predicting the future, employed by physicians to establish opportune times for procedures such as bloodletting and by political figures and the wealthier laity who sought to know their fate and answers to questions which troubled them.[68] In the late Middle Ages, the mendicant orders produced several notable figures in this context, such as John Somer, an astronomer based at the Franciscan convent of Bridgwater,

---

[64] Given-Wilson, *Chronicles*, p. 79; van Houts, *Memory and Gender*, p. 13.

[65] BI CP.F.89. For a detailed analysis of this case, see B. Kane, 'Return of the Native: Franciscan Education and Astrological Practice in the Medieval North of England', in M. Robson and J. Rohrkasten, eds., *Franciscan Organisation in the Mendicant Context: Formal and Informal Structures of the Friars' Lives and Ministry in the Middle Ages* (Berlin, 2010), pp. 281–306.

[66] D. L. d'Avray, with A. C. de la Mare, 'Portable *Vademecum* Books Containing Franciscan and Dominican Texts', in A. C. de la Mare and B. C. Barker-Benfield, eds., *Manuscripts at Oxford: An Exhibition in Memory of Richard William Hunt ... on Themes Selected and Described by Some of his Friends (1908–1979)* (Oxford, 1980), pp. 60–4, at p. 61.

[67] BI CP.F.89. 'disposiciones eventus et fortunas'.

[68] J. D. North, 'Astronomy and Mathematics', in J. I. Catto and R. Evans, eds., *The History of the University of Oxford*, vol. 2: *Late Medieval Oxford* (Oxford, 1992), pp. 103–74, at p. 104.

Orality, Written Memory, and Custom

whose activities in astronomy attracted aristocratic and royal patrons.[69] Other friars interested in the science of astronomy emerged from northern England in the same period, including Richard de Thorpe, an Augustinian friar in York, who compiled an astronomical calendar between 1381 and 1389.[70] Michael received his early education locally before entering the Franciscan friary of Hartlepool, where he studied arithmetic and domification (the division of astrological houses), later transferring to convents in Cambridge, Richmond, and Doncaster. During his period in Cambridge, he became a master of studies and spent a year serving as a regent lecturer, finally returning to Doncaster where he spent six years and was resident when he testified on Katherine Northefolk's birth.

Learned astrologists, like Michael Dawnay, trained in the friaries or the universities, could continue astrological practice outside their confines, casting horoscopes for clients with interests in predicting the future.[71] Michael's calculations were made in familial settings, however, as the first entry in his quire centred on a visit with his kinsmen, one of whom wished to have his own horoscope cast although he did not know the details of his own birth. The maintenance of a booklet on family births perhaps connected his personal memories with the family's wider history and growth, particularly in the absence of his own biological line and in the context of the religious vow of celibacy. Although these calculations aimed to forecast the future, such a written record provided a documentary survey of the family's past, in contrast with parental accounts of birth that were usually given in oral form. While depositions were based routinely on the speech responses of deponents, Michael recited text from his quire which was then inserted into his testimony.

Oral and written forms of memory existed on a spectrum shaped by a confluence of interrelated factors, including social hierarchy, status, and gender. Despite the appearance of recognisable cultural patterns, occasionally evident in the use of motifs associated with writing and orality, memories of this kind could also disclose complex subjectivities that conveyed strands of personal identities and experiences. The modes of expression used to communicate memories of writing and speech signified sets of power relations under dispute in legal contests, which were also present in conflicts encountered in daily life. Patriarchal attitudes and practices structured the way in which men and women engaged with the continuum of orality and writing. Gendered practices relating to work, and the application of canon law, circumscribed women's access to documentary culture, although status, religious profession, and the nature of women's social networks permitted higher levels of female

---

[69] *The Kalendarium of John Somer*, ed. L. Mooney (Athens, GA, 1998), p. 2.

[70] J. B. Friedman, 'Richard de Thorpe's Astronomical Kalendar and the Luxury Book Trade at York', *Studies in the Age of Chaucer*, 7 (1985), 137–60.

[71] S. Page, 'Richard Trewythian and the Uses of Astrology in Late Medieval England', *Journal of the Warburg and Courtauld Institutes*, 64 (2001), 193–228, at p. 208.

Popular Memory and Gender in Medieval England

agency. In this sense, literate habits were widespread in lower- and middling-status groups, yet the ability to read and write in Latin remained more restricted. In addition, literacy in Latin was not a necessity for laymen testifying in cases over benefices and church rights since knowledge of the law and its processes could be signified in other related ways.

Orality, literacy, and memory accrued particular importance in the fields of custom and local knowledge of rights. The organisation of custom was multi-valent in essence and its transmission depended on the constantly shifting relationship between speech and documentary evidence. Gendered patterns of land ownership and use intersected with memories of rights and practices, while patriarchal perceptions of oral authority also determined the degree of visibility that women experienced under the law.

CUSTOM AND MEMORY

Memories of law, custom, and practice drew on notions of legal rights that had developed in the late medieval parish and manor, characterised as practices that had supposedly existed from 'time immemorial' or since 'time out of mind of man'.[72] Late medieval and Tudor common lawyers associated ideas of custom with the coronation of King Richard I in 1189, a date identified in the late thirteenth century as the limit of legal memory. In the common-law courts, litigants gave oral testimony to the right of their ancestors to land since the Norman Conquest.[73] The growth of legal thought in the twelfth century, coupled with the expansion of royal and manorial law, tempered the extent to which custom influenced many facets of conflict settlement.[74] Yet unlike marriage suits that were usually settled by principles familiar to canonists, the law on tithes and parish rights drew on local custom as much as on canon law.[75] Helmholz notes that the settlement of disputes concerning tithes was achieved through a 'mixture of decretal and local customary law', with little intervention from common law.[76] Principles of canon law sat alongside local custom as inhabitants, and often the clergy themselves, drew on versions of the past that were regarded as meaningful, whether these were influenced by written law or established practice.[77]

---

[72] Brand, '"Time out of mind"', pp. 37–54.

[73] Brand, '"Time out of mind"', pp. 39, 45; J. Greenberg, *The Radical Face of the Ancient Constitution: St Edward's 'Laws' in Early Modern Political Thought* (Cambridge, 2001), pp. 21–4.

[74] D. J. Bederman, *Custom as a Source of Law* (Cambridge, 2010), p. 23.

[75] Helmholz, *Roman Canon Law*, pp. 8–9; Donahue, 'Roman Canon Law in the Medieval English Church', pp. 647–716.

[76] Helmholz, *Roman Canon Law*, p. 9.

[77] J. Porter, 'Custom, Ordinance and Natural Right in Gratian's *Decretum*', in A. Perreau-Saussine and J. B. Murphy, eds., *The Nature of Customary Law* (Cambridge, 2006), pp. 79–100, at p. 81.

Orality, Written Memory, and Custom

In the localities, popular politics was enacted through the peasantry's engagement with the organisation of labour and the economy, as power relations with institutions such as the manor and the Church were negotiated and redefined.[78] The legal authority of the Church framed some of the experiences of local customs, uses, and rights, primarily through the Church's financial dependence on customary payments, tithes, and, to a lesser extent, alms and gifts. Although accounts of parish customs and rights appeared in ecclesiastical testimony, they were situated in a wider network of related traditions from jurisdictions that overlapped in everyday life. Attempts by priests to recover tithes or legitimize parish boundaries elicited a lay reaction that ranged from cooperation to outright opposition. Uncertainty about the payment of tithes after the death of an incumbent, or the rendering of tithes to a distant church, may have encouraged individuals involved to come before the court. Despite localised friction, disputes over tithes were far from ubiquitous in the late medieval church courts. These scattered quarrels are often eclipsed by an upsurge in numbers of cases concerning tithes after the Reformation, with non-payment emerging as a major concern in the sectarian context following the civil wars of the seventeenth century. Few pre-Reformation tithe or mortuary cases contested the principle behind payment, but rather challenged the way that custom was interpreted.[79]

Customary rights extended beyond the realm of written law and shaped agrarian routines in European parishes. For E. P. Thompson, custom was the 'ambience' that governed daily experience, with local inhabitants evincing a profound understanding of its operation. Far from fact, it was instead 'a lived environment comprised of practices, inherited expectations, rules which both determined limits to usages and disclosed possibilities, norms and sanctions both of law and neighbourhood practices'.[80] Social experience, however, belied the language of custom that depicted its origins solely in a timeless and primarily oral past. The relationship between oral and written memory was a key element of custom in legal disputes. Written evidence of ancient and continuous use buttressed legal claims in a range of jurisdictions and implicitly contradicted the claim that custom was timeless and unwritten.

Gender influenced the choice of lay deponents, with cases concerning local custom relying on male deponents almost without exception. Despite the absence of female testimony from these suits, male witnesses acknowledged women as oral informants, either as mothers passing on generational memory or in their old age when elderly men were deceased. The parochial clergy figured prominently in these suits, with the beneficed clergy appearing

---

[78] J. Whittle and S. H. Rigby, 'England: Popular Politics and Social Conflict', in S. H. Rigby, ed., *A Companion to Britain in the Later Middle Ages* (Oxford, 2003), pp. 65–86.

[79] B. Reay, 'Quaker Opposition to Tithes, 1652–1660', *Past & Present*, 86 (1980), 98–120; Helmholz, *Roman Canon Law*, p. 91.

[80] E. P. Thompson, *Customs in Common* (New York, 1993), p. 102.

Popular Memory and Gender in Medieval England

as litigants and deponents usually drawn from the unbeneficed clergy or the laity. Religious houses acted as parties in tithe cases where a parish church had been appropriated to them. These suits captured memories that were contested between different groups, both lay and ecclesiastical, rather than comprehensive and unified parish histories. Memories of custom and church rights did not embody coherent or straightforward motives – in the comparable context of early modern England these claims were often 'highly ideological and quite fictional'.[81]

Customary rights were depicted as existing since 'time out of mind' in cases of disputed tithes and parochial rights as parties and witnesses sought to establish the history of their rights. The language of custom portrayed these practices as indistinguishable from living memory, which underscored their perpetual nature and transmission over generations, and claims were phrased in vague terms, reinforcing the 'timelessness' of customs and rights. The initial origins and possession of these rights usually remained obscure, which detached them from the chronological progression of time. In a tithe dispute initiated in 1340, John le Smale, canon of Ripon and prebendary of Studley, brought an action against William Boye, one of his tenants holding land in farm from him, in order to recover corn and hay owed in tithes from the grange of Havercroft. Hugh del Roche, chaplain, presented the rights of the church of Ripon as well established and having existed since 'time out of mind'. More recent memories of the status and rights of churches could supplement claims of antiquity, and Hugh asserted the church's 'ancient' customs, stating that he had witnessed the administering of church sacraments in the parish for the last thirty years.[82] In the same suit, Richard de Stowe deposed that John le Smale collected tithes in Ripon and its outlying areas until William Boye's recent incursions, when the latter seized the fruits of the lands of Havercroft for his own use. References to less distant events were used to emphasise the perpetual and continuing possession of tithes, while also underlining the recent nature of any challenges. Aside from the occasional use of stock phrases, such as 'time out of mind', deponents did not merely recite the static language of custom, but also drew on evidence of recent local practices as proof of the exercise of rights and custom.

Communities that owed dues and payments could capitalise on the unwritten, fluid nature of these burdens to resist payments to the Church. Parishioners emphasised the ambiguity of payments in cases where claims were made more explicitly on the basis of custom. In the early 1290s John, the vicar of Cuddesdon, initiated a suit against inhabitants of his Oxfordshire parish in the consistory court of Lincoln, claiming that he and his predecessors 'from old were in possession, and receiving as if by law, due and

---

[81] A. Wood, 'Custom and the Social Organisation of Writing in Early Modern England', *Transactions of the Royal Historical Society*, 6th series, 9 (1999), 257–69, at p. 261.

[82] BI CP.E.270.

Orality, Written Memory, and Custom

accustomed annual offerings' from these parishioners. Further, the vicar argued that these oblations were given 'according to the custom of the same place'.[83] The parishioners of Cuddeston challenged the payment of oblations in a way that may not have applied to tithes. Helmholz notes that although '[s]criptural justification was found for tithes; it was much harder to justify payments based simply on custom'.[84] The proctor acting for the parishioners made an exception to the vicar's claim on the grounds of its obscurity, noting that 'where it says "on the feast of St Martin-in-Winter according to the custom of the place" […] it does not say what that custom is or what or how much is owed on account of this custom'.[85] It was not uncommon for disputes over rights to be characterised by imprecision. In the thirteenth century, vague terms were still used to define the common rights of the peasantry to *estovers* – the combined rights of timber and wood for housebote, haibote, and firebote. Inhabitants were authorised to gather *estovers* that were '"reasonable", "sufficient", or "appropriate" to a certain size of tenement or amount of land'.[86] In contrast to the claims in Cuddeston, this imprecision may have signalled shifting demand for wood and the availability of its supply. It thus allowed custom to accommodate the contradictions inherent in customs related to shared resources or seasonally variable access to the land. The parishioners not only pointed out the vague foundations of the vicar of Cuddeston's claims, but also demanded an explanation of custom that explained its nature, its persistence, and how much was owed. Sections of the laity evidently understood that unwritten elements of custom could both support and destabilise legal claims.

Local inhabitants possessed enough knowledge of custom to infer related dues from other pre-existing rights. In a late thirteenth-century tithe suit from Oxfordshire, the payment of sheaves of corn to an abbey caused witnesses to conclude that the lord, Richard de St Valery, owed further payments from his other landholdings. Some testified that tithes were due from his meadow. 'It is commonly said in the country', claimed William Arundel, 'that the abbey and convent ought to receive the tithe of hay because they receive the tithe of sheaves'. Although Richard de St Valery was in dispute with the abbey, William stated that 'by right (*de iure*) he ought to pay tithes of hay from the meadow

---

83 CCA E.S. Roll 63; *Select Cases*, p. 400. 'ab antiquo fuerunt in posessione vel quasi iuris percipiendi annuatim oblaticiones debitas et consuetas'; 'secundum consuetudinem loci eiusdem'.

84 R. H. Helmholz, 'Mortuaries and the Law of Custom', in Helmholz, *The Ius Commune in England*, pp. 135–86, at p. 136.

85 CCA E.S. Roll 63; *Select Cases*, p. 403. 'ubi dicit "in festo Sancti Martini in yeme secundum consuetudinem loci" pro eo quod non dicit que est illa consuetudo seu quid aut auantum pretextu huiusmodi consuetudinis debetur'.

86 J. Birrell, 'Common Rights in the Medieval Forest: Disputes and Conflicts in the Thirteenth Century', *Past & Present*, 117 (1987), 22–49, at p. 29.

Popular Memory and Gender in Medieval England

lands to the abbey and convent of Ivry' in the diocese of Évreux.[87] This claim drew on local custom, but also alleged that the payment was due *de iure*, suggesting that nuanced understandings of the law underpinned lay perceptions of tithe payments. Even customs said to have existed 'time out of mind' required concrete examples of earlier practices.

Oral transmission between successive generations formed a significant element of witness testimony in customary disputes. The idea that memories of customs and rights were conveyed from the old to the young endowed witness testimony with additional authority, supporting claims that were depicted as timeless and widely accepted in the local community. The ancient nature of custom was corroborated by the advanced age of many deponents for whom knowledge of local practices was interlaced with their own personal histories and based on their established residence in the area. In 1356, a suit between the perpetual chaplain of the hospital and chapel of the Virgin Mary in Jesmond and the vicar of St Nicholas in Newcastle required witnesses to state their knowledge of the offerings that were under dispute.[88] William Nele, aged eighty, deposed on the status of the chapel that he claimed was an ancient parish church before the church of St Nicholas was founded. The transference of these memories was occasionally traced back to the earlier stages of childhood during detailed conversations about customs and privileges with elderly relatives and neighbours. When the examiner questioned William Nele on his knowledge of the chapel of the Virgin Mary, he testified that older inhabitants of the village had informed him of these rights and its status during his youth. Another deponent, Gilbert Jargonne, aged sixty-two, remembered older parishioners relating the chapel's history, although his father and mother had contributed their own memories of its ancient status. Each witness described how this knowledge was accrued when they were boys, in a juxtaposition of youth and old age that emphasised their seniority and reinforced their authority.[89]

The consequences of customs and rights, whether involving the collection of tithes or rendering dues and oblations, penetrated many corners of experience during this period, influencing the stability of the household economy, the way in which families and communities used land, and the nature of local relationships. The conscious instruction of youths on local boundaries may have depended on the gendered function of men and women in these cases. This type of knowledge was, however, imparted to girls and boys since women are shown to have acted as sources of memory later in their lives and instilled these details in their children and younger kin.

---

[87] CCA E.S. Roll 73ii; *Select Cases*, p. 455. 'hoc est commune dictum de patria illa quod dicti ... abbas et conventus debent percipere decimam feni quia percipient decimas garbarum'; 'dicit quod de iure debet solvere predicis ... abbati et conventui de Ybreio'.

[88] BI CP.E.78.

[89] BI CP.E.78. Gilbert Jargonne: 'quando fuerat unus puer'.

Orality, Written Memory, and Custom

Customs and rights concerning the Church were outlined in suits that involved both the secular clergy and parishioners, and testimony in these cases indicates the complex organization of parochial activities and the areas where clerical and lay knowledge overlapped or diverged. In 1199, parishioners of Nuthampstead in Hertfordshire were engaged in a suit with the rector of the nearby church of Barkway over the status of a local chapel.[90] Witnesses for the rector testified on his receipt of tithes and the provision of a chaplain for the chapel from Barkway as the mother church. Parishioners of Nuthampstead, however, asserted its independent status and its relationship to Barkway through its gift to a monastic house which farmed it to the rector of Barkway. The laymen described the historical freedom of the chapel and its possession of sacramental rights. One witness recalled that he had espoused his wife in the chapel and others noted its discharge of services apart from the burial of bodies, which was deferred freely to the church of Barkway. The exercise of other rights, like the collection of grain from demesne lands, was also remembered to prove the status of clergy in disputes over benefices. In a late thirteenth-century suit concerning a church in Gloucestershire, John de Kent claimed that Master William de Meriden had been the legitimate rector, and during his appointment he commanded the gathering of the fruits of the church and the sowing of lands belonging to the benefice.[91]

Local knowledge was central to testimony in suits over customs and rights, circulating beyond the immediate locale via communication networks that connected neighbouring villages. In the suit over tithes of hay allegedly owed to the abbey of Ivry, witnesses provided evidence that was highly dependent on their awareness of agrarian practices and traditions in adjacent vills and manors.[92] William Arundel noted that although he was not acquainted with Richard de St Valery, lord of the manor, he knew that the latter possessed lands and fields in the village of Fulbrook. They were tithes from Fulbrook that Richard de St Valery withheld, it was argued, despite the rightful claims of the abbey of Ivry. William Arundel testified that his knowledge of Richard's lands, including the tithes owed to the abbey, derived from his residence in the neighbouring village of Burford, not more than half a league from Fullbrook.[93] Other men were more explicit in connecting their places of dwelling with communication networks that bound the social memory of settlements to their environs, where they were publicized through oral exchanges between villagers. In a thirteenth-century suit over tithes from the watermill in Coddenham, John de Caxstrete, an inhabitant of another settlement, testified that as a near neighbour to Coddenham he '[knew] that the payments

---

[90] CCA E.S. Roll. 210; *Select Cases*, pp. 8–10.
[91] CCA E.S. Roll 349; *Select Cases*, pp. 258–9.
[92] CCA E.S. Roll 73ii; *Select Cases*, p. 455.
[93] CCA E.S. Roll 73ii; *Select Cases*, p. 455.

were made in this way, and it was public and notorious in these parts'.[94] Oral discussion of customs and rights in neighbouring areas were recalled even when witnesses had more specialized knowledge than other witnesses. Testifying in one such case, John Gale was asked how he knew that the party he supported was in possession of the disputed tithes, to which he responded that the papal judges' delegate had granted rights to the tithes to Master Peter de Wilton. The witness statement does not include details of John's position, but he appears to have been Master Peter's associate. Despite expertise gained in relation to the law, John obtained elements of his knowledge from conversations with other local inhabitants, stating that he heard about Master Peter's eviction 'from the men and near neighbours of this vill'.[95]

Memories of customs and ecclesiastical rights were situated in more expansive histories that incorporated developments beyond the manor and vill. National events emerged as reference points more often among higher-status and clerical witnesses, and social hierarchy as well as disparate cultural perspectives influenced the political parameters of men's memories in these suits. Social status sometimes mitigated patriarchal practices surrounding the selection of witnesses, which otherwise excluded women from cases that might demonstrate engagement with governmental politics. In a late thirteenth-century suit, Eleanor, wife of Sir Ralph Bassett of Welland, recalled that John de Arden had held the church of Steane in Northamptonshire, the possession of which was under dispute, before the battle of Evesham almost thirty years before. A kinsman of Eleanor's husband, Ralph Bassett, from the Drayton line, had fought and died at Evesham.[96] The suit concerned claims to a benefice where the opposing party alleged that John had married Eleanor's sister prior to his appointment, generating an inquiry into his marital status and his possession of the church. Female members of gentry and aristocratic families were expected to ensure the maintenance of family memory, and higher up the social scale its temporal intersection with national politics ingrained these events in generational lore.

Memories of political events could similarly involve references to the activities of royal women through their participation in Crown governance and diplomacy during the monarch's absence. In a case from the diocese of Bath in the early thirteenth century, one witness, Robert le Bule, recalled the resignation of the prebend in dispute during his visit to London on legal business ten years earlier. Robert described how this coincided with Eleanor of Aquitaine travelling to Germany to secure the release of her son, Richard I, following his

---

[94] CCA E.S. Roll 334; *Select Cases*, p. 439. 'sic facte fuerunt huiusmodi soluciones novit et ea sunt puplica [*sic*] et notoria in partibus illis'.

[95] CCA E.S. Roll 225a. 'Requisitus quomodo scit eum fuisse deiectum dixit quod audivit ab hominibus et vicinis proximis illius ville'.

[96] CCA E.S. Roll 57; *Select Cases*, p. 540; J. R. Maddicott, *Simon de Montfort* (Cambridge, 1994), p. 62.

Orality, Written Memory, and Custom

capture by the duke of Austria as Richard returned from crusade.[97] The raising of Richard's ransom was achieved through onerous taxation with the queen mother's approval. This type of fiscal burden in tandem with his imprisonment must have ensured widespread knowledge of the incident in the localities.[98]

Lower-status men seldom remembered customs and rights in connection with formal politics, and the battles and national events that gentry and aristocratic witnesses occasionally recalled were much less prevalent temporal referents outside of these groups. The relative absence of national politics at this social level does not connote a lack of awareness or even involvement in them. Peasant communities participated in military actions during periods of political turmoil, as well as in large-scale rebellions that saw higher degrees of non-elite involvement.[99] In contrast to these recollections of political events, non-elite memories of customs and dues were predominantly rooted in a form of popular politics that evinced a profound engagement with a variety of social and economic conflicts. While the peasantry and labourers adhered to different ideological boundaries, their perceptions of the past were multi-faceted and marked by memorial friction. Competing memories emerged not only between parishioners and the Church, but also within rival sections of the community and among men testifying in the same case.

Memories below the level of the gentry drew on lived experiences of events that had disturbed the exercise of customs and rights in local areas. In the suit over disputed offerings in 1356, William Nele described how the chapel of Jesmond was founded before the church of St Nicholas and possessed all of the markers of a parish church including a baptismal font. When he was a boy, thieves and bandits from the neighbouring forest had plagued the area, forcing inhabitants of the village to move elsewhere.[100] It was at this point that the chapel's rights and customs were obscured and contested due to the population's resettlement. Despite this time of upheaval, local men claimed that the offerings and dues in dispute continued to belong to the chapel of Jesmond. Memories of this period evoked the anxiety and disruption that residents experienced as patterns of worship and other activities were interrupted and households had to relocate to evade these problems.

Local politics informed the content and focus of lay testimony rather more than national events, not least because experiences in the parish, manor, and vill informed the initial mental and geographical tone of political experience for the majority of lower-status people. There were other ways that evidence was imbued with authority beyond its location in synchronic episodes, including the situation of these memories in timeless narratives intended to

---

[97] CCA E.S. Roll 1; *Select Cases*, p. 12.

[98] J. R. Maddicott, *The Origins of the English Parliament, 924–1327* (Oxford, 2010), p. 120.

[99] D. A. Carpenter, 'English Peasants in Politics, 1258–67', *Past & Present*, 136 (1992), 3–42.

[100] BI CP.E.78.

Popular Memory and Gender in Medieval England

underscore their eternal existence. Both of these methods contributed to the generational transmission of social memory, although local pasts gained new meanings in the present as the passage of time coincided with the immediate and mutable concerns of legal disputes. Documentary evidence supplemented the oral basis of custom, appearing in the memories of the laity and clergy alike and replicating the nexus of literacy, orality, and memory in local experiences of the law.

WRITING AND CUSTOM

The capacity of writing not only to record but also to generate and maintain custom was understood in parish communities. Patterns of memory were gendered in this setting since the law recognised and valued men's authority more often than women's in cases that pertained to custom, rights, and land use. Suits in these areas depended almost entirely on evidence from male witnesses, endowing memories of custom based on writing with a specifically masculine tone. Depictions of documents outside clerical and elite circles usually occurred between local men in narratives that concentrated on their production and use, especially the ways in which they were read, heard, and interpreted. The language of official legal processes was cited in these kinds of suits as evidence of the witnesses' knowledge, regardless of men's levels of literacy.

Despite its particular prominence in testimony from the clergy, the written word was not entirely absent from memories of custom among laymen. In a dispute over tithes in Hughlathes, South Yorkshire, written memory accompanied the oral transmission of popular beliefs in the evidence of lay witnesses.[101] In 1354, Hugh de Saxton, vicar of the church of All Saints in Pontefract, brought suit against Roger, the vicar of Darrington, over possession of tithes of wool from the sheep of Thomas de Greene in Hughlathes. The case was intended to determine whether the lands on which Thomas's sheep grazed lay in the parish of All Saints or of Darrington. The boundaries of the former parish were identified by deponents who testified on their perceptions of where the sheep grazed, noting through their knowledge of agrarian practices how these details had been gained. Local opinion about the extent of the parish limits stemmed from the men's memories of lordship under a branch of the Lacy family, baronial magnates with lands in England, Ireland, and Normandy, though this section held a more limited set of territories focused on the honour of Pontefract.[102]

A land grant associated with Hughlathes dominated the popular memory of inhabitants in both areas, with witnesses from each parish providing

---

[101] BI CP.E.67.

[102] C. Veach, *Lordship in Four Realms: The Lacy Family, 1166–1241* (Manchester, 2014), p. 21.

Orality, Written Memory, and Custom

contradictory accounts of the gift of land. According to Robert Colte of Darrington, a member of the Lacy family had endowed Hugh, his tailor, with the lands. Hugh then enclosed the fields and built his home there, paying tithes and receiving sacraments in the parish church of Darrington, where he was later buried. Robert's testimony emphasised the legitimacy of the gift in references to Hugh's established residency, signified in the attachment of his name to the fields and his integration into the sacramental and financial functions of the parish. Other witnesses recalled the existence of records that later circulated as part of the community's oral history. In his deposition in support of the vicar of All Saints, John Wyles testified that Henry de Lacy, earl of Lincoln, gave Hughlathes to his servant Walter Coterus for his good service. John deposed that he knew this from old charters of enfeoffment which he had seen and had heard recounted by his elders. John made specific reference to written evidence, but also stated that the content of the charters circulated orally in the parish. Cases concerning custom demonstrate the symbiosis of oral and textual memory as both forms of communication were regarded as authoritative means of proof. Popular traditions of rights accumulated around literate and oral channels, at the same time reflecting and reproducing sets of power relations based on seigneurial and ecclesiastical power.

Parishioners had access to written memory through official administrative roles as well as the confirmation of land grants and tenancies.[103] Yet there were crucial differences in the way that clerical (Latin-literate) and lay deponents framed memories of custom and parish rights. Most significantly, clerical and religious witnesses could remember their own involvement in the production of written records. In the case involving Katherine Northefolk, Michael Dawnay recalled the quire of births which he had produced with his own hand.[104] Perhaps intended to deflect accusations of forgery and to underscore the witness's memorial authority, the use of the phrase 'in manu suo' evoked the scribal signature and the reference 'manu propria' recalled the scribal seal that authenticated written documents. Physical descriptions of written documents appeared in clerical memories to a greater extent than in lay testimony, but certain of these characteristics bore resemblance to accounts of custom among rural labourers. Men who testified in disputes over tithes and parish boundaries legitimized their evidence in descriptions of their seasonal and annual experiences working the land. These physical practices were accompanied by accounts of how fathers, uncles, and grandfathers had similarly tended the land in preceding generations. These routine actions and gestures represented the 'bodily practices' of livelihood, forming a kind of habit memory established through physical repetition.[105] Such phrases

---

[103] Justice, *Writing and Rebellion,* p. 32.
[104] BI CP.F.89.
[105] Connerton, *How Societies Remember*, p. 77.

Popular Memory and Gender in Medieval England

communicated entire knowledge bases and sets of expertise, referencing family histories and long-established customs that were embedded in and shaped by the landscape. In this sense, lay and clerical witnesses used comparable methods of remembering that were solidified through bodily discipline and the mastery of physical practices.

Laymen framed local custom in the language of other legal jurisdictions, which emphasises the migration of terms and phrases from the common law to the church courts. In a tithe suit from 1338 between the abbot and convent of Furness and the archdeacon of Richmond, as rector of Clapham, several lay deponents testified on the rightful claim of the abbey to produce from lands in the local area.[106] Two men deposed that these were held 'pacifice et quiete' from the abbey for many years, using language reminiscent of land grants under the common law. The phrase may have entered the men's depositions through the mediation of clerical scribes familiar with the diplomatic used to draw up charters. Alternatively, the appearance of this phrase represented its vocalisation from one form of legal document, such as a land grant, either read aloud or discussed with others, after which it was transmitted orally and recorded in ecclesiastical testimony. The use of such terms could even point to experiences of the law among parishioners who were not schooled in legal doctrine, but remained highly competent in legal mechanisms used in different jurisdictions.

Laymen referred to a variety of legal processes in disputes over custom, which perhaps intensified the authority of their evidence. In the mid-fourteenth-century case over tithes in Hughlathes, one Edward, son of Germain, testified to his knowledge of parish boundaries, remembering that Hughlathes was in Darrington rather than Pontefract from a coroner's inquest that had taken place when he was a boy. Anthony Musson has argued that 'legal knowledge was acquired throughout a person's life concomitant with the level of his or her exposure to legal process'. Edward remembered the coroner's visit during a church-court dispute, indicating the 'incremental nature of legal experience' which developed into interwoven points of legal reference.[107] Edward recalled that after a local inhabitant had died in a heavy snow, an inquest was sought before the king's coroner, with men gathered from the vill of Darrington rather than Pontefract. Male villagers and townsmen usually acted as jurors to perform the judicial inquiry, yet women were restricted from these activities. This impediment may have limited the breadth of women's legal memory and caused it to diverge subtly from the experiences of their male neighbours and kin.

From an official perspective, parish histories depended on memories of specific customs and rights, some of which were expressed through the ability

---

[106] BI CP.E.45.

[107] Musson, *Medieval Law in Context*, both quotes at p. 84.

Orality, Written Memory, and Custom

to recall the identities of clergy appointed as rectors and vicars. Clerical witnesses understandably tended to provide detailed testimony on procedural matters in suits that involved or touched on appointments to benefices. The laity also remembered the minutiae of parochial issues, however, recalling significant details from memory, such as the names of former vicars and rectors. In the mid-fourteenth-century case over tithes in Hughlathes, Thomas, son of Jordan, and Nicholas Barbour, both laymen, confirmed that these were due to Hugh de Saxton, vicar of All Saints, Pontefract, as they had been to the other vicars who preceded him. When questioned, Thomas and Nicholas testified that they had known four vicars of the parish church, namely Nicholas de Englis, William the said Petit, Roger de Paxton, and Hugh de Saxton.[108] The men did not describe themselves as servants of Hugh de Saxton, nor did they refer to written documents to add substance to their memories. Their evidence, nevertheless, created a linear chronology of the payment of tithes, resembling the apparent precision found in muniments and parish documents. The laity had experiences with written memory that were less dependent on personal literacy than those of churchmen and clerical personnel, but they still retained knowledge of parish history through legal processes and its circulation and oral transmission in the local area.

During this period, clerical and monastic parties were more adept at erasing written evidence in ecclesiastical suits over customs in order to render them redundant. In 1200 witnesses in a suit concerning tithes testified that one party retracted his assent to an agreement and then burned the text that recorded the transfer and sale of tithes.[109] Destruction of the record was intended to reverse the arrangement, although memories of the agreement and its deliberate incineration eventually entered legal record through the action in the courts. Lay men and women engaged in the destruction of documents during the Peasants' Revolt, concentrating especially on manorial and ecclesiastical archives. As Justice notes, insurgents were involved in the widespread and selective destruction of institutional records, particularly those which dealt with judicial actions and customary rights.[110] The archives of monastic manors were targeted during attacks and their material embodiment of manorial and Church authority undoubtedly fostered a reticence among the laity to remember these events openly in legal contexts. The rebellion itself was absent as a temporal referent from church-court testimony after 1381.

Written documents were important as proof of rights and customs, but it was not sufficient for parties merely to present them in self-explanatory terms – they needed to be clarified and set in the context of their nature and use. The tithe dispute between the convent of Ivry and Richard de St Valery saw

---

[108] BI CP.E.67.
[109] CCA SVSB III, no. 4; *Select Cases*, pp. 6–7.
[110] Justice, *Writing and Rebellion*, pp. 41–51.

Popular Memory and Gender in Medieval England

the latter's counsel submit exceptions, one of which contested the veracity of the documents submitted by the monks. Despite claims in the *processus* of the case that monks of the house had provided 'certain instruments' on different occasions and in different ways, proctors acting on behalf of Richard de St Valery challenged their authenticity and claimed that the monks presented them without precise details of their contents and nature.[111] The written memory of rights and customs needed to be organised and demonstrated as relevant to legal disputes, otherwise parties were vulnerable to charges that the documents supplied only intended to obfuscate and delay judicial processes.

Written records were also used to disprove false testimony. In a late thirteenth-century dispute over the right of presentation to the church of Houghton in Leicestershire, one party alleged that the sentence was based on perjured evidence that was ultimately refuted by chirograph charters and letters of institution.[112] Written records were thus regarded as essential in court processes, as attested by numerous references to enrolling documents, the searching of archives, and their use as legal proof to combat official anxieties over the vagaries of custom. These records were only as reliable as the clerk who compiled, registered, or enrolled them. In the late thirteenth-century Fulbrook tithe dispute, Master John de Stokes, a clerk, testified that an appeal was made by Richard de St Valery's proctor in a public written instrument, but he was unable to remember if it was interposed in writing. Record-keeping could prove inconstant or fail, despite its role in producing and storing legal memory.[113] Where legal evidence depended on documents, that fallibility and partial nature alluded to the potential for alternative accounts of the past with their origins in oral tradition and memory.

GENDER AND CUSTOM

The evidence in preceding sections suggests that custom cohered into legal evidence primarily through its articulation in men's testimony, despite women contributing to its creation and maintenance in wider social and economic life. Indeed, work on early modern testimony relating to custom reveals that, while deponents claimed to represent the 'common voice' of an area and of the poor who depended on common rights, formal accounts of custom might also include the opinions of wealthier, settled, male inhabitants.[114] In addition, patriarchal assumptions and legal mechanisms reproduced gendered hierarchies in marital and household contexts, providing the contours for women's participation in agrarian labour and landholding. These constraints guided

---

[111] CCA Ch. Ant. M370; *Select Cases*, p. 472. 'quedam instrumenta'.

[112] CCA E.S. Roll 331c; *Select Cases*, p. 322.

[113] CCA E.S Roll 73i; *Select Cases*, p. 493.

[114] A. Wood, *The 1549 Rebellions and the Making of Early Modern England* (Cambridge, 2008), pp. 178–87; Sandall, *Custom and Popular Memory*, p. 50.

Orality, Written Memory, and Custom

the extent and representation of women's knowledge in legal situations concerning rights and customs. Yet these could be circumvented through female involvement in networks of speech and local knowledge where gendered experiences of customary spheres impinged on women's lives.

Rural women engaged directly in the negotiation and preservation of customs and traditions. As Whyte observes of early modern England, 'women were instrumental in the formation and continuity of oral memories relating to the economic terrain of local life'.[115] In manorial contexts, male and female tenants worked together to negotiate and challenge dues and services, occasionally appearing alongside one another in disputes. A late thirteenth-century anonymous poem recorded a seigneurial response to one such dispute between the inhabitants of the vill of Stoughton and their manorial lord, the abbot and convent of Leicester, over labour services on the manor. Although the majority of tenants identified in the Latin satirical poem were men, two female tenants perhaps based on local figures were referenced by name. The author of the text may have been part of the convent of Leicester, and the descriptions of these women are saturated in misogynistic and hierarchical motifs. Christina was depicted as dressed in 'old skins' and speaking empty words, while Maud was described as 'a diana' with few goods of value.[116] The denigration of speech and the emphasis upon their supposed poverty chimed with contemporary stereotypes of rural women's behaviour and socio-economic status. Both women were aligned with elements of peasant and forest culture, and the language used in the poem implied their inferior comprehension of legal processes. This was a negative characterisation, but the women were nevertheless depicted as active figures in the conflict, appearing before the king's court to assert the rights of serfs in defence of their autonomy.

Local custom, broadly defined, represented a central strand of communal memory and underpinned practices relating to the landscape and its history. Vills and manors possessed groups of men whose knowledge of the law was particularly respected, many of whom engaged in related activities from fiscal administration in the manor and parish to the legal role of juror.[117] Perceptions of their expertise in these areas ensured that they served to 'establish, safeguard, and alter local social memories about legal transactions'.[118] In a similar vein, the majority of suits over tithes and parochial rights were initiated by groups of male parishioners listed as parties by name though occasionally purporting to represent the parish. Elderly men were regarded as principle experts in local matters and, as Shepard notes of legal cases in

---

[115] Whyte, 'Custodians of Memory', p. 154.

[116] R. H. Hilton, 'A Thirteenth-Century Poem on Disputed Villein Services', *English Historical Review*, 56 (1941), 90–7, at p. 96.

[117] McSheffrey, 'Jurors, Respectable Masculinity, and Christian Morality', p. 269.

[118] P. Górecki, 'Communities of Legal Memory in Medieval Poland, c. 1200–1240', *Journal of Medieval History*, 24 (1998), 127–54, at p. 136.

Popular Memory and Gender in Medieval England

early modern England, 'the authority associated with longevity, at least in the formal setting of the courtroom, was also entirely gender specific'.[119] Age could compensate for men's lower social status as the knowledge of older men was allotted primacy regardless of their socio-economic standing.

Women's ability to contribute to local memory originated in their position in the community, especially through the informal role accorded to them in parochial organisation. Despite the prevalence of male parishioners in leadership positions, laywomen were able to exercise agency in a number of fiscal, spiritual, and administrative areas, by raising funds, organising events, and engaging in 'churchkeeping'.[120] Few women witnesses, however, were selected to give evidence in suits over tithes or other ecclesiastical dues. The degree of agency permitted to women in legal disputes was restricted in formal terms, but many elements of social memory had as their source the knowledge and experience of elderly female kin and neighbours.

Memories of custom and rights occasionally relied on 'common fame', a type of evidence which was regarded as more reliable than hearsay but less credible than eye-witness testimony.[121] Its construction drew on notions of communal knowledge circulating in the local area, producing testimony that perhaps included the perspectives of female inhabitants, albeit in anonymous terms. In a fourteenth-century suit between the rector of Warsop and the parishioners of nearby Sookholme in Nottinghamshire, William de Nettilworth stated that he heard 'from his elders that the said chapel was dedicated one hundred years before his birth'.[122] Other men were more explicit in supplying the source of their information, including in their testimony the memories of female parishioners from whom their knowledge was derived. In a late fourteenth-century case over church rights, Hugh de Rukby, a sixty-year-old chaplain, described hearing details of the collegiate church of Darlington from men and women of the parish who were more than eighty years old.[123] Women were only occasionally cited explicitly and references to female relatives tended to refer to ties of marriage or kinship rather than women's individual forenames. John de Peron, a witness in an early fifteenth-century case over tithes, stated that he heard about some of the customs surrounding tithes in the area from his wife.[124] Patterns of migration after marriage might disrupt the memories of men who settled outside their natal community, but ties of kinship allowed female relatives to impart important details to younger members of the family. In a suit initiated in York in 1496, male witnesses testified on the repairs

[119] Shepard, *Meanings of Manhood*, p. 222.
[120] French, *The Good Women of the Parish*, pp. 118–56.
[121] Wickham, '*Fama* and the Law', pp. 16–17.
[122] BI CP.E.151. 'a senioribus suis quod dicta capella fuerat dedicata per C annos ante originem istius iurati'.
[123] BI CP.E.99.
[124] BI CP.F.10.

Orality, Written Memory, and Custom

to the conventual church of Kirkham; Robert Bringham remembered that his mother, then aged eighty, had told him of the customs surrounding the church, while Robert Turnay recalled them with reference to where his aunt had lived and was buried.[125] Although informally barred from deposing on these matters, women's memories were integral to the inculcation of local knowledge among male witnesses.

Women's memories could centre on experiences of custom and rights acquired during instances where their life cycles intersected with Church sacraments. These interactions were cited in men's testimony most commonly in cases involving parish rights, where proof was needed of the church's dedication and its sacramental status. In 1357 John Pert, a layman, was accused of removing trees from lands of the church of Hovingham, which the prior and convent of Newburgh claimed as property following its appropriation to the religious house. Thomas Bast remembered hearing about the sacramental rights of the church of Hovingham from his mother, aged more than one hundred.[126] In a late thirteenth-century dispute over the prebend of Thame, several men recalled the opposing party's alleged incursion and violation of the church, which impeded its sacramental use. John de Clipston, a clerk, recalled that the purification after childbirth of a female parishioner could not be performed in the church belonging to the prebend of Thame and was instead conducted in a chapel elsewhere. The church's vicar received the payment associated with the purification on the orders of the rival claimant to the prebend.[127] Laywomen engaged with church ceremonies and the annual liturgy, participating in sacraments and rituals that held particular resonance for female parishioners at different points in the life cycle. Women aided in the demonstration of the status and authority of parish churches as these encounters sustained memories of rights and customs that were both personal and embedded in communal ties of kinship and community. These were later communicated to family and neighbours and cited as authoritative in men's testimony, implying recognition of women's distinctive and gendered experiences of parish life.

Despite the extent of women's involvement in parochial worship, men's versions of parish histories could still operate to exclude their participation from official memory. In a case of disputed parochial rights between the churches of Wawne and Sutton in the East Riding, elderly men who testified in an earlier inquiry erased the presence of women at the dedication of the parish church of Sutton fifty years before.[128] The dispute was brought before the dean and chapter in 1429 at the behest of Robert Tyas, vicar of Wawne, on account of encroachments on his church's parochial rights by the dependent chapel of

---

[125] BI CP.F.307.

[126] BI CP.E.75

[127] CCA E.S. Roll 79; *Select Cases*, p. 597.

[128] YMA M2 (3)c.

Popular Memory and Gender in Medieval England

Sutton. The quarrel between the church of Wawne and the chapel of Sutton was part of an established conflict over their status and relationship, and later stages of the dispute centred on competing claims to burial rights and associated oblations.[129] In 1346 a licence in mortmain had allowed the chapel to become a college with tithes of the chapel of Sutton, and cure of souls of the villages of Sutton and Stoneferry was granted to the college's masters and chaplains. The mortuaries and oblations of the college were reserved to the church of Wawne, but the college breached these conditions and was ordered to cease the interment of villagers of Sutton and Stoneferry in its cemetery. Evidence in the suit was gathered in two stages. An investigation into burial rights was held in 1402 after a complaint from the incumbent of Wawne, and the dispute resurfaced again in 1429.[130]

The inquiry initiated in October 1402 sought to establish the rights surrounding the burial of the laity in the surrounding areas. The function of the majority of the witnesses was to establish proof that the chapel and later college of St James in Sutton had been dedicated and regarded as a parish church and held parochial status. John Day of Halsham, for example, attested that the church had a baptismal font and a dedication feast, and that many parishioners had been buried in its cemetery.[131] A group of older men remembered their presence at the dedication of the church decades earlier. Peter Dowson, aged sixty-eight, stated that fifty-two years ago he had attended the ceremony with his fellow witnesses, John Dowson, Peter Spencer, and Robert Stevenson, during which the suffragan of the archbishop of York had dedicated and consecrated the church and cemetery in honour of St James the apostle.[132] Peter Spencer, more than sixty-four years old, recalled that he was present when the parish church of Sutton was dedicated fifty years earlier, with 'William Spencer, his father, Richard Baker, Peter Dowson, his fellow witness, and many others of the parish whose names he could not recall'.[133] Several other older men provided almost identical evidence that noted the attendance only of men in the village, some of whom acted as fellow witnesses in the case.

Among the men of the 1402 inquiry, most of whom were elderly, only one younger witness referred to the presence of women at the dedication. Henry Hobson, aged forty years and more, was not present but stated that his grandmother, Alice Gawnsted, attended the dedication and recounted to him details of the status of the chapel and its receipt of tithes.[134] Later evidence gathered

---

[129] C. Lutgens, 'The Case of Waghen vs. Sutton: Conflict over Burial Rights in Late Medieval England', *Mediaeval Studies*, 38 (1976), 145–84.

[130] Lutgens, 'The Case of Waghen vs. Sutton', p. 148.

[131] YMA M2 (3)c, fol. 35v.

[132] YMA M2 (3)c, fol. 180v.

[133] YMA M2 (3)c, fol. 194r. 'Willelmo Spencer patre suo Nicholo Baker Petro Dowson conteste suo et pluries ab parochis eiusdem ecclesie quorum nominum non recordatur'.

[134] YMA M2 (3)c, fols. 205v–207v.

Orality, Written Memory, and Custom

when the conflict flared once more in 1429–31, however, indicates that local women did participate in the dedication ceremony, but were omitted from the testimony of the older men in 1402. In the second set of statements, a group of younger men of Sutton gave evidence on recent burial practices and memories from parents and elders of their community. Fifteen of these men based their evidence on the accounts of several older women who recalled the dedication of the parish church eighty years before. John Hogeson stated that the church and cemetery were dedicated eighty years previously, 'according to an old woman, the wife of Peter Sayer', who attended the dedication and talked about it often.[135] William Wetwang and Thomas Dowson provided similar levels of detail, citing the names of the women in attendance at the ceremony.

The omission of female company from the earlier inquiry reflected the widespread view of men as more authoritative deponents when recounting past events. In the later evidence, the older men of the inquiry in 1402 were seldom mentioned as sources of memory about the dedication. From the fifteen deponents who testified on attendees at the ceremony, only John Hobson made reference to the older group of men, who were also accompanied by several women of the village, including Alice Sayer, Katherine Dowson, and Margaret Spencer.[136] The older men of the 1402 inquiry were probably already dead after the passage of a further thirty years, perhaps facilitating inclusion of the women's informal testimony as evidence from the oldest living inhabitants of the village. Similarly, as Everard observes, women testified as inquest-jurors in twelfth- and thirteenth-century legal disputes in Brittany when they represented the oldest living memory in the absence of male witnesses.[137]

The reliance of younger men upon the memories of elderly women, both neighbours and kin, instead of the accounts of local men, implies that female social status could shift in later stages of the life cycle, when increased age conferred greater authority on laywomen. Both Alice Sayer and Katherine Dowson were specifically identified as old women. During earlier stages in the life cycle, their presence at the dedication was perhaps not regarded as influential enough by their husbands and neighbours to be included in their legal testimony. As younger married women, neither were they exceptional as eye-witnesses, nor had they circumvented the constraints of patriarchal ideologies related to gender or marital status. In suits that dealt with memory in familial contexts, such as those relating to consanguinity or testamentary issues, younger women were employed as witnesses on matters of ancestry and patterns of marriage. Yet in cases concerning tithes and other ecclesiastical dues, the memories of older women in particular were transmitted to

---

[135] YMA M2 (3)c, fol. 39r. 'quamdam vetulam nuper uxorem petri sayer'.

[136] YMA M2 (3)c, fol. 70r.

[137] Everard, 'Sworn Testimony', p. 81.

men outside of their own families, serving as sources of custom in those men's legal evidence.

Laywomen could provide testimony themselves in cases relating to customs and rights, but only on rare occasions during their advanced age. For example, in 1404, Alice Baker, a seventy-eight-year-old widow testified alongside a group of younger men in a suit over tithes in the parish of Crayke, North Yorkshire.[138] Like others who deposed in the case, Alice described the tithes, rights, and oblations to which the rector was entitled, outlining in detail the boundaries and limits of the parish. Other witnesses recalled how John Craykeson, the farmer of the lands involved, had driven the rector's animals from pasture in a place called 'le Overfosse'. The only distinctive difference in Alice's account was her inability to offer eye-witness evidence on this event as she then 'lay gravely ill in bed', but she later heard about this event from her neighbours.[139] Alice's memories extended back further than those of much younger men in the suit, which endowed her testimony with greater validity in the local community and under the law. The physical debility that accompanied ageing corroborated her testimony further, serving as an embodied form of memory rooted in her illness and acting as justification for her absence during the incident.

The authority assigned to female witnesses in social and legal practice correlated with changing perceptions of women's function and role at different stages of the life cycle. Many widows were able to occupy a position outside the patriarchal household, in contrast to earlier points in life when familial and conjugal bonds commonly inhibited female autonomy. Although widows often struggled with households disrupted by loss and instability, some aspects of widowhood conveyed an improvement in status and public position, as well as the ability to exercise agency outside the confines of marriage.[140] Older and elderly women were burdened with fewer routines related to their perceived sexual function, such as the ability to menstruate and bear children. Misogynistic attitudes towards women's bodies interpreted this stage as one during which female sexual roles were seen to diminish in ways that ultimately made their sexuality less suspect and morally threatening to legal and ecclesiastical authorities. Patriarchal beliefs fuelled the heightened agency that women could exert as sources of memory, but female knowledge and their own personal longevity was the basis for their inclusion in local tradition.

Women transmitted memories of custom as parties and witnesses in cases over tithes where age was not the principal factor in their involvement. The issue of religious houses paying tithes meant that women resident in these

---

[138] BI CP.F.10.

[139] BI CP.F.10. 'ista iurata gravissime infirmata iacuit in lecto'.

[140] Bennett, *Women in the Medieval English Countryside*, pp. 149–50.

Orality, Written Memory, and Custom

institutions also brought suit and testified in legal disputes over their status.[141] In 1440 the prioress and convent of Thicket in the East Riding of Yorkshire declared their exclusion from the payment of tithes to the prior and convent of Ellerton.[142] Two female religious from Thicket testified with a group of older men, citing the appropriation of tithes by the convent of Ellerton and their own house's exemption based on its incorporation into the Cistercian order. Dame Margaret Broghton, aged forty-nine, stated that since her entry to Thicket forty years before the house had enjoyed immunity from these payments. The women's experiences of resisting these claims, by refusing direct demands during visits from the servants of Ellerton, were supplemented with institutional memories of legal immunity and evidence from local men who cultivated their lands. In this sense, the convent of Thicket defended the convent's tithes using methods of proof prevalent in cases where testimony came exclusively from men.

Women outside religious orders acted as parties in disputes over tithes and other dues, such as when aristocratic laywomen held landed estates for which payments were contested. In 1292 the prior and convent of Kyme in Lincolnshire were plaintiffs in a case against Lady Matilda de Croft for refusing to render tithes of swans and a windmill.[143] Matilda withheld these tithes for many years, it was alleged, a claim that her proctor challenged on several fronts, stating that they were based on ambiguous or inaccurate interpretations and that she retained rights over the tithes. The prior and convent of Kyme insinuated that she had intentionally relocated from her manor to better resist the men's suit, based on her absence when the local dean had visited to instruct her to make payments. Through her temporary departure and legal response, Matilda rejected the convent's demands, but her ability to sustain her position originated in her place within the social hierarchy. The social and economic influence intrinsic to aristocratic status worked to balance the power dynamics that existed between laywomen and the Church, which were otherwise rooted in clerical perceptions of gender difference and weighted towards churchmen in general.

Experiences of custom and dues among non-elite women were more common in cases concerning the payment of mortuary, rather than suits over tithes or ecclesiastical rights where gentry and clerical parties and witnesses predominated. Although its rendering no doubt burdened most households, entailing the donation of the second-best beast or garment to the local church, it was especially onerous for lower-status and recently widowed women.[144] The Church levied this initially voluntary fee using a range of justifications,

---

[141] For the fourteenth century, see BI CP.E.52, 81, 177, and 195.

[142] BI CP.F.221.

[143] CCA E.S. Roll 75; *Select Cases*, pp. 441–8.

[144] On mortuary payments in general, see P. Heath, *Medieval Clerical Accounts* (York, 1964), pp. 20–1; for regional variations in mortuary custom, see M. Harvey, 'Some

Popular Memory and Gender in Medieval England

including the argument that it was made to fulfil 'forgotten tithes' over the deceased's lifetime, yet parishioners with means occasionally left separate amounts for tithes and mortuary payments. While exceptions applied to certain groups in theory, most inhabitants were regarded as liable for this obligation.[145] Its significance among female parties and witnesses reflects women's roles in the management of the household economy and resources in the stage after spousal death. Mortuaries usually had a detrimental influence upon household wealth as its customary payment could exacerbate poverty during an already precarious period of financial instability.

The payment of tithes had a scriptural basis that was reinforced by canon law, but the rationale for rendering mortuary fees was more tenuous and depended on local practices rather than learned law. Although men dominated lists of witnesses in the majority of cases over customs and rights, both male and female parishioners brought cases over this particular payment. In 1367 the prior and chapter of Durham claimed that Alice, the widow of John Yeland, as a parishioner of the appropriated church of St Oswald's, owed the couple's best beast to the house, a custom that Alice challenged on several fronts.[146] The payment was not extracted from every inhabitant of the area of Framwellgate where she lived, it was stated, but only from those unable to challenge its imposition. In addition, she argued that mortuary was a recent obligation in the parish, instituted only in the last ten years, which failed to represent an established custom under the law. Fourteen witnesses gave evidence in the case, some of whom deviated from Alice's account of its limited use. Two women testified on the boundaries of the parish to establish liability for its payment and recalled the death and burial of neighbours in order to determine the location of their residence at their demise and where they had been interred. The male witnesses also included details of the animals that parishioners had rendered. The prior and convent countered that Alice withheld the animal that she owed, a horse valued at 13s. 4d., and that the collection of mortuaries had existed in the parish for over a hundred years. Although Alice failed in her attempt to resist payment, she situated her challenge to the priory's claims in the language of custom through references to practices in the community. Witnesses on both sides outlined the items given, how long mortuary payment had endured, and from whom it had been paid, and local women played a central part in its articulation, both as widows providing precedents and as legal witnesses in the case.

Widows were integral to the definition of mortuary fees as a recognised custom, but they possessed varying degrees of agency in resisting and negotiating the nature of its payment. In the late thirteenth century, Emma Paty

---

Comments on Northern Mortuary Customs in the Later Middle Ages', *Journal of Ecclesiastical History*, 59 (2008), 272–80.

[145] Helmholz, 'Mortuaries and the Law of Custom', pp. 169, 173.

[146] BI CP.E.101; see also, Helmholz, 'Mortuaries and the Law of Custom', pp. 175-6.

Orality, Written Memory, and Custom

and Robert Randulf refused to render a mortuary to the prior of Andover in Hampshire after the death of Emma's husband, for whom both defendants acted as executors. Although several men supporting the house recalled the type and colour of animals given as mortuaries, there were indications of discontent over its payment. Both Emma and Robert argued that other residents had left animals to the Church only as legacies. Witnesses for the prior noted that the local Foxcott family, manorial lords in the area, attempted to do the same, perhaps intending to weaken the custom, but the offer was rejected. When the prior's representatives approached Emma Paty threatening excommunication, she admitted the obligation to make the payment, but could not pay it 'for fear of her lady of Foxcote and, in this way, she resisted its payment and did not dare to render it'.[147] Although no sentence survives, Isabella de Foxcott, a landowner in Hampshire perhaps responsible for rejecting her husband's mortuary, became an additional named defendant in the case. Laywomen of greater means could subvert the activities of local religious houses and the Church by steering the actions of tenants and influencing arguments for the refusal of customs and dues. Lower-status women like Emma Paty had less agency when deciding whether to pay or withhold these sums, but her reference to Isabella's position might equally have concealed her own autonomy and masked the women's collusion in undermining the claim.

Despite its controversial reception among the laity, the levy of mortuary upon widowed spouses could be used to prove the existence of otherwise uncertain marital relationships. In a case of bastardy that reached the court of Canterbury in 1293 on appeal, witnesses testified that the marriage of Robert Dyne and Emma Handsacre was valid in order to prove their son's legitimacy in an inheritance case from the secular courts.[148] Several men recalled how Robert gave his local church a cow following the death of Emma Handsacre, in honour of the union which his son from the second marriage called into dispute. Witnesses noted that Emma had made a testament from the couple's shared goods before her death, and that Robert had rendered the customary payment of heriot to the manorial lord when she died. Walter de Brampton, a clerk, testified that the custom of that area meant that concubines could not make testaments and that no mortuary payment was given to the Church when they died; both practices applied only to wives who had married in the parish church. The payment of mortuary entered the written accounts of the parish upon its receipt, but it also became part of local memory as evidence of custom in practice.

Other customs relating to widowhood were cited as proof that a couple had made a valid marriage. These included memories of the groom assigning

---

[147] CCA E.S. Roll 77; *Select Cases*, pp. 425–6: 'pro timore domine sue de Foxcote que huiusmodi solutioni resistit solvere non audebat'.

[148] CCA E.S. Rolls 80, 184, 230, and 231; *Select Cases*, pp. 612–27.

Popular Memory and Gender in Medieval England

gifts of dower to his wife for her use after his death.[149] Both widows and rival claimants situated arguments about dower and the division of goods in terms of custom and legal precedent, and the widows' dower was cited as evidence that couples were validly married. In a case from around 1200 that originated in the diocese of Worcester, Richard Suel sought to disprove claims of bastardy made against him, perhaps in relation to a suit in another jurisdiction. Witnesses were questioned on whether Edith, Richard's mother, had married one Fulk before his death. Adam Tugge stated that he recalled seeing her 'recover her dower by writ of the lord king when her husband died'.[150] Customs related directly to widowhood were essential in establishing the legitimacy of a couple's marriage under the law. Memories of rights and customs similarly touched on the wealth of the marital household when goods were allocated after a husband's death. In 1427, Margaret, widow of John Colynson, initiated a suit against the executors of her late husband's testament, including Robert Colynson, his son from another union. Margaret's proctors stated that the third portion was owed to her, both 'by law and custom of the kingdom of England', which applied in the diocese of York since a time when the 'memory of man runs not to the contrary'.[151] William Eschedale stated that Margaret was owed half of her late husband's estate including money, according to the custom that he had known from the time of his discretion. Other witnesses based the extent of Margaret's rights on similar situations that had occurred recently in the area, noting that the respective wives of Richard Eschedale, Richard Cayens, Thomas Laster, and Thomas Preston each received the proper portion of their husbands' estates. Memories of women claiming dower were embedded in local networks, whether social or occupational, preserving its use and bolstering widows' claims. Cultural preferences for men as witnesses saw these memories expressed from patriarchal perspectives as the women's personal names were absorbed by their marital identity, perhaps due to the nature of the dispute that focused on marriage itself. Women's involvement in gendered customs around death and burial underscores the extent to which they shaped and used memory for concrete and material purposes.

CONCLUSION

Laywomen and female religious contributed to the development of a variety of customs and rights, despite their almost complete exclusion from litigation over these issues. Women were nevertheless central to the formation of these beliefs and practices at a local level, even where social habits relating

---

[149] See Walker, 'Litigation as Personal Quest'.

[150] CCA E.S. Roll 40v; *Select Cases*, p. 31. 'recuperare fotem suam per breve domini regis mortuo viro suo'.

[151] BI CP.F.163. 'de iure et consuetudine regni Anglie ... contrarii memoria hominis non existit'. See also BI CP.E.241Y.

Orality, Written Memory, and Custom

to the selection of witnesses had the power partially to obscure their agency. Gendered life events, rituals, and sacraments afforded laywomen the ability to underline the value of these experiences in maintaining the community's shared past. Women's memories of birth, baptism, life, and death were to an extent respected and these activities laid the foundations for the extension of their authority as they aged. At this stage in the life cycle, the narrowly defined and primarily reproductive roles allotted to women expanded to accommodate the breadth of their knowledge on the ownership and use of land, ecclesiastical customs and dues, and customary rights during widowhood.

Oral transmission was a central channel for circulating popular traditions of land use, from the communal narratives of anonymous older parishioners to accounts of parents and grandparents. The association of women with orality stereotyped and essentialised the remit of their actions, but it simultaneously confirmed their central role in preserving the past by facilitating their memories of customs and rights. The memories of non-elite men and women were also entwined with the production and function of institutional archives. Written records and oral recall coincided in the same nexus of proof, and speech was only one among several mechanisms that non-elite people used to organise perceptions of the past in popular contexts.

Many of the customs that men and women recalled did not emerge from ancient tradition but rather developed in the course of recent disagreements over changing power dynamics in local areas. Custom was often stabilised only during legal proceedings as parties challenged the validity of competing rights. Far from unified expressions of ancient tradition, statements of custom in the late medieval parish alluded to fragmentation as communities protected their subjective experience of custom against perceived encroachment. The malleable borders of written and oral memory, formal law and practice, and clerical and lay cultures unified many of the shared interests and experiences through which custom was defined.

Like perceptions of the past in general, the remembrance of documents, customs, and rights was situated in particular spaces and places. Men and women recalled the world around them in narratives that drew on gendered assumptions about the meaning and use of the physical environment. The implications of women's mobility attracted special comment in the realms of sexual activity and work, but the language of patriarchy was also concerned with men's itinerancy and use of the land. Memories of space, movement, and place were constructed to counter or reinforce gendered perceptions and tropes while, reciprocally, the past was recalled through traces of embodied experience in the material environment and surrounding landscape. The final chapter explores, in greater depth, the relation between place, landscape, and gendered forms of memory.

7

PLACE, LANDSCAPE, AND GENDER

From the emergence of classical architectures of memory to their medieval revival in modified form, the places and spatial tone of remembrance dominated discussion in intellectual treatises. Attributed most often to the ancient Greek poet Simonides, this system of learned mnemotechnics entailed the allocation of memory images to assigned places from which they could be retrieved with greater ease.[1] This elite practice declined as a method of recalling the past during the early and high Middle Ages, only becoming more widespread in schools and monasteries from the thirteenth century onwards. Despite the intellectual foundations of architectural memory, the local environment had long structured the memories of inhabitants regardless of their literate expertise. Literate practices were increasingly prevalent in late medieval culture but, as discussed in the previous chapter, the use of written records was not yet evenly distributed across the social levels. Familiar landscapes and places were therefore one of the most prominent ways of storing and prompting memories in everyday life.

The historical analysis of space, landscape, and place has developed in tandem with the expansion of tools for exploring the physical environment, resulting in the 'spatial turn' in history over the past two decades.[2] Earlier works in historical geography conceptualised physical pasts primarily through the static lens of place, but more recent studies in the social sciences note the extent to which space was a more active site of cultural and economic production, including the reification of class relations.[3] Sociologists and human geographers highlight the social construction of space and the landscape, emphasising their fluid nature and their ideological composition. Henri Lefebvre outlined an influential tripartite system which comprised practices of lived space and its accompanying routines; representational space which embodied knowledge about space and its construction; and

---

[1] Enders, *The Medieval Theater of Cruelty*, pp. 63–4.

[2] For an overview of theoretical developments, see F. Williamson, *Social Relations and Urban Space: Norwich, 1600–1700* (Woodbridge, 2014), pp. 1–10.

[3] See K. Beebe, A. Davis, and K. Gleadle, 'Space, Place and Gendered Identities: Feminist History and the Spatial Turn', *Women's History Review*, 21 (2012), 523–32.

Popular Memory and Gender in Medieval England

symbolic space expressed through ideological beliefs and images.[4] The shifting dynamics between narrative structure and the physical environment can also produce 'spatial stories', through the arrangement of places and spaces 'in linear or interlaced series'.[5] From the perspective of legal testimony presented to the church courts, witnesses recalled journeys between sites and spaces in ways that conveyed specific representations of past events and relationships.

Spatial theorists make distinctions between the terms used in analysing the physical world. The term 'landscape' has attracted multiple interpretations from theories that depict it as a natural – little changing – backdrop, while more recent studies focus on the role of human intervention in its development and, thus, the reciprocal role of the material environment in shaping human activity.[6] The latter approach is especially sensitive to the subtleties of agency and power relations which together produce space. 'Place' often refers to the attachment of social relationships to sites, entailing 'the creation of mutual, affective ties within a distinct locality'.[7] Numerous studies of social relations have explored the collective nature of local settlements through the concept of 'community', a notion that has drawn criticism for its expansive and somewhat illusory nature. In the past decade, the term has seen some rehabilitation as historians increasingly recognise its multivalence and utility in accommodating conflict as much as cooperation.[8]

Men and women in both rural and urban settlements interpreted the world around them through the built and natural environment which acted as a physical repository for the 'accumulation of social memory'.[9] In matrimonial and defamation suits, memories of birth, marriage, and work were attached to the places in which they occurred and situated in material environments that carried gendered meaning. Disputes over tithes and parish rights yielded particularly male versions of the environmental past, reflecting gendered perceptions of speech and authority that shaped the selection of witnesses. Urban spaces and buildings acted as sites of memory in ways akin to physical markers and the practical use of the landscape in rural areas. Fentress and Wickham underline the importance of the urban environment as a framework

---

[4] H. Lefebvre, *The Production of Space*, trans. D. Nicholson-Smith (Cambridge, MA, 1991), p. 33.

[5] M. de Certeau, *The Practice of Everyday Life*, trans. S. Rendall (Berkeley, 1984), p. 115.

[6] Wood, *The Memory of the People*, pp. 188–9.

[7] Wood, *The Memory of the People*, p. 188.

[8] For an important critique of this concept, see C. Carpenter, 'Gentry and Community in Medieval England', *Journal of British Studies*, 33 (1994), 340–80; see also P. Withington and A. Shepard, 'Introduction: Communities in Early Modern England', in A. Shepard and P. Withington, ed., *Communities in Early Modern England: Networks, Place, Rhetoric* (Manchester, 2000), pp. 1–15, at pp. 5–6.

[9] D. Keene, 'The Medieval Urban Landscape, AD 900–1540', in P. Waller, ed., *The English Urban Landscape* (Oxford, 2000), pp. 74–98, at p. 74.

Place, Landscape, and Gender

for memory, stating that 'people in towns locate their memories in space, as peasants do, with streets and squares replacing fields and hills'.[10] Past events were situated in spaces and places that were imbued with patriarchal ideologies, and engagement with their depiction allowed men and women to replicate, adapt, and challenge the salience of gendered norms in social practice.

The spatial dynamics of everyday life were far from neutral and the past was seen to flow from them constantly. Spaces and places assumed ideological roles in facilitating social hierarchies and maintaining 'moral geographies'.[11] Authorities enacted control through the organisation of space which accrued symbolic meaning and served as 'a metaphorical extension of the body'.[12] Institutional processes that gathered geographical information for cadastral purposes, as Daniel Lord Smail notes, also recorded power relations between people and places.[13] Spatial memory could both reflect and reinforce hierarchies of gender, status, and social and religious difference. The constitutive force of space 'determines the contexts in which men and women meet; it assists in defining a sexual division of labour; it reproduces attitudes toward sexuality and the body'.[14] Theorists of gender once emphasised the division of spatial practices in the interwoven areas of ideology and practice, whereby women were situated in domestic, private realms, while men occupied public and official spaces.[15] Although the abstract configuration of space could depend on gendered patterns of work and sociability, its arrangement was more fluid in everyday life than earlier models suggest. The power relations implicit in everyday cultural attitudes and more overtly expressed in social and legal structures, such as manorial society and the church courts, used perceptions of space and place to construct individuals as subjects. The ideological norms that placed women in domestic settings aimed to compensate for the liminal and fluid nature of space in everyday life. Men and women could, however, exercise agency through the negotiation of gendered norms related

---

[10] Fentress and Wickham, *Social Memory*, p. 121. See A. Classen, ed., *Urban Space in the Middle Ages and the Early Modern Age* (Berlin, 2009); B. Hanawalt and K. Reyerson, eds., *City and Spectacle in Medieval Europe* (Minneapolis, 1994).

[11] T. Cresswell, 'Moral Geographies', in D. Atkinson et al., eds., *Cultural Geography: A Critical Dictionary of Ideas* (London, 2005), pp. 128–34.

[12] R. Gilchrist, 'Medieval Bodies in the Material World: Gender, Stigma and the Body', in S. Kay and M. Rubin, eds., *Framing Medieval Bodies* (Manchester, 1994), pp. 43–61, at p. 45.

[13] D. L. Smail, *Imaginary Cartographies: Possession and Identity in Late Medieval Marseille* (Ithaca, NY, 2000), pp. 1–8.

[14] R. Gilchrist, *Gender and Material Culture: The Archaeology of Religious Women* (London, 1994), p. 17.

[15] For an overview of these approaches, see S. Rees Jones, 'Public and Private Space and Gender in Medieval Europe', in Bennett and Karras, eds., *The Oxford Handbook of Women and Gender*, pp. 246–61.

Popular Memory and Gender in Medieval England

to mobility and spatial practice – especially memory organised around space – situating past events in places that implied aspects of their personal and collective identities.

Spatial practices of gender have received some attention for the medieval period. Works on gendered experiences of space and place have addressed its composition and use in monasteries and religious culture in general.[16] Roberta Gilchrist observed differences in the construction of space in religious communities where the interiors of nunneries were arranged to segregate women in ways that reflected gendered attitudes towards female chastity and bodily enclosure.[17] Anchoritic space appears as the most intense form, where women's religious lives were enacted through contemplation, silence, and the 'insistently feminine hermeneutics' of enclosure.[18] Beyond these extremes, gender figures in relation to discussions of devotional space in general, the metaphorical and literal marginality of prostitutes, and in studies of the conceptualization of gendered space in domestic and more public places.[19] During the late Middle Ages, gender binaries were applied intensively as a 'heightened focus on procreative functions' led to the more defined order and use of space.[20] This chapter focuses on spatial practices in relation to non-elite memories and uses of space and place, exploring the way that men and women understood and mapped the physical environment and how this influenced perceptions of the past.

The majority of studies on place and memory in medieval English society focus on sacred space or on secular spatial practices in elite circles, while early modernists have only recently begun to explore popular memories of space and the landscape from gendered perspectives.[21] The agricultural landscape intersected with the remembrance of custom and labour, just as gendered social relations shaped material aspects of towns and suburbs. Memories of mobility similarly accommodated gendered patterns of movement, with journeys and other forms of relocation accruing different meanings. Sexual morality was associated with place and space, retaining particular resonance in constructing women's characters and gendered subjectivities. Manorial

---

[16] See, for example, L. V. Hicks, *Religious Life in Normandy: Space, Gender and Social Pressure, c. 1050–1300* (Woodbridge, 2007).

[17] Gilchrist, *Gender and Material Culture.*

[18] L. H. McAvoy, *Medieval Anchoritisms: Gender, Space and the Solitary Life* (Cambridge, 2011), p. 9.

[19] S. Stanbury and V. Raguin, eds., *Women's Space: Patronage, Place and Gender in the Medieval Church* (Albany, 2005); P. J. P. Goldberg, 'Pigs and Prostitutes: Streetwalking in Comparative Perspective', in Lewis, Menuge, and Phillips, eds., *Young Medieval Women*, pp. 172–93; P. J. P. Goldberg, 'Space and Gender in the Later Medieval English House', *Viator*, 42 (2011), 205–32.

[20] Rees Jones, 'Public and Private Space and Gender', p. 258.

[21] Rees Jones, 'Public and Private Space and Gender', p. 247; Wood, *The Memory of the People*, pp. 297–315; Whyte, 'Custodians of Memory', 153–73.

Place, Landscape, and Gender

power relations were also evident in cases that touched on production and use of the land, revealing memories that engaged with the assertion of hegemony and its resistance. In each of these areas of life, men and women recalled spatial pasts in ways that stressed the influence of gender on depictions of the environment as much as the diversity of their experiences.

SPACE, BOUNDARIES, AND PLACE

Spatial metaphors and practices were ubiquitous in late medieval society, both in intellectual spheres and in everyday life. Several models prevalent in learned memory centred on the relationship between remembrance and place. The image of the 'seal-in-wax' represented a means of recording memory and 'storing it in a place in the memory'.[22] The metaphor of the 'thesaurus' interpreted memory as a site for storage, or a treasury, where recollections were organised into smaller cells for ease of reference in the present. While classical and medieval thinkers urged the use of artificial locations as memory palaces, others such as Albertus Magnus recommended material rather than imagined buildings.[23] Familiar locations were considered more effective store-houses for memories, and the most appropriate places needed to evoke emotional responses.[24]

The language of spatiality and place was used in order to conceptualise memory in learned theory, with rural landscapes featuring in treatises on formal mnemonics. In these texts, the image of the 'silva' or forest represented the spatial tone of disordered memory in which recollection was made less problematic through the use of mnemonic practices.[25] In his early fourteenth-century *ars memorativa*, Thomas Bradwardine recommended the idea of a field in various stages of cultivation as a framework for the memory store.[26] Spatial and written forms of memory were interlaced as ideas of place and landscape worked alongside written records to order and shape memory. David Rollison, for instance, suggests that learned reliance on the landscape 'was a natural adaptation of a universal characteristic of the "aboriginal" oral cultures out of which, originally, the tools of literacy emerged'.[27] Documentary cultures were thus connected to notions of place at a fundamental level.

People rarely used maps, though numerous images of smaller settlements and cities have survived, and written descriptions were the usual method of representing places, property ownership, and the landscape in legal and

---

[22] Carruthers, *The Book of Memory*, p. 37.

[23] Coleman, *Ancient and Medieval Memories*, p. 417.

[24] Yates, *The Art of Memory*, p. 75; Carruthers, *The Book of Memory*, pp. 143–6.

[25] Carruthers, *The Book of Memory*, p. 33.

[26] Carruthers, *The Book of Memory*, p. 31.

[27] D. Rollison, *The Local Origins of Modern Society: Gloucestershire, 1500–1800* (London, 1992), p. 71.

Popular Memory and Gender in Medieval England

administrative records.[28] The language of spatial experience saturated the testimony of non-elite men and women, producing vernacular maps of communities that encompassed a full range of social and economic connections. Bonds and identities that mattered to legal claims were expressed through memories of the negotiation of space. Ties of property ownership, kinship, neighbourhood, or friendship, and places recognised by the occupation or identity of householders were usually depicted as discrete, yet local relationships were multidimensional and entwined in social life. Domestic buildings, workshops, and taverns noted in testimony were imbued with memories of their routine use, signalled in the performance of activities that held social, moral, and legal resonance both prior to and during suits.

Memories of journeys connoted spatial progression by drawing on landscape features, like rivers or ditches, sites of reference connected with individuals, such as the head of the household, master, or proprietor, or buildings with a discernible function, like the parish church or guild hall. The occupational significance of local figures could ensure their association with specific sites which had gained importance in the social memory of the community. Spatial references to labour and residency were more visible among men than women, but memories of where women lived and worked appeared incidentally in cases where witnesses recalled female heads of households or women living alone. In an early fifteenth-century marriage dispute from North Yorkshire, Alice Remyngton recalled her presence at a child's birth which took place 'in a house that a certain person called Little Cecilia inhabited in the vill of Sicklinghall, which the same Cecilia had from the leasing of Thomas Caltall'.[29] The delivery of a child in Cecilia's home, coupled with the absence of obvious ties of kinship or friendship with the women attending the birth, implies her employment as a midwife. Female occupational identities tended to be fragmented and composite in nature due to women's involvement in marginal, low-paid work. Women were integral to the economic operation of the household as wives, daughters, and servants, but patriarchal values interpreted the head of household as practicing an identifiable trade, married, and responsible for the governance of different sets of dependants. These ideological markers were prevalent primarily among men, and the identity, function, and location of the household was usually interpreted through this lens. The greater worth assigned to recognisably masculine forms of labour meant that women's work was less perceptible from a spatial perspective, except where their activities proved relevant to witnesses and especially to women.

---

[28] P. D. A. Harvey, 'Local and Regional Cartography in Medieval Europe', in J. B. Harley and D. Woodward, eds., *The History of Cartography*, vol. 1: *Cartography in Prehistoric, Ancient, and Medieval Europe and the Mediterranean* (Chicago and London, 1987), pp. 464–501.

[29] BI CP.F.79. 'in domo qua inhabitat quedam vocata parva cecilia in villa de Sykyngale quam domum habuit eadem Cecilia ex locacione Thome Caltall'.

Place, Landscape, and Gender

Where the principal issue was the position of boundaries between buildings or the extent of landholdings, local knowledge was cited to establish both use and ownership. Like other cases where customs and land rights were primary concerns, witnesses in these suits were usually male, although women in local communities no doubt knew the extent of landholdings from sight and hearsay. Several men gave evidence in a dispute initiated in the diocese of Coventry around 1200 where they recalled the boundaries between two properties after a fence was replaced with a stone wall.[30] The extent of land on either side was debated in relation to the latter's removal, as the men noted that one neighbour had intentionally expanded their own holdings. Perceptions of boundaries were presented in a context of geographical proximity and daily experience. For example, the proximity of witnesses' houses to the landholdings in question endowed their testimony with authority. In 1200, Walter de Etchilhampton, a layman in an appeal concerning tithes, testified that his property lay to the immediate west of the barns and house of the church of Etchilhampton, Wiltshire, with his courtyard adjacent to the tithe barn. The tithes owed from lands within the parish were paid to Master Peter de Wilton, whose men Walter frequently saw in the area as they conducted business related to gathering and safeguarding the tithes.[31] When servants of one Master Stephen broke into the buildings, seizing the produce and changing the bolts, Walter heard this from his own courtyard which abutted the barn from which the commotion arose. The choice of men as witnesses in cases of this kind generated memories of boundaries and the activities that defined them which appear distinctively male.

Boundaries between places were assigned symbolic as well as practical significance, and their infringement tended to stem from pre-existing relationships and power dynamics. Doorways and thresholds became areas of narrative action in suits over defamation as insults emanated from households and workshops. While their borders were porous, as Gowing notes for early modern London, references to physical boundaries could be used to construct the household as a closed space.[32] Memories of interpersonal violence between men included incidents where the site of attacks mattered as much as their severity. In 1354, several deponents testified on the reputation of John de Stanlay, a witness for the plaintiff in a marriage suit.[33] It was alleged that John de Stanlay had visited John de Walkington's house late at night, before breaking his door and injuring his hand with a knife, while Peter Webster claimed that he saw John de Stanlay insult John de Walkington

---

[30] CCA E.S. Roll 224; *Select Cases*, pp. 38–9.

[31] CCA E.S. Roll 2; *Select Cases*, p. 4.

[32] L. Gowing, '"The freedom of the streets": Women and Social Space, 1560–1640', in P. Griffiths and M. S. R. Jenner, eds., *Londinopolis: Essays in the Cultural and Social History of Early Modern London, 1500–1750* (Manchester, 2000), pp. 130–51.

[33] BI CP.E.82.

Popular Memory and Gender in Medieval England

in his own home. The men's stories portrayed John's violence not only as excessive in its wounding of John de Walkington, but also transgressive as it represented a challenge to the latter's patriarchal control. Doorways and walls were emblems of masculine household authority and attacks upon them symbolised another form of injury. Boundaries and borders were thus often reconstituted as impermeable in legal testimony, and their breach depicted as deliberate violation.

Beyond attempts to define boundaries in relation to the spatial expression of power, memories of places focused on events that were integral to personal and collective identities. A major site imbued with spiritual and social meaning was the parish church, which figured in a range of witnesses' memories and influenced the portrayal of past events that were alleged to have occurred in its confines. In defamation suits, the local church became the location for the exchange of insults, with the public nature of their declaration meeting the canon-legal requirement of intent to harm reputations. For instance, women used the occasion of church services to add legitimacy to accusations, and the location of these claims later provided plaintiffs with evidence of malice. Witnesses also remembered the appearance of neighbours and acquaintances before Church officials in cases where couples were made to abjure one another *sub pena nubendi*.[34] Events depicted as transpiring in the parish church were characterised as well known, representing part of the social memory of the community and made more authoritative by their sacred location.

The internal layout of parish churches surfaced in disputes that required proof of their ritual and liturgical functions. Men recalled these features more often than women due to their prevalence as witnesses in cases relating to ecclesiastical rights and customs. In the suit over burial rights in the Yorkshire village of Sutton, John Wylflete claimed that the church of Sutton had been dedicated eighty years previously. John recalled that twelve years before the case, the walls of the church had been painted white, and that prior to the white-washing the walls had old crosses and images painted upon them, perhaps to commemorate its consecration. These markers were cited in the dispute to underline the church's antiquity and its right to administer sacraments.[35] In the same case, Peter Schakyll of Stoneferry stated that on the feast of the dedication every year since he could remember, a banner with a small bell had hung by the window of the belfry.[36] The gendered nature of parochial worship meant that women recalled the layout and function of the parish church in relation to specific rituals. In 1496, William Addison testified in a suit involving the conventual church of Kirkham in which witnesses provided

---

[34] CCA E.S. Roll 272; BI CP.E.37.
[35] YMA M2 (3)c, fol. 135–6v.
[36] YMA M2 (3)c, fol. 84v.

Place, Landscape, and Gender

material proof of its sacramental function. William noted that his wife, aged more than sixty years, had recalled that when she was younger 'she saw an old baptismal font with a cover (*lez topynet*) standing where the new font now stands'.[37] Although less visible in these types of cases, women's experiences of the church building were perceived to be valuable even when recounted at a remove. Its spatial organisation could be understood through gendered subjective experiences, and memories of its use were substantiated by these social and religious practices.

The household was another site of memory that was ubiquitous in the narratives of nuclear families, kin, and dependants, including servants and apprentices. Despite the prohibition on clandestine marriages in the canons of the Fourth Lateran Council, men and women usually remembered contracts that occurred indoors and in private rather than public places. Memories enlisted in these suits referred to words of consent and the intercourse that followed, with alleged events glimpsed through doorways and windows or overheard through thin walls. In 1372, it was claimed that Thomas Walde had wed one Joan Suardby in his marital home, while his wife, Mariona, Margaret de Burton, and John Wald listened outside the room. Margaret recalled the location of the chamber, near the cellar where Thomas usually slept with his wife, and stated that 'John stood closest on the first step, and Mariona furthest away, with this witness in the middle'.[38] The distance between buildings could also be represented in legal testimony as the audibility of alleged contracts was rendered in spatial form. In 1418, several men and women testified in a marriage case where two female witnesses claimed they had overheard a contract made in a bedchamber within a neighbouring building. Witnesses for the opposing parties disagreed on the proximity of the two structures, providing approximate measurements of the distance between them. Alice Remyngton noted that this was no more than eight feet and that speech could be heard in each room from the adjacent building. Roger, her husband, testified that he had measured the space with a rod and later with a piece of cord, which he presented as evidence at his deposition.[39] This approach aimed to reduce the ambiguity inherent in spatial claims that were difficult to quantify, by employing physical means to convert distance into a material proxy and a more concrete form of proof.

Narratives of marriage in domestic settings similarly involved household spaces, and memories of conduct that occurred within this remit retained symbolic and moral meaning. Women recalled performing a variety of domestic tasks, moving between rooms with specific items for different

---

[37] BI CP.F.307. 'ipsa vidit unum fontem veterem baptismalem cum lez topynet stantem ubi novus fons modo stat'.

[38] BI CP.E.111. 'Johannes stetit propinquius super primum gradum et dicta Mariona remotius ista iurata in medio'.

[39] BI CP.F.79.

Popular Memory and Gender in Medieval England

purposes. In a marriage case initiated in 1269, Mariota de Hamstead described how she went to a store room to fetch cloths, but upon discovering the couple in question having sex, turned and went directly out again.[40] During the dispute between Joan Suardby and Thomas Walde, it was stated that Mariona Walde had fled to her spinning wheel to prevent her husband discovering her eavesdropping.[41] Everyday patterns of women's labour were cited as plausible explanations for their movements in domestic spaces, and references to household goods, their location, and use corroborated these accounts. These actions framed the behaviour of parties and witnesses and signified a lack of knowledge and intention where it was required.

Beds and chambers, in general, often provided the site for licit and illicit sex, but they also featured in memories of bed-sharing by servants, friends, and family members. Such arrangements facilitated private conversations between parties and witnesses, acting as additional proof of their presence in specific places. In a fourteenth-century case, Emma, wife of Thomas Cokfeld, claimed that she had shared a bed with Margaret Graystanes, while her husband slept alongside Thomas del Dale, before the couple supposedly made a contract of marriage.[42] In a late fourteenth-century suit, Idonya Bower, a single woman living in York, testified on the alleged union between Elena de Leyrmouth and William de Stokton. She recalled sharing a bed with the couple on one occasion when she overheard them having sex next to her.[43] Cultural practices of bed-sharing allowed men and women to root representations of the past in the spatial dynamics of the household. These habits brought bodies together physically and encouraged an emotional intimacy that was conducive to the disclosure of secrets.

Women demonstrated a high degree of physical displacement in relation to domestic ownership, with married women usually designating their homes as the 'domus' of their husband. Women's everyday use of conjugal goods and housing mitigated many elements of the theory of coverture, yet Gowing observes that female embodiment in general often conveyed a 'sense of space as not their own'.[44] Memories of marital abuse were portrayed in ways that referenced women's ambivalent relationship with domestic space. The escalation of attacks culminated in wives fleeing their homes suddenly, in clothing customarily worn in bedchambers or under their main apparel.[45] The domestic location of this violence occasionally precluded its comprehensive reporting, although men and women nevertheless testified in support of female plaintiffs. In 1500, deponents in a case from the diocese of Norwich

[40] CCA E.S. Roll 11.
[41] BI CP.E.111.
[42] BI CP.E.215.
[43] BI CP.E.126.
[44] Gowing, "'The freedom of the streets'", p. 131.
[45] See, for instance, BI CP.E.257.

Place, Landscape, and Gender

testified on the death of Thomas Banburgh's wife, after he brought suit following accusations that he was responsible for her murder. Simon Warner claimed that 'all men know not how she died, for [her husband] was her death', implying that the precise manner of her death was not widely known in the local community.[46] Household areas could be depicted as less accessible to other people, inverting ideas of marital intimacy in narratives where patriarchal violence obscured knowledge of enclosed domestic spaces.

SPACE AND MOBILITY

Descriptions of places and spaces alluded to gendered patterns of mobility, and these accounts reflected the extent to which social and economic relations depended on journeys and migration of various lengths and distances. Rollison notes that fixed local populations have generated a greater body of scholarship than studies of 'more mobile and dynamic communities', despite the significant role of movement and travel in late medieval and early modern culture.[47] The act of travelling also transformed the distance between sites into spaces, which Michel de Certeau described as 'practiced places'.[48] Memories of journeys thus recalled the circumstances in which they were remembered, including their experience, purpose, timing, and connection to wider narratives advanced in the courts. Men were the most common narrators of mobility, although both male and female witnesses used tropes and motifs to portray movement in ways that reinforced norms or emphasised their subversion.

Gendered attitudes influenced the portrayal of women's spatial practices, evident in conduct literature that associated female chastity and modesty with the home. Attempts to exert control over women's movements echoed broader patriarchal concerns about their submission to public and familial authority. One early fourteenth-century civic ordinance in York elided the disorder seen to accompany street-based prostitution with the disruption of untended pigs, aligning both types of activities with lust as well as concerns over 'transgressive wandering' in communal byways.[49] The impulse to limit women's mobility extended to the household and was enacted most fully in marital relationships where female subordination to husbandly authority was regarded as a natural facet of male dominance. In a fourteenth-century marriage suit from York, for instance, witnesses echoed the cautions of the

---

[46] Neal, *The Masculine Self*, p. 81.

[47] D. Rollison, 'Exploding England: The Dialectics of Mobility and Settlement in Early Modern England', *Social History*, 24 (1999), 1–16, at p. 2; see also Gowing, '"The freedom of the streets"'.

[48] Certeau, *The Practice of Everyday Life*, p. 117.

[49] Goldberg, 'Pigs and Prostitutes', p. 173.

Popular Memory and Gender in Medieval England

Book of Proverbs, whereby domestic violence was cast as a response to the wife's absence from the household without spousal consent.[50]

Depictions of mobility related to work, and the nature and geographical extent of these journeys, were determined by gendered attitudes towards labour. Servanthood was an accepted stage in the life cycle for young urban workers of both sexes, acting as a channel for courtship prior to marriage, and was congruent with the interests of the patriarchal household. Men recalled past events in relation to service; one such was William le Marchal, a witness in a late thirteenth-century case from the court of Canterbury. William stated that ten years before he had left service at the abbey of Pipewell in Northamptonshire and afterwards married his wife.[51] Periods of singleness and later ages of marriage accompanied life-cycle servanthood in regions where the north-west European marriage pattern prevailed, perhaps intensifying after the plague in towns and cities like York.[52]

Servants tended to enter contracts for set amounts of time, with a series of consecutive contracts acting as temporal referents for witnesses, and the regularity of annual hiring fairs meant that these periods of employment also ordered the memories of masters. In 1374, William Coke remembered hiring Joan, daughter of Peter atte Enges, thirteen years before in the week of Pentecost, on a contract of 6s. per year.[53] Indenture agreements between masters and their servants and apprentices recorded the conditions of employment, and these accounts could be retained and used as a form of proof in later disputes that might arise over the terms or length of service. Servants' memories depended more directly on personal experience than written documentation, by locating events with respect to movement between households at specific points of the hiring cycle and to major life events like marriage. The influence of gender upon rates of literacy, and women's social and economic marginalisation in many trades and guilds, perhaps intensified the differences in format between the memories of masters and female servants.

The ideological nature of legal testimony, and the pressures to align behaviour with gendered traits, meant that women's mobility was usually characterised as limited in extent and associated with specific spatial patterns. Service was particularly prevalent among young women in the late fourteenth and early fifteenth centuries, but other types of work were interpreted as detrimental to the integrity of the patriarchal household. Short-term harvest work was pervasive among women who were willing to travel outside of their residential towns and villages. This kind of employment was well remunerated and relied on sections of society who were not necessarily engaged in sustained

---

[50] BI CP.E.221; see also Goldberg, 'Masters and Men', pp. 62–3.

[51] CCA E.S. Roll 113i.

[52] Goldberg, *Women, Work, and Life Cycle*, pp. 204–32.

[53] BI CP.E.155.

Place, Landscape, and Gender

paid work, yet it could disrupt routines in the household and, more crucially, challenge patriarchal authority.[54] Witnesses recalled that in 1356, Lucy, wife of William Fentrice, left her marital household to engage in harvest work, and others remembered that she had incurred her husband's wrath since her decision was made without his permission.[55] In cases of this kind, women's journeys were framed in terms of their disruption to the work patterns of male members of the household, including husbands and fellow servants. Gendered norms linking honest womanhood to domestic containment were seen to be subverted especially where autonomous travel and temporary relocation accompanied their labour.

Memories of men's mobility included travel further afield than the majority of women's journeys, usually for the purposes of trade, with the duration and distance of these trips emphasised in cases where an alibi was required for the male party. In an early fifteenth-century suit, Thomas Cottesworth and John Thomeson, both in their twenties, recalled their absence from an alleged marriage because they had then been staying overseas. As the men sought to return to England, they had to wait in Calais due to a sickness in the area that had affected one of their party and necessitated a period of convalescence in the port town. Testifying in the same case, William Till stated that he remembered the marriage after so long because at that time 'he went to places overseas for the purpose of trading and stayed in the same parts, namely Finmark and Holland for two full years'.[56] Men's memories of travel overseas were recalled in reference to journeys and trading activities; Le Goff observed that mercantile measurements of time gradually eroded the prevalence of Church time in medieval culture. Feast days were still often referenced alongside trade and physical travel, suggesting that temporal systems continued to vary and coexisted in ways that reflected the subjective experience of time.[57]

Men's memories of mobility could centre on visits to local and regional centres of trade to buy and sell specialist goods. Hugh Swynflete remembered a contract because he was in Scarborough in order to purchase casks, while Richard Fowler recalled visiting the town to buy herring and salted fish.[58] Some of these recollections focused on commercial activity, such as markets and fairs which happened at regular intervals and could be dated to specific points in time. In 1432 Alexander Butler remembered an alleged contract because Robert, a monk, arrived at Pontefract with John Hereford, a party

---

[54] Goldberg, 'Migration, Youth and Gender', pp. 93–4.

[55] BI CP.E.77 and BI CP.E.159.

[56] BI CP.F.113. 'transivit ad partes transmarinas causa mercandizandi et in eisdem partibus via Ffymark et Holland expectavit per duos annos'.

[57] Le Goff, 'Merchant's Time and Church's Time in the Middle Ages', in Le Goff, *Time, Work and Culture*, pp. 29–42, at p. 36.

[58] BI CP.F.113.

Popular Memory and Gender in Medieval England

in the suit, during the horse fair to buy an ambling palfrey, but the fair had almost finished.[59] Women also engaged in local travel for the purpose of trade, and female servants claimed to have witnessed marriages and public disputes while carrying out errands to other households or workshops at the behest of their employers.[60] Women's journeys in relation to work were, however, usually shorter than men's and occurred as part of their dependent service for employers and heads of households.

Memories of journeys could be imbued with spiritual meaning in men and women's narratives. Experiences of pilgrimage were depicted in a spiritual time scheme in which the laity prepared their souls for the Day of Judgement. In a marriage suit brought in 1430, Henry Devyas recalled his pilgrimage to the church of St Theobald during a recent outbreak of plague. While visiting the site, Henry had made an oath to abstain from fish every Friday for the rest of his life, which he remembered in order to reference the marriage contract.[61] Such journeys accrued enduring significance as temporal markers in personal histories of religious belief. Despite the piety that this type of travel implied, the secular and the spiritual coalesced in many religious journeys – as when women prayed for conception and reproductive health, both for themselves and for kinswomen and friends.[62] In an early fifteenth-century case, one witness remembered a pilgrimage journey with a neighbour who commented that she would prefer to be tending to a kinswoman, recently delivered of a child.[63] Tensions could develop between gendered obligations of care and religious duties, even where pilgrimage tempered some of the domestic and familial pressures upon women's piety.

Memories of moving home appeared in the testimony of men and women, although there were gendered differences in the focus and content of these accounts. In 1367, William Sturgys recalled a marriage contract because he had been present, along with his wife, at the union of her sister, Agnes, to Walter de Tiryngton in Willsthorp one day around Michaelmas sixteen years before. William stated that near the time of the contract, two years after the first plague epidemic, he and his wife had moved to the home where the couple still lived. William used his marital relationship to reinforce memories of their move as he told the examiner that he 'calculated these years many times with his wife'.[64] William's wife, Maud, testified after him, yet the clerical scribe merely noted that her testimony agreed with her husband's account.

---

59 BI CP.F.104.
60 See, for example, BI CP.F.113.
61 BI CP.F.113.
62 S. S. Morrison, *Women Pilgrims in Medieval England: Private Piety as Public Performance* (London and New York, 2000), pp. 19–20.
63 BI CP.F.89. 'dixit quod libenter tunc vellet esse cum Agnete Northefolk uxore Thome Northefolk [illegible] sui et Katerina filia eorumdem'.
64 BI CP.E.95. 'istos annos pluries computavit cum uxore sua'.

Place, Landscape, and Gender

In legal suits, where evidence from both spouses was required, patriarchal assumptions about authority perhaps influenced how testimony from married couples was recorded, suppressing the memories of wives despite their active involvement in maintaining the couple's shared history.

Memories of domestic relocation among married women were occasionally noted alongside their husbands' testimony. In 1425, Margery Carbot, wife of John Carbot, aged more than sixty years, testified on Katherine Northefolk's birth, recalling that she and her husband moved to a house in the village of Naburn near York around the time Katherine was born. The couple still lived in the same house during the legal suit, holding their tenancy from one William Gascoigne. Margery emphasised her role in its arrangement, noting that both she and her husband 'paid an annual farm' for their house and because of these costs she remembered the passage of time.[65] Married women drew on domestic experiences apart from childbirth to identify past events, although a number of tasks deemed to be feminine were performed during relocation, such as the organisation of household items.[66] Margery's husband, John Carbot, also testified in the case, but gave more extensive detail, including a period living in 'the house and tenement of Henry Aclom, squire', the transportation of domestic goods, and the recent death overseas of their landlord.[67] Although wives worked with husbands to arrange the practicalities of relocation, men's memories were more precise, perhaps evoking aspects of legal negotiations and agreements made as head of household with different landlords.

Landlords equally recalled the names and order of tenants as referents for their memories. In the same case, Robert Souman remembered the men and women who had rented a house from him in the preceding twelve years, including one Joan Hurton, Laurence Forster and Agnes, his wife, William Parryerman, and a couple whose surname he could not recall. Robert used this list of residents to calculate the amount of time that had passed. Although only partial and from a landlord's perspective, it offered an oral memory of the house's previous residents, including a single woman and a single man who lived separately there at different points.

Collective events like the arrival of plague spurred various kinds of mobility in the immediate context of the disease, typically involving its avoidance and entailing residential resettlement in the longer term. Decreased population levels after the plague afforded tenants greater mobility as a number of manors offered more favourable rents and services.[68] Demographic decline from the mid-fourteenth century onwards intensified patterns of migration into

---

[65] BI CP.F.89. 'idem Johannes maritus suus et ipsa iurata solverunt annuatim firmam'.

[66] F. Riddy, 'Looking Closely: Authority and Intimacy in the Late Medieval Urban Home', in Kowaleski and Erler, eds., *Gendering the Master Narrative*, pp. 212–28.

[67] BI CP.F.89. 'a domo et tenemente henrici aclom domicelli usque ad tenementum'.

[68] Hatcher, 'England in the Aftermath of the Black Death', p. 26.

Popular Memory and Gender in Medieval England

urban areas, with young women and other workers drawn into a depopulated labour market.[69] Men and women remembered people relocating to different areas, as well as their own resettlement, after the initial visitation. In a late fourteenth-century suit, one Thomas Nade provided details of his residential movements, stating that he had lived in the parish of Althorp from the time of the first pestilence.[70] A fluid land and labour market encouraged more intense migration such that communities were remade in more accommodating urban environments. Length of residency was addressed in testimony, however, as witnesses recognised the implications of demographic disruption. In 1355, John de Hoperton attested to the good reputation of Maud Katersouth and her son, whom he claimed to have known 'from the time of the last mortality right up to the present day'.[71] Local memory was reconfigured during and after periods of plague in ways that weakened previous notions of 'common fame'. In many senses, the embedding of social relationships in more recent chronologies compounded the absence of long-term bonds, highlighting the temporal limits of personal and local knowledge.

The inverse of licit forms of mobility attached to work, marriage, and resettlement were spatial practices that were seen as disruptive and a threat to local cohesion. In one late thirteenth-century suit, interrogatories used for one set of witnesses asked if the men lived in specific places or were 'wanderers' without permanent households.[72] Residential status could reflect on the character of witnesses in legal disputes, since vagrancy connoted economic instability as well as the absence of 'common fame', which was usually shaped by personal histories built up within the local community. Poverty intersected with mobility through itinerant routines of begging for shelter and sustenance, yet it also shaped spatial practices among men and women with fixed households. Witnesses described Maud Katersouth, apparently a single mother, as performing menial work for others in her neighbourhood in exchange for money or food.[73] Other transgressive forms of mobility were less local in nature and extended further afield, but also intersected with marital status.[74] In 1364, Edmund Dronefeld sought a divorce *a vinculo* from Margaret de Donbarre as it had emerged that she had an earlier marriage in Scotland. Prior to her union with Edmund, Margaret had wed one William de Brigham during a period in her life when she had been known as Agnes.[75]

---

[69] Goldberg, 'Migration, Youth and Gender', pp. 85–99.

[70] BI CP.E.155.

[71] BI CP.E.82.

[72] CCA E.S. Roll 88; *Select Cases*, p. 551. 'Item an larem foveant in aliquo certo loco vel fuerint devagantes absque certo domicilio'.

[73] BI CP.E.82.

[74] On spousal desertion see S. Butler, 'Runaway Wives: Husband Desertion in Medieval England', *Journal of Social History*, 40 (2006), 337–59.

[75] BI CP.E.87; Owen, 'White Annays', pp. 331–4; Donahue, *Law, Marriage, and Society*, pp.

Place, Landscape, and Gender

Women could exploit or navigate the disturbance that accompanied episodes of plague and military activity to desert husbands and remarry, creating new social identities that omitted their recent marital pasts.

PLACE, SPACE, AND SEXUALITY

Memory intersected with spatial practice more explicitly in accounts of gendered forms of embodiment situated in particular places and landscapes. The spatial imaginaries of clergy and moral commentators imbued places and spaces with gendered associations, many of which were aligned with the ideological segregation of women within domestic spaces. Biblical models of appropriate feminine behaviour located respectable women in the household in comparison with their sexually loose counterparts who wandered the streets. The implications of this strand of patriarchal control meant that certain spaces and places were judged more or less appropriate for female use. Women's reputations were composed of shared memories from neighbours, kin, and acquaintances that referenced their past behaviour through accounts of their actions and speech. Witnesses also composed spatial histories for men and women in legal disputes that acted as evidence of character and respectability.

The establishment of conjugal households functioned as a central form of proof in suits over disputed marriages, while in cases of defamation, and exceptions against witnesses, marital status and maintenance of a shared household became a symbol of female respectability. If abiding within the marital home saw women adhere to appropriate gendered norms of mobility, then residence in another household under adulterous circumstances represented its antithesis. In 1357, Lucy, wife of William Fentrice, sought restitution of goods from her husband after the failure of their marriage.[76] Witnesses recalled William's cruelty towards Lucy and noted that while she was absent from the couple's household during the previous harvest, William had kept a woman named Alice in their home where they engaged in a sexual relationship. Thomas Dogeson deposed that he saw Alice serving William, working in his fields and driving his plough. The subversion of sexual norms in the household underlined the illegitimacy of William's behaviour, and Alice's performance of household labour reinforced depictions of their relationship as illicit and adulterous.

Different kinds of sexual activity were situated in the built environment and mapped onto the landscape in ways that embodied perceptions and ideologies of gendered behaviour. Narratives that depicted sex as the consummation of marriage usually located these events in domestic rooms, but accounts of

141–2.
[76] BI CP.E.77.

non-marital sex were recalled in other locations where illicit activity more commonly took place. In a marriage suit initiated in 1292, Senicla de Suffolk remembered a sexual encounter between Elias de Suffolk and Christine de Thorley in a bath house near the Tower of London.[77] Public baths were often unofficial sites of prostitution and illicit sex, containing beds and located close to brothels and streets used for trading sex.[78] Senicla described the events she claimed to have witnessed, but stated that she had only visited the bath house because she had recently injured her hand. Despite the brothels of Southwark falling within the liberty of the bishop of Winchester, justification was needed to explain why she had frequented the establishment and observed the illicit sexual activity.[79]

In urban and rural environments, drinking houses offered young people, servants, and apprentices an alternative place in which to socialize and engage in courtship, prior to the formation of independent households. Despite their ideological association with criminality and prostitution, taverns and ale-houses represented an extension of the domestic sphere where marriages were more commonly formalised.[80] As communal spaces, these sites were central to testimony where marriages or personal disputes were the focus of litigation. In a late thirteenth-century suit that reached the court of Canterbury, several women recalled meeting in a local tavern to witness an alleged marriage contract at the request of Agnes King. Geoffrey le Brewere stated that he remembered this event as he had worked in the tavern selling ale for some time, but finished working there in the year before the couple wed.[81] Although licit marriages were sometimes formed in taverns, they were also places in which young men and women socialised accompanied by the consumption of alcohol. In 1269, several women claimed to have seen Johanna de Clopton and Richard de Bosco having sex near a tavern where they had spent the evening. Male witnesses in the same case recalled a similar occasion in which Richard had sex with a different woman, as the men left another tavern in the area.[82] Courtesy manuals, like the mid-fourteenth-century text *How the Goode Wife Taught hyr Doughter*, advised young women to avoid socializing in taverns, yet as Felicity Riddy notes, these moral anxieties reflected clerical and civic attempts to control the conduct of young, unmarried women.[83]

---

[77] CCA E.S. Roll 69; *Select Cases*, p. 359.

[78] R. M. Karras, *Common Women: Prostitution and Sexuality in Medieval England* (Oxford, 1996), pp. 17–18.

[79] Karras, *Common Women*, p. 23.

[80] McSheffrey, *Marriage, Sex, and Civic Culture*, p. 132.

[81] CCA E.S. Roll 239.

[82] CCA E.S. Roll 310.

[83] 'How the Goode Wife Taught hyr Doughter', in *The Trials and Joys of Marriage*, ed. E. Salisbury (Kalamazoo, MI, 2002), pp. 219–24; Riddy, 'Mother Knows Best', pp. 66–86.

Place, Landscape, and Gender

The reluctance of many young men to marry was acknowledged through the association of illicit sex with secrecy, as well as its spatial occurrence in suspect places outside the domestic and marital household. In contemporary lyrics and ballads, illicit sex was often depicted as occurring outdoors in marginal environments. The young female narrator in *A Betrayed Maiden's Lament* told how Sir John, her suitor, had lain her against the bank during their sexual encounter. Likewise, in *The Serving Maid's Holiday*, the young woman's lover, Jack, was described as placing her 'on the lond / that al my buttockus ben of sond'.[84] Accounts of sex in fields and under hedges perhaps also reflected clerical associations of female desire with the natural environment, simultaneously echoing misogynistic fantasies of sexual promiscuity among young single women.

Memories of sex in rural spaces or on the outskirts of settlements were occasionally used in legal cases as proof of consummation, but they were also cited in order to underline the illicit nature of the relationship in question. The marriage suit between Johanna de Clopton and Richard de Bosco was heard in the court of the bishop of Salisbury on the grounds of fornication following an oath of *sub pena nubendi*, prior to its referral on appeal to Canterbury.[85] A number of deponents who testified on behalf of Johanna remembered seeing the parties having sex in a field. Witnesses used the location of sex to depict the presence of young couples alone in remote areas as morally dubious, and occasionally had to explain how they came to observe these events. During a late thirteenth-century case, several men deposed on a sexual encounter they asserted took place between one William and Alice three years before in a field near Liss in Hampshire.[86] Asked why he had followed the couple, John le Longe claimed that he was suspicious of them entering the field alone, and wished to investigate to discover the purpose of their actions. Other men in the suit offered more circumstantial reasons for pursuing the pair, like Henry Wollemelk, who described how he was leading a bull towards the village when it broke loose near where the couple lay. The appearance of secluded places in legal testimony demonstrates the practical concerns that determined the location of sexual practices, especially among young unmarried men and women without independent households. These claims were positioned in plausible narratives of sexual relationships, yet focused only on the later stages in order to portray them as transitory rather than part of the progression of courtship.

Women also demonstrated narrative agency in recounting their own premarital sexual activities. In a marriage case from Kent brought in 1293, Juliana, the daughter of William le Granger, told the court that her sexual

[84] *Secular Lyrics of the XIV and XV Centuries*, ed. R. Hope Robbins (Oxford, 1955), p. 19, line 6; p. 25, lines 30–1.

[85] CCA E.S. Roll 310.

[86] CCA E.S. Roll 181.

Popular Memory and Gender in Medieval England

encounter with William de Stonham rendered his marriage to her sister invalid. Juliana testified that she had known William carnally in a grange belonging to their father before his contract with her sister.[87] Although men tended to make claims of affinity through sexual contact with kin, women could similarly advance this argument to form an impediment to marriage. Juliana admitted to sex with William in a setting which emphasised its illicit nature, adopting a subject position more often assigned to women in confessional settings. The location of their encounter intimated its sinfulness, as well as the lack of sexual control which they both exhibited. Women could thus appropriate the moral and spatial connotations of sexual activity, drawing on narrative strategies that commonly appeared in testimony for male parties.

Urban and rural environments retained mnemonic resonance in disputes where sex and marriage were primary concerns, allowing witnesses to rely on gendered social perceptions to construct narratives that signified elements of social experience.[88] Men and women also represented past events in spatial terms more explicitly through descriptions of boundaries, animal husbandry, and the cultivation of the land through arable farming. Writing of agrarian communities in sixteenth- and seventeenth-century Gloucestershire, Rollison observes that 'the land was a memory palace' that provided a store-house for popular remembrance.[89] Landscape features and artificial markers were everyday components of men and women's lives in this period, and fields, ditches, rivers, and crosses were the very substance of non-elite memory in rural communities.

LANDSCAPE AND MEMORY

The relationship of the peasantry to the landscape depended on the terms and restrictions of their landholdings, which intersected with the material conditions of tenure and wider fluctuations in social, economic, and demographic conditions.[90] The spatial organisation of the rural landscape supplemented claims of customs and rights, recalling them synchronically in relation to the agricultural year, seasonal cycles, and local histories of land use. Gender influenced depictions of the natural and cultivated environment, producing memories in which physical locations, local customs, and boundaries were articulated primarily through men's testimony. Patriarchal ideologies asserted women's domestic enclosure, reiterating paternalistic and misogynistic

---

[87] CCA E.S. Roll 292.

[88] Wood, 'The Place of Custom in Plebeian Political Culture', pp. 46–60; N. Whyte, 'Landscape, Memory and Custom: Parish Identities c. 1550–1700', *Social History*, 32 (2007), 166–86.

[89] Rollison, *The Local Origins of Modern Society*, p. 73.

[90] T. H. Aston, ed., *Landlords, Peasants and Politics in Medieval England* (Cambridge, 1987); Bailey, *The Decline of Serfdom*.

Place, Landscape, and Gender

attempts to contain female bodies and speech.[91] The remit of women's daily movements thus often appears to centre on activities performed in domestic environs, with doorways and streets forming the backdrop to networks of female neighbours and kin.[92] Disparities in the selection of deponents reinforced these assumptions as women appeared most often in disputes over marriage and defamation. Although less prominent than men in memories of the rural landscape, women are nevertheless perceptible, performing agricultural labour and keeping animals in ways that defined that landscape's use and contributed to local accounts of its history.

Men and women were often questioned about the weather on the days which they recalled in their testimony, as examiners attempted to establish the precise circumstances of the events described. In a late thirteenth-century case, Matilda Corneys noted that it was raining during the marriage contract she claimed to have witnessed, while John le Longe described the weather as beautiful on the day he recalled in his evidence.[93] Poor weather and storms were generic temporal referents in proofs of age from the early fourteenth century onwards, perhaps retaining the same narrative function in evidence from witnesses in the church courts. Yet, in some instances, memories of the weather signalled its ability to disrupt the material survival and composition of local communities in physical and affective ways. Unsettled weather where water levels rose or rivers broke their banks punctuated personal and local versions of the past. In 1435, John Cotrell remembered a marriage contract because around the feast of St Peter's Chains four years before 'notorious floods befell these parts of northern England from which the greater part of the crops and hay-harvest growing in that year was destroyed'. John stated that about the same time 'a certain Richard Park of Lepyngton was lamentably drowned in the waters of Derwent, near Kexby bridge'.[94] The area where Richard Park drowned was identified in approximate terms, 'near' the bridge which served as a physical structure to which later accounts of his death were attached.

Conflict surrounding the extent of parish boundaries produced more intricate accounts of the landscape that navigated larger segments of land. Markers, landscape features, and buildings were referenced in geographical order to create the appearance of a continuous legal border. In 1457 an

---

[91] S. Salih, 'At Home; Out of the House', in Dinshaw and Wallace, eds., *The Cambridge Companion to Medieval Women's Writing*, pp. 124–40.

[92] Gowing, '"The freedom of the streets"', pp. 130–51; Whyte, 'Custodians of Memory', p. 154.

[93] CCA E.S. Roll 11.

[94] BI CP.F.179. 'contingebat diluvia famosa in istis partibus borialis anglie quibus maior pars messum et feni illo anno proveniens fuit destructa ... quidam Ricardus Park de Lepyngton in aqua de Derwent prope pontem de Kexby fuit lamentabiliter submersus citra qua diluvia et submersione'.

Popular Memory and Gender in Medieval England

ongoing conflict between St Mary's abbey in York and the dean and chapter of the cathedral church developed into a legal dispute over rights to tithes and oblations in the Green Dykes area outside the city. Twelve men from the parish of St Lawrence testified that Greek Dykes came within their parish's limits.[95] It was claimed that, by agreement with the nearby hospital of St Leonard's, the parish of St Lawrence was paid the minor tithes, while the greater were owed to the dean and chapter of York as appropriators of the parish church. Thomas Stokton recalled that a certain long ditch separated Green Dykes from the lands of St Mary's abbey. This began at the corner of the close of St Nicholas's hospital, extending to Tilmire marsh, with boundary stones on the bank of the ditch that separated the parish of St Lawrence from a neighbouring parish.[96] Aside from identifying spatial limits, agricultural activities were also described in this type of suit to underline the routine processes that claimants carried out, sometimes by legal agreement. Richard More recalled that the master and brothers of St Leonard's hospital transported manure from the city, depositing it in a great ditch near Green Dykes for composting and spreading on fields. This was in exchange for the grant of tithes to the parish of St Lawrence and the dean and chapter, and Richard stated that 'no one spoke against' the dumping of manure in the ditch near Green Dykes, indicating widespread knowledge of the arrangement.

The landscape was an agricultural and economic resource, ensuring that custom operated against a backdrop of the 'workaday routine of livelihood'.[97] Memories were depicted in relation to seasonal patterns of labour and tasks that were performed at specific times in the farming year. Agrarian societies drew on a 'measurement of time [that] is commonly related to familiar processes in the cycle of work or of domestic chores' and extended to annual patterns of labour.[98] In an early fifteenth-century suit, Robert Dalton recalled his presence at his sister's marriage to John Warde in the field of North Hill in the Yorkshire village of Burnby. Robert stated that he remembered the time of the union because crops were then growing and 'now it is sown with grain'.[99] Memories of the landscape were nevertheless mutable, despite their reliance on material forms of proof. Other men in the case testified that the field of North Hill 'lay sterile, not sown, namely fallow' during the period that Robert claimed it had been sown.[100] Other stages of the agricultural cycle featured in alibis that sought to establish the whereabouts of parties and witnesses. In a

---

95 BI CP.F.342.

96 K. J. Allison, ed., *VCH: A History of the County of York East Riding*, vol. 3 (London, 1976), pp. 31–2; see F. Drake, *Eboracum, or the History and Antiquities of the City of York*, with a new introduction by K. J. Allison (London, 1736), p. 251.

97 Thompson, *Customs in Common*, p. 102.

98 Thompson, *Customs in Common*, p. 355.

99 BI CP.F.200. 'nunc est cum frumento seminatus'.

100 BI CP.F.200. John Fawden: 'iacuit sterilis non seminatus viz falgh'.

Place, Landscape, and Gender

thirteenth-century suit from Canterbury, witnesses stated that Alice Peytevyn was working in a field called 'Westherpyng' on the day that it was alleged she had sex with William Bandely.[101] Deponents stated that Emma Peytevyn had planted beans alongside Alice, while William Peytevyn harrowed the land and Robert Denays carried the goad for driving the horse and cart. During periods of agricultural intensity, women's labour supplemented heavier farming tasks usually performed by men.[102] Memories that depended on evocations of the landscape acknowledged the gendered dynamics of agrarian labour, situating them in recognisable narratives of seasonal work within the peasant household economy.

Customs relating to land use were rooted in particular spaces through references to animal husbandry as much as arable farming. One way of asserting claims over rights to tithes was through knowledge of the animals that were tended in the parish. In a mid-fourteenth-century case, witnesses reported that the vicar of All Saints, Pontefract, was entitled to tithes from sheep in Hughlathes since they were fed and grazed there. The mobility of livestock meant that customs attaching them to the landscape were multiple and dispersed, generating ample occasion for disputes over their ownership. This method of establishing rights produced detailed accounts of husbandry in the form of narrative maps of their movement through fields and common areas.[103] During an appeal suit over tithes of herbage and pasture in 1407, witnesses outlined the pasture of animals belonging to local residents in a close called 'le Carre' in the East Riding of Yorkshire, which the rector of Wheldrake claimed made them liable for payment.[104] The animals had allegedly been kept in the field during birthing and while being fattened for milking, where they were pastured and identified 'horne be horn' and 'fote be fote', perhaps a method of counting that implied detailed knowledge of herds and flocks.

Memories of the ownership of cows, bulls, and horses in the parish were cited as evidence of customs attached to the land on which they were kept and grazed. In a late thirteenth-century suit over marriage, John le Longe stated that he recalled the events about which he deposed as that same day he had found submerged in a marsh a cow that he kept in the royal forest of Woolmer in Hampshire.[105] Memories of this kind were embedded in a variety of rights and customs related to tenure and status that encompassed common pasture, pannage, and the use of wood for different purposes.[106] Men in cases over tithes and parochial rights constructed narratives of their own personal

---

[101] CCA SVSB III, no. 33.

[102] Bennett, *Women in the Medieval English Countryside*, p. 116.

[103] BI CP.E.67.

[104] BI CP.F.29.

[105] CCA E.S. Roll 181.

[106] Birrell, 'Common Rights in the Medieval Forest', p. 27.

Popular Memory and Gender in Medieval England

and familial expertise in the management of local animals. In the dispute over tithes owed from Green Dykes in York, Thomas Stokton recalled his father's stint as herder of the common cows of the city. During this time, one of Alice Gare's cows gave birth and Thomas' father returned the animals to her, collecting a penny in tithes for the new calf which he paid to the parish priest of St Lawrence's.[107] Men's memories took account of women's experiences of rights and custom, whether in relation to Church or manorial authority, to an extent mitigating the more generalised suppression of female perceptions of the past. The rural environment was narrated in ways that evoked the financial and legal consequences of land use, which in turn depended on the jurisdictions that men and women used and inhabited.

Alterations to the landscape reconfigured its role and use, especially in rural areas where the land was integral to patterns of subsistence and employment among small-holders and landless workers engaged in agricultural wage labour. Human intervention could act to adjust elements of local memory when resources and features, like rivers and other bodies of water, were redirected and the customs attached to them changed. In 1357 John, son of James of Reedness, recalled when a marriage had occurred from his memory of a watercourse begun the same year at a place called 'Merskelande' in the East Riding, probably an area of marsh, for the purpose of drainage.[108] Adaptations of the landscape on this scale formalised new patterns of land use perhaps already reflected in provisional work practices and variations to routes of travel. Perceptions of the landscape were transformed in some instances since 'to alter or destroy a land form [...] was to erase a part of the collective memory'.[109] Substantial changes of this nature became embedded in local histories as inhabitants recalled environmental habits that prevailed before and after these developments.

The extent of customs and rights varied, despite assertions of their timelessness in litigation. Natural features and resources were mutable and liable to environmental transformations which in turn disturbed the balance of local power dynamics beyond the immediate economic context. In a mid-thirteenth-century suit over tithes from a watermill in Coddenham, near Ipswich, witnesses recalled how a bank known locally as 'Schaldeforde' separated the parishes of Baylham and Coddenham, a function perhaps signalled in its name, which meant 'shallow ford'.[110] A scarcity of water led the farmer of the mill, William le Fleyer, to transfer operations across a waterway from the parish of Baylham to the neighbouring parish of Coddenham. The mill had been established in Coddenham for twelve years by the time

---

[107] BI CP.F.342.

[108] BI CP.E.76.

[109] Rollison, *The Local Origins of Modern Society*, p. 70.

[110] CCA E.S. Roll 334. The probable meaning of 'shallow ford' is suggested in *Select Cases*, p. 434 n. 2.

Place, Landscape, and Gender

the conflict entered the courts. After rendering payment to the vicar of Coddenham for much of this period, Alan Baday, the new farmer, began to pay the tithes to the vicar of Baylham once more. John de Caxstrete noted that although he did not witness the tithes being rendered to the vicar of Coddenham, their transition to the vicar of Baylham led to a 'great tumult' in the neighbourhood.[111] Although the mill had been transferred across the river in recent memory, a pre-existing conflict between the communities over landed resources and boundaries may have engendered an intense awareness of rights among residents of both parishes. John Eldevik describes the material nature of these types of custom, noting that 'tithe rights were sites of memory and power that could be erected, changed, enlarged and manipulated'.[112] Such histories depended on oral accounts circulating in the area, whether customs were cast as 'ancient' or as the more recent result of changes in the environment that weakened rival claims. Local communities exercised agency in building identities, sometimes anew, from rights associated with the landscape.

Customs and rights were usually narrated by men in legal testimony, but alterations to the landscape held gendered implications for laywomen as well. These could be cited in cases where periods of environmental stress rendered water levels unstable and restricted the delivery of the *cura animarum*. In 1487, parishioners from Temple Sowerby in Westmorland brought a suit against Henry Wherton, the parish rector of Kirby Thore, perhaps seeking independent status for the existing chapel. The plaintiffs requested a chaplain to replace the visiting priest, claiming that the river often overflowed, obstructing passage to the church, with inhabitants of Temple Sowerby unable to hear services or receive sacraments.[113] The parishioners claimed that the geographical location of the church of Kirby Thore, about two miles away, impeded the rector's pastoral care. This meant that the sacraments were not reliably administered, resulting in a lack of baptism for infants, a failure to attend to women in distress during childbirth, as well as the absence of clergy for marriage contracts and funerals. Disruption of this nature undermined the spiritual comfort of the laity during life events that aroused powerful psychological and emotional responses. Anxieties that were more specific – of mortal danger and spiritual peril – were attached to women in labour who were not recently confessed and newborn infants who were unbaptised. The experiences of laywomen were seldom cited in this type of dispute, but parties could exploit the Church's desire to mediate key life events by emphasising the sacramental needs of distinct sections of the parish.

---

[111] CCA E.S. Roll 334.

[112] Eldevik, 'Driving the Chariot of the Lord', p. 173.

[113] BI CP.F.260; see also R. N. Swanson, 'Fissures in the Bedrock: Parishes, Chapels, Parishioners and Chaplains in Pre-Reformation England', in A. Morton and N. Lewycky, eds., *Getting Along? Religious Identities and Confessional Relations in Early Modern England: Essays in Honour of W. J. Sheils* (Farnham, 2012), pp. 77–95.

Uses of the land were also integral to memories of religious practice, producing memory maps composed of sites related to worship and parish rights. In the dispute over tithes in the Green Dykes area of York, it emerged that local inhabitants had established a shrine to the Blessed Virgin Mary along the roadside which attracted worship and gifts that the vicar of St Lawrence collected on behalf of the parish. William Paton, one of the twelve parishioners who testified, described the shrine as a small house to which oblations were made in the form of money and miniature wax figures of eyes, arms, and legs, perhaps the impaired body parts mentioned in prayers.[114] Despite the prominence given to sites of spiritual significance, the men's accounts of parish boundaries also incorporated natural and artificial features of the landscape that held little religious import, including ditches, roads, and a mill known as 'Howmilne'. Parochial memory maintained a reciprocal relationship with the secular and agricultural topographies that formed part of the wider environment beyond jurisdictional limits.

Each generation of men was responsible for transmitting details of parish bounds to younger male parishioners when they reached adulthood. Like other witnesses in the suit over tithes from Green Dykes, Thomas Stokton drew on his father's knowledge of the parish and its landscape in order to substantiate his testimony. Thomas recalled his father's occupation as herder of the cows of the city of York for twenty years before his death, with whom he had worked during his childhood when his father taught him about aspects of the area's history.[115] In other cases, the memories of fathers and other relatives, some of whom were older female kin, functioned as a link with the distant past when deponents lacked personal familiarity with land use.[116] The limits of parishes were imparted both through conversation and during informal and official perambulation and inspection of their perimeters. In the dispute over tithes in Green Dykes, Thomas Brown claimed to recall the boundaries of the parish of St Lawrence because two elderly men, aged eighty and one hundred respectively, had shown younger laymen the stones that indicated its limits some sixty years before. Richard More knew Green Dykes was in the parish of St Lawrence's because he had participated in Rogation processions when he lived in neighbouring Fulford, and on one occasion bore the procession banner on their route. The performance of rogation rituals marginalised some sections of the community, such as women and 'strangers', from the formation of the parish's social memory.[117] Yet in social practice the circulation of knowledge about parish limits did not exclude women entirely.

---

[114] BI CP.F.342.

[115] BI CP.F.342.

[116] Everard, 'Sworn Testimony', p. 82.

[117] M. Rubin, 'Religious Culture in Town and City: Reflections on a Great Divide', in D. Abulafia, M. Franklin, and M. Rubin, eds., *Church and City, 1000–1500: Essays in Honour of Christopher Brooke* (Cambridge, 1992), pp. 3–22, at p. 12.

Place, Landscape, and Gender

Sermons to be preached on Rogation days were occasionally addressed to wives as well as husbands, while the material culture of the parish, such as the religious imagery on baptismal fonts, implies that in certain situations women participated in religious processions.[118]

Rituals related to boundaries that might be cited later in legal disputes may have excluded the contributions of women to formal versions of parish memory, but other religious practices tied to places in the parish were more overtly connected with the female laity, appearing in suits where their activities were usually overlooked. One of the few references to women in the case over rights in Green Dykes centred on the presence of parishioners and pilgrims 'of both sexes' at the shrine to the Image of the Blessed Virgin in Heslington. The devotional attachment of laywomen to the Marian cult was manifested in maidens' guilds, as well as the permeation of Marian worship in many realms of parish life.[119] Although female parishioners were omitted from more official accounts that marked and reinforced boundaries, they were central to other shared rituals rooted in the landscape. Some of these activities aided in the demarcation of parish limits and highlight women's contact with places where memory, worship, and local identity overlapped.

The burial of neighbours and kin was a central part of local memory, serving as proof of existing customs and practices in disputes over parish rights. These were established in ways that signalled the corporeal bond that the laity retained with the sacred landscape after death. Accounts of interment underlined the subterranean tone of parish memory, where the burial of laymen and women was seen to mark the physical and spiritual space of the churchyard, literally embodying the church's status and rights. In the fifteenth-century case between the churches of Wawne and Sutton in the East Riding, older male parishioners of Sutton provided evidence on the burial of the village's dead, many of whom perished in the mortality crisis of 1429, to establish common consensus on the burial place of parishioners.[120] Lists of the dead incorporated into local memory large numbers of laypeople buried in the cemetery of St James in Sutton-on-Hull, whose presence in the parish was usually omitted from written records, including children and laywomen. Burial practices elsewhere referred to traditions that linked memory and burial in a more immediate sense. Parishioners in the Green Dykes area of York identified the boundaries of the parish of St Lawrence in relation to Heslington Cross, where funeral processions paused en route to the parish church to pray and affix small wooden crosses in memory of the dead. Thomas

---

[118] Barr, *The Pastoral Care of Women*, pp. 55–6; R. Gilchrist, *Medieval Life: Archaeology and the Life Course* (Woodbridge, 2012), p. 186. Gilchrist notes the presence of a woman carrying a procession flag on a stone font in the parish church of Burnham Deepdale, Norfolk.

[119] Phillips, *Medieval Maidens*, pp. 77–80.

[120] YMA, M2 (3)c.

Popular Memory and Gender in Medieval England

Stokton, aged more than eighty, testified that this was 'according to the custom of that parish and other surrounding churches and villages' which shared the same use and observance.[121] The funerary practice was described as an ancient custom, existing 'time out of mind' in the local area. Memories of burial thus functioned as embodied maps of parish rights and boundaries, as well as commemorative sites associated with the deceased.

LANDSCAPE AND AUTHORITY

The landscape was fundamental to the multitude of legal relationships in manorial communities, and the performance of labour services and dues was derived from this personal status. Patriarchal hegemony was exerted through a dynamic that operated between uses of the landscape and their connection to seigneurial authority. In manorial society, disputes over landed resources appeared in tandem with lordly attempts to control the autonomy of tenants in the areas of work and mobility. Land tenure was often proven through memories of customs and services which acted as evidence of the personal status of witnesses. Although married women in rural areas were seldom directly liable for labour services, by virtue of their marital status, female heads of households were held accountable for any failure to provide these duties.[122] In addition, both men and women could commute these duties into payments or hire labourers to perform them in their stead.

Despite these similarities in the treatment of men and women in manorial settings, the gendered allocation of labour meant that men performed a wider range of activities for the lord, which coincided with the greater prevalence of male witnesses generally in church-court litigation. Memories of unfreedom thus tended to focus on men's experiences of labour services, with their servility evidenced through accounts which centred on agricultural work. The completion of these duties acted as a central means of proof in suits where the testimony of witnesses was undermined on the basis of alleged servility. In a late thirteenth-century dispute over the church of Ratley in Warwickshire, several men were alleged to be unfree from birth as they were seen transporting manure, ploughing, sowing, and reaping for the manorial lord. Richard Alfrey, a former forester in the area and witness in the case, described his knowledge of the men's legal status and the works they performed in reference to his own occupation.[123] The remit of the forester's role depended on the nature of the appointment, but knowledge of the surrounding landscape and the status of

---

[121] BI CP.F.342. 'secundum consuetudinem illius parochie ac aliarum ecclesiarum et villarum circumvicinorum'. For a treatment of popular religion and folk practices see A. Vauchez, *The Laity in the Middle Ages: Religious Beliefs and Devotional Practices*, trans. M. J. Schneider (London, 1993), pp. 129–39.

[122] Müller, 'Peasant Women, Agency and Status', p. 102.

[123] CCA E.S. Roll 95ii.

Place, Landscape, and Gender

its inhabitants underpinned the enforcement of forest law and the prosecution of offenses.[124]

Local people also distinguished between the discharge of labour services and paid employment based on the work that men had historically performed. In the same case, Thomas Wellemakere recalled how several men had carried out different tasks for John de Arden, noting that they had worked only as day labourers and that their employer could not behave towards them as their lord.[125] Peasant uses of the land were construed through accounts of their work, which in turn signified the limits and nature of lordly authority.

Seigneurial control over men's spatial movements and legal agency was also used as proof of their servile pasts. In the suit over the church of Ratley, John de Arden brought exceptions against the witnesses of Ralph, the clerk, claiming that several were serfs of the lord of the neighbouring manor of Upton. Ralph de Cheesebrak told the court that Thomas atte Hulle's parents were serfs, and that the manorial lord could 'dispose of his goods and of his body freely, legally remove him from the lands he holds and sell his body if he pleases'.[126] Being unfree meant the witnesses lacked legal and bodily autonomy, which fell under the control of the seigneurial lord, a condition that acted as evidence of servility and subordination. Other men in the case were described as liable for payments upon the marriages of their sons and daughters, unable to leave the manor without rendering this sum, and as working at the will of the lord. The subordinate position of male serfs implicated them in socio-economic power relations that were patriarchal in essence, mirroring some of the structural and legal constraints upon married women and dependants. Limitations imposed on these men held gendered connotations, including the inability to discharge the responsibilities associated with adult married men. These further emphasised the potential for conflict between unfree, free, and seigneurial heads of household, rooted in the intersection of gender relations and hierarchical difference. Ralph de Cheesebrak recalled the development of an unspecified 'enmity' between Thomas atte Hulle and his manorial lord in the year preceding, which had been resolved only recently. The denigration of witnesses' legal capacity through their association with serfdom did not entirely mask histories of hostility between serfs and manorial lords, signalling tensions in the seigneurial system while reinforcing its existence.

Memories of personal status were cited in suits that involved claims of serfdom. References to servile pasts could touch on the legal condition of the serf's children as much as their own ancestry, since evidence of unfreedom

---

[124] J. R. Birrell, 'The Medieval English Forest', *Journal of Forest History*, 24 (1980), 78–85.

[125] CCA E.S. Roll 95ii.

[126] CCA E.S. Roll 95i; the English translation follows *Select Cases*, p. 558. 'de bonis que tenet prefatus Thomas et eciam de corpore ipsius Thome libere disponere potest, et ipsum Thomam a terra quam tenet licite removere et corpus suum vendere cum sibi placuerit'.

was traced for various administrative purposes in English manors.[127] In 1269, a suit was initiated over the possession of the church of Houghton in Leicestershire.[128] William, son of the steward of Houghton, made an exception against the evidence of one Geoffrey Sampson, a neighbour from the vill of Houghton, on the grounds that he was a villein. William alleged that Geoffrey's status meant that he could be 'sold as if he was an ox or an ass, with or without the glebe land, along with his sons and daughters, his household and all his chattels'.[129] The legal status of unfree peasantry was established in part through the transactional language of animal husbandry that interpreted tenants as resources for labour. Non-elite men and women recognised the association between land and personal status, a mutual relationship that became embedded in the memory of local communities. William also referred to the status of another witness, named Ralph, who had previously been a villein, despite his later manumission and tenure of free land.[130] By the second half of the fourteenth century, labour services and dues associated with manorial authority had entered a period of decline, although memories of unfreedom persisted. In a marriage suit initiated in 1372, Simon de Sketeby described himself as servile in condition as he held his lands in bondage.[131] Even after the manorial system began to weaken in earnest, personal and family memories of serfdom were transmitted across generations and remained part of the social memory of local communities. Servile pasts were signified in numerous ways, yet their basis lay in the legal relationship between the peasantry and the rural landscape.

Manorial authority was established in part through rights related to the cultivation of the land, and this was the case where different jurisdictions overlapped or villages were administered by several manors. Conceptions of lordship in legal suits sought to resist the permeability of the natural and worked landscape, by referring to the boundaries and judicial processes that gave its physical limits a greater degree of solidity.[132] In the case over tithes in Green Dykes, Thomas Brown recalled that years before, John Langwath, the bailiff of the manor of Heslington and minister of St Leonard's hospital,

---

[127] On servile genealogies, see Bailey, *The Decline of Serfdom*, pp. 95–6; Cam, 'Pedigrees of Villeins and Freemen', pp. 124–35.

[128] CCA E.S. Roll 9ii and Ch. Ant. Z. no. 183. See also, in 1374, for instance, Thomas Nash deposed in a marriage case in the Court of York, despite informing them of his own servility.

[129] CCA E.S. Roll 9ii and Ch. Ant. Z. 183; *Select Cases*, p. 288. 'potest vendi cum gleba cum filiis et filiabus et cum omnibus catallis suis et cum tota sua sequela ac si esset bos vel asinus'.

[130] CCA E.S. Roll 9ii and Ch. Ant. Z. 183; *Select Cases*, p. 288.

[131] BI CP.E.114.

[132] For an interesting analysis of jurisdiction as a process, see T. Johnson, 'The Tree and the Rod: Jurisdiction in Late Medieval England', *Past & Present*, 237 (2017), 13–51, at pp. 11–13.

Place, Landscape, and Gender

had seized his horse and cart for digging clay in their jurisdiction.[133] The experience of official and financial punishment formed the basis for knowledge about the manor and the extent of its boundaries.

Judicial violence meted out by manorial authorities was also enacted in ways that left a physical impression on the local environment. In the same dispute, the gallows erected by the hospital of St Leonard's, lords of the manor of Heslington, were remembered in conjunction with the execution of thieves and other criminals. Several men testified to the hanging of five thieves by the sheriff of York on the gallows of St Leonard's thirty or forty years earlier, after which the men claimed that the site was known as 'Seynt Leonard's Gallowes'.[134] Thomas Brown stated that the hospital had erected the gallows on the edge of the manor as a sign of their lordship, an act that aimed to inscribe its extent on the landscape. In scholastic treatises on memory, violent imagery was regarded as a powerful mnemonic, and evidence from land disputes in medieval France provides instances in which children were beaten so that the boundaries would be remembered in the future.[135] The focus upon judicial violence in the dispute involving St Leonard's hospital not only encoded in its name the punitive nature of its authority, but also referred to the judicial processes that underpinned the manor's extent. Boundaries were thus memorialised through punishment for transgressing their limits, while popular memory reiterated both experiences of and opposition to legal authority.

Since custom was established in part through practice, the agricultural use of the land was the primary means of proof for the majority of witnesses, and familiarity with the land through labour was valued highly in legal cases. Men of higher status who held some literate expertise underlined the authoritative nature of their knowledge by drawing on legal documents that recorded jurisdictional boundaries from an official perspective. John Shirwood, common clerk of the city of York for over thirty years, and described as a freeman and gentleman in the civic records, lent weight to the claims of the parishioners of St Lawrence.[136] Earlier in his career, John had held the court of St Leonard's hospital in Heslington, an administrative position which entailed working with its accounts, where he recalled seeing details of their landholdings. John had read in a written agreement, dated June 1252, that the dean and chapter of the cathedral church of York were named proprietors of St Lawrence's church. The same agreement with St Leonard's hospital assigned tithes in the area to

---

[133] BI CP.F.342.

[134] On the gallows, see P. M. Tillott, ed., *VCH: A History of the County of York, the City of York* (Oxford, 1961), pp. 497–8.

[135] Carruthers, *The Book of Memory*, p. 134; van Houts, 'Gender and Authority', pp. 206–7.

[136] B. Dobson, 'John Shirwood of York: A Common Clerk's Will of 1473', in M. Aston and R. Horrox, eds., *Much Heaving and Shoving: Late Medieval Gentry and their Concerns: Essays for Colin Richmond* (Lavenham, 2005), pp. 109–20.

Popular Memory and Gender in Medieval England

the dean and chapter from the hospital's lands in Heslington. John stated that he had also read in several civic registers that the gallows were commonly known to belong to St Leonard's. From the same records, he gave details of the ditch that several non-elite men described in almost identical terms. Having served as common clerk of the city of York, the 'civic official most directly responsible for the town's many written communications', John was central to the construction and maintenance of its legal memory, which shaped his knowledge of the landscape.[137]

Written records were cited as authorities more often in men's legal accounts of jurisdictional boundaries, with few laywomen referring to texts in testimony related to the environment. Although the use of documentary evidence operated as a gendered form of expertise, connoting respectable masculinity and perhaps clerical status, it was not the only way in which literate men recalled the landscape. Richard Thornton, another witness in the dispute over Green Dykes and a former sheriff of York with experience of the city's archives, attested to parish boundaries without reference to written registers, while John Shirwood also relied on oral memory to imbue his account with greater authority. In disputes concerning tithes and rights, the memories of ordinary inhabitants who cultivated the land formed an essential cornerstone of proof. Experiences of funeral and Rogation processions, agricultural practice, and the payment of tithes verified descriptions of parish limits. Methods of conceptualising the landscape were diverse and fluid with boundaries closely entwined, a pattern that was mirrored in men and women's experiences of the law and different jurisdictional processes. Written legal records were by no means favoured over oral tradition, and although their formal expression issued from men, women's memories and experiences were occasionally referenced and gendered norms of custom, work, and legal status had considerable bearing on relationships between men.

CONCLUSION

Men's memories were endowed with greater legal capacity than women's in relation to custom and the landscape as non-elite male experiences of the law were often more visible and sustained. Men's communal testimony resulted in the inscription of apparently male places of memory on the landscape, yet women were also involved in the transmission of social memory, engaging with and reconstructing the landscape through their labour and the remembrance of local custom. Male deponents might still efface the presence of

---

[137] G. Rosser, 'Myth, Image and Social Process in the English Medieval Town', *Urban History*, 23 (1996), 5–25, at p. 6; Dobson, 'John Shirwood of York', p. 114; D. O'Brien, '"The veray registre of all trouthe": The Content, Function and Character of the Civic Registers of London and York, c. 1274–c. 1482' (PhD thesis, University of York, 1999), pp. 242–3.

Place, Landscape, and Gender

women, socially and spatially, giving depictions of female memory an unstable quality reflective of social marginalisation. Women's journeys were characterised as local in nature, entailing support for friends and kin during birth, visits to parish churches for baptisms, to taverns, and in relation to patterns of work. Memories of spatial practices were used to establish and reconfigure power dynamics in cases where women's movements exposed the instability of patriarchal authority. In this manner, testimony that recalled the free and unfree status of male labourers demonstrates the social potency of memory in defining the limits of seigneurialism under the law.

Building on the conclusions of Chapter 3, this chapter has shown that legal testimony which drew on the material environment to reconstruct the past was dependent not only on textual memory but also on a variety of other practices that resisted the masculine tone of more diachronic histories. Material memories of the rural environment were largely based on male ownership and use of the land, farms, and individual fields, while the urban environment held mnemonic traces which reflected the diversity and fluidity of these communities. In short, towns and cities were far more likely than rural areas to be inflected with memories of women's working and social lives. This was echoed more broadly in the tendency of men's testimony towards traditional homosocial narratives and the written record, whereas women and more marginal men tended to refer to physical experience and memories of the world around them.

CONCLUSION

The aim of this book has been to explore everyday perceptions and manifestations of the past in England from the early thirteenth to the late fifteenth centuries. Memory was ubiquitous in many strands of life during this period, underpinning the shape of religious, economic, and social institutions, and accruing new kinds of gendered meaning for men and women with each stage of the life cycle. Most significant, though, was its prevalence in everyday situations where the past was used to make sense of the present and to plan for the future. Custom, rights over land and property, memories of life events, and commemoration depended on types of remembrance – social, environmental, personal, or generational – that overlapped, but were organised and deployed in distinctive ways. Gender was a central influence upon attitudes towards the past, both reinforcing patriarchal values through normative models of behaviour, and offering a field in which these could be contested and redefined.

Versions of the past conveyed strands of men and women's gendered experiences in subjectivities that revealed the anticipation of the law in everyday life. The intrinsic function of the law influenced people's social, economic, and religious behaviour from the outset, while awareness of its nuances and malleability saw the emergence and use of recognisable motifs and tropes in narratives that shifted subtly over time. Representations of the past in witness testimony did not signify the existence of unmediated discourses, but instead contained interpretations of the law based on the perceptions of litigants, witnesses, and their counsel.[1] Social experience was formed in part through contact with and apprehension of the law both inside and outside the courts, and legal processes developed and adapted in turn through their use in local communities.

A mounting interest in the circumstances of sin by the late twelfth century, coupled with a growing emphasis on conscience and intention in pastoral theology, fostered a fixation with memory in church-court testimony. In these nascent judicial contexts, examiners trialled novel ways of eliciting testimony, using methods which had perhaps been transmitted by learned churchmen

---

[1] Johnson, 'The Preconstruction of Witness Testimony', pp. 144–5.

Popular Memory and Gender in Medieval England

and administrators schooled in canon law and theology. Experiments in the application of canon law coincided with a marked expansion in pastoral literature from the early thirteenth century onwards, which had a pervasive influence on many facets of social and spiritual experience. The habit of questioning men and women on why they recalled past events receded in the church courts by the early to mid-fifteenth century, although the stories that people told remained detailed in content and sets of questions continued to guide their responses.

This book has analysed attitudes towards memory among non-elite men and women in litigation from the church courts, yet this was only one strand of a legal network made up of numerous intertwined processes through which grievances were pursued. Rural settlements were composed of several overlapping jurisdictions, and the extent to which people could use different courts both embodied and reified forms of socio-economic disparity rooted in legal status and gender. Men and women depicted the past using language and tropes that demonstrated the centrality of the law to their experiences. People understood canon law and applied their knowledge of it to these situations, referring to a body of knowledge that amalgamated practices from several legal systems.

Laypeople used the law to shape and reflect relationships between acquaintances, neighbours, and kin, and cited interpersonal histories that had developed over periods ranging from days or months to decades. Daily sight of, and contact with, 'enemies' occurred at the same time as people used the law against them.[2] The distinctive qualities that infused local contexts, such as the nature of the landscape, its history, and personal or collective ties, pervaded quarrels and determined how behaviour was characterised in the legal cases that followed. Accounts of arguments over insults, and disagreements over marriage, rights to tithes, and the extent of parish boundaries were framed with specific reference to their spatial and embodied contours.

The memory practices of non-elites maintained an intimate and complex relationship with the habits of the clergy and wealthier groups, demonstrating the way in which the practicalities of daily life could limit the potentially polarising effects of social stratification. Despite a greater propensity for the citation of written records in clerical or more elite settings, townspeople and the peasantry inhabited social and religious spaces where the written word was commonly used, taking part in cultural experiences that underlined the expansive nature of many facets of literacy. Literate forms of memory may have appeared more durable and culturally dominant in relation to the growing bureaucracy of Church and State in this period, yet even apparently ephemeral types of memory left their traces. Many of these were orally

---

[2] D. L. Smail, *The Consumption of Justice: Emotions, Publicity, and Legal Culture in Marseille, 1264–1423* (Ithaca, NY, 2003), pp. 100–17.

Conclusion

based but alluded to both the material and ideological elements that made up daily life. Domestic habits and work routines were recalled with reference to the minutiae of these activities – the objects, textiles, and surfaces that were handled on a regular basis and the meanings which they amassed and continued to accrue upon their donation and re-imagining in testimony. The spatial organisation of houses, fields, streets, and taverns was also described in language that carried moral values, and gave a sense of the personal and collective identities of lower-status people and their everyday concerns.

Even where memory practices were shared or appropriated, this did not signify the absence of conflict, and people evinced varying degrees of familiarity with perceptions of the past that were often contradictory at an ideological level. Memories of local custom referred to claims of long-term land use which could represent different economic interests, whether those of parishioners or the parish clergy. Antagonisms between manorial lords and the free and unfree peasantry often stemmed from and were communicated through visions of the past that engaged with existing sets of power relations. Memories of conflict with manorial or Church authorities tended to reify the oppositional tone of this contact to construct a set of events that did not entirely undermine official perceptions of the social hierarchy. Where non-elite men and women observed these distinctions, their characterisation as compliant afforded them increased agency to support their own legal positions. Wood observes that class relations in early modern England were not marked only by deference or resistance, but that 'the lower orders ... both contested and constituted the terms of their subordination'.[3] Popular reactions to the threatened loss of rights and traditions, and the levying of new dues, thus depended on the local dynamics that engendered men and women's senses of the past. These memories were multifaceted, defined through internal conflict within the lower orders as well as through struggles with authorities and groups higher in the social hierarchy. In this sense, political and economic marginalisation intensified through intermittent erosions of autonomy, and this encouraged strategic collusion in the production of testimony as much as it did narratives of direct resistance.

The reconstruction and remembrance of past events in these records demonstrates how people understood and depicted their actions in culturally meaningful ways. Many of these memories implied the meaning of behaviour in language that communicated men and women's moral and social worth, using tropes and motifs that indicate how perceptions of social and cultural values changed in this period. Misogynistic norms permeated characterisations of women's attitudes and actions in these areas of activity, yet both genders were adept at negotiating the ideological and practical limits of the

---

[3]   A. Wood, 'Fear, Hatred and the Hidden Injuries of Class in Early Modern England', *Journal of Social History*, 39 (2006), 803–26, at p. 817.

Popular Memory and Gender in Medieval England

law. The meaning and form of memories fluctuated in these centuries despite the overall resilience of the traditional gender order, and the behaviour that witnesses described was the corollary of these wider social and economic developments. Accounts of courtship, marriage, sexual activity, and other aspects of daily life were organised through references to masculinity and femininity, and many of the norms that defined conventional gender roles centred on marriage and work. These held different implications for men and women and across social and legal hierarchies, and their subversion or adaptation, especially where claims were used to impugn the reputations of parties and witnesses, acted as challenges to patriarchal control.

Women's memories were particularly valued in cases which dealt with marriage, childbirth, and the ages of children, as well as suits related to spousal impotence and defamation. The appearance of female witnesses, and the nature and foci of their evidence, thus reflected and reified normative perceptions of women's social function, which in turn aligned them with embodied and reproductive spheres. Memories which centred on the sight and function of female body parts related to their perceived purpose and were framed in gendered terms. Pregnancy and reproduction were seen to mark women's bodies, impressing sexual histories upon their bodily tissue and altering the appearance of genitals and breasts. While this ideological focus upon their sexual potential could perpetuate patriarchal assumptions about women's social role, it also highlighted the value of their sensory experiences beyond their personal generative pasts. Women could occasionally appear in cases that required similarly embodied types of testimony that drew on the evidence of the landscape and material environment. Although more limited than in men's testimony, women's memories relied on the physical world as a residual store of memory as much as the human body to support claims in court. The realms of emotional and sensory experience were more accessible to non-elite men and women than chronological narratives that were rooted in literacy, political events, and hegemonic forms of male behaviour.

Men with claims to respectability were able to draw on communal experiences and accompanying forms of male sociability to confer public legitimacy upon their arguments. An increased concern with recording memories afforded female parties and witnesses degrees of agency in constructing their pasts, but the negative connotations attached to some forms of women's mobility outside the home restricted their capacity to cite narratives grounded in a similar range of activities. The linear, diachronic, and causal narratives adopted by groups of male parishioners were less accessible to women and non-elite men, although subaltern memories occasionally disrupted the patriarchal language used to describe the passage of time.

Patriarchal attitudes and norms infused accounts of men's past behaviour, depictions of which often drew on markers associated with dominant models of masculinity. These assumptions generated tropes of men's behaviour and language which intersected with the rules of canon law. Male identities which

Conclusion

failed to embody patriarchal values of economic, legal, and occupational independence were scrutinised during litigation. Where men deviated from these expectations, opposing parties and witnesses portrayed their identities and behaviour in negative language to reflect the absence of manliness. Moral perceptions of poverty and the notion of 'dependence' cast doubts upon the testimony of more marginalised men. Poor, vagrant, and unfree men were situated outside normative timelines as accounts of their past behaviour focused on their lack of means, residency, and restrictions upon their bodily autonomy. Gendered perceptions of witnesses did not simply distinguish between the authority of men and women, but also privileged the testimony of men who could depict themselves as more respectable while dismissing the evidence of women and the poor.

A major distinction in the treatment of men and women's testimony was the tendency towards the sexualisation of female poverty. Bennett has emphasised the prevalence of misogynistic tropes in lyrics and religious texts about young single women of marriageable age.[4] The expansion of pastoral reform into an established programme supported by a wealth of media allowed the clergy to monitor the moral and spiritual behaviour of the laity more closely. Sex and its relationship with morality 'occupied a substantial position in the literature of confession', as Pierre J. Payer observes, and was a central theme in pastoral advice aimed at the laity.[5] Clerical attitudes towards gender relations acted as the scaffold for treatments of fornication, marriage, adultery, and other sexual practices that were frequently misogynistic in language and tone. Penitential discourse interpreted laywomen as especially susceptible to sexual sin, regarding them as morally responsible for prompting sexual memories among the clergy and laymen alike. Pastoral literature aligned women with cultural tropes that stoked fears of the untrustworthy woman, more disposed to the concealment of sexual misdeeds than their confession.

Depictions of past events in litigation emphasise that constructions of masculinity, like representations of femininity, were by no means homogeneous in this period.[6] As Shepard notes for the period 1560–1640, the characterisation of manliness from the thirteenth to the fifteenth centuries was 'contingent and multifaceted [...] and also often contradictory in its different emphases'.[7] In later medieval England, patriarchal attitudes and structures were reinforced by men who derived considerable benefits from

---

4   J. M. Bennett, 'Ventriloquisms: When Maidens Speak in English Songs, c. 1300–1550', in A. M. Rasmussen and A. Klinck, eds., *Medieval Women's Song: Cross-Cultural Approaches* (Philadelphia, 2002), pp. 187–204, at pp. 194–5.

5   P. J. Payer, *Sex and the New Medieval Literature of Confession, 1150–1300* (Toronto, 2009), p. 4.

6   For a critique of hegemonic notions of masculinity, see Neal, *The Masculine Self*, pp. 243–4.

7   Shepard, *Meanings of Manhood*, p. 247.

249

Popular Memory and Gender in Medieval England

the maintenance of gendered hierarchies. Despite a general tendency in medieval culture to embrace gender ideologies centred on male hegemony and a belief in women's natural inferiority, conflict at times marked exchanges between men from different status and occupational groups, in part due to the exclusion of non-elite men from the advantages of patriarchal power.

Men's evidence occasionally referred to the prospect of disharmony as the overlapping boundaries of social attitudes and the law produced testimony that imbued their accounts with gendered implications. The enforcement of these hierarchies generated social and economic segregation between men, but masculine identities could reside in traits and activities outside of dominant forms of male authority. Shepard observes that men from lower social groups developed gender ideologies 'either in explicit resistance or as independent alternatives to patriarchal codes'.[8] Yet, in certain circumstances non-elite men nevertheless endorsed these attitudes and beliefs. Gender ideologies in peasant communities, for example, were marked by patriarchal practices such as leyrwite, merchet, and manorial control over the right to marry that disadvantaged women in social and economic terms. Other strands of peasant women's experiences were less overtly related to the fiscal operation of the manor, like restrictions related to law and governance, which as S. H. Rigby puts it, 'worked primarily "for the benefit of men" rather than for that of feudalism'.[9] In this sense, peasant masculinities remained intimately connected to patriarchal ideologies that constrained elements of peasant women's autonomy, limiting their full participation in administrative activities and, on some manors, their right to inherit and transfer landholdings.[10] This was the case even where practices did not directly profit the manorial lord and might simultaneously alienate men from their own labour and political and legal freedom. There was, of course, variation between manors, and numerous modes of tenure based on personal status and local forms of landholding existed among the free and unfree. This internal hierarchy became more visible in suits that touched on legal status. Men and women remembered labour services and legal restrictions attached to other residents of the manor, framing them in language and motifs that signalled subtle differences in position and obligations that often related directly to gender.

On a broader scale, peasant attitudes towards the past were embedded in the dynamics of custom and common rights, as well as memories surrounding the legal status of neighbours and kin which, at times, underpinned this knowledge. Custom was most often construed as long-held traditions and practices that existed regardless of written memory. Patriarchal social attitudes

---

[8] Shepard, *Meanings of Manhood*, p. 249.

[9] S. H. Rigby, *English Society in the Later Middle Ages: Class, Status and Gender* (New York, 1995), p. 262.

[10] On legal and economic restrictions, see Bennett, *Women in the Medieval English Countryside*, pp. 27–36.

Conclusion

drew inherent associations between masculinity and traits of authority and respectability. These perceptions lay behind the selection of male witnesses in cases that touched upon manorial custom, the rights of the Church to tithes and dues, and the geographical extent of parish boundaries. Canon law preferred evidence from men and the entrenched nature of these gender hierarchies, particularly in rural areas, compounded this pattern. Women's recollections were occasionally cited in suits, but this was typically within the confines of masculine authority and with the approval of male parties. Although their knowledge was usually disregarded during cases of this kind, peasant women possessed a detailed body of information about the local landscape derived in part from the seasonal routines of agricultural labour. The operation of the rural economy depended on the joint labour of married couples and, while the allocation of work was occasionally gendered and the female peasantry oversaw numerous domestic activities, women also contributed to the cultivation of the land and participated in animal husbandry. In addition, the boundaries between physical households, farmyards, and fields were porous because the shared use of space for different purposes rendered their margins ill-defined. Social gatherings among non-elite neighbours and kin occurred in both communal places and the home, holding the potential for mixed-sex groups to meet and converse.[11] Memories of local matters – custom, aspects of the landscape, noteworthy events – were diffused and reified in spaces that accommodated women's narratives about their lived environments.

Beyond memories embedded in the natural and built world, the laity in towns and the countryside had to negotiate their own relationships with local Church authorities, and again, assumptions about gender guided the tone of these encounters. Past experiences with the church courts permeated men and women's assumptions about their own behaviour and influenced its depiction in testimony. This included citations for moral and spiritual crimes and involvement in private suits, in tandem with knowledge of the courts' activities garnered from neighbours or kin. Despite the distinctive piety ascribed to laywomen in this period, many pastoral and popular texts presented their relationship with the parish clergy as problematic, typified by sexual danger and the suppression of sin.

Comparable difficulties were a feature of exchanges between local churchmen and male parishioners. The summoners, proctors, judges, and other officials of the church courts settled disputes regarding the sexual and marital lives of the laity, producing sentences that elicited hostility from parishioners, including men pursued for fornication or alleged marriage contracts. In the vernacular alliterative poem *Satire on the Consistory Courts*, composed in the early fourteenth century, the male narrator recounts his appearance before the church court over a sexual relationship with a woman, which later

---

[11] Goldberg, 'Space and Gender', p. 215.

Popular Memory and Gender in Medieval England

developed into the legal case or citation that he describes.[12] Although the narrator claims not to have made promises to the female character in the poem, he complains that the courts persecute men if they lie with women upon the ground. The language of transitory sexual ties is contrasted with the learning of clerks, while the legal men of the court are dismissed as low in social status in comparison with the narrator. The text concentrates primarily on male experiences of canon law on sex and marriage, but the narrator also references anxieties specific to women involved in cases and citations, noting that the female character 'scrynketh for shome ant shometh for men'.[13] Literacy, social standing, legal status, and gender intersected in ways that reflected the individual circumstances of witnesses and parties. Knowledge of how the courts were used, whether acquired personally or from neighbours and kin, produced a cultural memory of legal experience which highlighted the vulnerabilities that each gender confronted.

Contemporary literature tended to caricature as acute and static the differences that men and women experienced during their contact with the church courts. Despite the persistence of specific tropes and social patterns, there were changes in the narratives presented to the courts during these centuries. Some of these were apparent in the application of canon law, which in turn absorbed subtle adjustments in popular opinion and social practice. One such example was the declining use of abjuration *sub pena nubendi* to formalise sexual unions by the beginning of the fifteenth century. The significance assigned to the mutual consent of both parties in a marriage contract had begun to outweigh the Church's objections to informal relationships and the belief that marriage could be used to alleviate these moral crimes.[14] At the same time, concubinage was increasingly prohibited and markers like co-residence or the birth of children were treated as evidence of marriage.[15] The language of paternity and domestic partnership was increasingly common in suits where women sought to enforce contracts, and witnesses recalled long-established ties that were often indistinguishable from wedlock. Other legal arguments were explicit in their evocation of gendered stereotypes, as in cases where alleged husbands asserted their absence from marriage contracts, for example. The activities recalled in this type of testimony conformed to traditionally masculine forms of sociability and work, situating young men in same-sex groups engaged in sports and drinking, as well as inherently respectable duties like legal or guild administration. These alibis appeared in a higher proportion

---

[12] For a discussion of this poem, see V. J. Scattergood, 'The "Lewed" and the "Lerede": A Reading of Satire on the Consistory Courts', in V. J. Scattergood, *The Lost Tradition: Essays on Middle English Alliterative Poetry* (Dublin, 2000), pp. 27–42.

[13] 'Ne mai no lewed lued libben in londe', in *The Complete Harley*, ed. Fein, Raybin, and Ziolkowski, p. 190, line 59.

[14] Helmholz, *Marriage Litigation*, pp. 177–8.

[15] Brundage, *Law, Sex, and Christian Society*, pp. 515–16.

Conclusion

of marriage cases during the fifteenth century, as Donahue's statistical analysis has demonstrated.[16] This pattern coincided with heightened male paranoia about the prospect of women colluding to fabricate their own testimony, perceptible from the early part of that century.

Broader social and economic shifts impinged on the practical and ideological shape of gender relations from the second half of the fourteenth century onwards. Bernard Capp has demonstrated the imperceptible rate of change in patriarchal structures during the early modern period as they adapted to their potential erosion.[17] The gradual decline of serfdom intensified in the second half of the fourteenth century, and the demographic shock of the plague led to opportunities for enhanced wages and conditions outside the manor. Improved economic agency among non-elites threatened the existing social equilibrium and weakened manorial authority, while better working conditions outside the manor afforded the peasantry and labourers greater levels of mobility in relation to work. Villein tenure slowly began to diminish, works were increasingly commuted into payments, and certain fines and dues were gradually retired on many manors, especially leyrwite, which was seldom levied upon poor single mothers after the late fourteenth century.[18] These apparent gains were counterbalanced through manorial and governmental efforts to reassert control over a labour force seen to be exploiting the shortage of workers to extract higher wages. In 1349 the Ordinance of Labourers was issued to address some of these problems by coercing unemployed, able-bodied men and women into compulsory service, thus alleviating the pressures associated with the weakening of serfdom. Poor single women living in rural communities were especially susceptible to compelled labour. Requests and indictments under this law performed the additional task of extending control over unmarried women and inducing them to join a specific household where male authority could be exerted on a daily basis.[19]

The patriarchal systems that prevailed in urban households were similarly vulnerable to modification during this period as a result of various social and economic factors, and these shifts presumably influenced perceptions of women's function and their authority under the law. Female labour was integral to the operation of craft workshops, and the central role of wives and daughters was acknowledged in guild regulations, although formal recognition of their role through membership of guilds was more limited. Some

---

[16] Donahue, *Law, Marriage, and Society*, p. 71.

[17] B. Capp, *When Gossips Meet: Women, Family, and Neighbourhood in Early Modern England* (Oxford, 2003), pp. 374–5; see also A. Fletcher, *Gender, Sex and Subordination in England, 1500–1800* (New Haven, 1995).

[18] Bailey, *The Decline of Serfdom*, pp. 307–37; on the decline of leyrwite, see Bennett, 'Writing Fornication', pp. 152–3.

[19] Bennett, 'Compulsory Service', pp. 25–6, 33–41.

groups of women perhaps experienced a brief improvement in economic power during the late fourteenth century, albeit only to a similar extent as male workers. This, however, was balanced against limitations upon women's legal activities and, subsequently, their declining position in the economy and the labour market.[20] Female workers also experienced a deteriorating status in many regions of Europe during the late fifteenth century as the twin pressures of economic contraction and demographic growth restricted their involvement in the labour market.[21] Guild ordinances prohibited women from service in specific trades from the second half of the fifteenth century, for instance in the weavers' guilds of Coventry, Bristol, and Hull.[22] Some types of service may have become more feminised professions, suggests Goldberg, since women were especially prominent in mercantile households and performed 'unskilled, non-industrial or domestic functions' and were marginalised from specialised labour in artisan workshops.[23]

The adaptation of the patriarchal order not only impinged on women's participation in the economy, their social status, and position in the household, but also had a bearing on their legal activities. Although non-elite women from labouring and peasant groups, and those employed in service, could exert mediated forms of agency in the courts, gendered socio-cultural values influenced the relative proportions of male and female litigants and witnesses, and restricted the narratives that were presented in legal suits. Women initiated marriage cases in greater numbers than men throughout this period, but this pattern was not as pronounced during the fifteenth century as the numbers of female plaintiffs in suits to enforce contracts fell.[24] Female plaintiffs from rural communities were more common throughout this century, as the frequency with which women in urban areas brought suit decreased. Goldberg found that parties of both sexes opted for male witnesses in higher numbers, and the peasantry were especially likely to select men rather than women. This preference became more distinct by the end of the fifteenth century. Social attitudes towards gender in this context had apparently grown increasingly dichotomous, and many parties regarded men's testimony as the default choice, rendering women's perceptions of the past less visible in the courts.[25] Despite the apparent stasis and even weakening of women's social

---

[20] S. Bardsley, 'Women's Work Reconsidered: Gender and Wage Differentiation in Late Medieval England', *Past & Present*, 165 (1999), 3–29; on women's declining economic power in York after the plague, as demonstrated in rental accounts, see Rees Jones, *York: The Making of a City*, pp. 296–8.

[21] For an outline of regional differences in women's economic experiences, see M. C. Howell, *Women, Production, and Patriarchy in Late Medieval Cities* (Chicago, 1986).

[22] Goldberg, *Women, Work, and Life Cycle*, pp. 200, 354–5.

[23] Goldberg, *Women, Work, and Life Cycle*, pp. 201–2.

[24] Donahue, *Law, Marriage, and Society*, pp. 84–9.

[25] Goldberg, 'Gender and Matrimonial Litigation', pp. 44–7.

Conclusion

and economic position, Church authorities were not necessarily prejudiced against female parties, however, and tended to favour plaintiffs regardless of their gender.[26]

Similar patterns can be observed in other jurisdictions. A reduced level of legal activity for women is evident in some manorial courts in England by the end of the fourteenth century.[27] Quantitative analysis of London women's involvement in litigation, undertaken by Matthew Stevens, shows that numbers of female plaintiffs in the sheriff's court fell by the 1460s while the proportion of women acting as defendants increased.[28] From this perspective, women's engagement with canon law may offer evidence of the 'progressive tightening up of patriarchal dominance' throughout the late medieval period and the fifteenth century in particular.[29] Yet although these patterns indicate a demonstrable shift in uses of the law, focusing only on legal workings of cases can obscure the breadth of women's activities – in the related areas of custom, household management, social policing, and the formation of local memory – all of which varied by region and jurisdiction. Some courts granted women a wider range of legal options, for example, where manorial custom permitted their legal participation despite the theoretical limits of coverture under common law.[30]

The practical and discursive constraints imposed on female testimony, as well as evidence from the poor and unfree, only partially impeded their ability to communicate their identities and subject positions. For instance, single women engaged in poorly paid work were conscious of the negative connotations ascribed to their marital and socio-economic status, and often anticipated attacks upon their reputations by reframing their sexual and labour activities as legitimate or at least morally explicable. Narratives that witnesses recounted in testimony captured moments where men and women reviewed their personal histories, emphasising action that acknowledged points of canon law from the outset, such as the preference for two or more witnesses to marriage contracts. The language of emotion and embodiment allowed people to exert agency in more complex depictions of the past that required detailed explanation. In many marriage suits, former relationships were recast as bonds based on mutual affection or dismissed as transitory

---

[26] See the contrasting arguments in Donahue, *Law, Marriage, and Society*, pp. 77–8; Goldberg, 'Gender and Matrimonial Litigation', pp. 43–59.

[27] C. Briggs, 'Empowered or Marginalized? Rural Women and Credit in Later Thirteenth- and Fourteenth-Century England', *Continuity and Change*, 19 (2004), 13–43.

[28] M. F. Stevens, 'London Women, the Courts and the "Golden Age": A Quantitative Analysis of Female Litigants in the Fourteenth and Fifteenth Centuries', *The London Journal*, 37 (2012), 67–88.

[29] Stevens, 'London Women, the Courts and the "Golden Age"', p. 70.

[30] For a discussion of the breadth of peasant-women's activities and the limits of common law, see Müller, 'Peasant Women, Agency and Status', pp. 91–113, at p. 103.

Popular Memory and Gender in Medieval England

sexual ties. Both of these positions referred to recognisable gendered motifs and behaviours that cohered into portrayals of personal intentions, whether those of parties or witnesses.

The past mattered in material and emotional terms. Common undercurrents in the testimony of both men and women were concerns about the present and anxieties about the future, perceptible in cases over marriage and defamation, tithes, and testamentary issues. To use one example, marriage was often integral to women's economic survival and its absence could determine their trade, living standard, and reputation especially where sex had already occurred outside wedlock. Men too depended on the acquisition of marital status as this aided in the formation of a viable patriarchal household and workshop. Quarrels that escalated into suits over defamation were also approached through the economic problems and social exclusion that potential damage to an individual's public identity could inflict.

Yet there were undercurrents of optimism as well as disquiet. While focusing on the late eighteenth and nineteenth centuries after enclosure, Wood makes the important observation that hope for the future among non-elite communities was sustained through popular memories of traditional rights.[31] For lower-status men and women in later medieval society, the act of remembering sought to ameliorate current situations and improve future prospects by challenging alternative ways of viewing the past. Memories of marginality – stemming from gender relations, legal status, or economic standing – engaged with existing power structures as opposing parties sought their reinforcement while non-elite men and women aimed to regain control over depictions of their pasts. There were, of course, exceptions to this pattern that underscore the heterogeneity and competing interests of the peasantry, and women could also ensure the endurance of patriarchal attitudes and systems through assessments of other people's actions that drew on gendered norms.

It has been argued in this study that testimony was shaped in the interactions between the courts and the people who used them, generating accounts of past experiences from which the law itself was inseparable. It was in this context that the prevalence of gendered stereotypes exerted influence on perceptions of female deponents and contributed to the marginalisation of women's testimony. As noted in the Introduction, it would be misleading to interpret the church courts as a legal arena which enforced only a dominant vision of social relations. It is more accurate to view them as a field of contest in which women negotiated social and legal constraints to shape their lives and the world around them. While gendered cultural tropes rooted in socio-economic hierarchies had a negative influence on the legal agency of non-elite men, and women in particular, the clerical obsession with recording

---

[31] Wood, *The Memory of the People*, pp. 351–2.

Conclusion

memories as a form of evidence opened a space in which their experiences could be validated.

These accounts of the past were only partial and exist as subjective representations of a dense series of processes and relationships. They were nevertheless articulated in an official setting and recorded in writing, thus gaining a degree of formality and the opportunity to influence legal judgements. Most significantly, this testimony alludes to the vibrant and diverse nature of women's contributions to non-elite memory at a point when legal, social, and religious structures otherwise curtailed their choices and actions. Through the examination of church-court testimony in this period, this book has explored the nuances of power relations between men and women of differing status. Ultimately, it expands interpretations of gendered agency in the courts and social life, treating testimony as a crucial space in which women could resist linear and patriarchal narratives about the past.

BIBLIOGRAPHY

MANUSCRIPT SOURCES

Borthwick Institute, York
  CP.E. series
  CP.F. series
Canterbury Cathedral Archives
  Chartae Antiquae
  Christ Church Letters
  Ecclesiastical Suit Rolls
  Sede Vacante Scrapbooks, 1–3
East Riding Archive Office
  DDRI/22/33
Kent Archives and Local History Service
  X.10.1. (deposition book)
Oxford, Bodleian Library
  Douce 60 (SC 21634)
York Minster Archive
  L2 (4)
  M2 (3)c

PRINTED PRIMARY SOURCES

Alberti Magni opera omnia, vol. 12: *Quaestiones super De Animalibus*, ed. E. Filthaut (Münster, 1955)

The Book of Margery Kempe, ed. B. Windeatt (Harlow, 2000)

Chronica de Monasterii de Melsa a fundacione usque ad annum 1396, ed. E. A. Bond, Rolls Series, 43, 2 vols. (London, 1866–88)

The Complete Harley 2253 Manuscript, ed. S. Greer Fein, with D. Raybin and J. Ziolkowski (Kalamazoo, MI, 2014), vol. 2

The Complete Works of Aristotle: The Revised Oxford Translation, ed. J. Barnes (Princeton, 1984), vol. 1

Concilia Magnae Britanniae et Hiberniae, 446–1718, ed. D. Wilkins (London, 1737; repr. Brussels, 1964), vol. 2

Dan Michel's Ayenbite of Inwyt or Remorse of Conscience, ed. R. Morris and P. Gradon (Oxford, 1979)

Bibliography

Decrees of the Ecumenical Councils, ed. N. P. Tanner (London and Georgetown, 1990), vol. 1

Drake, F., *Eboracum, or the History and Antiquities of the City of York*, with a new introduction by K. J. Allison (London, 1736)

The Early English Versions of the Gesta Romanorum, ed. S. J. H. Herrtage, EETS, extra series, 33 (London, 1879)

English and Scottish Popular Ballads, ed. F. J. Child (Boston, 1869), vol. 1

Gower, John, *Mirour de l'Omme*, trans. W. Burton Wilson, rev. N. Wilson Van Baak (East Lansing, MI, 1992)

Grosseteste, Robert, *Templum Dei*, ed. J. Goering and F. A. C. Mantello (Toronto, 1984)

Hostiensis, *Lectura in Decretales (in primum ... librum decretalium commentaria)* (Venice, 1581; repr. Turin, 1965)

—— *Summa Aurea* (Venice, 1574)

John Mirk's Festial, ed. S. Powell (Oxford, 2011)

John Mirk's Instructions for Parish Priests, ed. G. Kristensson, Lund Studies in English, 49 (Lund, 1974)

The Kalendarium of John Somer, ed. L. Mooney (Athens, GA, 1998)

The Medieval Craft of Memory: An Anthology of Texts and Pictures, ed. M. Carruthers and J. M. Ziolkowski (Philadelphia, 2002)

Pilii, Tancredi, Gratiae, Libri de iudiciorum ordine, ed. F. Bergmann (Gottingen, 1842)

Polychronicon Ranulphi Higden monachi Cestrensis; Together with the English Translations of John Trevisa and of an Unknown Writer of the Fifteenth Century, ed. C. Babington, Rolls Series, 41 (London, 1865)

The Prose Salernitan Questions: Edited from a Bodleian MS (Auct. F.3.10), an Anonymous Collection Dealing with Science and Medicine Written by an Englishman c. 1200, ed. B. Lawn (Oxford, 1979)

The Riverside Chaucer, ed. L. D. Benson, 3rd edition (Boston, 1987)

Robert of Brunne's Handlyng Synne, ed. F. J. Furnivall, EETS, original series, 119, 123 (London, 1901, 1903; repr. Millwood, 1975)

Robert of Flamborough, *Liber Poenitentialis*, ed. J. J. Francis Frith (Toronto, 1971)

Sancti Bernardi Opera Omnia, vol. 4, ed. J. Leclercq and H. M. Rochais (Rome, 1966)

Secular Lyrics of the XIV and XV Centuries, ed. R. Hope Robbins (Oxford, 1955)

Select Cases on Defamation to 1600, ed. R. H. Helmholz, Selden Society, 101 (London, 1985)

Speculum vitae: A Reading Edition, ed. R. Hanna, 2 vols. (Oxford, 2008)

A Talk of Ten Wives on their Husbands' Ware [in] Jyl of Breyntford's Testament ... and Other Short Pieces, ed. F. J. Furnivall (London, 1871)

Thomas of Chobham, *Summa Confessorum*, ed. F. Broomfield (Paris, 1968)

The Trials and Joys of Marriage, ed. E. Salisbury (Kalamazoo, MI, 2002)

The Trotula: A Medieval Compendium of Women's Medicine, ed. and trans. M. Green (Philadelphia, 2001)

Bibliography

Women in England, c. 1275–1525: Documentary Sources, ed. and trans. P. J. P. Goldberg (Manchester, 1995)

Women's Secrets: A Translation of Pseudo-Albertus Magnus's De Secretis Mulierum with Commentaries, ed. H. Rodnite Lemay (Albany, 1992)

SECONDARY WORKS

Acheson, E., *A Gentry Community: Leicestershire in the Fifteenth Century, c. 1422–c. 1485* (Cambridge, 1992)

Allison, K. J., ed., *Victoria County History: A History of the County of York East Riding*, vol. 3 (London, 1976)

Archer, R. E., and B. E. Ferme, 'Testamentary Procedure with Special Reference to the Executrix', *Reading Medieval Studies*, 15 (1989), 3–34

Armitage, S., 'The Stages of Women's Oral History', in D. A. Ritchie, ed., *The Oxford Handbook of Oral History* (Oxford, 2011), pp. 169–85

Arnold, J. H., *Inquisition and Power: Catharism and the Confessing Subject in Medieval Languedoc* (Philadelphia, 2001)

Aston, T. H., ed., *Landlords, Peasants and Politics in Medieval England* (Cambridge, 1987)

d'Avray, D. L., *Medieval Marriage: Symbolism and Society* (Oxford, 2005)

——— 'Peter Damian, Consanguinity and Church Property', in L. M. Smith and B. Ward, eds., *Intellectual Life in the Middle Ages: Essays Presented to Margaret Gibson* (London, 1992), pp. 71–80

d'Avray, D. L., with A. C. de la Mare, 'Portable *Vademecum* Books Containing Franciscan and Dominican Texts', in A. C. de la Mare and B. C. Barker-Benfield, eds., *Manuscripts at Oxford: An Exhibition in Memory of Richard William Hunt ... on Themes Selected and Described by Some of his Friends (1908–1979)* (Oxford, 1980), pp. 60–4

Baildon, W. P., and J. W. Walker, eds., *Notes on the Religious and Secular Houses of Yorkshire*, Yorkshire Archaeological Society Record Series, 17 and 81, 2 vols. (London, 1895 [vol. 1], and Wakefield, 1931 [vol. 2])

Bailey, J., *Parenting in England, 1760–1830: Emotion, Identity, and Generation* (Oxford, 2012)

Bailey, M., *The Decline of Serfdom in Late Medieval England: From Bondage to Freedom* (Woodbridge, 2014)

Baker, K. M., 'Memory and Practice', *Representations*, 11 (1985), 134–59

Baldwin, J. W., *Masters, Princes and Merchants: The Social Views of Peter the Chanter and his Circle*, 2 vols. (Princeton, 1970)

Barclay, K., *Love, Intimacy and Power: Marriage and Patriarchy in Scotland, 1650–1850* (Manchester, 2011)

Bardsley, S., 'Peasant Women and Inheritance of Land in Fourteenth-Century England', *Continuity and Change*, 29 (2014), 297–324

——— *Venomous Tongues: Speech and Gender in Late Medieval England* (Philadelphia, 2006)

Bibliography

—— 'Women's Work Reconsidered: Gender and Wage Differentiation in Late Medieval England', *Past & Present*, 165 (1999), 3–29

Barr, B. A., *The Pastoral Care of Women in Late Medieval England* (Woodbridge, 2008)

Barron, C. M., 'The "Golden Age" of Women in Medieval London', *Reading Medieval Studies*, 15 (1989), 35–58

Barron, C. M., and C. Burgess, eds., *Memory and Commemoration in Medieval England* (Donington, 2010)

Bartlett, F. C., *Remembering: A Study in Experimental and Social Psychology*, 2nd edition (Cambridge, 1964)

Bartlett, R., *Trial by Fire and Water: The Medieval Judicial Ordeal* (Oxford, 1986)

Beattie, C., *Medieval Single Women: The Politics of Social Classification in Late Medieval England* (Oxford, 2007)

—— 'The Problem of Women's Work Identities in Post Black Death England', in J. Bothwell, P. J. P. Goldberg, and W. M. Ormrod, eds., *The Problem of Labour in Fourteenth-Century England* (York, 2000), pp. 1–19

—— 'Your Oratrice: Women's Petitions to the Late Medieval Court of Chancery', in B. Kane and F. Williamson, eds., *Women, Agency and the Law, 1300–1700* (London, 2013), pp. 17–30

Beattie, C., and M. F. Stevens, eds., *Married Women and the Law in Premodern Northwest Europe* (Woodbridge, 2013)

Beckwith, S., *Christ's Body: Identity, Culture and Society in Late Medieval Writings* (New York, 1993)

Bedell, J., 'Memory and Proof of Age in England, 1272–1327', *Past & Present*, 162 (1999), 3–27

Bederman, D. J., *Custom as a Source of Law* (Cambridge, 2010)

Beebe, K., A. Davis, and K. Gleadle, 'Space, Place and Gendered Identities: Feminist History and the Spatial Turn', *Women's History Review*, 21 (2012), 523–32

Bennett, J. M., *Ale, Beer, and Brewsters in England: Women's Work in a Changing World, 1300–1600* (Oxford, 1996)

—— 'Compulsory Service in Late Medieval England', *Past & Present*, 209 (2010), 7–51

—— 'Medieval Women, Modern Women: Across the Great Divide', in D. Aers, ed., *Culture and History, 1350–1600: Essays on English Communities, Identities, and Writing* (London, 1992), pp. 147–75

—— 'Ventriloquisms: When Maidens Speak in English Songs, c. 1300–1550', in A. M. Rasmussen and A. Klinck, eds., *Medieval Women's Song: Cross-Cultural Approaches* (Philadelphia, 2002), pp. 187–204

—— *Women in the Medieval English Countryside: Gender and Household in Brigstock before the Plague* (Oxford, 1987)

—— 'Writing Fornication: Medieval Leyrwite and its Historians', *Transactions of the Royal Historical Society*, 6th series, 13 (2003), 131–62

Berger Gluck, S., 'Women's Oral History: Is it So Special?', in T. L. Charlton, L. E.

Bibliography

Myers, and R. Sharpless, eds., *Handbook of Oral History* (Lanham, MD, 2006), pp. 357–83

Berger Gluck, S., and D. Patai, eds., *Women's Words: The Feminist Practice of Oral History* (New York, 1991)

Bernstein, S. D., *Confessional Subjects: Revelations of Gender and Power in Victorian Literature and Culture* (Chapel Hill, NC, and London, 1997)

Biancalana, J., *The Fee Tail and the Common Recovery in Medieval England, 1176–1502* (Cambridge, 2002)

Biller, P., *The Measure of Multitude: Population in Medieval Thought* (Oxford, 2000)

Birkett, H., 'The Pastoral Application of the Lateran IV Reforms in the Northern Province, 1215–1348', *Northern History*, 43 (2006), 199–219

Birrell, J., 'Common Rights in the Medieval Forest: Disputes and Conflicts in the Thirteenth Century', *Past & Present*, 117 (1987), 22–49

—— 'The Medieval English Forest', *Journal of Forest History*, 24 (1980), 78–85

Blamires, A., 'Beneath the Pulpit', in C. Dinshaw and D. Wallace, eds., *The Cambridge Companion to Medieval Women's Writing* (Cambridge, 2003), pp. 141–58

Bloch, D., *Aristotle on Memory and Recollection: Text, Translation, Interpretation and Reception in Western Scholasticism* (Leiden, 2007)

Bolton, J., '"The world upside down": Plague as an Agent of Economic and Social Change', in W. M. Ormrod and Phillip Lindley, eds., *The Black Death in England* (Stamford, 1996), pp. 17–78

Bourdieu, P., *The Logic of Practice*, trans. R. Nice (Stanford, CA, 1990)

Boydston, J., 'Gender as a Question of Historical Analysis', *Gender & History*, 20 (2008), 558–83

Boyle, L., 'The Fourth Lateran Council and Manuals of Popular Theology', in T. J. Heffernan, ed., *The Popular Literature of Medieval England* (Knoxville, TN, 1985), pp. 30–43

—— 'The Inter-Conciliar Period, 1179–1215, and the Beginnings of Pastoral Manuals', in F. Liotta, ed., *Miscellanea Rolando Bandinelli, Papa Alessandro III* (Siena, 1986), pp. 43–56

—— 'The "Oculus Sacerdotis" and Some Other Works of William of Pagula: The Alexander Prize Essay', *Transactions of the Royal Historical Society*, 5th series, 5 (1955), 81–110

—— 'A Study of the Works Attributed to William of Pagula: With Special Reference to the "Oculus Sacerdotis" and "Summa Summarum"' (DPhil thesis, University of Oxford, 1956)

Bradbury, J., *Philip Augustus: King of France, 1180–1223* (New York, 1998)

Brand, P., '"Deserving" and "Undeserving" Wives: Earning and Forfeiting Dower in Medieval England', *Journal of Legal History*, 22 (2001), 1–20

—— 'Lawyers' Time in England in the Later Middle Ages', in C. Humphrey and W. M. Ormrod eds., *Time in the Medieval World* (York, 2001), pp. 73–104

—— '"Time out of mind": The Knowledge and Use of the Eleventh- and Twelfth-Century Past in Thirteenth-Century Litigation', *Anglo-Norman Studies* XVI (1994), 37–54

Bibliography

Breen, K., *Imagining an English Reading Public, c. 1150–1400* (Cambridge, 2010)

Brenner, E., M. Cohen, and M. Franklin-Brown, eds., *Memory and Commemoration in Medieval Culture* (Farnham, 2013)

Briggs, C., 'Empowered or Marginalized? Rural Women and Credit in Later Thirteenth- and Fourteenth-Century England', *Continuity and Change*, 19 (2004), 13–43

Britnell, R. H., ed., *Pragmatic Literacy, East and West, 1200–1300* (Woodbridge, 1997)

Brooke, C. N. L., *The Medieval Idea of Marriage* (Oxford, 1989)

Brundage, J. A., 'Juridical Space: Female Witnesses in Canon Law', *Dumbarton Oaks Papers*, 52 (1998), 147–56

—— *Law, Sex, and Christian Society in Medieval Europe* (Chicago, 1987)

—— *Medieval Canon Law* (London and New York, 1995)

—— *The Medieval Origins of the Legal Profession: Canonists, Civilians, and Courts* (Chicago, 2008)

—— 'Neuton, John (c. 1350–1414)', *Oxford Dictionary of National Biography* (Oxford, 2004)

Bruner, J., 'The Narrative Construction of Reality', *Critical Inquiry*, 18 (1991), 1–21

Burgess, C., 'Pre-Reformation Churchwardens' Accounts and Parish Government: Lessons from London and Bristol', *English Historical Review*, 117 (2002), 306–22

Burrow, J. A., *The Ages of Man: A Study in Medieval Writing and Thought* (Oxford, 1996)

Burton, J., 'The Convent and the Community: Cause Papers as a Source for Monastic History', in P. Hoskin, C. Brooke, and B. Dobson, eds., *The Foundations of Medieval English Ecclesiastical History: Studies Presented to David Smith* (Woodbridge, 2005), pp. 63–76

—— 'Priory and Parish: Kirkham and its Parishioners, 1496–7', in B. Thompson, ed., *Monasteries and Society in Medieval Britain* (Stamford, 1999), pp. 329–47

Butler, J., *Excitable Speech: A Politics of the Performative* (New York, 1997)

Butler, S., *The Language of Abuse: Marital Violence in Later Medieval England* (Leiden and Boston, 2007)

—— 'Runaway Wives: Husband Desertion in Medieval England', *Journal of Social History*, 40 (2006), 337–59

Bynum, C. W., 'The Female Body and Religious Practice in the Later Middle Ages', in C. W. Bynum, *Fragmentation and Redemption: Essays on Gender and the Human Body in Medieval Religion* (New York, 1991), pp. 181–238

Cadden, J., *Meanings of Sex Difference in the Middle Ages: Medicine, Science, and Culture* (Cambridge, 1993)

Cam, H., 'Pedigrees of Villeins and Freemen in the Thirteenth Century', in H. Cam, ed., *Liberties and Communities in Medieval England: Collected Studies in Local Administration and Topography* (London, 1963), pp. 124–35

Campbell, B. M. S., *The Great Transition: Climate, Disease and Society in the Late-Medieval World* (Cambridge, 2016)

Bibliography

Campbell, B. M. S., ed., *Before the Black Death: Studies in the 'Crisis' of the Early Fourteenth Century* (Manchester, 1991)

Campbell, E., *Medieval Saints' Lives: The Gift, Kinship and Community in Old French Hagiography* (Cambridge, 2008)

Campbell, W. H., *The Landscape of Pastoral Care in Thirteenth-Century England* (Cambridge, 2018)

Canning, K., 'The Body as Method? Reflections on the Place of the Body in Gender History', in K. Canning, *Gender History in Practice: Historical Perspectives on Bodies, Class, and Citizenship* (Ithaca, NY, 2005), pp. 168–88

—— 'Difficult Dichotomies: "Experience" between Narrativity and Materiality', in K. Canning, *Gender History in Practice: Historical Perspectives on Bodies, Class, and Citizenship* (Ithaca, NY, 2005), pp. 101–20

—— 'Feminist History after the Linguistic Turn: Historicizing Discourse and Experience', in K. Canning, *Gender History in Practice: Historical Perspectives on Bodies, Class, and Citizenship* (Ithaca, NY, 2005), pp. 63–100

Cannon, D., 'London Pride: Citizenship and the Fourteenth-Century Custumals of the City of London', in S. Rees Jones, ed., *Learning and Literacy in Medieval England and Abroad* (Turnhout, 2003), pp. 179–98

Capp, B., *When Gossips Meet: Women, Family, and Neighbourhood in Early Modern England* (Oxford, 2003)

Carpenter, C., 'Gentry and Community in Medieval England', *Journal of British Studies*, 33 (1994), 340–80

Carpenter, D. A., 'English Peasants in Politics, 1258–67', *Past & Present*, 136 (1992), 3–42

Carrel, H. M., 'Civic Government and Identity in the Provincial Towns of Late Medieval England, c. 1370–c. 1500' (PhD thesis, University of Cambridge, 2007)

Carruthers, M., *The Book of Memory: A Study of Memory in Medieval Culture* (Cambridge, 1990)

Cartlidge, N., '"Alas, I go with chylde": Representations of Extra-Marital Pregnancy in the Middle English Lyric', *English Studies*, 79 (1998), 395–414

Cassidy-Welch, M., *Monastic Spaces and their Meanings: Thirteenth-Century English Cistercian Monasteries* (Turnhout, 2001)

Certeau, M. de, *The Practice of Everyday Life*, trans. S. Rendall (Berkeley, 1984)

Champeaux, E., '*Jus sanguinis*: Trois façons de calculer la parenté au Moyen Age', *Revue historique de droit francais et étranger*, 4th series, 12 (1933), 241–90

Champion, M. S., *The Fullness of Time: Temporalities of the Fifteenth-Century Low Countries* (Chicago, 2017)

Ciappelli, G., 'Family Memory: Functions, Evolution, Recurrences', in G. Ciappelli and P. Rubin, eds., *Art, Memory and Family in Renaissance Florence* (Cambridge, 2000), pp. 26–38

Ciappelli, G., and P. Rubin, eds., *Art, Memory and Family in Renaissance Florence* (Cambridge, 2000)

Bibliography

Clanchy, M. T., *From Memory to Written Record: England 1066–1307*, 2nd edition (Oxford, 1993)

Clark, E., 'Social Welfare and Mutual Aid in the Medieval Countryside', *Journal of British Studies*, 33 (1994), 381–406

—— 'Some Aspects of Social Security in Medieval England', *Journal of Family History*, 7 (1982), 307–20

Classen, A., ed., *Urban Space in the Middle Ages and the Early Modern Age* (Berlin, 2009)

Coleman, J., *Ancient and Medieval Memories: Studies in the Reconstruction of the Past* (Cambridge, 2005)

Coleman, J., *Public Reading and the Reading Public in Late Medieval England and France* (Cambridge, 1996)

Connerton, P., *How Societies Remember* (Cambridge, 1989)

—— 'Seven Types of Forgetting', *Memory Studies*, 1 (2008), 59–71

Cox, E., L. H. McAvoy, and R. Magnani, eds., *Reconsidering Gender, Time and Memory in Medieval Culture* (Cambridge, 2015)

Crane, S. A., 'Writing the Individual Back into Collective Memory', *The American Historical Review*, 102.5 (1997), 1372–85

Crehan, K., *Gramsci, Culture and Anthropology* (London, Sterling, and Virginia, 2002)

Cresswell, T., 'Moral Geographies', in D. Atkinson et al., eds., *Cultural Geography: A Critical Dictionary of Ideas* (London, 2005), pp. 128–34

Cressy, D., 'Purification, Thanksgiving and the Churching of Women', in D. Cressy, *Birth, Marriage and Death: Ritual, Religion and the Life-Cycle in Tudor and Stuart England* (Oxford, 1997), pp. 197–228

Crick, J. C., and A. Walsham, 'Introduction: Script, Print and History', in J. C. Crick and A. Walsham, eds., *The Uses of Script and Print, 1300–1700* (Cambridge, 2004), pp. 1–28

Crossley, N., *The Social Body: Habit, Identity and Desire* (London, 2001)

Cullum, P. H., 'Clergy, Masculinity and Transgression in Late Medieval England', in D. M. Hadley, ed., *Masculinity in Medieval Europe* (London, 1999), pp. 178–96

Daniell, C., *Death and Burial in Medieval England, 1066–1550* (London, 1997)

Dobson, B., 'Contrasting Chronicles: Historical Writing at York and Durham at the Close of the Middle Ages', in I. Wood and G. A. Loud, eds., *Church and Chronicle in the Middle Ages: Essays Presented to John Taylor* (London, 1991), pp. 201–18

—— 'John Shirwood of York: A Common Clerk's Will of 1473', in M. Aston and R. Horrox, eds., *Much Heaving and Shoving: Late Medieval Gentry and their Concerns: Essays for Colin Richmond* (Lavenham, 2005), pp. 109–20

Donahue, C., Jr., 'Female Plaintiffs in Marriage Cases in the Court of York in the Later Middle Ages: What Can We Learn from the Numbers?', in S. S. Walker, ed., *Wife and Widow in Medieval England* (Ann Arbor, 1993), pp. 183–213

Bibliography

—— *Law, Marriage, and Society in the Later Middle Ages: Arguments about Marriage from Five Courts* (Cambridge, 2007)

—— 'Procedure in the Courts of the *Ius Commune*', in W. Hartmann and K. Pennington, eds., *The History of Courts and Procedure in Medieval Canon Law* (Washington, DC, 2016), pp. 74–124

—— 'Proof by Witnesses in the Church Courts of Medieval England: An Imperfect Reception of the Learned Law', in M. S. Arnold et al., eds., *On the Laws and Customs of Medieval England: Essays in Honor of Samuel E. Thorne* (Chapel Hill, NC, 1981), pp. 127–58

—— 'Roman Canon Law in the Medieval English Church: *Stubbs* vs. *Maitland* Re-Examined after 75 Years in the Light of Some Records from the Church Courts', *Michigan Law Review*, 72 (1974), 647–716

Duby, G., 'Lineage, Nobility and Knighthood: The Mâconnais in the Twelfth Century – A Revision', in G. Duby, *The Chivalrous Society*, trans. C. Postan (London, 1977), pp. 59–80

Duffy, E., *The Stripping of the Altars: Traditional Religion in England, 1400–1580*, 2nd edition (New Haven and London, 2005)

Durkheim, É., *The Elementary Forms of Religious Life*, trans. C. Cosman (New York, 1995)

Dyer, C., *Everyday Life in Medieval England* (London, 1994)

—— *Standards of Living in the Later Middle Ages: Social Change in England, c. 1200–1520*, revised edition (Cambridge, 1998)

Einbinder, S. L., *No Place of Rest: Jewish Literature, Expulsion, and the Memory of Medieval France* (Philadelphia, 2009)

Eldevik, J., 'Driving the Chariot of the Lord: Siegfried I of Mainz (1060–1084) and Episcopal Identity in an Age of Transition', in J. S. Ott and A. Trubore Jones, eds., *The Bishop Reformed: Studies of Episcopal Power and Culture in the Central Middle Ages* (Aldershot, 2007), pp. 161–88

Elliot, D., 'Women and Confession: From Empowerment to Pathology', in M. C. Erler and M. Kowaleski, eds., *Gendering the Master Narrative: Women and Power in the Middle Ages* (Ithaca, NY, 2003), pp. 31–51

Elsakkers, M., '"In pain you shall bear children" [Gen. 3:16]: Medieval Prayers for a Safe Delivery', in A. Korte, ed., *Women and Miracle Stories: A Multidisciplinary Exploration* (Leiden, 2001), pp. 179–209

Enders, J., 'Cutting off the Memory of Women', in C. Mason Sutherland and R. Sutcliffe, eds., *The Changing Tradition: Women in the History of Rhetoric* (Calgary, 1999), pp. 47–55

—— *The Medieval Theater of Cruelty: Rhetoric, Memory, Violence* (Ithaca, NY, 1999)

Everard, J., 'Sworn Testimony and Memory of the Past in Brittany, c. 1100–1250', in E. van Houts, ed., *Medieval Memories: Men, Women and the Past, 700–1300* (London, 2001), pp. 72–91

Fantham, E., 'The Concept of Nature and Human Nature in Quintilian's Psychology and Theory of Instruction', *Rhetorica: A Journal of the History of Rhetoric*, 13 (1995), 125–36

Bibliography

Farmer, S., 'Persuasive Voices: Clerical Images of Medieval Wives', *Speculum*, 61 (1986), 517–43

—— *Surviving Poverty in Medieval Paris: Gender, Ideology, and the Daily Lives of the Poor* (Ithaca, NY, 2002)

Fentress, J., and C. Wickham, *Social Memory* (Oxford, 1992)

Finnegan, R., *Literacy and Orality: Studies in the Technology of Communication* (Oxford, 1988)

Fletcher, A., *Gender, Sex and Subordination in England, 1500–1800* (New Haven, 1995)

Fletcher, A., and J. Stevenson, 'Introduction', in A. Fletcher and J. Stevenson, eds., *Order and Disorder in Early Modern England* (Cambridge, 1985), pp. 1–40

Ford, J. A., *John Mirk's Festial: Orthodoxy, Lollardy and the Common People in Fourteenth-Century England* (Cambridge, 2006)

Forrest, I., *The Detection of Heresy in Late Medieval England* (Oxford, 2005)

—— 'English Provincial Constitutions and Inquisition into Lollardy', in M. C. Flannery and K. C. Walter, eds., *The Culture of Inquisition in Medieval England* (Cambridge, 2013), pp. 45–59

—— 'The Politics of Burial in Late Medieval Hereford', *English Historical Review*, 125 (2010), 1110–38

—— *Trustworthy Men: How Inequality and Faith Made the Medieval Church* (Princeton, 2018)

Foucault, M., 'Film and Popular Memory: An Interview with Michel Foucault', trans. Martin Jordan, *Radical Philosophy*, 11 (1975), 24–9

—— *The History of Sexuality*, vol. 1: *An Introduction*, trans. R. Hurley (New York, 1990)

—— 'Nietzsche, Genealogy, History', in P. Rabinow, ed., *The Foucault Reader* (New York, 1984), pp. 76–100

Fowler-Magerl, L., *Ordo iudiciorum vel ordo iudiciarius: Begriff und Literaturgattung* (Frankfurt, 1984)

Freedman, P. H., *Images of the Medieval Peasant* (Stanford, 1999)

Freeman, E., 'Cistercian Nuns, Cause Papers and the York Consistory Court in the Fourteenth and Fifteenth Centuries', *Australia and New Zealand Law and History E-Journal* (2006), 1–14

French, K. L., *The Good Women of the Parish: Gender and Religion after the Black Death* (Philadelphia, 2007)

—— 'Maidens' Lights and Wives' Stores: Women's Parish Guilds in Late Medieval England', *Sixteenth-Century Journal*, 29 (1998), 399–425

—— *The People of the Parish: Community Life in a Late Medieval English Diocese* (Philadelphia, 2001)

—— '"To free them from binding": Women in the Late Medieval English Parish', *Journal of Interdisciplinary History*, 28 (1997), 387–412

Friedman, J. B., 'Richard de Thorpe's Astronomical Kalendar and the Luxury Book Trade at York', *Studies in the Age of Chaucer*, 7 (1985), 137–60

Bibliography

Geary, P. J., *Living with the Dead in the Middle Ages* (Ithaca, NY, and London, 1994)

—— *Phantoms of Remembrance: Memory and Oblivion at the End of the First Millennium* (Princeton, 1994)

Gee, E. A., 'The Painted Glass of All Saints' Church, North Street, York', *Archaeologia*, 102 (1969), 151–202

Gee, S., 'Parochial Libraries in Pre-Reformation England', in S. Rees Jones, ed., *Learning and Literacy in Medieval England* (Turnhout, 2003), pp. 199–222

Geiger, S., 'What's So Feminist About Women's Oral History?', *Journal of Women's History*, 2.1 (1990), 161–82

Gibbs, M., and J. Lang, *Bishops and Reform 1215–1272, with Special Reference to the Lateran Council of 1215* (Oxford, 1934)

Gilchrist, R., *Gender and Material Culture: The Archaeology of Religious Women* (London, 1994)

—— 'Medieval Bodies in the Material World: Gender, Stigma and the Body', in S. Kay and M. Rubin, eds., *Framing Medieval Bodies* (Manchester, 1994), pp. 43–61

—— *Medieval Life: Archaeology and the Life Course* (Woodbridge, 2012)

Gillespie, V., 'The Literary Form of the Middle English Pastoral Manual, with Particular Reference to the *Speculum Christiani* and Some Related Texts' (DPhil thesis, University of Oxford, 1981)

Given-Wilson, C., *Chronicles: The Writing of History in Medieval England* (London and New York, 2004)

Goering, J., 'The Summa of Master Serlo and Thirteenth-Century Penitential Literature', *Mediaeval Studies*, 40 (1978), 290–311

—— 'Thomas of Chobham', *Oxford Dictionary of National Biography* (Oxford, 2004)

—— 'When and Where did Grosseteste Study Theology?', in J. McEvoy, ed., *Robert Grosseteste: New Perspectives on his Thought and Scholarship* (Turnhout, 1995), pp. 17–51

—— *William de Montibus (c. 1140–1213): The Schools and the Literature of Pastoral Care* (Toronto, 1992)

Goering, J., and P. J. Payer, 'The "Summa Penitentie Fratrum Predicatorum": A Thirteenth-Century Confessional Formulary', *Mediaeval Studies*, 55 (1993), 1–50

Goering, J., and D. S. Taylor, '*Summulae* of Bishops Walter de Cantilupe (1240) and Peter Quinel (1287)', *Speculum*, 67 (1992), 576–94

Goldberg, P. J. P., *Communal Discord, Child Abduction, and Rape in the Later Middle Ages* (New York, 2007)

—— 'Female Labour, Service and Marriage in the Late Medieval Urban North', *Northern History*, 22 (1986), 18–38

—— 'Fiction in the Archives: The York Cause Papers as a Source for Later Medieval Social History', *Continuity and Change*, 12 (1997), 425–45

—— 'Gender and Matrimonial Litigation in the Church Courts in the Later

Middle Ages: The Evidence of the Court of York', *Gender & History*, 19 (2007), 43–59

—— 'John Skathelok's Dick: Voyeurism and "Pornography" in Late Medieval England', in N. McDonald, ed., *Medieval Obscenities* (York, 2006), pp. 105–23

—— 'Masters and Men in Later Medieval England', in D. M. Hadley, ed., *Masculinity in Medieval Europe* (New York, 1999), pp. 56–70

—— 'Migration, Youth and Gender in Later Medieval England', in P. J. P. Goldberg and F. Riddy, eds., *Youth in the Middle Ages* (York, 2004), pp. 85–99

—— 'Pigs and Prostitutes: Streetwalking in Comparative Perspective', in K. J. Lewis, N. J. Menuge, and K. M. Phillips, eds., *Young Medieval Women* (Stroud, 1999), pp. 172–93

—— 'Space and Gender in the Later Medieval English House', *Viator*, 42 (2011), 205–32

—— 'Women', in R. Horrox, ed., *Fifteenth-Century Attitudes: Perceptions of Society in Late Medieval England* (Cambridge, 1994), pp. 112–31

—— *Women, Work, and Life Cycle in a Medieval Economy: Women in York and Yorkshire c. 1300–1520* (Oxford, 1992)

Goody, J., *The Development of Family and Marriage in Europe* (Cambridge, 1983)

Goody, J., ed., *Literacy in Traditional Societies* (Cambridge, 1968)

Górecki, P., 'Communities of Legal Memory in Medieval Poland, c. 1200–1240', *Journal of Medieval History*, 24 (1998), 127–54

Gowing, L., *Common Bodies: Women, Touch and Power in Seventeenth-Century England* (New Haven, 2003)

—— *Domestic Dangers: Women, Words, and Sex in Early Modern London* (Oxford, 1996)

—— '"The freedom of the streets": Women and Social Space, 1560–1640', in P. Griffiths and M. S. R. Jenner, eds., *Londinopolis: Essays in the Cultural and Social History of Early Modern London, 1500–1750* (Manchester, 2000), pp. 130–51

—— 'Language, Power and the Law: Women's Slander Litigation in Early Modern London', in J. Kermode and G. Walker, eds., *Women, Crime and the Courts in Early Modern England* (Chapel Hill, NC, and London, 1994), pp. 26–47

Graham, H., '"A woman's work …": Labour and Gender in the Late Medieval Countryside', in P. J. P. Goldberg, ed., *Woman is a Worthy Wight: Women in English Society, c. 1200–1500* (Stroud, 1992), pp. 126–48

Gransden, A., *Historical Writing in England*, vol. 2: *c. 1307 to the Early Sixteenth Century*, 2nd edition (London, 1996)

Green, M., *Making Women's Medicine Masculine: The Rise of Male Authority in Pre-Modern Gynaecology* (Oxford, 2008)

Green, R. F., *Elf Queens and Holy Friars: Fairy Beliefs and the Medieval Church* (Philadelphia, 2016)

Green, W. M., 'Hugo of St. Victor: *De tribus maximis circumstantiis gestorum*', *Speculum*, 18 (1943), 484–93

Greenberg, J., *The Radical Face of the Ancient Constitution: St Edward's 'Laws' in Early Modern Political Thought* (Cambridge, 2001)

Bibliography

Gurevich, A., *Medieval Popular Culture: Problems of Belief and Perception*, trans. J. M. Bak and P. A. Hollingsworth (Cambridge, 1988)

Haggerty, G. E., 'Keyhole Testimony: Witnessing Sodomy in the Eighteenth Century', *Eighteenth Century: Theory and Interpretation*, 44 (2003), 167–82

Halbwachs, M., *On Collective Memory*, ed. and trans. L. A. Coser (Chicago, 1992)

Hamilton, S., 'Penance in the Age of Gregorian Reform', in K. Cooper and J. Gregory, eds., *Retribution, Repentance, and Reconciliation* (Woodbridge, 2004), pp. 47–73

—— *The Practice of Penance, 900–1050* (Woodbridge, 2001)

Hanawalt, B. A., 'Peasant Women's Contribution to the Home Economy in Late Medieval England', in B. A. Hanawalt, ed., *Women and Work in Preindustrial Europe* (Bloomington, IN, 1986), pp. 3–19

—— *The Ties that Bound: Peasant Families in Medieval England* (Oxford, 1986)

—— *Women and Work in Preindustrial Europe* (Bloomington, IN, 1986)

Hanawalt, B. A., and K. Reyerson, eds., *City and Spectacle in Medieval Europe* (Minneapolis, 1994)

Haren, M., 'Confession, Social Ethics and Social Discipline in the *Memoriale Presbiterorum*', in P. Biller and A. J. Minnis, eds., *Handling Sin: Confession in the Middle Ages* (York, 1998), pp. 109–22

—— 'The Interrogatories for Officials, Lawyers and Secular Estates of the *Memoriale Presbiterorum*', in P. Biller and A. J. Minnis eds., *Handling Sin: Confession in the Middle Ages* (York, 1998), pp. 123–63

—— *Sin and Society in Fourteenth-Century England: A Study of the Memoriale Presbiterorum* (Oxford, 2000)

Harris-Stoertz, F., 'Remembering Birth in Thirteenth- and Fourteenth-Century England', in E. Cox, L. H. McAvoy, and R. Magnani, eds., *Reconsidering Gender, Time and Memory in Medieval Culture* (Cambridge, 2015), pp. 25–59

Harvey, M., 'Some Comments on Northern Mortuary Customs in the Later Middle Ages', *Journal of Ecclesiastical History*, 59 (2008), 272–80

Harvey, P. D. A., 'Local and Regional Cartography in Medieval Europe', in J. B. Harley and D. Woodward, eds., *The History of Cartography*, vol. 1: *Cartography in Prehistoric, Ancient, and Medieval Europe and the Mediterranean* (Chicago and London, 1987), pp. 464–501

Hatcher, J., 'England in the Aftermath of the Black Death', *Past & Present*, 144 (1994), 3–35

Hawkes, E., '"[S]he will … protect and defend her rights boldly by law and reason": Women's Knowledge of Common Law and Equity Courts in Late-Medieval England', in N. J. Menuge, ed., *Medieval Women and the Law* (Woodbridge, 2000), pp. 145–61

Heath, P., *Medieval Clerical Accounts* (York, 1964)

Helmholz, R. H., 'Abjuration *sub pena nubendi*', *The Jurist*, 32 (1972), 80–90

—— 'The Bible in the Service of the Canon Law', *Chicago-Kent Law Review*, 70 (1995), 1557–81

—— *Canon Law and the Law of England* (London, 1987)

Bibliography

—— 'Infanticide in the Province of Canterbury during the Fifteenth Century', *History of Childhood Quarterly*, 2 (1975), 379–90

—— *The Ius Commune in England: Four Studies* (Oxford, 2001)

—— 'John de Burgh', *Ecclesiastical Law Journal*, 18 (2016), 67–72

—— *Marriage Litigation in Medieval England* (Cambridge, 1974)

—— 'Mortuaries and the Law of Custom', in R. H. Helmholz, *The Ius Commune in England: Four Studies* (Oxford, 2001), pp. 135–86

—— *The Oxford History of the Laws of England: The History of the Canon Law and Ecclesiastical Jurisdiction from 597 to the 1640s* (Oxford, 2004)

—— *Roman Canon Law in Reformation England* (Cambridge, 1990)

Herlihy, D., 'The Making of the Medieval Family: Symmetry, Structure, and Sentiment', *Journal of Family History*, 8 (1983), 116–30

—— *Women, Family and Society in Medieval Europe: Historical Essays, 1978-1991*, ed. A. Molho (Providence, RI, and Oxford, 1995)

Herlihy, D., and C. Klapisch-Zuber, *Tuscans and their Families: A Study of the Florentine Catasto of 1427* (New Haven and London, 1985)

Hicks, L. V., *Religious Life in Normandy: Space, Gender and Social Pressure, 1050-1300* (Woodbridge, 2007)

Hilton, R. H., *Bondmen Made Free: Medieval Peasant Movements and the English Rising of 1381* (New York, 1973; repr. London and New York, 2003)

—— 'A Thirteenth-Century Poem on Disputed Villein Services', *English Historical Review*, 56 (1941), 90–7

Hirsch, M., and V. Smith, 'Feminism and Cultural Memory: An Introduction', *Signs: Journal of Women in Culture and Society*, 28.1, special issue: *Gender and Cultural Memory* (2002), 1–19

Hofmeyer, I., *'We spend our years as a tale that is told': Oral Historical Narrative in a South African Chiefdom* (Johannesburg and London, 1994)

Howell, M. C., *Women, Production, and Patriarchy in Late Medieval Cities* (Chicago, 1986)

Hughes, J., 'The Administration of Confession in the Diocese of York in the Fourteenth Century', in D. M. Smith, ed., *Studies in Clergy and Ministry in Medieval England* (York, 1991), pp. 87–163

Hunt, A., 'The New Legal History: Prospects and Perspectives', *Crime, Law, and Social Change*, 10 (1986), 201–8

Hutton, P. H., *History as an Art of Memory* (Hanover, 1993)

Hyams, P. R., 'Deans and their Doings: The Norwich Inquiry of 1286', *Proceedings of the Sixth International Conference on Canon Law, Berkeley* (Vatican City, 1985), pp. 619–46

—— 'The Legal Revolution and the Discourse of Dispute in the Twelfth Century', in A. Galloway, ed., *The Cambridge Companion to Medieval English Culture* (Cambridge, 2011), pp. 43–65

Innes, M., 'Keeping it in the Family: Women and Aristocratic Memory, 700-1200', in E. van Houts, ed., *Medieval Memories: Men, Women and the Past, 700-1300* (London, 2001), pp. 17–35

Bibliography

—— 'Memory, Orality and Literacy in an Early Medieval Society', *Past & Present*, 158 (1998), 3–36

Jacquart, D., and C. Thomasset, *Sexuality and Medicine in the Middle Ages*, trans. M. Adamson (Cambridge, 1988)

Jennings, M., 'Tutivillus: The Literary Career of the Recording Demon', *Studies in Philology*, 74 (1977), 1–95

Jewell, H., 'Women at the Courts of the Manor of Wakefield, 1348–1350', *Northern History*, 26 (1990), 59–81

—— *Women in Medieval England* (Manchester, 1996)

Johnson, T., 'Medieval Law and Materiality: Shipwrecks, Finders, and Property on the Suffolk Coast, ca. 1380–1410', *American Historical Review*, 120 (2015), 407–32

—— 'The Preconstruction of Witness Testimony: Law and Social Discourse in England before the Reformation', *Law and History Review*, 32 (2014), 127–47

—— 'The Tree and the Rod: Jurisdiction in Late Medieval England', *Past & Present*, 237 (2017), 13–51

Jones, A. R., and P. Stallybrass, *Renaissance Clothing and the Materials of Memory* (Cambridge, 2000)

Jones, K., *Gender and Petty Crime in Late Medieval England: The Local Courts in Kent, 1460–1560* (Woodbridge, 2006)

Jussen, B., 'Challenging the Culture of *Memoria*: Dead Men, Oblivion, and the "Faithless Widow" in the Middle Ages', in G. Althoff, J. Fried, and P. J. Geary, eds., *Medieval Concepts of the Past: Ritual, Memory, Historiography* (Cambridge, 2002), pp. 215–32

Justice, S., *Writing and Rebellion: England in 1381* (Berkeley, 1994)

Kane, B., 'Custom, Memory and Knowledge in the Medieval English Church Courts', in R. Hayes and W. J. Sheils, eds., *Clergy, Church and Society in England and Wales, c. 1200–1800* (York, 2013), pp. 61–81

—— *Impotence and Virginity in the Late Medieval Ecclesiastical Court of York* (York, 2008)

—— 'Reading Emotion and Gender in the Later Medieval English Church Courts', *Frühneuzeit-Info*, 12 (2012), 53–63

—— 'Return of the Native: Franciscan Education and Astrological Practice in the Medieval North of England', in M. Robson and J. Rohrkasten, eds., *Franciscan Organisation in the Mendicant Context: Formal and Informal Structures of the Friars' Lives and Ministry in the Middle Ages* (Berlin, 2010), pp. 281–306

—— 'Women, Memory and Testimony in the Medieval Ecclesiastical Courts of Canterbury and York', in B. Kane and F. Williamson, eds., *Women, Agency and the Law, 1300–1700* (London, 2013), pp. 43–62

Kane, B., with F. Williamson, 'Introduction', in B. Kane and F. Williamson, eds., *Women, Agency and the Law, 1300–1700* (London, 2013), pp. 1–16

Karras, R. M., *Common Women: Prostitution and Sexuality in Medieval England* (Oxford, 1996)

Bibliography

—— *From Boys to Men: Formations of Masculinity in Late Medieval Europe* (Philadelphia, 2003)

—— *Unmarriages: Women, Men, and Sexual Unions in the Middle Ages* (Philadelphia, 2012)

Keene, D., 'The Medieval Urban Landscape, AD 900–1540', in P. Waller, ed., *The English Urban Landscape* (Oxford, 2000), pp. 74–98

Kelly, K. C., *Performing Virginity and Testing Chastity in the Middle Ages* (London, 2001)

Kent, G. H. R., ed., *Victoria County History: A History of the County of York East Riding*, vol. 7: *Holderness Wapentake, Middle and North Divisions* (London, 2002)

Kerby-Fulton, K., 'Piers Plowman', in D. Wallace, ed., *The Cambridge History of Medieval English Literature* (Cambridge, 1999), pp. 513–38

Klapisch-Zuber, C., 'The "Cruel Mother": Maternity, Widowhood, and Dowry in Florence in the Fourteenth and Fifteenth Centuries', in L. Hutson, ed., *Feminism and Renaissance Studies* (Oxford, 1999), pp. 186–202

—— *L'Ombre des ancêtres: Essai sur l'imaginaire médiéval de la parenté* (Paris, 2000)

—— *Women, Family, and Ritual in Renaissance Italy*, trans. L. Cochrane (Chicago and London, 1985)

Koslofsky, C., *Evening's Empire: A History of the Night in Early Modern Europe* (Cambridge, 2011)

Kounine, L., 'Emotions, Mind, and Body on Trial: A Cross-Cultural Perspective', *Journal of Social History*, 51 (2017), 219–30

Kowaleski, M., and J. M. Bennett, 'Crafts, Gilds, and Women in the Middle Ages: Fifty Years after Marian K. Dale', in J. M. Bennett et al., eds., *Sisters and Workers in the Middle Ages* (Chicago, 1989), pp. 11–38

Kowaleski, M., and P. J. P. Goldberg, 'Introduction. Medieval Domesticity: Home, Housing and Household', in M. Kowaleski and P. J. P. Goldberg, eds., *Medieval Domesticity: Home, Housing and Household in Medieval England* (Cambridge, 2008), pp. 1–13

Kristeva, J., 'Women's Time', *Signs*, 7 (1981), 13–35

Krug, R., *Reading Families: Women's Literate Practices in Late Medieval England* (Ithaca, NY, and London, 2002)

Kuehn, T., '*Fama* as a Legal Status in Renaissance Florence', in T. Fenster and D. L. Smail, eds., *Fama: The Politics of Talk and Reputation in Medieval Europe* (Ithaca, NY, and London, 2003), pp. 27–46

Kümin, B., *The Shaping of a Community: The Rise and Reformation of the English Parish, c. 1400–1560* (Aldershot, 1996)

Larson, A. A., *Master of Penance: Gratian and the Development of Penitential Thought and Law in the Twelfth Century* (Washington, DC, 2014)

Larson, P. L., *Conflict and Compromise in the Late Medieval Countryside: Lords and Peasants in Durham, 1349–1400* (New York, 2006)

Latham, R. E., ed., *Revised Medieval Latin Wordlist from British and Irish Sources* (Oxford, 1965; repr. with supplement, 1999)

Bibliography

Le Goff, J., *Histoire et mémoire* (Paris, 1988)

—— 'Merchant's Time and Church's Time in the Middle Ages', in J. Le Goff, *Time, Work and Culture in the Middle Ages*, trans. A. Goldhammer (Chicago and London, 1980), pp. 29–42

—— *Time, Work and Culture in the Middle Ages*, trans. A. Goldhammer (Chicago and London, 1980)

Lea, H. C., *A History of Auricular Confession and Indulgences in the Latin Church* (Philadelphia, 1896), vol. 1

Lee, B. R., 'A Company of Women and Men: Men's Recollections of Childbirth in Medieval England', *Journal of Family History*, 27 (2002), 92–100

—— 'Men's Recollections of a Women's Rite: Medieval English Men's Recollections Regarding the Rite of the Purification of Women after Childbirth', *Gender & History*, 14 (2002), 224–41

Lefebvre, H., *The Production of Space*, trans. D. Nicholson-Smith (Cambridge, MA, 1991)

Leitao, D. D., *The Pregnant Male as Myth and Metaphor in Classical Greek Literature* (Cambridge, 2012)

Lemmings, D., 'Law', in S. Broomhall, ed., *Early Modern Emotions: An Introduction* (Abingdon, 2017), pp. 192–5

Leydesdorff, S., L. Passerini, and P. Thompson, eds., *Gender and Memory*, 2nd edition (New Brunswick, NJ, and London, 2007)

Lightfoot, D. W., *Women, Dowries and Agency: Marriage in Fifteenth-Century Valencia* (Manchester, 2013)

Lipsitz, G., *Time Passages: Collective Memory and American Popular Culture* (Minneapolis, 1990)

Lohr, C. H., *Latin Aristotle Commentaries*, vol. 5: *Bibliography of Secondary Literature* (Florence, 2005)

Lourie, M. A., D. C. Staunton, and M. Vicinus, 'Introduction: Women and Memory', *Michigan Quarterly Review*, 26 (1987), 1–8

Lutgens, C., 'The Case of Waghen vs. Sutton: Conflict over Burial Rights in Late Medieval England', *Mediaeval Studies*, 38 (1976), 145–84

Lutton, R., *Lollardy and Orthodox Religion in Pre-Reformation England* (Woodbridge, 2006)

McAvoy, L. H., 'Introduction. *In Principio*: The Queer Matrix of Gender, Time and Memory in the Middle Ages', in E. Cox, L. H. McAvoy, and R. Magnani, eds., *Reconsidering Gender, Time and Memory in Medieval Culture* (Cambridge, 2015), pp. 1–12

—— *Medieval Anchoritisms: Gender, Space and the Solitary Life* (Cambridge, 2011)

McDougall, S., 'Women and Gender in Canon Law', in J. M. Bennett and R. M. Karras, eds., *The Oxford Handbook of Women and Gender in Medieval Europe* (Oxford, 2013), pp. 163–78

McIntosh, M. K., 'The Benefits and Drawbacks of *Femme Sole* Status in England, 1300–1630', *Journal of British Studies*, 44 (2005), 410–38

Bibliography

McMurray Gibson, G., 'Blessing from Sun and Moon: Churching as Women's Theater', in B. A. Hanawalt and D. Wallace, eds., *Bodies and Disciplines: Intersections of Literature and History in Fifteenth-Century England* (Minneapolis, 1996), pp. 139–54

McSheffrey, S., *Marriage, Sex, and Civic Culture in Late Medieval London* (Philadelphia, 2006)

—— 'Jurors, Respectable Masculinity, and Christian Morality: A Comment on Marjorie McIntosh's *Controlling Misbehavior*', *The Journal of British Studies*, 37.3: *Controlling (Mis)Behavior: Medieval and Early Modern Perspectives* (1998), 269–78

Maddicott, J. R., *The Origins of the English Parliament, 924–1327* (Oxford, 2010)

—— *Simon de Montfort* (Cambridge, 1994)

Makowski, E. M., *English Nuns and the Law in the Middle Ages: Cloistered Nuns and their Lawyers, 1293–1540* (Woodbridge, 2011)

Matsuda, M. K., *The Memory of the Modern* (New York, 1996)

Menuge, N. J., ed., *Medieval Women and the Law* (Woodbridge, 2000)

Middleton, D., and D. Edwards, 'Conversational Remembering: A Social Psychological Approach', in D. Middleton and D. Edwards, eds., *Collective Remembering* (London, 1990), pp. 23–45

Miller, N. J., *Winestead and its Lords: A History of a Holderness Village* (Hull, 1933)

Misztal, B. A., *Theories of Social Remembering* (Maidenhead, 2003)

Moi, T., *What is a Woman? And Other Essays* (Oxford, 1999)

Montaigne, M. de, *Les Essais* (Paris, 2007), vol. 2

Morenzoni, F., *Des écoles aux paroisses: Thomas de Chobham et la promotion de la prédication au début du XIIIe siècle* (Paris, 1995)

Morrison, S. S., *Women Pilgrims in Medieval England: Private Piety as Public Performance* (London and New York, 2000)

Moss, R. E., *Fatherhood and its Representations in Middle English Texts* (Cambridge, 2013)

Müller, M., 'A Divided Class? Peasants and Peasant Communities in Later Medieval England', in C. Dyer, P. Coss, and C. Wickham, eds., *Rodney Hilton's Middle Ages: An Exploration of Historical Themes*, Past & Present Supplements, 2 (Oxford, 2007), pp. 115–31

—— 'Peasant Women, Agency and Status in Mid-Thirteenth to Late Fourteenth-Century England: Some Reconsiderations', in C. Beattie and M. F. Stevens, eds., *Married Women and the Law in Premodern Northwest Europe* (Woodbridge, 2013), pp. 91–113

Murchison, K. A., 'The Readers of the *Manuel des Péchés* Revisited', *Philological Quarterly*, 95 (2016), 161–99

Murray, A., *Conscience and Authority in the Medieval Church* (Oxford, 2015)

Murray, J., 'Gendered Souls in Sexed Bodies: The Male Construction of Female Sexuality in Some Medieval Confessors' Manuals', in P. Biller and A. J. Minnis, eds., *Handling Sin: Confession in the Middle Ages* (York, 1998), pp. 79–93

—— '"The law of sin that is in my members": The Problem of Male Embodiment',

Bibliography

in S. J. E. Riches and S. Salih, eds., *Gender and Holiness: Men, Women and Saints in Late Medieval Europe* (Abingdon, 2002), pp. 9–22

—— 'On the Origins and Role of "Wise Women" in Causes for Annulment on the Grounds of Male Impotence', *Journal of Medieval History*, 16 (1990), 235–51

Musson, A., 'Law and Text: Legal Authority and Judicial Accessibility in the Late Middle Ages', in J. C. Crick and A. Walsham, eds., *The Uses of Script and Print, 1300–1700* (Cambridge, 2004), pp. 95–115

—— *Medieval Law in Context: The Growth of Legal Consciousness from Magna Carta to the Peasants' Revolt* (Manchester, 2001)

Neal, D. G., *The Masculine Self in Late Medieval England* (Chicago, 2008)

North, J. D., 'Astronomy and Mathematics', in J. I. Catto and R. Evans, eds., *The History of the University of Oxford*, vol. 2: *Late Medieval Oxford* (Oxford, 1992), pp. 103–74

O'Brien, D., '"The veray registre of all trouthe": The Content, Function and Character of the Civic Registers of London and York, c. 1274–c. 1482' (PhD thesis, University of York, 1999)

O'Mara, V. M., 'Female Scribal Ability and Scribal Activity in Late Medieval England: The Evidence?', *Leeds Studies in English*, new series, 27 (1996), 87–130

Olsan, L. T., 'Charms in Medieval Memory', in J. Roper, ed., *Charms and Charming in Europe* (Basingstoke, 2004), pp. 59–88

Ong, W., *Orality and Literacy: The Technologizing of the Word* (London, 1982)

Owen, D. M., 'The Canonists' Formularies', in D. M. Owen, *The Medieval Canon Law: Teaching, Literature and Transmission* (Cambridge, 1990), pp. 30–42

—— 'White Annays and Others', in D. Baker, ed., *Medieval Women: Dedicated and Presented to Professor Rosalind M. T. Hill on the Occasion of her Seventieth Birthday*, Studies in Church History Subsidia, 1 (Oxford, 1978), pp. 331–46

Page, S., 'Richard Trewythian and the Uses of Astrology in Late Medieval England', *Journal of the Warburg and Courtauld Institutes*, 64 (2001), 193–228

Palmer, R. C., *Selling the Church: The English Parish in Law, Commerce and Religion, 1350–1550* (Chapel Hill, NC, 2002)

Pantin, W. A., 'Instructions for a Devout and Literate Layman', in J. J. G. Alexander and M. T. Gibson, eds., *Medieval Learning and Literature* (Oxford, 1976), pp. 398–422

Parkes, M. B., 'The Literacy of the Laity', in M. B. Parkes, *Scribes, Scripts and Readers: Studies in the Communication, Presentation and Dissemination of Medieval Texts* (London, 1991), pp. 275–97

Pasnau, R., *Thomas Aquinas on Human Nature: A Philosophical Study of Summa Theologiae, 1a 75–89* (Cambridge, 2002)

Passerini, L., *Fascism in Popular Memory: The Cultural Experience of the Turin Working Class* (Cambridge, 1987)

Payer, P. J., *Sex and the New Medieval Literature of Confession, 1150–1300* (Toronto, 2009)

Pedersen, F., 'Demography in the Archives: Social and Geographical Factors in

Bibliography

Fourteenth-Century York Cause Paper Litigation', *Continuity and Change*, 10 (1995), 405–36

—— *Marriage Disputes in Medieval England* (London, 2000)

Peel, J. D. Y., 'For who hath despised the day of small things? Missionary Narratives and Historical Anthropology', *Comparative Studies in Society and History*, 37 (1995), 581–607

Pennington, K., 'Henricus de Segusio (Hostiensis)', in K. Pennington, *Popes, Canonists and Texts, 1150–1550* (Aldershot, 1993), no. 16, pp. 1–12

—— *The Prince and the Law, 1200–1600: Sovereignty and Rights in the Western Legal Tradition* (Berkeley, 1993)

Phillips, K., 'Maidenhood as the Perfect Age of a Woman's Life', in K. Lewis, N. J. Menuge, and K. Phillips, eds., *Young Medieval Women* (Stroud, 1999), pp. 1–24

—— *Medieval Maidens: Young Women and Gender in England, c. 1270–1540* (Manchester, 2003)

Poleg, E., *Approaching the Bible in Medieval England* (Oxford, 2016)

Pollman, J., *Memory in Early Modern Europe, 1500–1800* (Oxford, 2017)

Pollock, F., and F. W. Maitland, *History of English Law*, 2nd edition (Cambridge, 1968)

Poos, L. R., *A Rural Society after the Black Death: Essex, 1350–1525* (Cambridge, 1991)

—— 'Sex, Lies, and the Church Courts of Pre-Reformation England', *Journal of Interdisciplinary History*, 25 (1995), 585–607

Popular Memory Group, 'Popular Memory: Theory, Politics, Method', in R. Perks and A. Thomson, eds., *The Oral History Reader* (London, 1998), pp. 75–86

Porter, J., 'Custom, Ordinance and Natural Right in Gratian's *Decretum*', in A. Perreau-Saussine and J. Bernard Murphy, eds., *The Nature of Customary Law* (Cambridge, 2006), pp. 79–100

Powell, S., 'The Transmission and Circulation of *The Lay Folks' Catechism*', in A. J. Minnis, ed., *Late Medieval Religious Texts and their Transmission: Essays in Honour of A. I. Doyle* (Cambridge, 1994), pp. 67–84

Quirk, K., 'Men, Women and Miracles in Normandy, 1000–1150', in E. van Houts, ed., *Medieval Memories: Men, Women and the Past, 700–1300* (London, 2001), pp. 53–71

Radulescu, R., 'Literature', in R. Radulescu and A. Truelove, eds., *Gentry Culture in Late Medieval England* (Manchester, 2005), pp. 100–18

Reay, B., *Popular Cultures in England, 1550–1750* (London and New York, 1998)

—— 'Quaker Opposition to Tithes, 1652–1660', *Past & Present*, 86 (1980), 98–120

Rees Jones, S., 'Public and Private Space and Gender in Medieval Europe', in J. M. Bennett and R. M. Karras, eds., *The Oxford Handbook of Women and Gender in Medieval Europe* (Oxford, 2013), pp. 246–61

—— *York: The Making of a City, 1068–1350* (Oxford, 2013)

—— 'York's Civic Administration, 1354–1464', in S. Rees Jones, ed., *The*

Government of Medieval York: Essays in Commemoration of the 1396 Royal Charter (York, 1997), pp. 108–40

Reeves, A., *Religious Education in Thirteenth-Century England: The Creed and Articles of Faith* (Leiden, 2015)

Reeves, A. C., 'Lawrence Booth: Bishop of Durham (1457–76), Archbishop of York (1476–80)', in S. D. Michalove and A. C. Reeves, eds., *Estrangement, Enterprise and Education in Fifteenth-Century England* (Stroud, 1998), pp. 63–88

Richardson, C., 'Having nothing upon hym saving onely his sherte': Event, Narrative and Material Culture in Early Modern England', in C. Richardson, ed., *Clothing Culture, 1350–1650* (Aldershot, 2004), pp. 209–22.

Richmond, C., *The Paston Family in the Fifteenth Century: Fastolf's Will* (Cambridge, 1996)

Riddy, F., 'Looking Closely: Authority and Intimacy in the Late Medieval Urban Home', in M. C. Erler and M. Kowaleski, eds., *Gendering the Master Narrative: Women and Power in the Middle Ages* (Ithaca, NY, 2003), pp. 212–28

——— 'Mother Knows Best: Reading Social Change in a Courtesy Text', *Speculum*, 71 (1996), 66–86

——— '"Women talking about the things of God": A Late Medieval Sub-Culture', in C. M. Meale, ed., *Women and Literature in Britain, 1150–1500* (Cambridge, 1993), pp. 104–27

Rider, C., 'Lay Religion and Pastoral Care in Thirteenth Century England: The Evidence of a Group of Short Confession Manuals', *Journal of Medieval History*, 36 (2010), 327–40

Rigby, S. H., *English Society in the Later Middle Ages: Class, Status and Gender* (New York, 1995)

Robertson, D. W., 'A Note on the Classical Origin of "Circumstances" in the Medieval Confessional', *Studies in Philology*, 43 (1946), 6–14

Rollison, D., 'Exploding England: The Dialectics of Mobility and Settlement in Early Modern England', *Social History*, 24 (1999), 1–16

——— *The Local Origins of Modern Society: Gloucestershire, 1500–1800* (London, 1992)

Rosenthal, J. T., *Social Memory in Late Medieval England: Village Life and Proofs of Age* (New York, 2018)

——— *Telling Tales: Sources and Narration in Late Medieval England* (Philadelphia, 2003)

Rosser, G., 'Myth, Image and Social Process in the English Medieval Town', *Urban History*, 23 (1996), 5–25

Rubin, M., *Corpus Christi: The Eucharist in Late Medieval Culture* (Cambridge, 1991)

——— 'Religious Culture in Town and City: Reflections on a Great Divide', in D. Abulafia, M. Franklin, and M. Rubin, eds., *Church and City, 1000–1500: Essays in Honour of Christopher Brooke* (Cambridge, 1992), pp. 3–22

Rublack, U., 'Pregnancy, Childbirth and the Female Body in Early Modern Germany', *Past & Present*, 150 (1996), 84–110

Bibliography

Ruiz, T. F., 'Elite and Popular Culture in Late Fifteenth-Century Castilian Carnivals: The Case of Jaén', in B. Hanawalt and K. Reyerson, eds., *City and Spectacle in Medieval Europe* (Minneapolis, 1994), pp. 296–318

Salih, S., 'At Home; Out of the House', in C. Dinshaw and D. Wallace, eds., *The Cambridge Companion to Medieval Women's Writing* (Cambridge, 2003), pp. 124–40

Sandall, S., 'Custom, Common Right and Commercialisation in the Forest of Dean, c. 1605–1640', in J. P. Bowen and A. T. Brown, eds., *Custom and Commercialisation in English Rural Society, c. 1350–c. 1750: Revisiting Tawney and Postan* (Hatfield, 2016), pp. 161–79

—— *Custom and Popular Memory in the Forest of Dean, c. 1550–1832* (Saarbrücken, 2013)

Saul, N., 'Bold as Brass: Secular Display in English Medieval Brasses', in P. Coss and M. Keen, eds., *Heraldry, Pageantry, and Social Display in Medieval England* (Woodbridge, 2002), pp. 169–94

Scattergood, V. J., 'The "Lewed" and the "Lerede": A Reading of Satire on the Consistory Courts', in V. J. Scattergood, *The Lost Tradition: Essays on Middle English Alliterative Poetry* (Dublin, 2000), pp. 27–42

Scott, J., 'The Evidence of Experience', *Critical Inquiry*, 17 (1991), 773–97

—— 'Gender: A Useful Category of Historical Analysis', *The American Historical Review*, 91 (1986), 1053–75

Sheehan, M. M., 'The Formation and Stability of Marriage in Fourteenth-Century England', in M. M. Sheehan, *Marriage, Family and Law in Medieval Europe: Collected Studies*, ed. J. K. Farge (Toronto, 1996), pp. 38–76

—— *Marriage, Family and Law in Medieval Europe: Collected Studies*, ed. J. K. Farge (Toronto, 1996)

—— 'Marriage Theory and Practice in the Conciliar Legislation and Diocesan Statutes of Medieval England', in M. M. Sheehan, *Marriage, Family and Law in Medieval Europe: Collected Studies*, ed. J. K. Farge (Toronto, 1996), pp. 118–76

—— *The Will in Medieval England from the Conversion of the Anglo-Saxons to the Thirteenth Century* (Toronto, 1963)

Sheingorn, P., 'Appropriating the Holy Kinship: Gender and Family History', in C. Neel, ed., *Medieval Families: Perspectives on Marriage, Household and Children* (Toronto, 2004), pp. 273–301

Shepard, A., *Accounting for Oneself: Worth, Status, and the Social Order in Early Modern England* (Oxford, 2017)

—— *Meanings of Manhood in Early Modern England* (Oxford, 2003)

Skinner, P., 'Gender and Memory in Medieval Italy', in E. van Houts, ed., *Medieval Memories: Men, Women and the Past, 700–1300* (London, 2001), pp. 36–52

—— 'The Pitfalls of Linear Time: Using the Medieval Female Life Cycle as an Organising Strategy', in E. Cox, L. H. McAvoy, and R. Magnani, eds., *Reconsidering Gender, Time and Memory in Medieval Culture* (Cambridge, 2015), pp. 13–28

Bibliography

Skoda, H., *Medieval Violence: Physical Brutality in Northern France, 1270–1330* (Oxford, 2013)

Smail, D. L., *The Consumption of Justice: Emotions, Publicity, and Legal Culture in Marseille, 1264–1423* (Ithaca, NY, 2003)

—— *Imaginary Cartographies: Possession and Identity in Late Medieval Marseille* (Ithaca, NY, 2000)

Smith, D. M., *The Court of York, 1400–1499: A Handlist of the Cause Papers and an Index to the Archiepiscopal Court Books* (York, 2003)

—— *Ecclesiastical Cause Papers at York: The Court of York, 1301–99* (York, 1988)

Spiegel, G. M., 'Genealogy: Form and Function in Medieval Historiography', *History and Theory*, 22 (1983), 43–53

Stahuljak, Z., *Bloodless Genealogies of the French Middle Ages: Translatio, Kinship and Metaphor* (Gainesville, FL, 2005)

Stallybrass, P., 'Worn Worlds: Clothes, Mourning, and the Life of Things', *Yale Review*, 81 (1993), 35–50

Stanbury, S., and V. Raguin, eds., *Women's Space: Patronage, Place and Gender in the Medieval Church* (Albany, NY, 2005)

Steiner, E., *Documentary Culture and the Making of Medieval English Literature* (Cambridge, 2003)

Stevens, M. F., 'London Women, the Courts and the "Golden Age": A Quantitative Analysis of Female Litigants in the Fourteenth and Fifteenth Centuries', *The London Journal*, 37 (2012), 67–88

Stone, D., 'The Reeve', in S. H. Rigby, with A. J. Minnis, ed., *Historians on Chaucer: The 'General Prologue' to the Canterbury Tales* (Oxford, 2014), pp. 399–420

Stothers, R. B., 'Climatic and Demographic Consequences of the Massive Volcanic Eruption of 1258', *Climatic Change*, 45 (2000), 361–74

Strathern, M., *The Gender of the Gift: Problems with Women and Problems with Society in Melanesia* (Berkley, 1988)

Summerlin, D., 'The Canons of the Third Lateran Council of 1179: Their Origins and Reception, ca. 1148–ca. 1191' (PhD thesis, University of Cambridge, 2012)

Swanson, R. N., 'Fissures in the Bedrock: Parishes, Chapels, Parishioners and Chaplains in Pre-Reformation England', in A. Morton and N. Lewycky, eds., *Getting Along? Religious Identities and Confessional Relations in Early Modern England: Essays in Honour of W. J. Sheils* (Farnham, 2012), pp. 77–95

Tanner, N., and S. Watson, 'Least of the Laity: The Minimum Requirements for a Medieval Christian', *Journal of Medieval History*, 32 (2006), 395–423

Tentler, T. N., *Sin and Confession on the Eve of the Reformation* (Princeton, 1977)

Thomas, H. M., *The Secular Clergy in England, 1066–1216* (Oxford, 2014)

Thomas, K., 'Age and Authority in Early Modern England', *Proceedings of the British Academy*, 62 (1976), 205–48

Thompson, E. P., *Customs in Common* (New York, 1993)

Tillott, P. M., ed., *Victoria County History: A History of the County of York, the City of York* (Oxford, 1961)

281

Bibliography

Truelove, A., 'Literacy', in R. Radulescu and A. Truelove, eds., *Gentry Culture in Late Medieval England* (Manchester, 2005), pp. 84–99

van Houts, E., 'Gender and Authority of Oral Witnesses in Europe, 800–1300', *Transactions of the Royal Historical Society*, 6th series, 9 (1999), 201–20

—— *Memory and Gender in Medieval Europe, 900–1200* (Basingstoke, 1999)

van Houts, E., ed., *Medieval Memories: Men, Women and the Past, 700–1300* (London, 2001)

Vauchez, A., *The Laity in the Middle Ages: Religious Beliefs and Devotional Practices*, trans. M. J. Schneider (London, 1993)

Veach, C., *Lordship in Four Realms: The Lacy Family, 1166–1241* (Manchester, 2014)

Walker, G., *Crime, Gender and Social Order in Early Modern England* (Cambridge, 2003)

—— 'Just Stories: Telling Tales of Infant Death in Early Modern England', in M. Mikesell and A. Seeff, eds., *Culture and Change: Attending to Early Modern Women* (Newwark, NJ, 2003), pp. 98–115

Walker, S. S., 'Litigation as Personal Quest: Suing for Dower in the Royal Courts, circa 1272–1350', in S. S. Walker, ed., *Wife and Widow in Medieval England* (Ann Arbor, 1993), pp. 81–108

Walsham, A., *The Reformation of the Landscape: Religion, Identity, and Memory in Early Modern Britain and Ireland* (Oxford, 2011)

Warren, N. B., *Spiritual Economies: Female Monasticism in Later Medieval England* (Philadelphia, 2001)

Watkins, C., *History and the Supernatural in Medieval England* (Cambridge, 2007)

Waugh, S. L., *The Lordship of England: Royal Wardships and Marriages in English Society and Politics, 1217–1327* (Princeton, 1998)

Wei, I., *Intellectual Culture in Medieval Paris: Theologians and the University, c. 1100–1330* (Cambridge, 2012)

Weldon, M. S., 'Remembering as a Social Process', *The Psychology of Learning and Motivation*, 40 (2001), 67–120

White, H., 'The Historical Text as Literary Artefact', in H. White, ed., *Tropics of Discourse: Essays in Cultural Criticism* (Baltimore, 1978), pp. 81–100

Whittle, J., and S. H. Rigby, 'England: Popular Politics and Social Conflict', in S. H. Rigby, ed., *A Companion to Britain in the Later Middle Ages* (Oxford, 2003), pp. 65–86

Whyte, N., 'Custodians of Memory: Women and Custom in Rural England c. 1550–1700', *Cultural and Social History*, 2 (2011), 153–73

—— 'Landscape, Memory and Custom: Parish Identities c. 1550–1700', *Social History*, 32 (2007), 166–86

—— '"With a sword drawne in her hande": Defending the Boundaries of Household Space in Early Modern Wales', in B. Kane and F. Williamson, eds., *Women, Agency and the Law, 1300–1700* (London, 2013), pp. 141–55

Wickham, C., '*Fama* and the Law in Twelfth-Century Tuscany', in T. Fenster and D. L. Smail, eds., *Fama: The Politics of Talk and Reputation in Medieval Europe* (Ithaca, NY, and London, 2003), pp. 15–26

Bibliography

—— 'Gossip and Resistance among the Medieval Peasantry', *Past & Present*, 160 (1998), 3–24

Williamson, F., *Social Relations and Urban Space: Norwich, 1600–1700* (Woodbridge, 2014)

Winroth, A., *The Making of Gratian's 'Decretum'* (Cambridge, 2000)

Withington, P., and A. Shepard, 'Introduction: Communities in Early Modern England', in A. Shepard and P. Withington, eds., *Communities in Early Modern England: Networks, Place, Rhetoric* (Manchester, 2000), pp. 1–15

Wogan-Browne, J., '"Cest livres liseez … chescun jour": Women and Reading c. 1230–1430', in J. Wogan-Browne et al., eds., *Language and Culture in Medieval Britain: The French of England, c. 1100–c. 1500* (York, 2009), pp. 239–53

Wood, A., *The 1549 Rebellions and the Making of Early Modern England* (Cambridge, 2008)

—— 'Custom and the Social Organisation of Writing in Early Modern England', *Transactions of the Royal Historical Society*, 6th series, 9 (1999), 257–69

—— 'Fear, Hatred and the Hidden Injuries of Class in Early Modern England', *Journal of Social History*, 39 (2006), 803–26

—— *The Memory of the People: Custom and Popular Senses of the Past in Early Modern England* (Cambridge, 2013)

—— 'The Place of Custom in Plebeian Political Culture: England, 1550–1800', *Social History*, 22 (1997), 46–60

—— *The Politics of Social Conflict: The Peak Country, 1520–1770* (Cambridge, 2004)

Wood, S., *Conscience and the Composition of* Piers Plowman (Oxford, 2012)

Woodcock, B. L., *Medieval Ecclesiastical Courts in the Diocese of Canterbury* (Oxford, 1952)

Woods, M. Curry, and R. Copeland, 'Classroom and Confession', in D. Wallace, ed., *The Cambridge History of Medieval English Literature* (Cambridge, 1999), pp. 376–406

Woolf, D. R., 'A Feminine Past? Gender, Genre, and Historical Knowledge in England, 1500–1800', *American Historical Review*, 102 (1997), 645–79

Worby, S., 'Kinship: Canon Law and the Common Law in Thirteenth-Century England', *Historical Research*, 80 (2007), 443–68

—— *Law and Kinship in Thirteenth-Century England* (Woodbridge, 2010)

Wright, S. H., 'Women in the Northern Courts: Interpreting Legal Records of Familial Conflict in Early Fifteenth-Century Yorkshire', *Florilegium*, 19 (2002), 27–48

Wright, S. M., *The Derbyshire Gentry in the Fifteenth Century* (Chesterfield, 1983)

Wrightson, K., and D. Levine, *Poverty and Piety in an English Village: Terling, 1525–1700* (London, 1979)

Yates, F. A., *The Art of Memory* (Chicago, 1966)

Youngs, D., *The Life Cycle in Western Europe, c. 1300–1500* (Manchester, 2006)

ACKNOWLEDGEMENTS

The work of this book has dominated my research efforts since 'time out of mind', existing as a project in progress for longer than I care to admit. A doctoral research award from the Arts and Humanities Research Council supported the initial research for the study. The task of writing the book saw the project develop into a somewhat different endeavour, and included the integration of records from Canterbury Cathedral Archive, the earliest surviving ecclesiastical proceedings for England. A Power Fellowship from the Economic History Society, a postdoctoral fellowship from the Institute for Advanced Studies in the Humanities (IASH) at the University of Edinburgh, and a Leverhulme Early Career Fellowship facilitated key archival research at Canterbury Cathedral Archive. A year of research leave at Cardiff University permitted the completion of final chapters, and I am very grateful to my medieval colleagues for their work in my absence. A period at Gladstone's Library in Hawarden, holding a Canon Symonds scholarship, enabled critical revisions in a peaceful environment.

Sections of Chapter 2 appeared in 'Courtship, Childbearing and Gender in Late Medieval England', *Frühneuzeit-Info*, 26 (2015), and parts of Chapter 6 were drawn from 'Custom, Memory and Knowledge in the Medieval English Church Courts', in R. C. E. Hayes and W. Sheils, eds., *Clergy, Church and Society in England and Wales c. 1200–1800* (York, 2013). I am grateful for permission to include some of this material in the present volume.

The greatest debts I owe to Jeremy Goldberg, who supervised my doctoral thesis, and to Miri Rubin, who examined the final version. Both Jeremy and Miri have shaped the project's development in untold ways. I first encountered Jeremy's work when I was an undergraduate at Queen's University, Belfast, and his path-breaking studies on medieval women, work, and the economy have long provided the backdrop to my research. Miri taught me how to be a more confident academic, while making me more aware of the routines that shaped the medieval parish, and we continue to enjoy visits and conferences filled with fun, conversation, and good food. The happiest element of academia is the transition of mentors into dear friends who make up the patchwork of social and working life.

One of the most humbling aspects of this process has been the willingness of friends and colleagues to read and comment on my work. These offers are especially generous in the face of the growing marketization of university culture and increasing pressures on academic time. Miri Rubin and Simon

Acknowledgements

Sandall commented on the entire manuscript, while Fergus Kane and Mark Williams also read chapters. Guidance from the anonymous reviewer aided the final preparation of the book, and I am particularly thankful to Caroline Palmer for her advice, patience, and good humour as I came close to submission. Earlier versions of this work were presented at too many conferences to name, but the Social Church meetings at Oxford and York, and conversations with John Arnold, Ian Forrest, and Simon Yarrow, were especially useful. I am also grateful to Mark Ormrod for his early support and to Philippa Hoskin for her guidance on ecclesiastical archives. My colleagues in the History department at Cardiff have offered moral support and friendship. Jasmine Kilburn-Toppin, James Ryan, Lisa Watkins, David Doddington, Mark Williams, and Keir Waddington provided company in finishing the project. Students on my units at Cardiff University and Bath Spa University asked critical questions and embraced the use of documents chosen with the themes of this study in mind.

The writing of this book has unfortunately taken precedence over family and social events many times. Helen Birkett has raised spirits on her stopovers, while Rosalyn Murtagh, Victoria Reynolds, Lisa Benz, Barbara Gribling, Karen Doherty, Aoife Morgan, Niamh and Connor Quinn, Ronan Kane, and their families, have visited and offered hospitality. Sally Sandall, Chris Barnard, Jeanette, Stuart, and Theo Sandall, Janka Rodziewiecs, Sam Earl, and Gesine Oppitz-Trotman have acted as hosts on many occasions. My god-daughter, Zahra Beattie, is owed many more visits, as are the rest of her family. Cordelia Beattie offered encouragement at critical points and my time at IASH was much improved by our after-work 'meetings' in the pub. Miri Rubin and Gareth Stedman-Jones have offered company many times, and visits to Llangrove are always joyous and memorable.

Periods of illness punctuated the writing process, and I will always be grateful to my husband and the NHS for their care. My parents-in-law, Barbara and Roger Sandall, tolerated visits that seemed to entail only writing and sleeping, and also provided ice-cream and humour when needed. My own parents, Christina and Fergus, and my sisters, Shauna and Fiona, have offered support over the years, and my mother's growing interest in her family's history has been a timely coincidence. My upbringing in Northern Ireland during the Troubles sharpened my awareness of power relations in the midst of social and religious conflict. So much of the region's history shaped the themes of this book, and the process of researching memory studies has helped me better understand the role of conflict and trauma in forming identity.

The greatest contribution has come from Simon Sandall, my husband and a brilliant early modern historian of memory and class conflict. Our scholarship has developed in tandem and our shared passion for history, politics, and music provides much conversation in our happy household. It is to Simon, Miri, and Jeremy that I dedicate this book. Despite the input of others to this volume, all errors herein are my own.

INDEX

Acle, Christina de 95
Acton, John 46
Addison, William 218–9
affinity 55, 70, 138, 145–6, 148–9, 152, 154
agency 5, 21–2, 235, 247, 256–7
  discursive (including narrative) 21–2, 58, 229, 255
  economic 88, 253
  generative 156–7
  identity and 21, 82, 135
  materiality
    embodiment 82, 101, 110, 123, 126, 135, 255
    objects 94–5
    spatial experience and 212–3
  non-elite men 22, 125, 171, 239–40
  women 3, 126, 185–6, 200, 204, 248, 257
    courtship 67, 69
    custom and 174, 206–9
    during litigation 58, 66, 123, 138, 254
    negotiating patriarchy 22, 38
    widowhood 204
ages of man 111
agnus dei 95 *see also* birth charms
Alexander III, pope 116
Alfrey, Richard 238–9
Andover priory, Hants. 206–7
apprentices 79, 89, 90, 139, 219, 222, 228
apprenticeship
  household memory 138–9, 219
  marriage *see under* courtship
  masculinity 79, 90
  occupational identity 89–90
  personal memory 90
Aquinas, Thomas 40, 84, 113

Summa Theologiae 84
Arden, John de 192, 239
Aristotle 112, 113, 114
  De Memoria 112, 113
  History of Animals 112
Arnold, John 21, 33–4, 42
ars memoria see under trained memory
Arundel, William 189, 191
Aslebery, Denis de 177
Aslowe, Thomas 95
Atehide, Alice 129
Atehulle, Matilda 129
Attebury, Adam 61, 62
Augustodunensis, Honorius, *De Philosophia Mundi* 125
Aunger, William 106
aurality 182
autobiography 6
Awne
  Agnes de 183
  Avice de 183
  William de 183
Awner, Robert 179
Ayenbite of Inwit 37

Bacon, Agnes, wife of John 129
Baker, Alice 204
Bakhtin, Mikhail 21
Ball, William 77
Bande of Lovynge, The 46
baptism 209, 243
  baptismal fonts 193, 202, 219, 237
  memory 13, 79, 96, 130–1, 154
  pastoral duties 235
  pastoral literature 46, 149
  spiritual affinity 145, 149, 154
Barbour
  Nicholas 197
  Robert 76, 77

Index

Bardsley, Sandy 19
Barking abbey, Essex 37
Barlay, Katherine 121–3, 128
Barley, Margaret 77
Barron, Caroline 18, 19
Bartlett, Frederic C. 5, 20
Barton
 Alice 38
 Eleanor de 55
 William 119–20, 121
Bassett
 Eleanor 66, 192
 Ralph 192
Bast, Thomas 201
Baxter, Thomas 79
Beattie, Cordelia 64
Bedell, John 13, 98
beds 96, 204
 bed-sharing 78, 116, 140, 166, 220
 child-bed 109
 deathbed 105, 166–7
 marriage contracts 92, 94
 sexual activity 134, 220, 227–8
Belamy
 Alice, daughter of Thomas 118, 134
 Richard 134
Bello, Stephen de 154
Bennett, Judith 19, 249
bereavement 14, 83, 101–2, 104, 162
 see also children, death; death;
  emotion, grief
Bernard of Clairvaux 115
Betrayed Maiden's Lament, A 229
Beveridge, William 69
Bewmond, John 134
Billyng, John 179
Blakeden, Anabel 148
Blayke, Katherine 141
Blyth priory, Notts. 182
bodies
 clothing 28, 83
 habit memory 91
 injury 98, 107
 men's 87–8, 111
  see also genital inspection;
   impotence
 proof 86–7
 women's 109–13, 117, 121–3

work 88, 91–3
Bogher, Peter le 156
Bolacer, Reginald le 183
Bolendene, Hugh, son of William de 98
Bolton, Alice, wife of Robert 102, 132
Booth
 Lawrence, archbishop of York 150,
  161
 William, archbishop of York 150
Bosco, Richard de 70, 71, 96, 117, 118,
  123, 228
Boton, John 62, 65, 93
Botry, William 148
boundaries 17, 97, 230, 235, 240, 242,
  251
 manorial 241
 markers 232, 236, 237
 parish 87, 187, 190, 194, 195, 196,
  204, 206, 231, 236, 237, 246,
  251
 property 217–8
Bower
 Idonya 220
 Robert 63
 Thomas 76, 77
Boydston, Jeanne 4
Boy, William 168
Boye, William 188
Boyle, Leonard 35, 45
Bradwardine, Thomas 215
 De Memoria Artificiali 126
Brampton, Walter de 207
Brand, Paul 165
breasts 28, 121–3, 248
 physical examination 121–3, 128
breastfeeding 133
 wet-nursing 109, 133
Brenlay, James de 125
Brerelay, Joan de 79
Brewere, Geoffrey le 88, 228
Bridelyngton, Alice de 61, 63
Bridsall, William 62
Bringham, Robert 201
Broghton, Margaret 205
Brown, Thomas 236, 240, 241
Brun
 (of Beckton), William 53
 (of Weldon), William 66

288

Index

Brundage, James 153
Brunne, Geoffrey de 142
Bruno, Giordano 9
Bryscow, Ralph 167
Bule, Robert le 192
Burges, Alice, wife of Robert 86
Burgh, John de 36
burial 83, 105, 206
  landscape 237
  processions 237–8
  rights 106, 172, 191, 202–3, 208, 218
Burton
  Alice 91
  Margaret de 219
Bury, Richard, bishop of Durham 46
Butler, Alexander 223–4
Butler
  Judith 22
  Sara 100
Buttercram, John de 183

Cadden, Joan 112, 115
calendars 11, 54, 172, 180, 185
Calthorne
  Thomas 78
  William 47, 59, 60, 77, 78
Cambridge
  Franciscan friary 185
  university 36, 47
Canning, Kathleen 21–2
canon law 2, 3, 20, 29, 58, 71, 73, 100,
    140, 147, 150, 151, 152, 158,
    161, 165, 166, 169, 185
  knowledge of 116, 186, 246, 252–3, 255
  pastoral care 44–7, 55, 149–50
  procedure 22, 23-7, 34, 74, 141, 145,
    149
    testimony 32, 43, 49, 51, 53, 56,
      59, 65, 69, 86, 110, 114–5, 116,
      141, 153
  see also defamation; genital
    inspection; impotence; kinship,
    proof of; marriage; mortuaries;
    tithes
  texts
    De vera et falsa poenitentia 41
    Gratian's *Decretum* 40, 41, 43, 49,
      153

    Tractatus de penitentia 41, 43
    Ordo iudiciarius 49
    Liber Extra 86, 121
    Summa Aurea 151
Cant, Alice 68
Canterbury
  St Augustine's abbey 37
Cantilupe, Walter de, bishop of
    Worcester 31, 39, 42
Capellanus, Andreas 113, 114
  De Amore 113
Capp, Bernard 253
Carbot
  John 225
  Margery 113, 225
Carlton, Alan de 99
Carrow
  John 144
  Margaret 68
Carruthers, Mary 9
Catryk, Thomas 91
Caxstrete, John de 191, 235
Cecilia, daughter of Bartholomew 1,
    54, 109
Certeau, Michel de 221
chambers 93, 96, 219
Chapelayn, John 75
Chapman, Thomas 98
charters 175, 195, 196, 198
Charters of Christ 81
Chaucer, Geoffrey 57, 114, 177
  Friar's Tale, The 177–8
  Wife of Bath's Prologue 57
Cheesebrak, Ralph de 239
childbirth 115, 225
  birth attendants 129
  charms and prayers 95, 158, 179
  confession 127
  death 127
  gendered embodiment 14, 81, 125,
    128
  horoscopes 184–5
  intellectual metaphor 126
  memory 13, 28, 90, 96, 102, 110, 126,
    127
    in cases concerning child's age 1,
      90, 96, 102–3, 109, 129, 131–3,
      184–5, 225

289

Index

men's personal 130, 144
women's personal 14, 54, 59, 79,
102, 103, 104, 109
postnatal body 28, 107, 128
proof of sexual relationships 69, 72,
73
temporality 109, 112, 126, 128
trauma 127, 235
women's testimony 14, 59, 79, 106,
126, 143, 248
childlessness 136
children 12, 37, 54, 104, 119–20, 237,
239, 252
death 102, 105
lying over 103
illegitimate 1, 59, 69–73
memory
church rights 190, 202
tithes 195, 234
paternity of 72, 73, 95–6, 123, 125
provision of clothing 133
physical chastisement 241
testimony from 49, 132–3
see also childbirth, memory
church courts
administration 10, 34, 44–8, 54, 56
consistories 23, 24, 26
Ely 44
Lincoln 188
London 96
Salisbury 70, 123
York 27, 178
personnel
advocates 26, 27, 44, 47, 51, 52, 79
apparitors (including summoners)
26, 178, 251
Officials (including judges) 26, 45,
46, 61, 62, 66, 182, 218
proctors 26, 27, 36, 46, 47, 51, 52,
79, 124, 164, 177, 189, 198,
205, 208, 251
proctor-general 47, 77
Clapton, Nicholas 117, 123
Cleansyng of Man's Soule, The 37
Clerk, John 183
Clifton, William de 180
Clipston, John de 99, 201
Cloghton, Margaret de 152

Clopton, Johanna de 70–2, 96, 117, 123,
228, 229
clothing 28, 63, 72, 75, 83, 94–7, 117,
133, 163, 199, 220
identity 96
items of clothing
chemise 97
girdle 96, 117
gown 96
swaddling cloth 96
tunic 96
recognition 94
see also work, spinning
Coke
Michael 11
William 222
Cokfield, Emma, wife of Thomas 220
Colnvill, John 166
Colte, Robert 195
Colynson
Margaret, widow of John 208
Robert 208
common fame 123, 141, 142, 155, 159,
175, 200
see also gossip; orality; reputation;
rumour, speech
concubinage 46, 69, 72, 73, 207, 252
confession 54–5, 56
circumstances of sin 40, 41–2, 43, 53
gender 48, 111, 116
men 47
women 38–9, 40, 127, 230, 249
introspection 43 *see also* conscience
manuals 39, 40, 45, 46, 85–6, 149-50
memory 39, 53
secrecy 39
testimony 43
see also sin, sexual
Connerton, Paul 7, 82
consanguinity 26, 70, 74, 145–9, 155,
165, 167, 203
see also affinity; kinship
conscience 32–3, 37, 39–43, 45, 48, 53,
55–56, 148, 245
contrition 34, 40–2, 44, 55–6
Copyn, Thomas 72
Corneys, Matilda 231
Corpus Christi 83

Index

Cotrell, John 231
Cottesworth, Thomas 182, 223
councils
    London (1102) 148
    Lateran III (1179) 34
    Lateran IV (1215) 34, 35, 55, 85, 141,
        146, 150, 158, 178, 219
    Salisbury (1217 X 1219) 35
    Oxford (1222) 87
    Lambeth (1281) 37
    Exeter (1287) 31, 42
    London (1329) 141
    London (1342) 44
    see also synodal decrees
countermemory 6-7
courtship 28, 67, 95, 124, 222
    narratives 67–73, 74, 89, 229, 248
    see also taverns
coverture 67, 111, 140, 220, 255
Crane, William 130, 131
Crehan, Kate 29
Crips, Robert 62
Croft, Matilda de 205
Crossley, Nick 82
Croxton, Isabel, wife of John 102, 128
Croydon, Avice de 89
Cullum, Patricia 46, 99
custom 3, 11, 14, 19, 25, 28, 44, 51, 87,
        97, 100, 123, 134, 172–82, 186,
        191–4, 234, 250
    gender and 198–209, 242
    manorial 15, 17, 207, 233, 234,
        239–40, 251, 255
    relating to land 214, 217, 230–35,
        238, 241–2, 247
    writing and 194–8
    see also burial, rights; mortuaries;
        tithes; written records

Dale, Thomas del 220
Dalton
    Alice, wife of Robert 89
    Robert 89, 232
Daly
    Anabilla 124
    Isabella 124
Damian, Peter 146
Danby, Nicholas 77

Dawnay, Michael 184–5, 195
Day, John 202
De Memoria Artificiali 126
death 1, 28, 37, 39, 40–1, 83, 97, 101–2,
        107, 150, 151, 152, 154, 172,
        187, 225, 231, 237
    family 104–5, 149
    parental 77, 236
    spousal 102, 144, 161, 162, 163, 167,
        206
    testaments 163–4, 183, 207
    women and 1, 14, 39–41, 104–6, 127,
        149, 167, 208–9, 220-1
    see also beds, deathbed; childbirth,
        death; children, death
defamation 14, 25, 50, 51, 58, 59, 60,
        61, 87, 116, 124, 212, 217, 218,
        227, 231, 248, 256
Derham, William de 163
Devoine, Margery de 97
Devyas, Henry 224
Dolling, Alice 75, 80
Donahue Jr., Charles 24, 50, 53, 74, 147,
        253
Donbarre, Margaret de 226
Doncaster
    John de 156, 161
    Stephen de 156
Doncaster friary, Yorks. 184
doorways 116, 118, 134, 166, 217–8,
        219, 231
Doune, William 46
Dowson
    John 202
    Katherine 203
    Peter 202
    Thomas 203
Draycote
    Alice, daughter of Richard de 131
    John de 131
Dronefeld, Edmund 226
Durham priory, Durham 206
Dyer, Christopher 163
Dyne, Robert 207

Eastleigh, Alexander de 178
Edward, son of Germain 196
Eldevik, John 235

291

Index

Eleanor of Aquitaine 192–3
Ellerton priory, Yorks. 205
Ely, John 96
embodiment 22, 78, 81–82, 110, 111,
117, 127, 135, 183, 220, 227,
255
emotion 7, 23, 28, 59, 73, 78, 79, 82, 83,
84, 85, 87, 89, 106, 107, 117–8,
132, 215, 220, 235, 248, 255,
256
emotional abuse 97, 100–1
grief 14, 102, 104, 105, 133, 162
love 68, 69, 73, 95, 110, 142
objects 95–97
shame 1, 39, 71, 112, 118, 121
see also children, death
Enders, Jody 97
Eschedale, William 208
Estthorp, John de 148
Etchilhampton, Walter de 217
Eukeston, William 64
Everard, Judith 13, 203
Everard, Richard 125

family memory 7, 12, 137–40, 141, 148,
153
gentry 155, 157, 158, 160, 163, 164,
167, 168
social status 137–9, 147, 158, 160, 184
women and 156, 161–70, 183, 192
see also genealogies; inheritance;
kinship; widows
Farmer, Sharon 62
fathers
absent 144 *see also* children,
illegitimate
ancestry 150, 151, 157, 158
commemoration 148, 162
death 47, 77, 163, 167
pastoral literature 37, 40
see also children, paternity of;
fatherhood
fatherhood
children *see* children, paternal
recognition of
genital size 119–20
masculinity 144
memory 130

conversation with children 123,
132
transmission 138, 141
serfdom 66
female religious 2, 131, 183, 205, 208,
214
literacy 180–1
memories of documents 181
femme coverte 174
femme sole 67, 174
Fentress, James 5, 212
Fentrice, Lucy, wife of William 223, 227
Feraunt, John 55
Ferrur, John le 159
Finnegan, Ruth 176
Flemyng, Walter 105
Flixton, Alice, wife of Robert de 142
Forrest, Ian 76
Forster, Thomas 105
Fossard, Joan 47, 59, 60, 78
Foucault, Michel 6, 32–3, 160, 176
Fowler, Richard 223
Foxcott, Isabella de 207
Foxholes, Isabella 63–4
Franciscans 184–5
Freedman, Paul H. 111
Freman, William 176
French, Katherine 75, 174
Furness abbey, Lancs. 196

Galt, Margaret, wife of John 130
Gamell, John 133
Garde, Emmota 119
Gaytenby, Robert 182
Geary, Patrick 9–10, 12, 102, 138, 162,
183
genealogy 12, 138, 139, 140, 146, 147,
150, 153, 156, 157, 158, 160–1,
168, 169, 183, 240 n. 127
genital inspection 87, 119-23
see also impotence
gentry 12, 16, 137–9, 147, 147 n. 50,
155, 157, 158, 159, 160, 163,
164, 176, 180, 182, 183, 193
marriage 26, 66, 140, 167, 168
women 64, 66, 177, 179, 180, 183,
192, 205
Gertham, John de 98

292

Index

Gilchrist, Roberta 214, 237 n. 118
Gilt, Hugh 168
Given-Wilson, Christopher 12
god-parents 69, 70, 129, 130, 131, 145,
    148, 149, 152, 154
Goderhele, Matilda 70, 117, 118
Goering, Joseph 43, 85–6
Goldberg, P.J.P. 14, 18, 19, 26, 50, 89,
    115, 153, 254
Goldesmyth, Margery 150, 155, 161
gossip 48, 55, 74, 141
gossips' genre 60
    see also Talk of Ten Wives on their
        Husbands' Wares, A
Gower, John, *Mirour de l'Omme* 114
Gowing, Laura 58, 67, 82, 122, 174, 217,
    220
Grandisson, John, bishop of Exeter 45,
    46
Granger, Juliana, daughter of William le
    229–30
Gratian's *Decretum see under* canon law
Gray, Walter, archbishop of York 45
Graystanes, Margaret 220
Green, Monica 121
Greene, Thomas de 194
Gretehed, William 119, 120
Grosseteste, Robert 36, 37, 39
Gudale, William 144
Gudechilde, Henry de 183
guilds 237, 254
    craft 83, 222, 253–4
    parish 75, 76, 98, 174, 252
Gurevich, Aaron 15
Gyll, Christopher 78
Gylton, John de 105
Gyselay, Thomas 90, 133

Hacchys, Agnes 61, 72
Halbwachs, Maurice 5, 138
Hall, Margaret 155
Hamilton, Sarah 34
Hamstead, Mariota de 220
Handlyng Synne 45, 149
Handsacre, Emma 207
Hanna, Ralph 46
Hartlepool friary, Durham 185
harvest 231

see also work, harvest
Harwod, Robert de 69
Helay
    Adam de 130
    Richard de 130
Helis, Mariona, wife of John 91
Helmholz, Richard 27, 67, 147, 186,
    189
Helwysson, John 168
Hereford, John 223–4
heriot 207
Herlihy, David 139, 149
Heyndon, Walter de 129
Higden, Ranulph, *Polychronicon* 137
Higham priory, Kent 52
Hildyard
    John 151, 166
    John, senior 55, 148, 160, 165, 167,
        168
    Katherine 148, 160, 165–8
    Peter 153, 165, 166, 167, 168
    Richard 151
Hill, Joan del 63
Hilton, Rodney 17
Hilton, Walter 44
Hinteworth
    Matilda 109
    Sibilla de 1
Hobbedoghter, Margaret 69
Hobson
    Henry 202
    John 203
Hofmeyer, Isabel 8
Hogeson, John 203
Hoghton, Alice 64
Holmcultram abbey, Cumberland 164
homosociality 74, 77, 78, 79, 80, 243
Honilane, Emma de 163
Hoperton, John de 226
Hopton, William 130
Hornby, junior, Thomas de 92
Hostiensis 49, 150, 151
household 14, 16, 38, 60, 79, 80, 89, 92,
    103, 104, 131, 228, 229, 251,
    256
    composition 224, 227, 233, 239, 254
    economy 88, 190, 206, 233
    moving 224–6

Index

see also migration

women and 60, 63, 65, 88, 96–7, 120, 130, 137, 223, 225, 226, 238, 253, 255

see also patriarchal authority, household

How the Goode Wife Taught hyr Doughter 228

Hugh of St Victor 84

Hunte, Johanna 129

Huntington, Agnes 100

Huntyngton, Alice 64-5

husbands 38, 49, 51, 57, 60, 63, 67, 75, 79, 86, 87, 90, 96–7, 101, 103, 104, 111, 118, 119, 121, 130–3, 138, 142, 155, 156, 157, 163–70, 203, 207–8, 220–1, 223, 224–5, 226–7, 237, 252

impotence 43, 59, 87, 119–21, 123, 126, 127 n. 75, 145, 248

In a fryht as Y con fare fremede 71

Ingeborg of Denmark 44

Ingram, Agnes, wife of John 102

inheritance 139, 146, 147, 155, 165, 167–9, 173, 184, 207

Instructions for a Devout and Literate Layman 39

Instructions for Parish Priests 127, 149

Ivry abbey, Évreux 189–90, 191, 197–8

Jakson, Alice, wife of John 95, 103

Jargonne, Gilbert 190

John the blacksmith 140, 142

Johnson, Tom 21, 93

Justice, Steven 172, 178, 197

Katersouth

Maud 132, 226

Robert 132

Kempe, Margery, *The Book of Margery Kempe* 40

Kenlay, William 144

Kent, John de 105, 191

kinship 2, 79, 118, 125, 138–9, 140, 145–6, 147–8, 165, 169, 200, 216

litigation 155–61, 168

memory 12, 153, 166, 201

pastoral advice 149

proof of 55, 59, 152

Kirkham priory, Yorks. 218-9

Kristeva, Julia 8

Krug, Rebecca 177

Kydde, John 75, 76, 78, 80

Kyghley

Emmota 157

Robert 155

Kyme priory, Lincs. 205

Kyrkeby, Nicholas 144

labour services 199, 238, 239, 240, 250

Lacy family 194–5

landholding 65, 76, 165, 189, 217, 230, 241

women 173, 179, 198, 250

Langdale, Agnes 87

Langton, Stephen, archbishop of Canterbury 49

Larson, Atria A. 43

Lay Folks' Catechism, The 37

Le Goff, Jacques 11, 16, 223

Leicester abbey, Leics. 199

legal documents *see* written records

legal memory 11, 85, 86, 124, 138, 153, 173, 175, 176, 186, 196, 198, 242

Lefebvre, Henri 211

Leye, Matilda de la 61

Leyrmouth, Elena de 220

leyrwite 65, 250, 253

Liber Poenitentialis 103

Lightfoot, Dana Wessell 22

literacy 16, 28, 35, 160, 175, 176–86, 194, 197, 215, 246, 248, 252

pragmatic 159, 161 n. 118, 177

women 158, 177–8, 179, 181, 222

see also orality; speech; written records

Lockwood family 66

Lombard, Peter 40–1

Long, Cecilia, daughter of Richard 75

Longe, John le 117, 229, 231, 233

Lorymer, Katherine 91–2

Lucy, wife of Richard the ploughman 62

Lytsone, William 124

Lyttster, John 63, 66, 68

294

Index

Magnus, Albertus 113, 215
Malcake, Johanna 123
Malton priory, Yorks. 180
Man, Christina de 68
Manchester, George de 159
Mannyng, Robert 149
Manuel des péchés 45, 48
Marchal, William le 222
Marche, John 120
Marescalle, Matilda, wife of John 152
marital status 47, 48, 64, 67, 122, 143, 155,
  170, 192, 203, 226, 227, 238, 256
 see also husbands; marriage; wives
marriage 1, 2, 8, 13, 18, 22, 24, 28, 32,
  37, 41, 49, 51, 53, 55, 59, 65,
  111, 120, 127, 138, 139, 140–5,
  219, 226
 custom 143
 disputes 14, 25, 44, 47, 50, 54, 58, 61,
  63, 66–73, 74–80, 86, 116, 118,
  119, 133, 134, 142, 227, 228
 impediments
  see affinity; consanguinity; genital
  inspection; impotence; kinship;
  servility
 memory 102, 112, 145–7, 156–8,
  203–4
 parental involvement 134, 147, 181
 social status 12, 26
  see also gentry, marriage
 sub pena nubendi 43, 69, 70, 73, 116,
  123, 218, 252
 witnesses to contract 68–9
 see also courtship; emotion, objects;
  husbands; servants, life-cycle;
  sex; sexuality; widows; wives
Marston, Robert de 179
masculinity 4, 74, 77, 78–9, 90, 99, 112,
  119, 135, 144, 169, 242, 248,
  249–51
Mass 38, 55, 76, 78, 80, 99, 104, 148,
  172
Mathew, William 72
Melksham, Richard de 165
Mellerby, Walter de 92
Memoriale Presbiterorum 42, 46, 103
memory studies 4–5, 7, 21
 feminist theory and 5–8, 20

menses 126
Meriden, William de 105, 191
Meriot, Hugh 78
Metelay, John de 120
Michael of Northgate 37
migration 18 n. 85, 151, 200, 221
 plague 89, 106–7, 225–6
mills 174, 191, 205, 234–5, 236
Mirk, John 37, 38, 127, 149
miscarriage 130
misogyny 32, 41, 48, 56, 57, 60, 63, 79,
  100, 110, 111, 113, 114, 199,
  204, 229, 230, 247, 249
mobility 28, 209, 214, 221–3, 225, 226,
  227, 233, 238, 248, 253
Monk Bretton priory, Yorks. 77
Montibus, William de 85
Mordon, Alice de 109
More, Richard 232, 236
mortuaries 106, 172, 187, 202, 205–7
motherhood 14, 102, 125, 131, 133, 137,
  143, 166–7, 169
 desire for 102–3, 126–7
 uterine memory 128
Müller, Miriam 17
Munkton, Simon de 100
Murray, Jacqueline 38
Musson, Anthony 196
Mycholson, John 38
Myton, Thomas de 104

Nade, Thomas 226
Nassington, William 46
Nayler, Joan, wife of Thomas 129
Nebb, Roger 141
Nele, William 190, 193
Nesfeld
 Margery 101
 Thomas 101
Nettilworth, William de 200
Neuton
 John 44
 John de 160
Newburgh priory, Yorks. 201
Newham, Patrick de 59
Norfolk
 St Margaret and St Remigius Church,
  Seething 48

295

Index

Norman Conquest 186
Norman, Robert 75
Northeby, Thomas 144
Northefolk
 Agnes 128, 129, 131, 133
 Katherine 90, 96, 102, 103, 128, 129,
  131, 132, 133, 184, 185, 195,
  225
Norton
 Joan 132
 John 132

Oculus Sacerdotis 36, 43, 45
old age 8, 13, 55, 151, 155, 163 n. 125,
  190, 199, 201, 202, 203, 236
 women's testimony 187, 200, 203–4
oral history 6, 195
orality 7, 10, 16, 28, 98, 160, 176, 178,
  181, 182, 185–6, 194–6, 209,
  225, 242, 246–7
 see also common fame; rumour;
  speech
Ordinance of Labourers 253
Owen, Dorothy M. 44

Palmer, William 124
Parage, Agnes de 142
parenting 14, 28, 95, 103, 110, 132–5,
  162, 185
 see also children; death, children;
  fathers; fatherhood; mothers
Paris 41, 44
parish church 75, 76, 180, 188, 201, 207,
  216, 218, 243
 dedication 201–3, 218
 interior of 193, 218–9
 wall-paintings 48, 178, 218
Parkes, M.B. 177
Passerini, Luisa 6
Paston
 John 162
 Margaret 162
pastoral
 care 27, 31–2, 34–5, 41, 44–6, 48,
  54–6, 85, 99, 149, 235
 literature 2, 34, 36, 43, 47, 56, 97, 111,
  115–6, 246, 249
 manuals for parish priests 32, 34,

  35–43, 50, 53, 85, 103, 111,
  149
Paton, William 235
patriarchal
 attitudes 51, 59–60, 66, 80, 83, 87,
  107, 114, 122, 134, 170, 174,
  175, 185, 186, 198, 203, 204,
  208, 213, 225, 230, 249, 250–1
 authority 50, 63, 79, 82, 90, 101,
  110–1, 120, 125, 140, 155, 169,
  173, 181, 223, 227, 238, 239,
  243, 245, 248, 250, 255, 257
 household 60, 96, 134, 138, 144–5,
  216, 218, 221, 222, 253, 256
Paty, Emma 206–7
Payer, Pierre J. 249
Peasants' Revolt 172, 178, 197
Pecham, John, archbishop of Canterbury
  36
Peniteas cito 85–6
perjury 26, 38, 59, 61, 63, 64, 74, 78, 79
Peron, John de 200
Pert, John 201
Peter the Chanter 41, 44, 45
Peytevyn
 Alice 233
Philip II of France 44
Phillip, son of Richard 118
Phillips, Kim 47, 111
Pickworthe, Margaret de 124
Piers Plowman 48
pilgrimage 75, 129, 224
plague 18–9, 89, 106–7, 180, 222, 224–7,
  253–4
political events 8, 53, 172, 184, 192–3,
  248
Polychronicon 137
Poore, Richard, bishop of Salisbury 35
popes 24, 34, 116, 181
Popilton, Robert de 63
popular culture 15–6, 116
Popular Memory Group 7
poverty 65, 76, 82, 198, 206, 226, 255
 female 28, 47, 62–4, 71, 79, 103, 124,
  132, 199, 249, 253
 male 98, 249
Prat, Juliana 72
preaching 37

296

Index

vernacular 35
see also sermons
pregnancy 14, 47, 59, 67, 70–3, 109,
        117, 122, 124, 128, 130, 149,
        158, 183, 248
  pastoral care 127
  personal memories of 102
Prick of Conscience, The 40, 48
proofs of age 13, 53–4, 98, 231
prostitution *see under* work, types of
Prudfoot, Emma 75
Pseudo-Albertus *De Secretis Mulierum*
        121
Pupilla Oculi 36
purification 100, 102, 127–8, 130, 201
Pykburn, Agnes 156, 157
Pynder, Anabilla 158

queer theory 4, 8

Randulf, Robert 206
rape 1, 14
Raynald, William 123
Rayneson, George 65
reading 9, 16, 64, 181
  aloud 37, 179, 181–3, 196
  clerical men 46–8, 57
  memory and 64, 84
  women 48, 175, 177, 179, 180
Rede, William 72
Redyng, Alice 62, 65, 93
Reedness, John, son of James 234
Remyngton
  Alice 216, 219
  Roger 219
reputation 14, 19, 27, 50, 58, 60–2, 65,
        72, 73, 76, 82, 93, 121, 124,
        143, 166, 175, 217, 218, 226,
        227, 248, 255, 256
Rhetorica novissima 100
Richard I 192–3
Richmond friary, Yorks. 185
ricordanze 12
Riddy, Felicity 228
Rigby, S.H. 250
Rikedon, Robert 61
Robert, John 96
Robert of Flamborough 103, 116

Roche, Hugh del 188
rogation processions 236, 242
  see also parish boundaries
Rolle, Richard 44
Rollison, David 215, 221, 230
Rosenthal, Joel 13
Rosyn, William 130
Rouclif
  Alice de 86
  Ellen de 133
  Margery de 179
Routh, Cecilia, daughter of William 92
Rubin, Miri 54
Rublack, Ulinka 130
Rukby, Hugh de 200
rumour 71, 123–5, 142
Rydyng, Alice 128

Salisbury 45
Sampson, Geoffrey 240
Sandall, Simon 15
Sandes
  Margaret, widow of Richard del
      163–4
  Richard del 163–4
  Thomas del 163
Satire on the Consistory Courts 251–2
Savage, Joan 120
Saxton, Hugh de 194–5, 197
Sayer, Alice 203
Saylbury, Christopher 160
Sayvell, John 66
Schakyll, Peter 218
Schilbottil, Agnes 91, 95, 181
Schilton, John de 164
Schyltelye, Alice, daughter of Robert de
      117
Scot, Robert 98
Scott, Joan 4, 21
seasons 11, 62, 189, 195, 230, 232, 233,
      251
secrecy 70, 121, 122, 166, 220, 229
Selby abbey, Yorks. 76
Selow, John 69
Selybarn, John 92
Semanson, William 180
Septuplum 46
Sereby, Richard 181–2

Index

serfdom 14, 27, 65, 66, 147, 175, 199, 239–40, 253
sermons 37–8, 40, 42, 44, 83, 87, 111, 115, 165, 178, 237
  exempla 35, 37, 39, 40, 47, 83, 97, 111
servants 3, 13, 18, 27, 48, 101, 132, 195, 205, 217, 220, 223
  female 47, 92–3
  hiring 222
  household composition 138–9, 219
  life-cycle 89, 132, 222
  memory 92, 222
  patriarchal authority 144, 216
  plague 106
  sexuality 70, 71, 124
  singleness 79 *see also* servants, life-cycle
  testimony 197, 224
Serving Maid's Holiday, The 71, 229
sex 43, 47, 48, 49, 56, 60, 61, 64–8, 69, 70–3, 75, 81, 87, 89, 92–4, 99, 103 n. 110, 104, 116–21, 124, 128, 140–41, 143, 145, 149, 220, 227–30, 233, 248, 252, 255–6
  difference 47, 113, 120, 121
sexual
  assault *see under* rape
  histories 58, 59, 62, 82, 114–6, 121, 124–5, 133, 143, 166, 248
sexuality 2, 28, 32, 46, 110, 111, 114, 213, 214
  gendered depictions of 22, 58, 65, 70, 71 n. 54, 79, 93, 115, 117, 122–3, 135, 157, 204, 209, 227, 249
Sharpe, Alice 127
Sheath and the Knife 149
Sheehan, Michael M. 44
Shepard, Alexandra 47, 78, 199, 249, 250
Shirburn, Roger 64
Shirwood, John 241–2
Shorwode, Adam de 106
shrines 224, 236, 237
Signa, Boncompagno da 100
Simonides 97, 211
sin 10, 31, 32, 33, 35, 36, 37, 39, 40, 41, 47, 116, 148, 245

sexual 34, 38, 39, 40, 115, 149–50, 230, 249, 251
singleness 222
  men 79, 132, 144, 225
  women 3, 18, 18 n. 85, 63, 71, 71 n. 54, 104, 111, 122, 220, 225, 226, 229, 249, 251, 253, 255
  see also servants
Sketeby, Simon de 240
skin 83, 95, 100, 117, 120, 122, 133
  complexion 87–8
  scarring 98, 101, 107
Skoda, Hannah 97
Smail, Daniel Lord 213
Smale, John le 188
Smelt, John 150–1, 157
Smith, William 75, 78, 80
Somer, John 184–5
Somme le roi 37
Souman
  Joan 129, 131, 132, 224
  Robert 96, 129, 131, 132, 225
Sparuwe, Matilda 125
spatial theory 211–4
Speculum Vitae 45–6
speech 55, 56, 87, 160, 175, 176, 178, 183, 185, 186, 209, 219
  women's 1, 18, 38, 57, 60, 66, 78, 100, 110, 112, 199, 212, 227, 231
  see also orality
Spencer
  Margaret 203
  Peter 202
Sprotburgh, Agnes, wife of William de 156, 159
Sprottelay, John de 151, 166, 168
Spuret, Margery 92
St Augustine 49
St John, Edward de 99
St Leonard's hospital, York 232, 240–2
St Lucy 100
St Mary's abbey, York 231–2
St Nicholas's hospital, York 232
St Valery, Richard de 189, 191, 197–8
Stanlay, John de 217–8
Stevens, Matthew 255
Stevenson, Robert 202
Stodlay, Alice de 94

Index

Stokes, John de 198
Stokton
  Thomas 232, 234, 236, 238
  William de 220
Stonham, William de 230
Stowe, Richard de 188
Strathern, Marilyn 94
Strete, Thomas 61
Stry, Hugh 92
Sturgys
  Maud, wife of William 224
  William 224
Suardby, Joan 219, 220
subjectivity 20, 21–3, 29, 31, 82, 88, 107,
    110, 185, 245, 257
  experience 6, 67, 209, 219, 223
  subject positions 93, 126, 255
Suel, Richard 208
Suffolk, Senicla de 228
Summa Confessorum 38, 45
Summa Penitentie Fratrum Predicatorum
    39
Summula (of Walter de Cantilupe) 31,
    39, 42
Susanna and the Elders 114
Sutton, Holderness, Yorks.
  St James, college 201–3
Sutton, Thomas de 99
Swynflete, Hugh 223
Symson, Nicholas 131
synodal decrees 35, 42
Syward, Petronilla, wife of Richard 70,
    94

Tailour
  John 87, 130
  Margaret, wife of Hugh 90, 144
  Thomas 118
Talbot, Roger 167
Talk of Ten Wives on their Husbands'
    Wares, A 60
Tancred 49, 50
taverns 216, 228, 243, 247
  female speech 60
  morality 228
Tayliour, William 90
Templum Dei 36–7, 39
testimony *see* canon law, testimony;

childbirth, women's testimony;
children, testimony from;
confession, testimony;
servants, testimony
textiles 22, 83, 91, 95, 96, 162, 247
  see also clothing
theology (including pastoral) 20, 32,
    34, 35, 38, 41, 43–5, 49, 56, 85,
    245–6
  Peter Lombard's *Sentences* 41
Thicket priory, Yorks. 205
Thomas of Chobham 38, 45
Thomas, son of Jordan 197
Thomeson
  John 182, 223
  Robert 118
Thompson, E.P. 187
Thoresby
  John, archbishop of York 37
  Richard 87
Thorley, Arnold de 142
Thornburgh, William 95
Thornton, Richard 242
Thorp, John 95, 181
Thorpe, Richard de 185
Thweng, Robert de 158
Till, William 223
time 8, 9, 11, 42, 53, 61, 78, 80, 85, 92,
    99, 106, 126, 128, 143, 161,
    180, 186, 188, 194, 223, 224,
    232, 248, 249
  calculation of time 53, 54, 102, 184–5,
    224–5
  timelessness 187, 188, 190, 193, 208,
    234, 238
tithes 17, 187, 189, 202, 234–5, 236, 246,
    251, 256
  disputes 14, 25, 50, 51, 106, 134, 154,
    173, 180, 186, 188, 194, 217,
    232
  proof in cases of 181, 189–92, 195–7,
    199, 233, 240–1, 242
  records 182
  women 51, 55, 57, 174, 200, 203–7,
    212, 234
Towneley cycle 48
Townley, Alice 167
Towton, Alice, wife of John 129

Index

trained memory (including *ars memoria*) 9, 10, 41, 64–5, 81, 84, 97, 110, 112, 114, 125–6, 176, 211, 215
  learned metaphors 43, 81, 112, 113, 125, 127, 176, 215
Tree of Jesse 146
Trevisa, John 137
Trotula 126
Tugge, Adam 142, 208
Turnay, Robert 201
Tutivillus 38, 48
Twyselton, Christopher 68
Tyas, Robert 201
Tykton, William 92

van Houts, Elisabeth 12
Vavasour, Agnes 72
vernacular *see* literacy; orality; written records
Vescy, Eustace de 180
violence 14, 22, 28, 46, 47, 81, 83, 98–99, 107, 126, 134, 217–8, 241
  domestic 19, 100–1, 142, 220–2
Virgin Mary's hospital and chapel, Jesmond, Northumberland 190
virginity 1, 14, 46, 72, 86, 121–3, 124

Waddington, William 45
Walde, Thomas 219, 220
Waldingsend, Thomas de 54
Waleys, Adam le 96
Walker, Alice 76, 78
Walker
  Garthine 19, 21, 58
  Sue Sheridan 165
Walkington, John de 217–8
Wallingwells priory, Notts. 184
Walter, Hubert, archbishop of Canterbury 24, 54
Warner, Simon 221
Warthill, William 72
Waryner, Walter 93
Wawne, Yorks. 106, 201–3, 237
weather 104, 231
Webster, Peter 217–8

Wele, Katherine, daughter of Roger de 59
Wellemakere, Thomas 239
Wetwang, William 203
Wherton, Henry 235
White, Hayden 20
Whitingdon, Agnes 96
Whyte, Nicola 15, 174, 199
Whytell, Margaret 133
Wickham, Chris 5, 212
widows 8, 49, 67, 126, 137–8, 143, 161, 178, 183, 204, 205, 206, 209
  dower 165–6, 167, 168, 169, 170, 207–8
  memory 12, 14, 161-70
  urban 173
  see also death, testaments; heriot; mortuaries
Wighton
  Johanna, wife of William 128, 131
  William 131
William of Pagula 36, 45
William, son of the steward of Houghton 240
Willyamson, John 87
Wilton
  Emma de 181
  Peter de 192, 217
Wimel, Mabila de 89, 102
Winchester, Henry, son of Henry de 165
wives 49, 120, 144, 207, 225, 237, 253
  household 96, 130, 131, 216, 220
  influence over husbands 38
  legal theories 19, 67
    see also coverture
  memory 28, 68
    family 156, 157, 168, 169, 170
  speech 60
  witnesses 121, 143
  see also violence, domestic
Wodecok, Hugh 130
Wodeham, Felicia de 88
Wogan-Browne, Jocelyn 48
Wollemelk, Henry 229
Wood, Andy 15, 172–3, 247, 256
Woolmer forest, Hants. 233
wombs 117, 128
  learned memory 125
women
  parish life 75, 174, 200

Index

work 1, 63–4, 82, 88–93, 130, 174, 185, 199, 213, 216, 222–3, 225, 251, 253–4, 255
see also agency, women and; bodies, women; breastfeeding; breasts; childbirth; death, women and; family memory, women and; household, women and; landholding, women; literacy, women; misogyny; motherhood; old age, women's testimony; poverty, female; pregnancy; purification; reading, women; sexuality, gendered depictions of; singleness, women; speech, women's; tithes, women; violence, domestic; widows; wives; wombs; written records, women
Worby, Sam 169
work 8, 14, 15, 17, 18, 28, 43, 47, 62, 80, 81, 83, 208, 209, 212, 222, 226, 242, 243, 247, 248, 253
accidents *see under* bodies, injury
identity 88–90, 216, 249, 250
types of
brewer 228
day labourer 18, 138–9
farming (agrarian and animal husbandry) 92, 162, 174, 195, 199, 227, 232, 238
forester 238–9
harvest 62, 92, 174, 222, 223, 227, 232
herder 236
landless rural worker 17, 234
plumber 91
prostitution 40, 61, 62, 63, 124, 214, 221, 228
reeve 90, 177
spinning 63, 91–2, 220
thatcher 91

workshops 90, 92, 93, 216, 217, 224, 253, 256
see also apprentices; apprenticeship; labour services; servants; women, work
written records 9–10, 16, 150, 153, 159, 211, 215, 243, 250
archives 160, 180, 241
civic 242
clerical contexts 180, 182, 207, 246
legal 31, 53, 77, 186, 187, 198, 237
see also charters
literate practices 177, 183
memory 175, 250
non-elites 48, 139, 179, 188–9, 194–7, 209, 246
patriarchy 174, 176
proof 84, 95, 177, 182, 198
vernacular 16, 26, 31, 35, 37, 38, 40, 45, 47, 48, 56, 114, 121, 137, 158, 175, 177, 182, 251
women 57–8, 66, 114, 138, 158, 177–8, 181, 183, 185, 222, 243
Wycombe, Elias de 183
Wykeham priory, Yorks. 181
Wyles, John 195
Wylflete, John 218
Wyman, John 144
Wynerthorp, Agnes de 181
Wyvell
Cecilia, wife of Henry 101, 142
Henry 101, 142

Yeland, Alice, widow of John 206
Yonge, Isabel, daughter of Henry 155
Yonger
Agnes 51, 147–8, 155
John, husband of Agnes 51–2, 155
York
All Saints Church 48
Minster 44
York, Richard de 104

301

GENDER IN THE MIDDLE AGES

I   *Gender and Medieval Drama*, Katie Normington, 2004

II   *Gender and Petty Crime in Late Medieval England: The Local Courts in Kent, 1460–1560*, Karen Jones, 2006

III   *The Pastoral Care of Women in Late Medieval England*, Beth Allison Barr, 2008

IV   *Gender, Nation and Conquest in the Works of William of Malmesbury*, Kirsten A. Fenton, 2008

V   *Monsters, Gender and Sexuality in Medieval English Literature*, Dana M. Oswald, 2010

VI   *Medieval Anchoritisms: Gender, Space and the Solitary Life*, Liz Herbert McAvoy, 2011

VII   *Middle-Aged Women in the Middle Ages*, edited by Sue Niebrzydowski, 2011

VIII   *Married Women and the Law in Premodern Northwest Europe*, edited by Cordelia Beattie and Matthew Frank Stevens, 2013

IX   *Religious Men and Masculine Identity in the Middle Ages*, edited by P. H. Cullum and Katherine J. Lewis, 2013

X   *Reconsidering Gender, Time and Memory in Medieval Culture*, edited by Elizabeth Cox, Liz Herbert McAvoy and Roberta Magnani, 2015

XI   *Medicine, Religion and Gender in Medieval Culture*, edited by Naoë Kukita Yoshikawa, 2015

XII   *The Unspeakable, Gender and Sexuality in Medieval Literature, 1000–1400*, Victoria Blud, 2017

XIII   *Popular Memory and Gender in Medieval England: Men, Women, and Testimony in the Church Courts, c.1200–1500*, Bronach C. Kane, 2019

XIV   *Authority, Gender and Space in the Anglo-Norman World, 900–1200*, Katherine Weikert, 2020

XV   *Female Desire in Chaucer's* Legend of Good Women *and Middle English Romance*, Lucy M. Allen-Gross, 2020

XVI   *Treason and Masculinity in Medieval England: Gender, Law and Political Culture*, E. Amanda McVitty, 2020

XVII   *Holy Harlots in Medieval English Religious Literature: Authority, Exemplarity and Femininity*, Juliette Vuille, 2021

XVIII   *Addressing Women in Early Medieval Religious Texts*, Kathryn Maude, 2021

Printed in the United States
by Baker & Taylor Publisher Services